WE CAN NEVER GO HOME

WHAT WE DO IS SECRET

BOSS

CAMPBELL

HOOD

KINDLON

ROSENBERG

SCURTI

TODD

WALSH

THIS BOOK WAS WRITTEN, DRAWN, AND COLORED IN APARTMENTS, COFFEE SHOPS, DINERS, MOTEL ROOMS, HOTEL ROOMS & FRIENDS HOUSES IN DANBURY, BOSTON, SEATTLE, LOS ANGELES, SAN DIEGO, CHICAGO, ANAHEIM, SAN FRANCISO, PORTLAND, LAS VEGAS, BALTIMORE, CINCINNATI, SAVANNAH, LONDON, ESSAOUIRA, MARAKECH AND NEW YORK.

THANKS FOR PUTTING UP WITH US.

BLACKMASK

PUBLISHED BY BLACK MASK STUDIOS LLC
MATT PIZZOLO | BRETT GUREWITZ | STEVE NILES

CHAPTER 1

WHAT WE DO IS SECRET

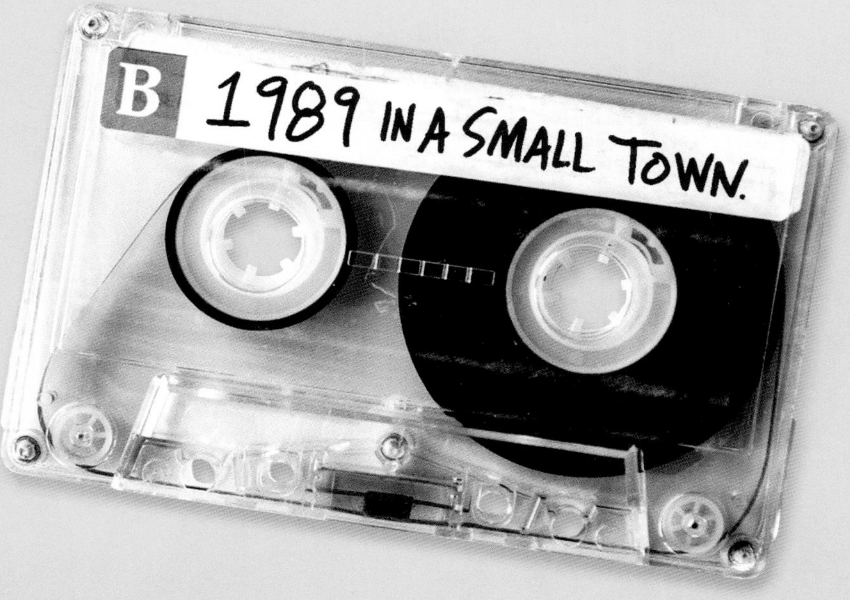
B
1989 IN A SMALL TOWN.

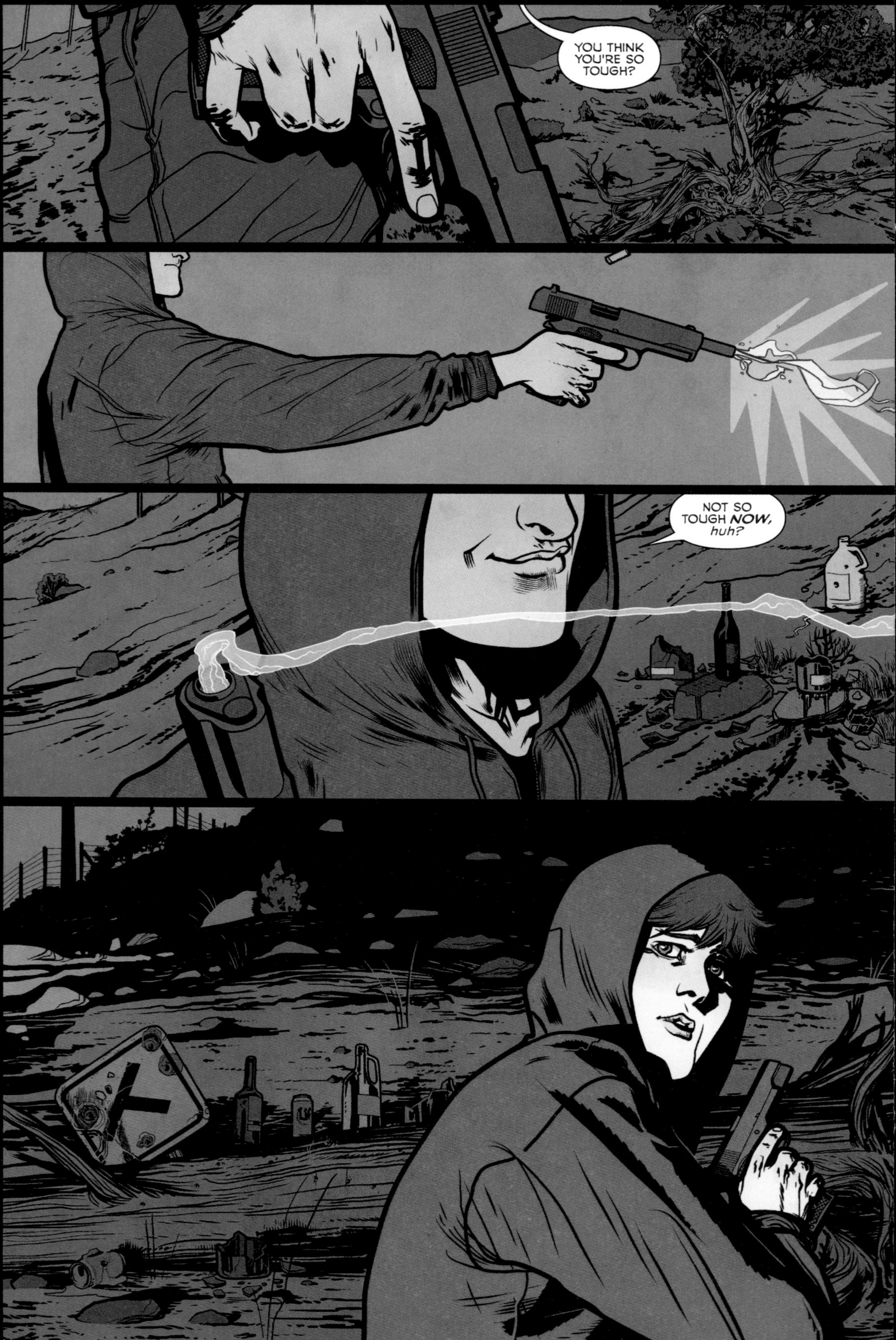
YOU THINK YOU'RE SO TOUGH?
NOT SO TOUGH **NOW,** *huh?*

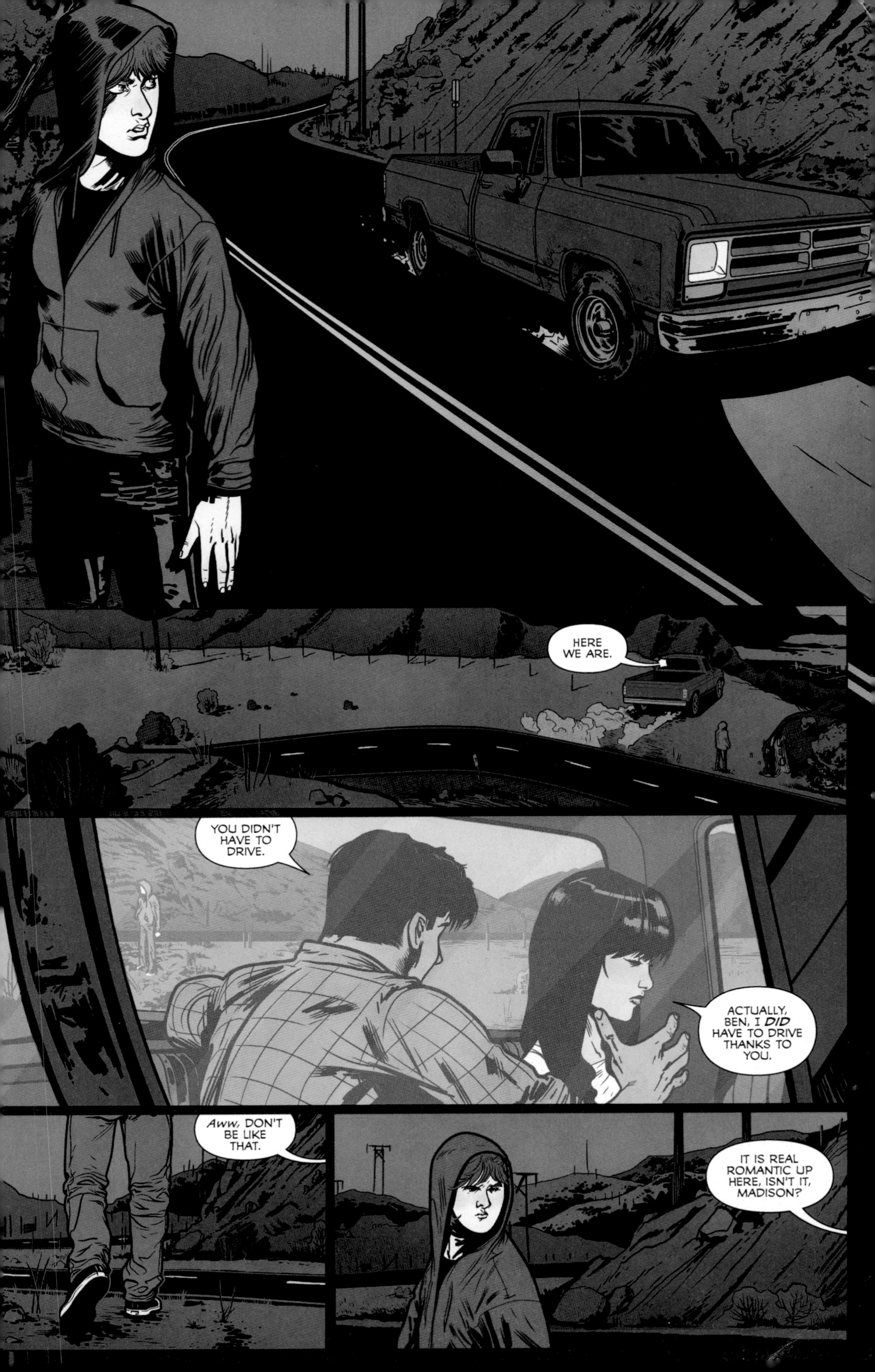
HERE WE ARE.
YOU DIDN'T HAVE TO DRIVE.
ACTUALLY, BEN, I *DID* HAVE TO DRIVE THANKS TO YOU.
Aww, DON'T BE LIKE THAT.
IT IS REAL ROMANTIC UP HERE, ISN'T IT, MADISON?

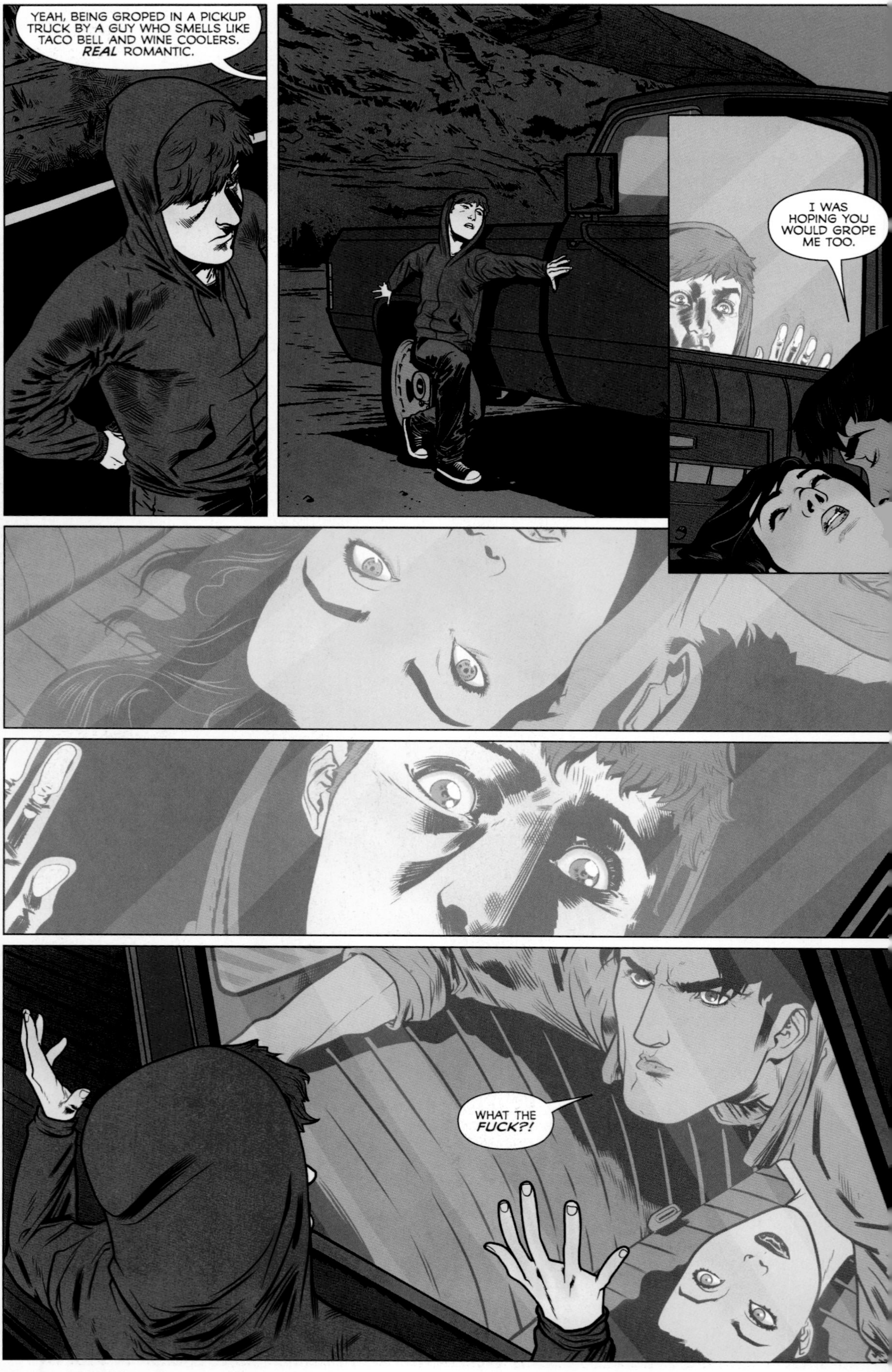
YEAH, BEING GROPED IN A PICKUP TRUCK BY A GUY WHO SMELLS LIKE TACO BELL AND WINE COOLERS. *REAL* ROMANTIC.
I WAS HOPING YOU WOULD GROPE ME TOO.
WHAT THE *FUCK?!*

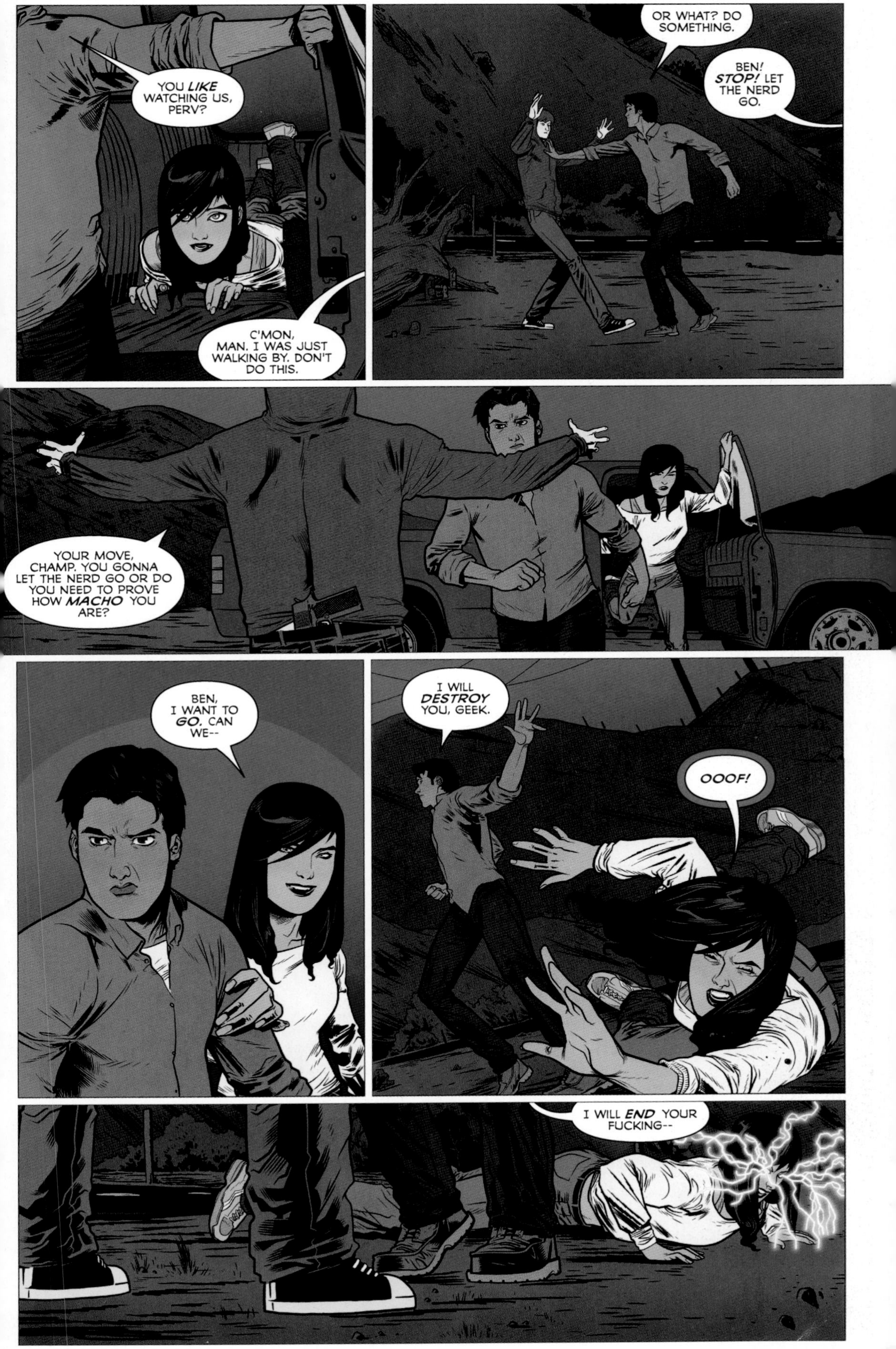
YOU *LIKE* WATCHING US, PERV?
C'MON, MAN. I WAS JUST WALKING BY. DON'T DO THIS.
OR WHAT? DO SOMETHING.
BEN! *STOP!* LET THE NERD GO.
YOUR MOVE, CHAMP. YOU GONNA LET THE NERD GO OR DO YOU NEED TO PROVE HOW *MACHO* YOU ARE?
BEN, I WANT TO *GO.* CAN WE--
I WILL *DESTROY* YOU, GEEK.
OOOF!
I WILL *END* YOUR FUCKING--

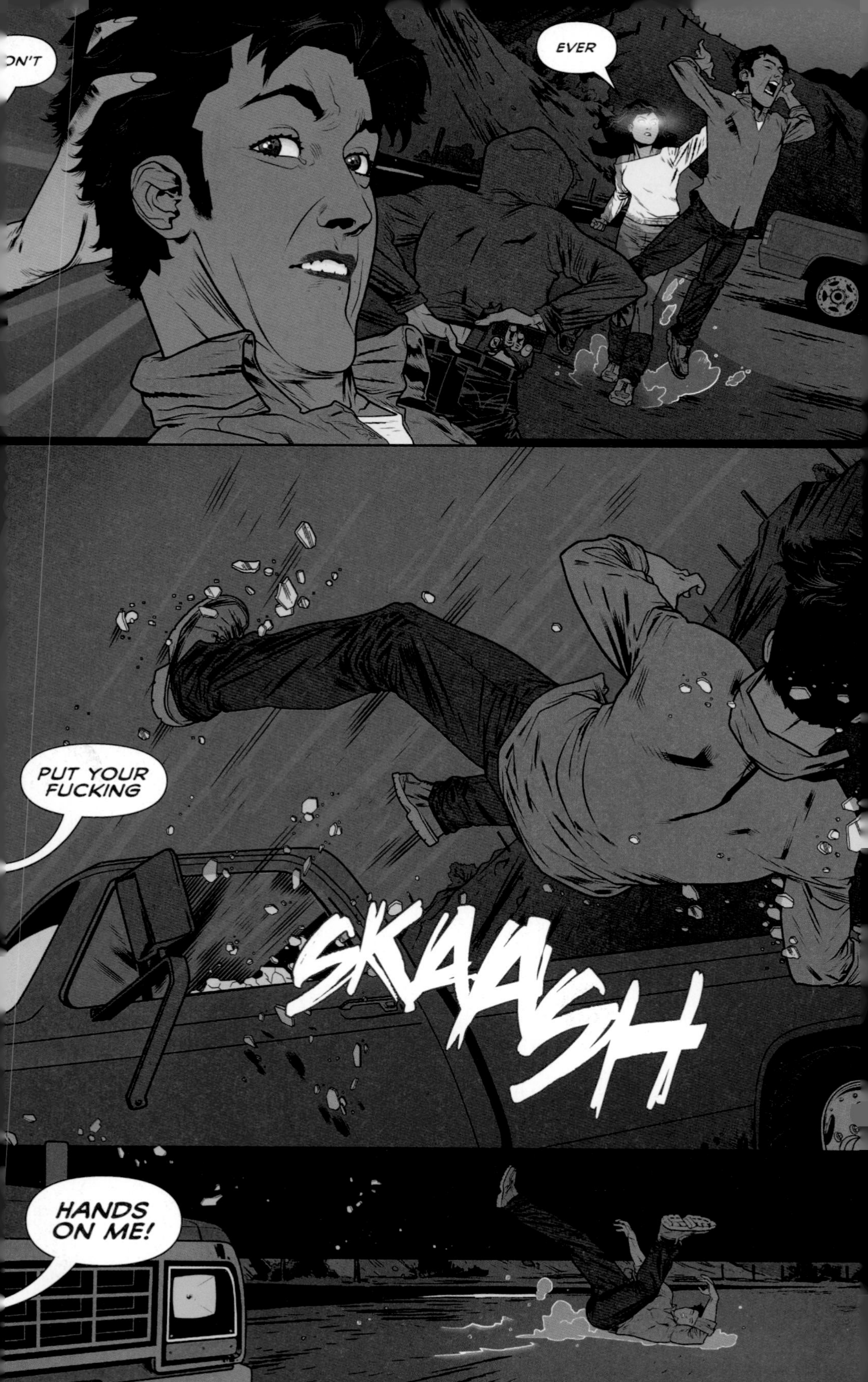

ON'T
EVER
PUT YOUR FUCKING
SKAASH
HANDS ON ME!

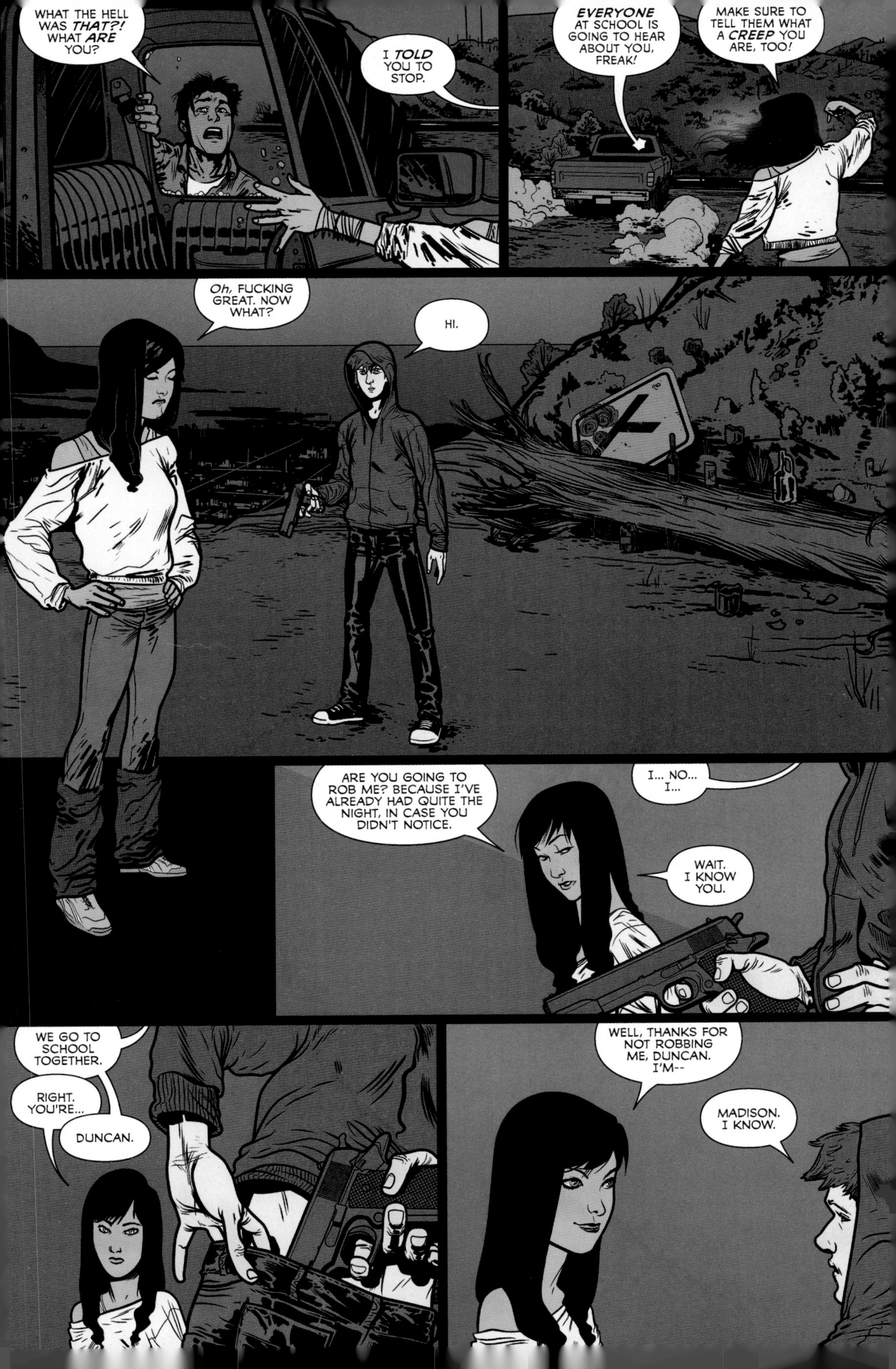
WHAT THE HELL WAS *THAT?!* WHAT *ARE* YOU?
I *TOLD* YOU TO STOP.
EVERYONE AT SCHOOL IS GOING TO HEAR ABOUT YOU, FREAK!
MAKE SURE TO TELL THEM WHAT A *CREEP* YOU ARE, TOO!
Oh, FUCKING GREAT. NOW WHAT?
HI.
ARE YOU GOING TO ROB ME? BECAUSE I'VE ALREADY HAD QUITE THE NIGHT, IN CASE YOU DIDN'T NOTICE.
I... NO... I...
WAIT. I KNOW YOU.
WE GO TO SCHOOL TOGETHER.
RIGHT. YOU'RE...
DUNCAN.
WELL, THANKS FOR NOT ROBBING ME, DUNCAN. I'M--
MADISON. I KNOW.

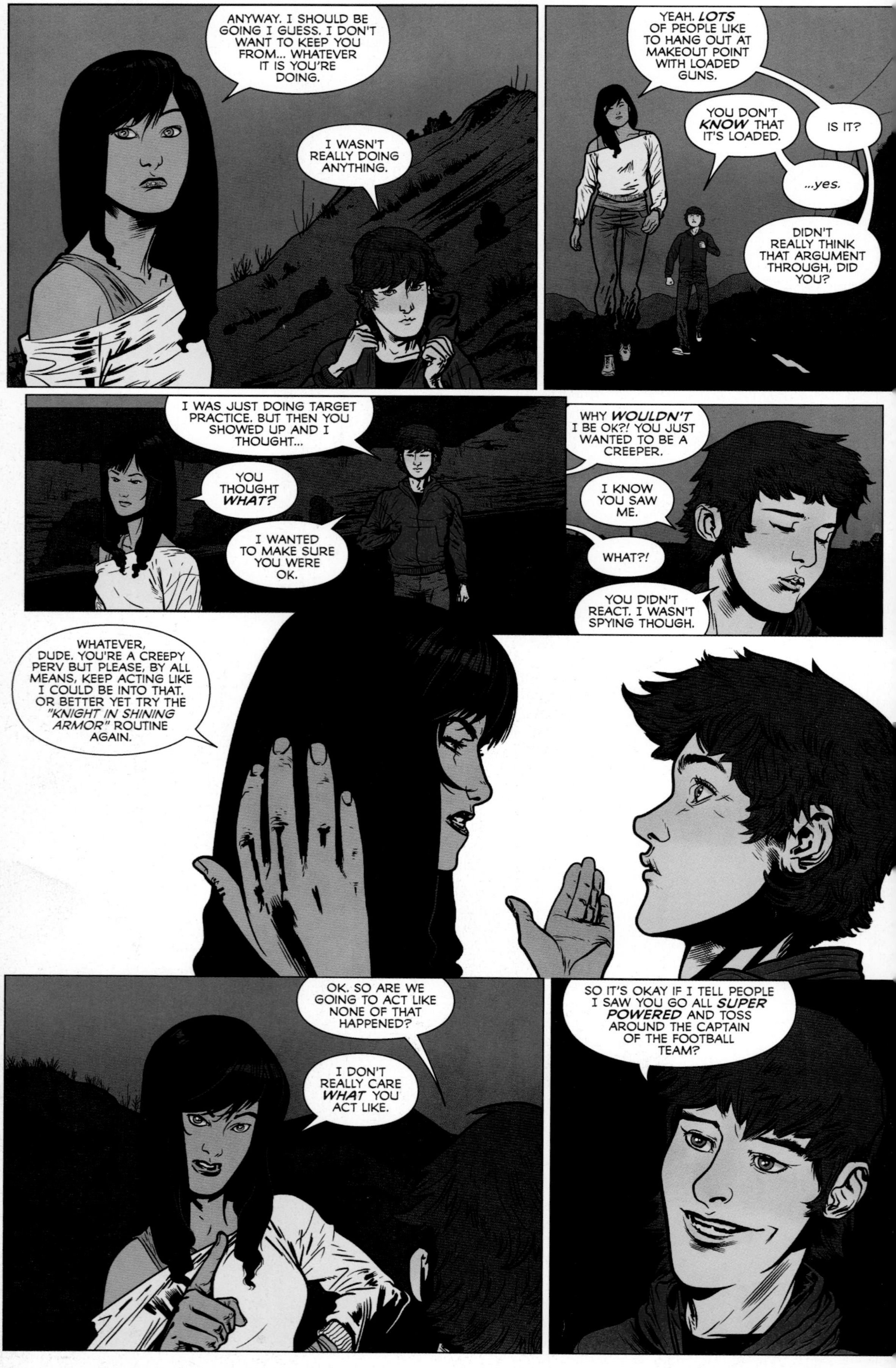
ANYWAY. I SHOULD BE GOING I GUESS. I DON'T WANT TO KEEP YOU FROM... WHATEVER IT IS YOU'RE DOING.
I WASN'T REALLY DOING ANYTHING.
YEAH. *LOTS* OF PEOPLE LIKE TO HANG OUT AT MAKEOUT POINT WITH LOADED GUNS.
YOU DON'T *KNOW* THAT IT'S LOADED.
IS IT?
...yes.
DIDN'T REALLY THINK THAT ARGUMENT THROUGH, DID YOU?
I WAS JUST DOING TARGET PRACTICE. BUT THEN YOU SHOWED UP AND I THOUGHT...
YOU THOUGHT *WHAT?*
I WANTED TO MAKE SURE YOU WERE OK.
WHY *WOULDN'T* I BE OK?! YOU JUST WANTED TO BE A CREEPER.
I KNOW YOU SAW ME.
WHAT?!
YOU DIDN'T REACT. I WASN'T SPYING THOUGH.
WHATEVER, DUDE. YOU'RE A CREEPY PERV BUT PLEASE, BY ALL MEANS, KEEP ACTING LIKE I COULD BE INTO THAT. OR BETTER YET TRY THE *"KNIGHT IN SHINING ARMOR"* ROUTINE AGAIN.
OK. SO ARE WE GOING TO ACT LIKE NONE OF THAT HAPPENED?
I DON'T REALLY CARE *WHAT* YOU ACT LIKE.
SO IT'S OKAY IF I TELL PEOPLE I SAW YOU GO ALL *SUPER POWERED* AND TOSS AROUND THE CAPTAIN OF THE FOOTBALL TEAM?

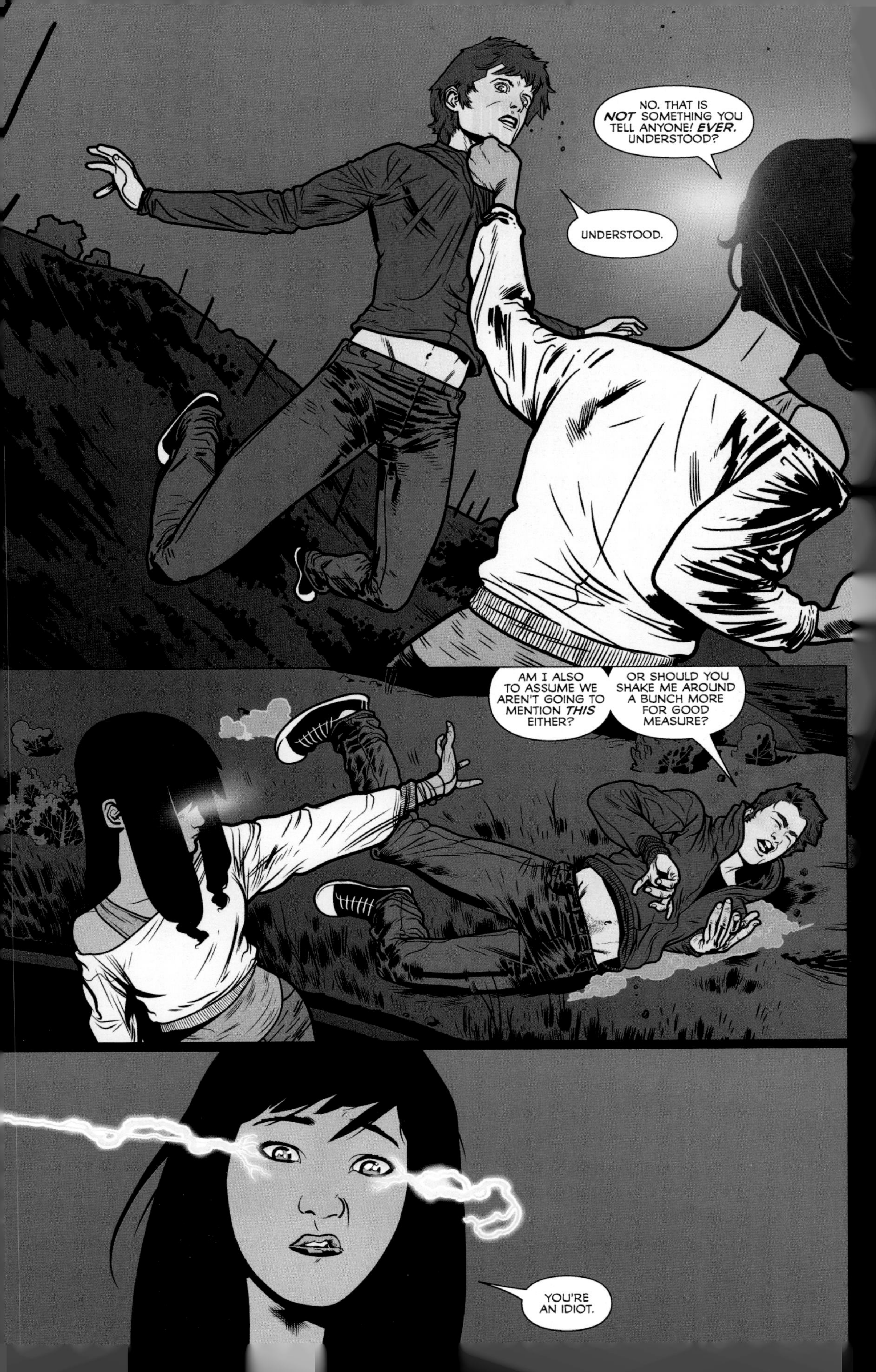
NO. THAT IS NOT SOMETHING YOU TELL ANYONE! EVER. UNDERSTOOD?
UNDERSTOOD.
AM I ALSO TO ASSUME WE AREN'T GOING TO MENTION THIS EITHER?
OR SHOULD YOU SHAKE ME AROUND A BUNCH MORE FOR GOOD MEASURE?
YOU'RE AN IDIOT.

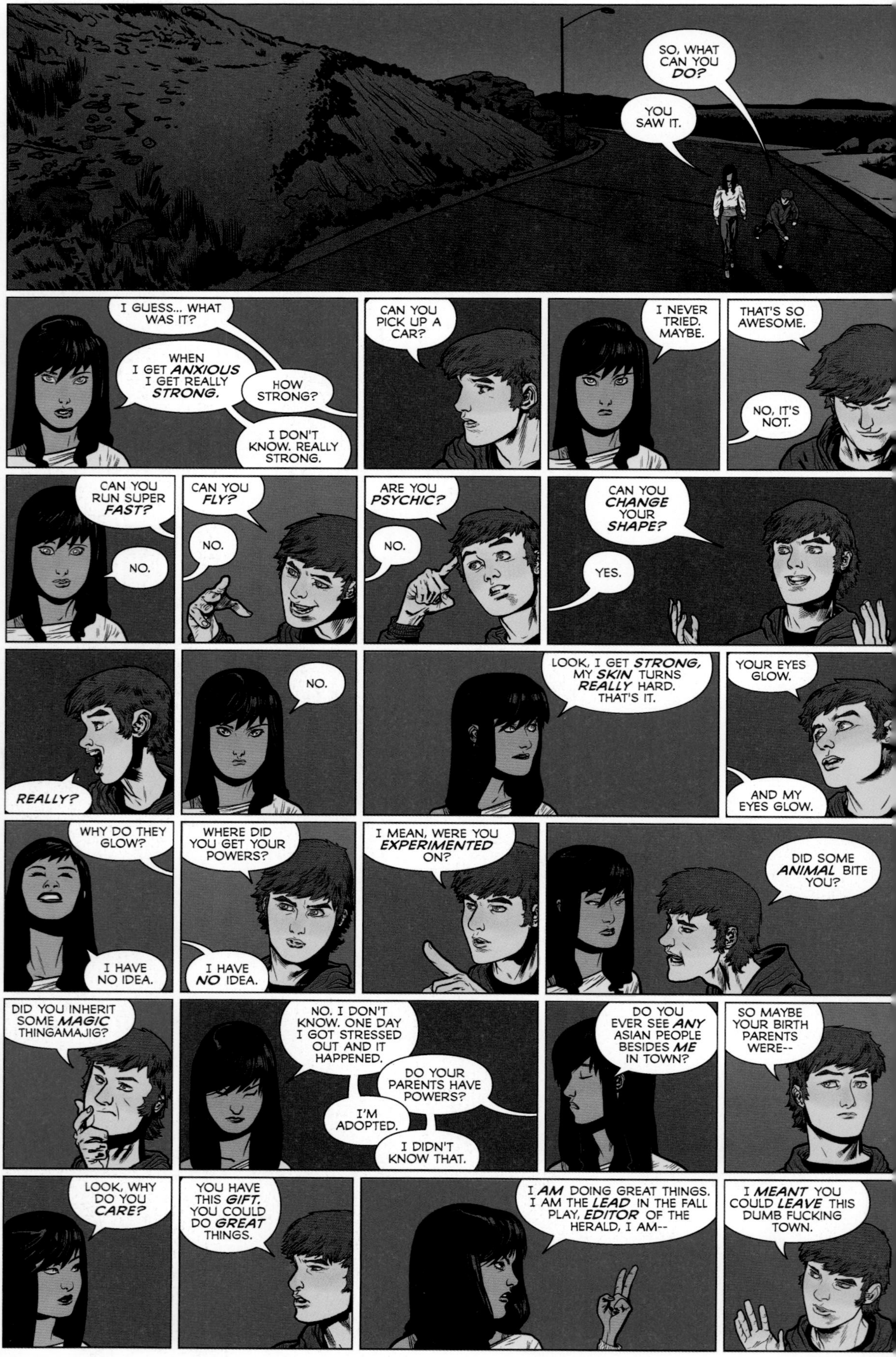
SO, WHAT CAN YOU DO?
YOU SAW IT.
I GUESS... WHAT WAS IT?
WHEN I GET ANXIOUS I GET REALLY STRONG.
HOW STRONG?
I DON'T KNOW. REALLY STRONG.
CAN YOU PICK UP A CAR?
I NEVER TRIED. MAYBE.
THAT'S SO AWESOME.
NO, IT'S NOT.
CAN YOU RUN SUPER FAST?
NO.
CAN YOU FLY?
NO.
ARE YOU PSYCHIC?
NO.
CAN YOU CHANGE YOUR SHAPE?
YES.
REALLY?
NO.
LOOK, I GET STRONG, MY SKIN TURNS REALLY HARD. THAT'S IT.
YOUR EYES GLOW.
AND MY EYES GLOW.
WHY DO THEY GLOW?
I HAVE NO IDEA.
WHERE DID YOU GET YOUR POWERS?
I HAVE NO IDEA.
I MEAN, WERE YOU EXPERIMENTED ON?
DID SOME ANIMAL BITE YOU?
DID YOU INHERIT SOME MAGIC THINGAMAJIG?
NO. I DON'T KNOW. ONE DAY I GOT STRESSED OUT AND IT HAPPENED.
DO YOUR PARENTS HAVE POWERS?
I'M ADOPTED.
I DIDN'T KNOW THAT.
DO YOU EVER SEE ANY ASIAN PEOPLE BESIDES ME IN TOWN?
SO MAYBE YOUR BIRTH PARENTS WERE--
LOOK, WHY DO YOU CARE?
YOU HAVE THIS GIFT. YOU COULD DO GREAT THINGS.
I AM DOING GREAT THINGS. I AM THE LEAD IN THE FALL PLAY, EDITOR OF THE HERALD, I AM--
I MEANT YOU COULD LEAVE THIS DUMB FUCKING TOWN.

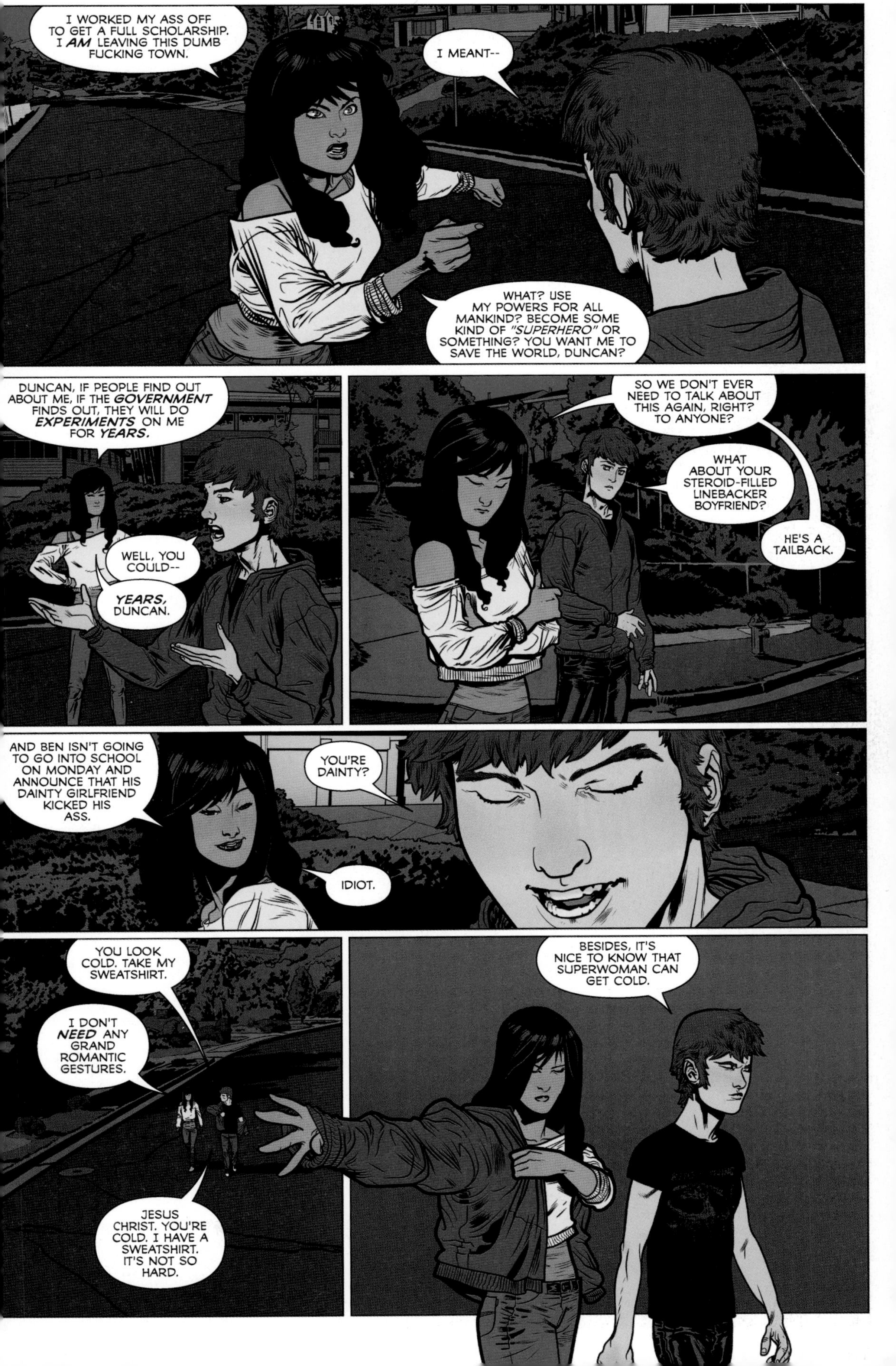

I WORKED MY ASS OFF TO GET A FULL SCHOLARSHIP. I *AM* LEAVING THIS DUMB FUCKING TOWN.
I MEANT--
WHAT? USE MY POWERS FOR ALL MANKIND? BECOME SOME KIND OF *"SUPERHERO"* OR SOMETHING? YOU WANT ME TO SAVE THE WORLD, DUNCAN?
DUNCAN, IF PEOPLE FIND OUT ABOUT ME, IF THE ***GOVERNMENT*** FINDS OUT, THEY WILL DO ***EXPERIMENTS*** ON ME FOR ***YEARS.***
WELL, YOU COULD--
YEARS, DUNCAN.
SO WE DON'T EVER NEED TO TALK ABOUT THIS AGAIN, RIGHT? TO ANYONE?
WHAT ABOUT YOUR STEROID-FILLED LINEBACKER BOYFRIEND?
HE'S A TAILBACK.
AND BEN ISN'T GOING TO GO INTO SCHOOL ON MONDAY AND ANNOUNCE THAT HIS DAINTY GIRLFRIEND KICKED HIS ASS.
YOU'RE DAINTY?
IDIOT.
YOU LOOK COLD. TAKE MY SWEATSHIRT.
I DON'T ***NEED*** ANY GRAND ROMANTIC GESTURES.
JESUS CHRIST. YOU'RE COLD. I HAVE A SWEATSHIRT. IT'S NOT SO HARD.
BESIDES, IT'S NICE TO KNOW THAT SUPERWOMAN CAN GET COLD.

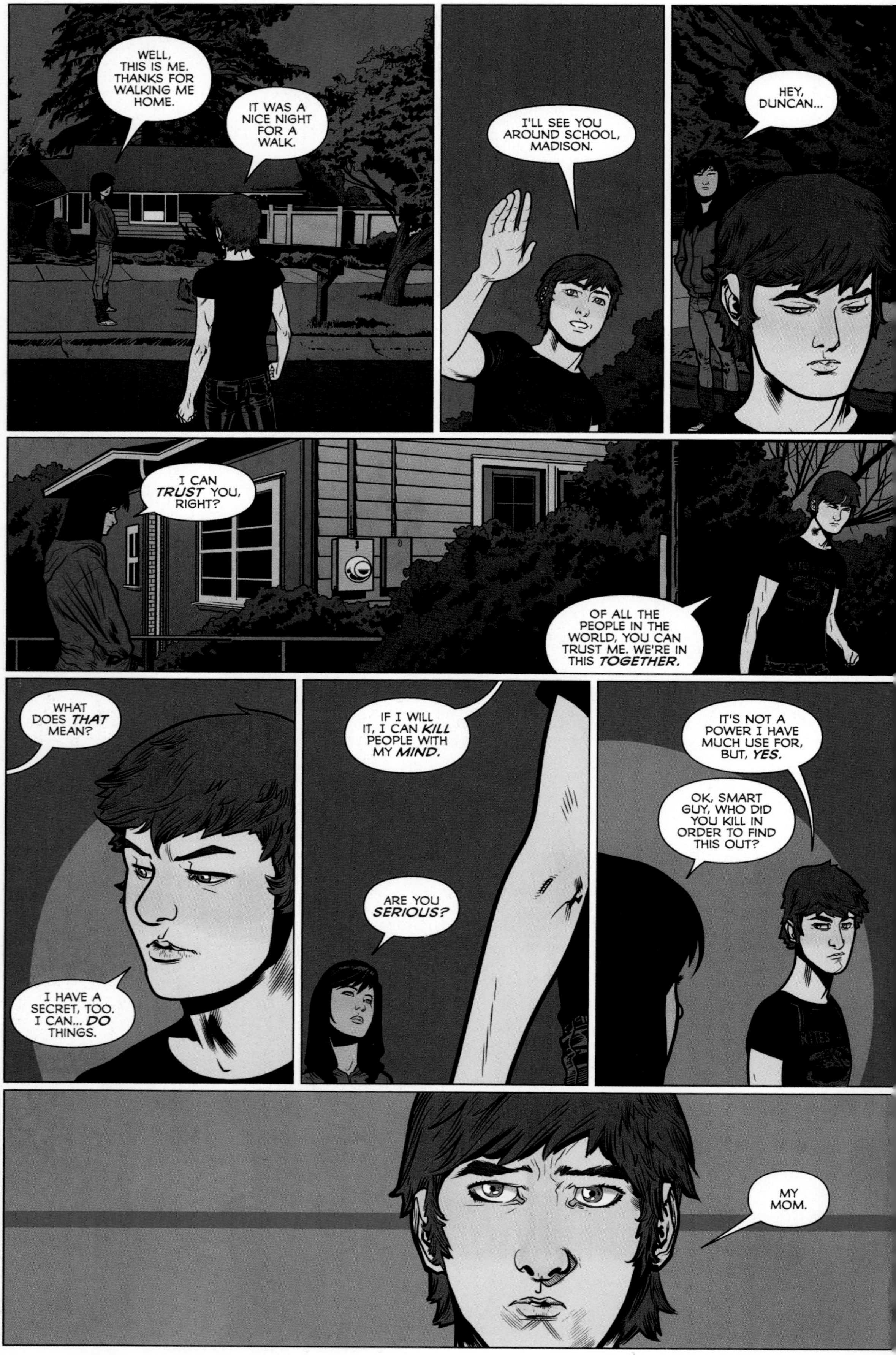
WELL, THIS IS ME. THANKS FOR WALKING ME HOME.
IT WAS A NICE NIGHT FOR A WALK.
I'LL SEE YOU AROUND SCHOOL, MADISON.
HEY, DUNCAN...
I CAN *TRUST* YOU, RIGHT?
OF ALL THE PEOPLE IN THE WORLD, YOU CAN TRUST ME. WE'RE IN THIS *TOGETHER.*
WHAT DOES *THAT* MEAN?
I HAVE A SECRET, TOO. I CAN... *DO* THINGS.
IF I WILL IT, I CAN *KILL* PEOPLE WITH MY *MIND.*
ARE YOU *SERIOUS?*
IT'S NOT A POWER I HAVE MUCH USE FOR, BUT, *YES.*
OK, SMART GUY, WHO DID YOU KILL IN ORDER TO FIND THIS OUT?
MY MOM.

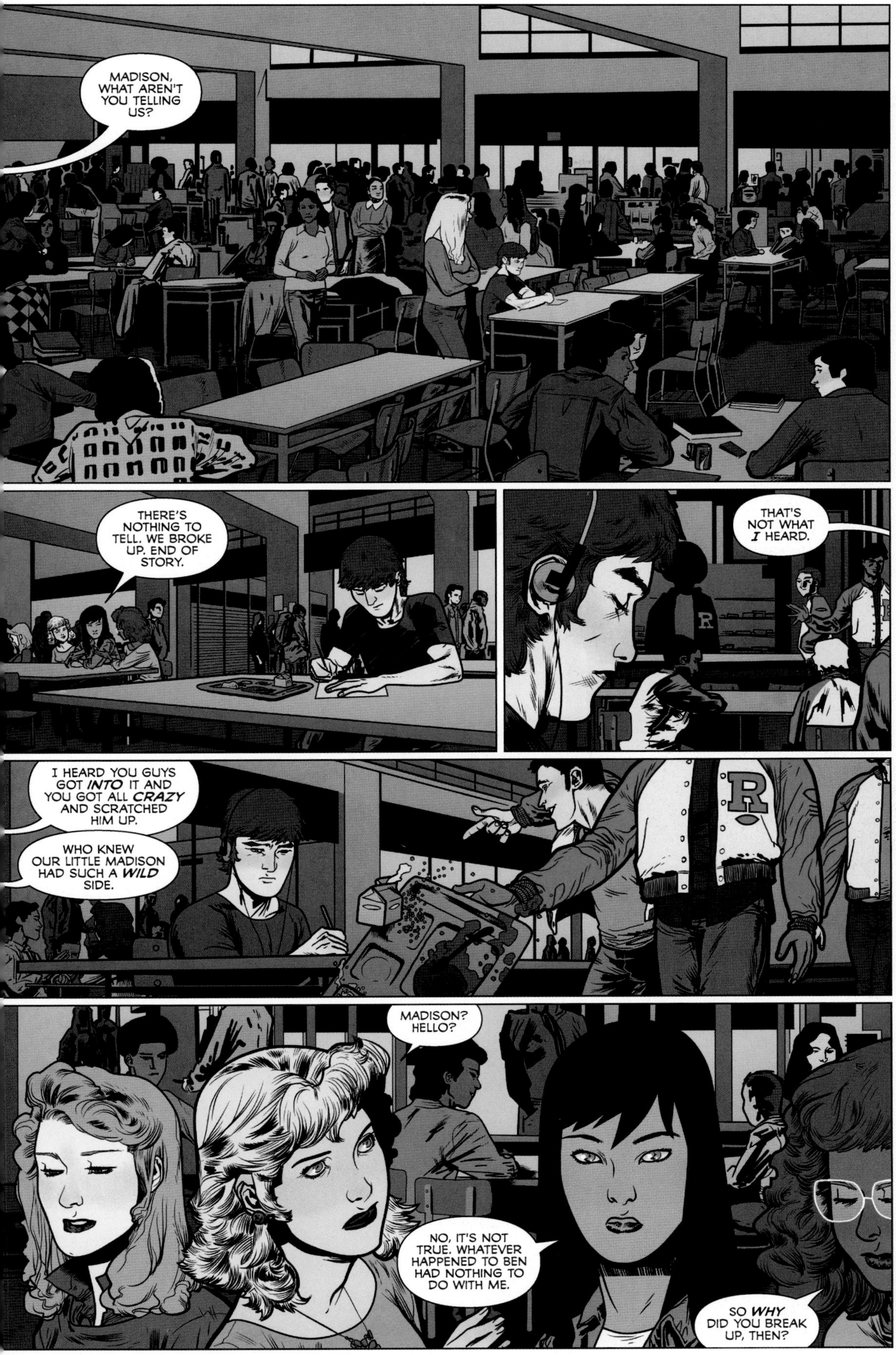
MADISON, WHAT AREN'T YOU TELLING US?
THERE'S NOTHING TO TELL. WE BROKE UP. END OF STORY.
THAT'S NOT WHAT *I* HEARD.
I HEARD YOU GUYS GOT *INTO* IT AND YOU GOT ALL *CRAZY* AND SCRATCHED HIM UP.
WHO KNEW OUR LITTLE MADISON HAD SUCH A *WILD* SIDE.
MADISON? HELLO?
NO, IT'S NOT TRUE. WHATEVER HAPPENED TO BEN HAD NOTHING TO DO WITH ME.
SO *WHY* DID YOU BREAK UP, THEN?

WHAT'UP, FREAK?

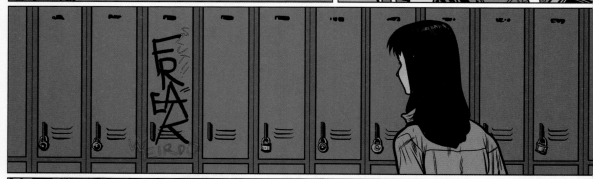

SHH! SHH! HERE SHE IS.

THEN SHE STARTS HOWLING LIKE AN *ANIMAL.* I DON'T GO IN FOR THAT KIND OF STUFF, YA KNOW?

YOU ARE *QUITE* THE TOPIC OF CONVERSATION TODAY, MISS.

AND I'M ALL *"BABY, WHY DON'T I GET ON TOP?"* AND SHE SAYS--

THIS SEEMS *TOTALLY* BELIEVABLE.

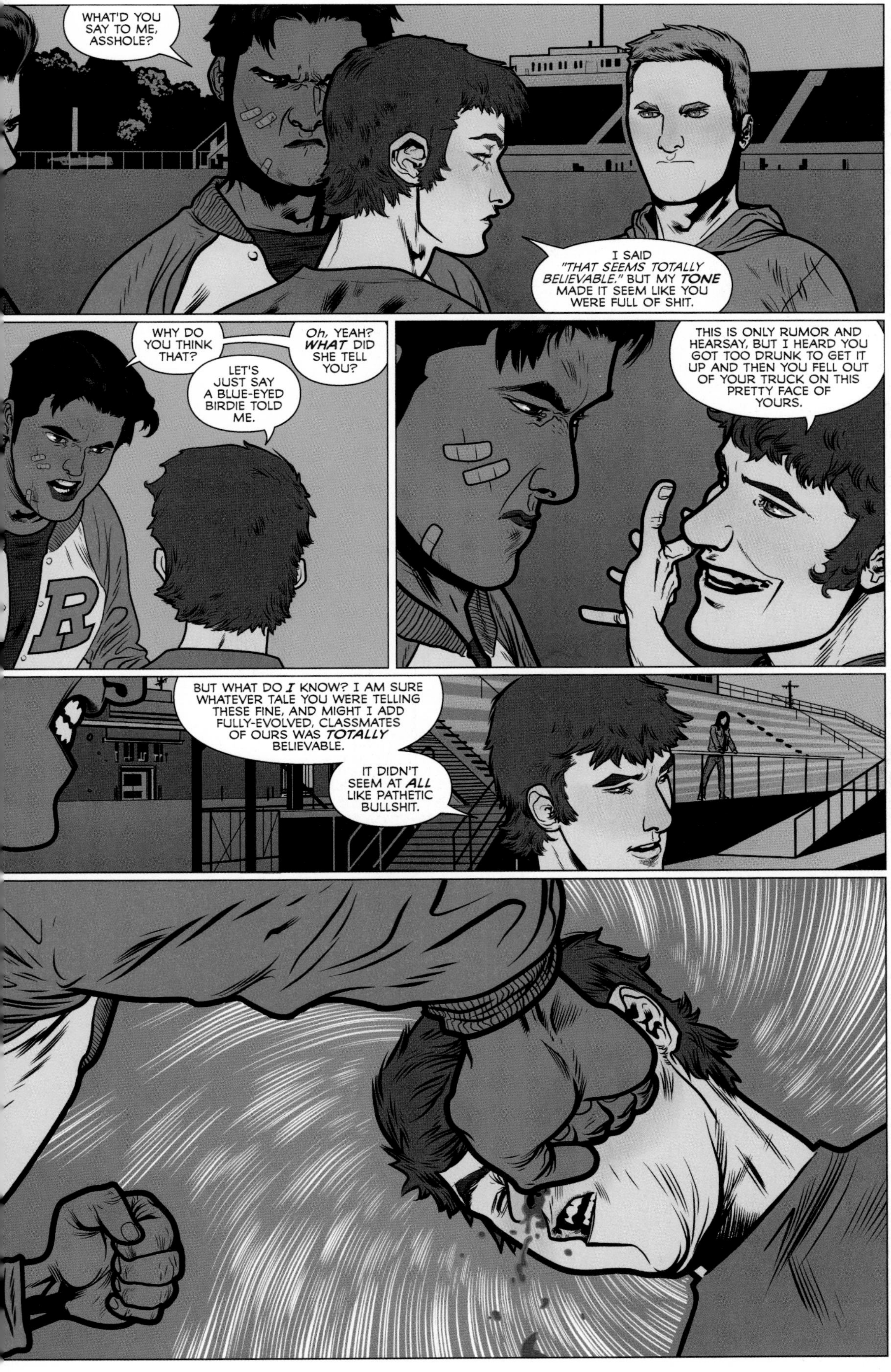
WHAT'D YOU SAY TO ME, ASSHOLE?
I SAID "THAT SEEMS TOTALLY BELIEVABLE." BUT MY TONE MADE IT SEEM LIKE YOU WERE FULL OF SHIT.
WHY DO YOU THINK THAT?
LET'S JUST SAY A BLUE-EYED BIRDIE TOLD ME.
Oh, YEAH? WHAT DID SHE TELL YOU?
THIS IS ONLY RUMOR AND HEARSAY, BUT I HEARD YOU GOT TOO DRUNK TO GET IT UP AND THEN YOU FELL OUT OF YOUR TRUCK ON THIS PRETTY FACE OF YOURS.
BUT WHAT DO I KNOW? I AM SURE WHATEVER TALE YOU WERE TELLING THESE FINE, AND MIGHT I ADD FULLY-EVOLVED, CLASSMATES OF OURS WAS TOTALLY BELIEVABLE.
IT DIDN'T SEEM AT ALL LIKE PATHETIC BULLSHIT.

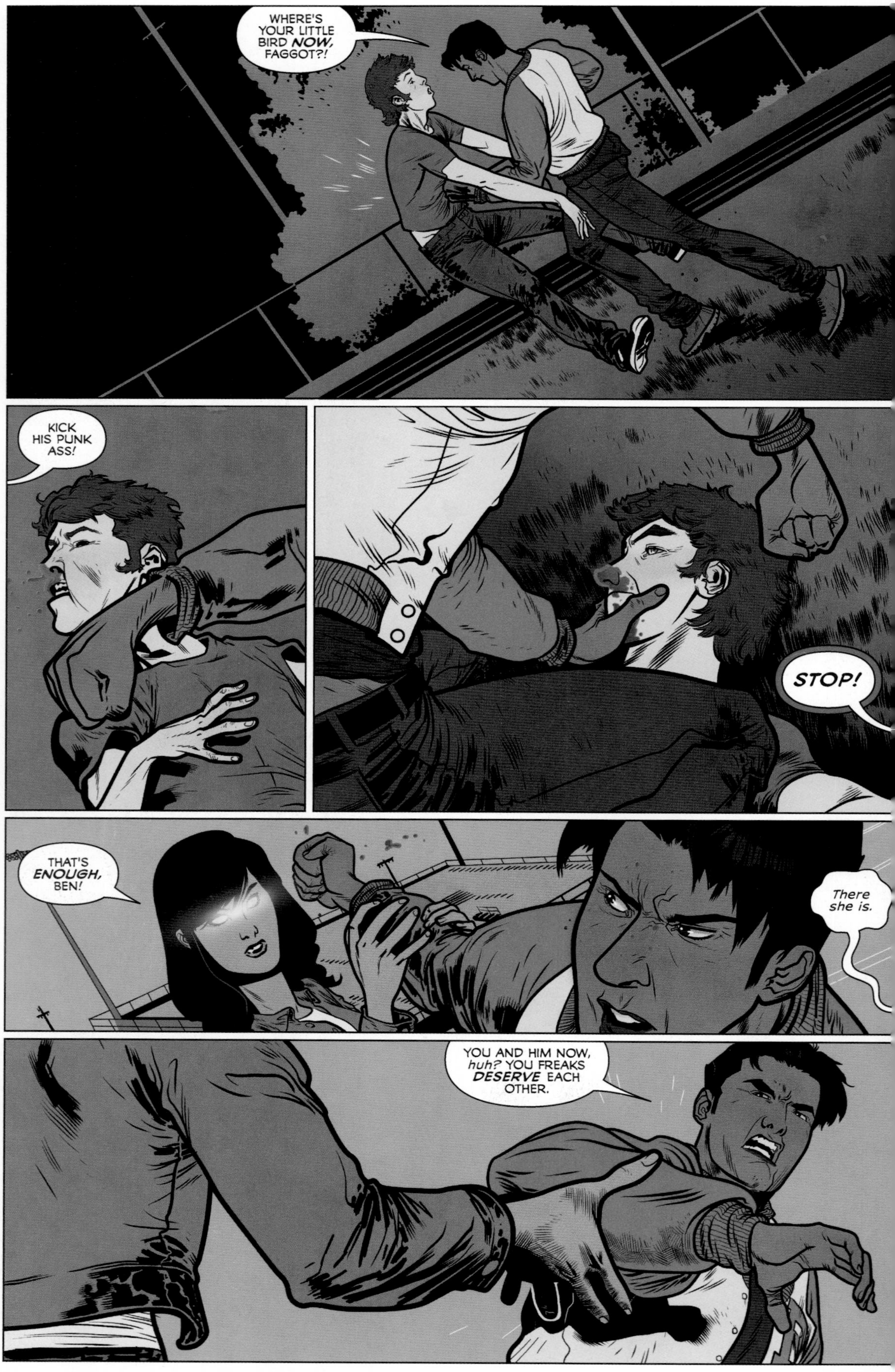
WHERE'S YOUR LITTLE BIRD NOW, FAGGOT?!
KICK HIS PUNK ASS!
STOP!
THAT'S ENOUGH, BEN!
There she is.
YOU AND HIM NOW, huh? YOU FREAKS DESERVE EACH OTHER.

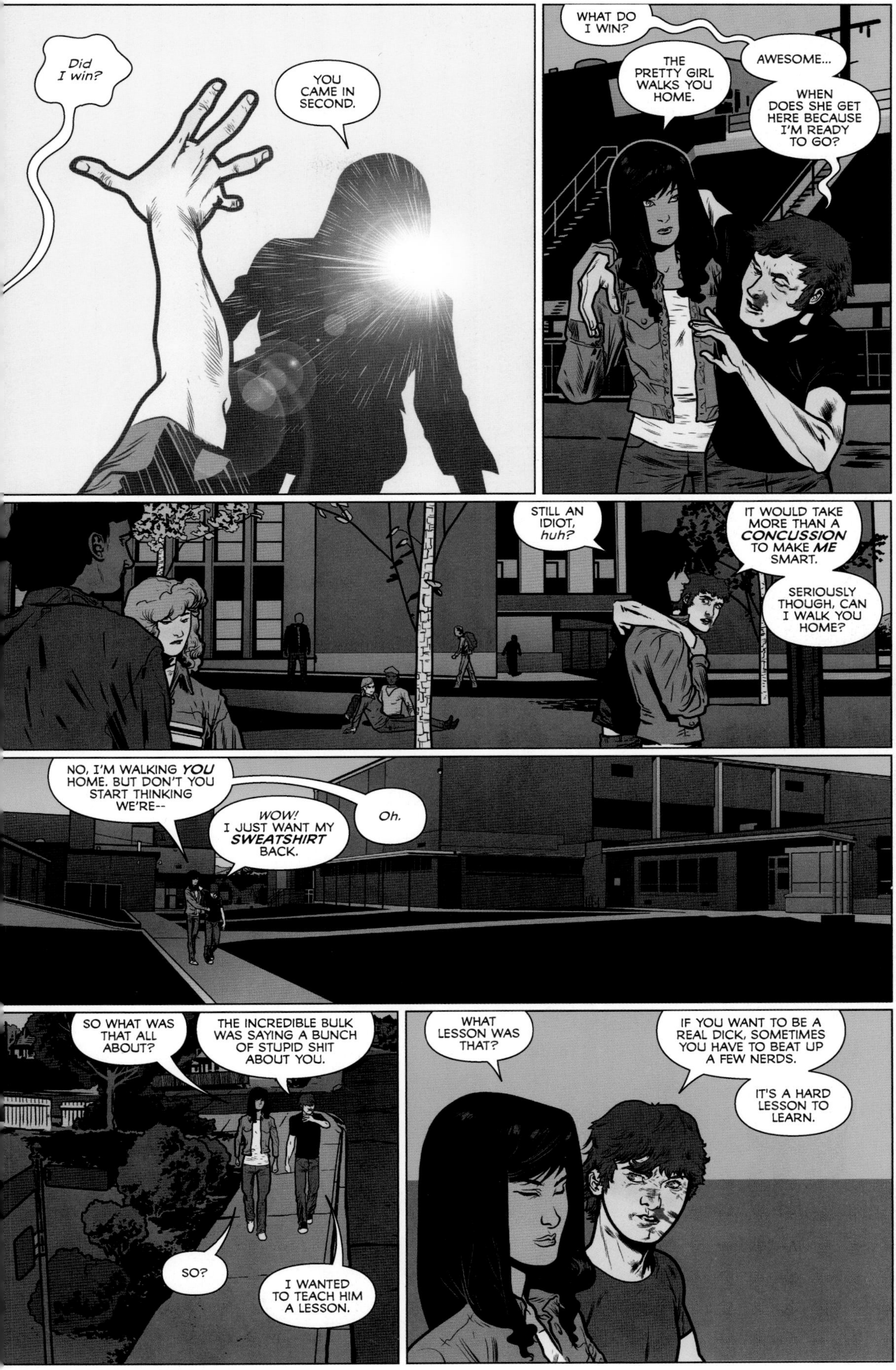
Did I win?
YOU CAME IN SECOND.
WHAT DO I WIN?
THE PRETTY GIRL WALKS YOU HOME.
AWESOME...
WHEN DOES SHE GET HERE BECAUSE I'M READY TO GO?
STILL AN IDIOT, *huh?*
IT WOULD TAKE MORE THAN A ***CONCUSSION*** TO MAKE ***ME*** SMART.
SERIOUSLY THOUGH, CAN I WALK YOU HOME?
NO, I'M WALKING ***YOU*** HOME. BUT DON'T YOU START THINKING WE'RE--
WOW! I JUST WANT MY ***SWEATSHIRT*** BACK.
Oh.
SO WHAT WAS THAT ALL ABOUT?
THE INCREDIBLE BULK WAS SAYING A BUNCH OF STUPID SHIT ABOUT YOU.
SO?
I WANTED TO TEACH HIM A LESSON.
WHAT LESSON WAS THAT?
IF YOU WANT TO BE A REAL DICK, SOMETIMES YOU HAVE TO BEAT UP A FEW NERDS.
IT'S A HARD LESSON TO LEARN.

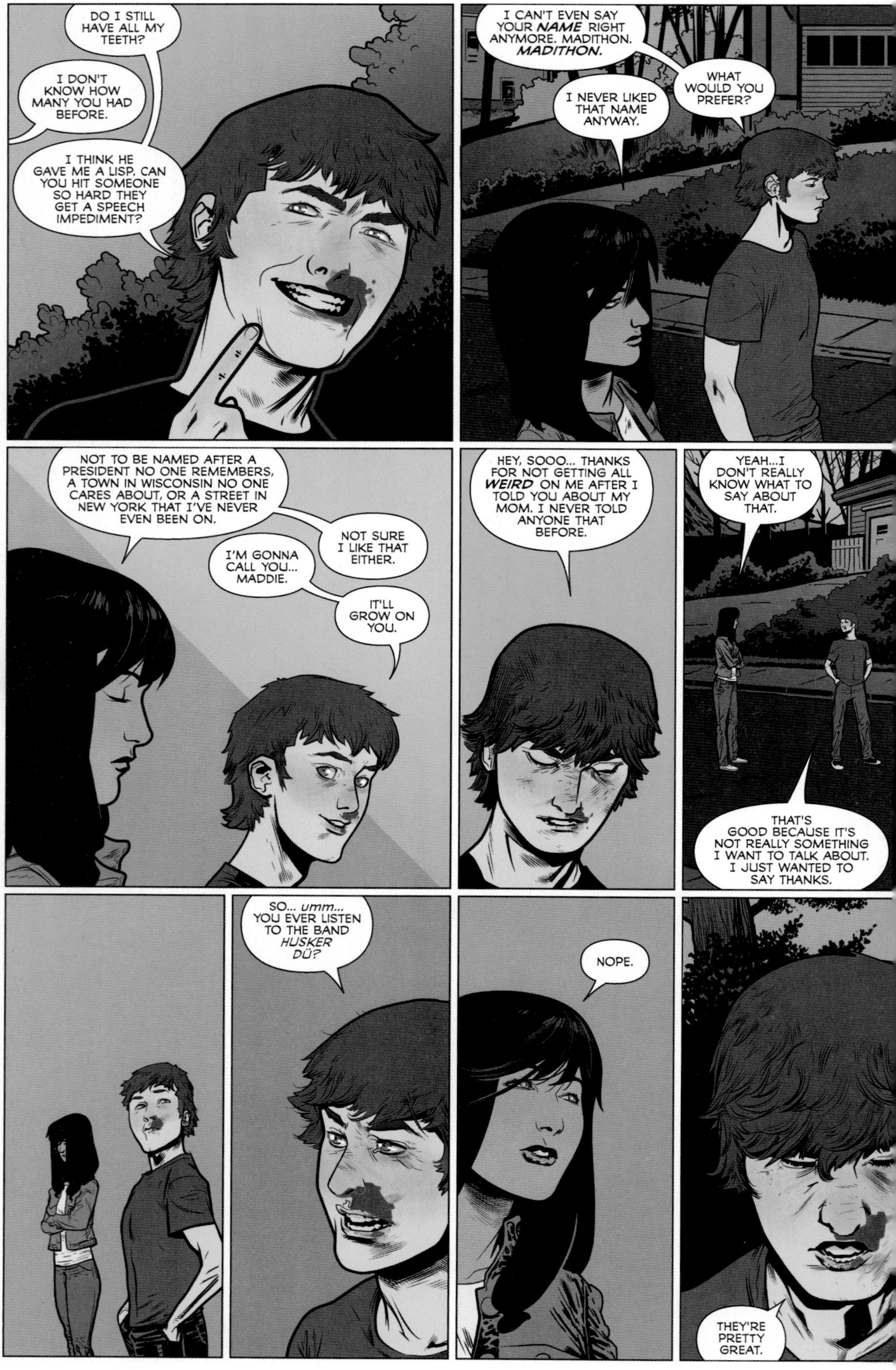
DO I STILL HAVE ALL MY TEETH?
I DON'T KNOW HOW MANY YOU HAD BEFORE.
I THINK HE GAVE ME A LISP. CAN YOU HIT SOMEONE SO HARD THEY GET A SPEECH IMPEDIMENT?
I CAN'T EVEN SAY YOUR ***NAME*** RIGHT ANYMORE. MADITHON. ***MADITHON.***
I NEVER LIKED THAT NAME ANYWAY.
WHAT WOULD YOU PREFER?
NOT TO BE NAMED AFTER A PRESIDENT NO ONE REMEMBERS, A TOWN IN WISCONSIN NO ONE CARES ABOUT, OR A STREET IN NEW YORK THAT I'VE NEVER EVEN BEEN ON.
I'M GONNA CALL YOU... MADDIE.
NOT SURE I LIKE THAT EITHER.
IT'LL GROW ON YOU.
HEY, SOOO... THANKS FOR NOT GETTING ALL ***WEIRD*** ON ME AFTER I TOLD YOU ABOUT MY MOM. I NEVER TOLD ANYONE THAT BEFORE.
YEAH...I DON'T REALLY KNOW WHAT TO SAY ABOUT THAT.
THAT'S GOOD BECAUSE IT'S NOT REALLY SOMETHING I WANT TO TALK ABOUT. I JUST WANTED TO SAY THANKS.
SO... *umm...* YOU EVER LISTEN TO THE BAND *HUSKER DÜ?*
NOPE.
THEY'RE PRETTY GREAT.

WHAT? WHY WOULD *I* APOLOGIZE TO *HIM*?

BEN IS STILL A PRETTY BIG DEAL IN CASE YOU FORGOT.

HE'S A PRETTY BIG ASSHOLE IN CASE YOU FORGOT.

STILL, YOU NEED TO GO WITH SOMEONE. UNLESS YOU WANT TO GO TO FALL FLING WITH ONE OF THE MUTANTS FROM A/V CLUB, MAYBE--

I HEARD HE MIGHT ASK ANNA.

ANNA WILL DEFINITELY PUT OUT. SHE'S EASIER THAN MR. SILK'S MIDTERM.

SHE'S EASIER THAN YOU, BETHANY.

FUCK YOU, JULIA.

I DON'T *CARE* WHO BEN GOES TO THE STUPID DANCE WITH. I DON'T *CARE* WHO HE *FUCKS*. I HOPE SHE *DOES* PUT OUT. I HOPE SHE GETS *PREGNANT* AND HAS TRIPLETS AND THEY GET MARRIED AND LIVE HAPPILY EVER AFTER. CAN WE *PLEASE* STOP FUCKING *TALKING* ABOUT THIS?

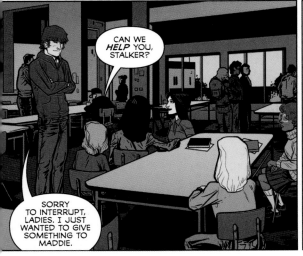

JEEZE. BITCHY, MUCH?

THOSE WOULD BE SOME *DUMB* BABIES.

DUMB *AND* SLUTTY. ANYWAY, WHAT *WOULD* PRECIOUS MISS MADISON LIKE TO TALK---

CAN WE *HELP* YOU, STALKER?

SORRY TO INTERRUPT, LADIES. I JUST WANTED TO GIVE SOMETHING TO MADDIE.

MADDIE? I DON'T THINK *MADISON* WANTS YOUR ANIMAL SACRIFICE OR WHATEVER... SO YOU CAN RUN ALONG NOW, WEIRDO.

WHAT IS IT, DUNCAN?

I MADE YOU A MIX. I THINK YOU'LL LIKE IT.

...I HOPE YOU WILL.

A *TAPE?* WHAT'S WRONG WITH YOU?

I DON'T HAVE A TAPE PLAYER.

YOU'LL FIND A WAY TO LISTEN TO IT.

HEY, DIDN'T HER BOYFRIEND BEAT THE *SHIT* OUT OF YOU YESTERDAY?

I DON'T THINK HE'S HER BOYFRIEND ANYMORE.

IS THAT BAND YOU WERE TELLING ME ABOUT ON HERE?

FIRST SONG ON THE B-SIDE.

YOU MUST FEEL LIKE A REAL *HOMO,* GETTING BEAT UP IN FRONT OF THE WHOLE *SCHOOL?*

I THINK THERE WERE ONLY TWENTY-FIVE PEOPLE THERE.

SO YOU HEAR SHE'S SINGLE AND YOU MAKE A STUPID *MIXTAPE* SO MADISON WILL GO TO *FALL FLING* WITH YOU?

IF SHE WANTS TO GO, I AM SURE MADDIE CAN GO WITH WHOMEVER SHE WANTS.

THE ONLY REASON *I* WOULD EVER GO IS TO WATCH *YOU* GET COVERED IN *PIG'S BLOOD.*

HA!

WHAT A FUCKING CREEP. A MIX TAPE?

I THOUGHT IT WAS KINDA SWEET.

AND WHAT WAS ALL THAT *"BAND YOU TOLD ME ABOUT"* STUFF? MADISON? *HELLO?*

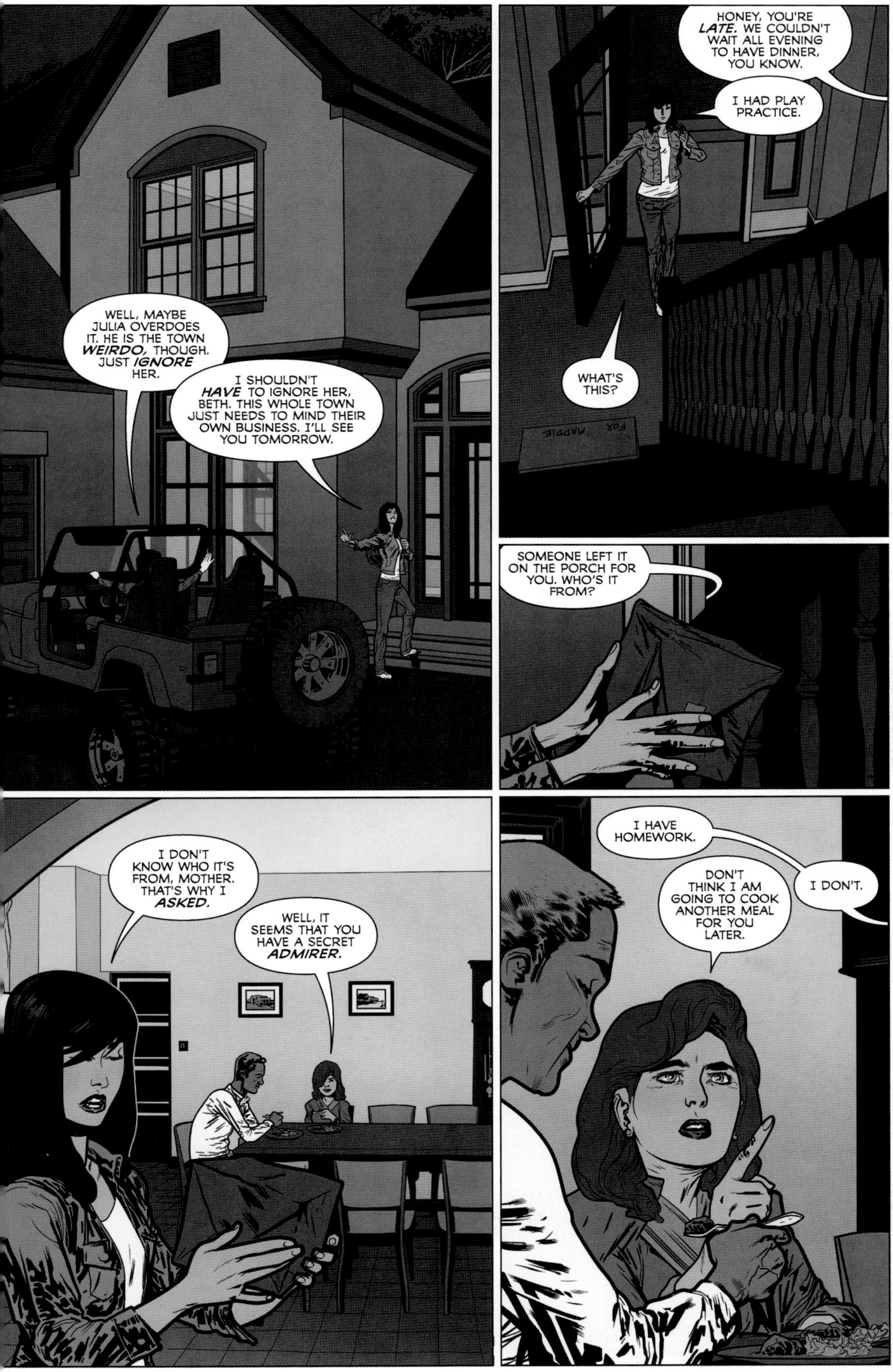
WELL, MAYBE JULIA OVERDOES IT. HE IS THE TOWN *WEIRDO,* THOUGH. JUST *IGNORE* HER.
I SHOULDN'T *HAVE* TO IGNORE HER, BETH. THIS WHOLE TOWN JUST NEEDS TO MIND THEIR OWN BUSINESS. I'LL SEE YOU TOMORROW.
HONEY, YOU'RE *LATE.* WE COULDN'T WAIT ALL EVENING TO HAVE DINNER, YOU KNOW.
I HAD PLAY PRACTICE.
WHAT'S THIS?
FOR MADDIE
SOMEONE LEFT IT ON THE PORCH FOR YOU. WHO'S IT FROM?
I DON'T KNOW WHO IT'S FROM, MOTHER. THAT'S WHY I *ASKED.*
WELL, IT SEEMS THAT YOU HAVE A SECRET *ADMIRER.*
I HAVE HOMEWORK.
DON'T THINK I AM GOING TO COOK ANOTHER MEAL FOR YOU LATER.
I DON'T.

8:57
STOP
PLAY
Death or Glory – The Clash
Germ Free Adolescents
– X-Ray Spex
Secret – Germs
Head
Etiquette
Tamer – Wire
When I Reach For My Revolver
Attitude – Bad Brains
Out of Step – Minor Threat
Stand Still – Gorilla Biscuits
Young Til I Die – 7 Seconds
SIDE B
Terms of Psychic Warfare
– Husker Du
Said Gun – Embrace
Good Good Things – Descendants
Because You're Frightened
– Magazine
Left of The Dial
– The Replacements
Bigmouth Strikes Again
– The Smiths
Help Save The Youth of America
– Billy Bragg
Psycho Killer – Talking Heads
Blues From A Gun – J.A.M.C.
Dumb Waiters – Psychedelic Furs
WHAT WE DO IS SECRET
GOING OUT!
WHERE ARE YOU GOING? IT'S ELEVEN O'CLOCK!

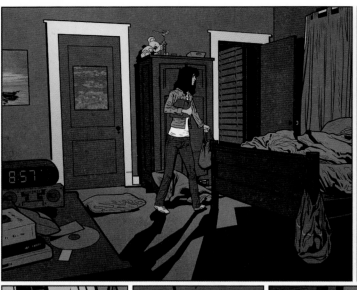

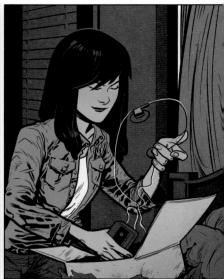

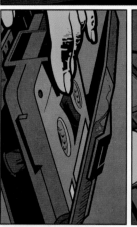

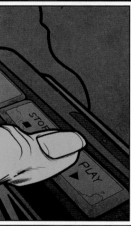

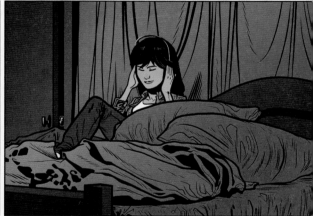

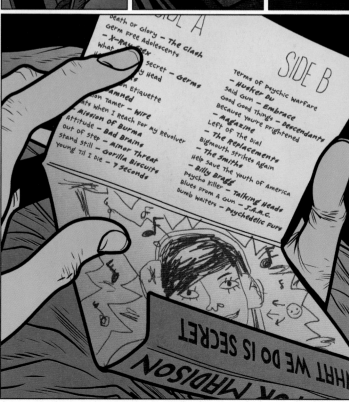

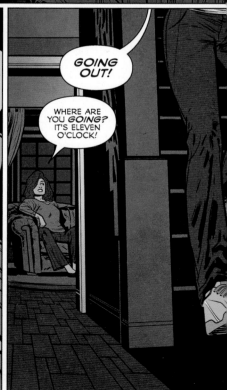

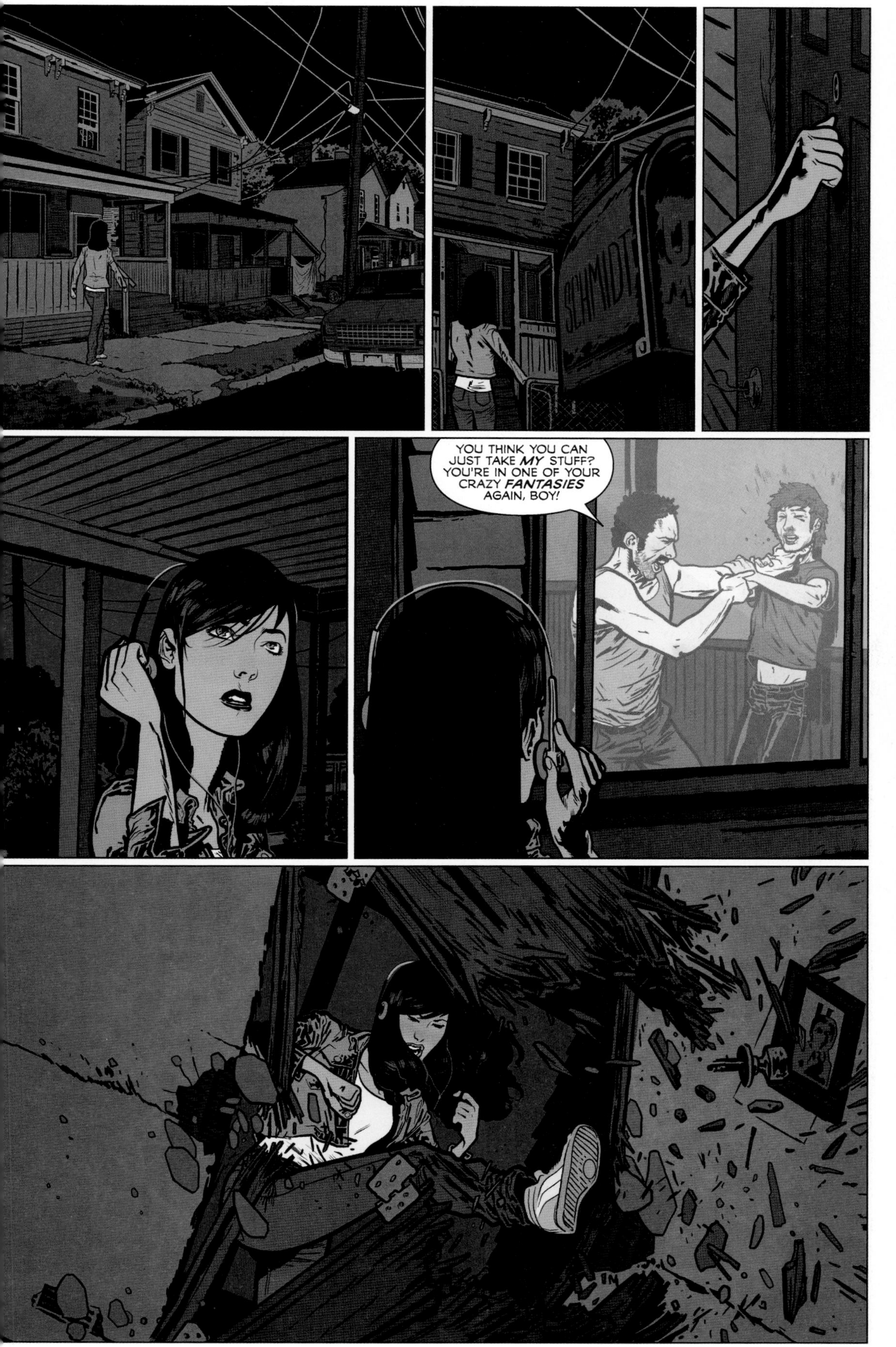
SCHMIDT
YOU THINK YOU CAN JUST TAKE *MY* STUFF? YOU'RE IN ONE OF YOUR CRAZY *FANTASIES* AGAIN, BOY!

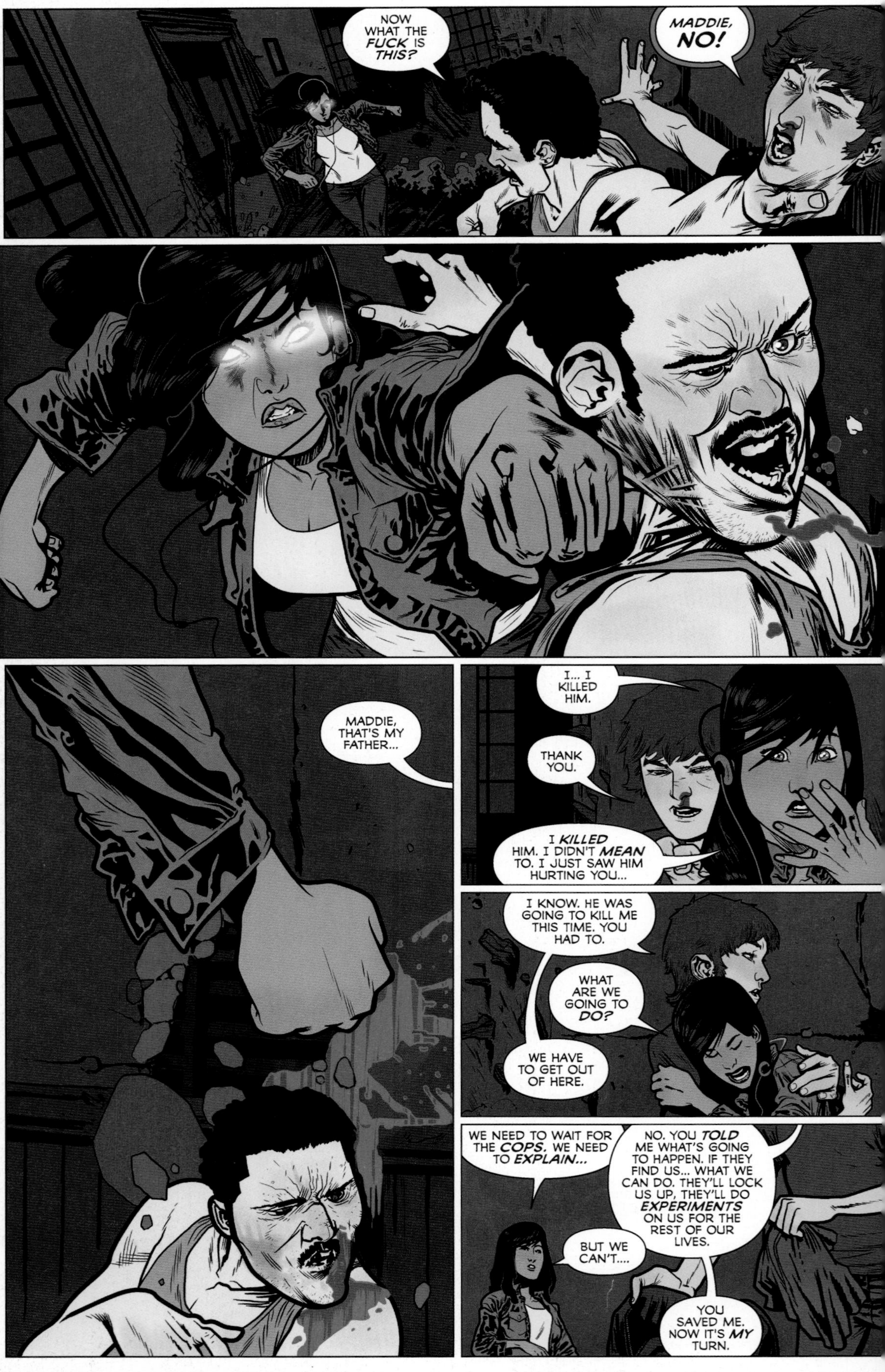
NOW WHAT THE *FUCK* IS *THIS?*
MADDIE, ***NO!***
MADDIE, THAT'S MY FATHER...
I... I KILLED HIM.
THANK YOU.
I *KILLED* HIM. I DIDN'T *MEAN* TO. I JUST SAW HIM HURTING YOU...
I KNOW. HE WAS GOING TO KILL ME THIS TIME. YOU HAD TO.
WHAT ARE WE GOING TO *DO?*
WE HAVE TO GET OUT OF HERE.
WE NEED TO WAIT FOR THE ***COPS.*** *WE NEED TO* ***EXPLAIN...***
NO. YOU ***TOLD*** ME WHAT'S GOING TO HAPPEN. IF THEY FIND US... WHAT WE CAN DO. THEY'LL LOCK US UP, THEY'LL DO ***EXPERIMENTS*** ON US FOR THE REST OF OUR LIVES.
BUT WE CAN'T....
YOU SAVED ME. NOW IT'S *MY* TURN.

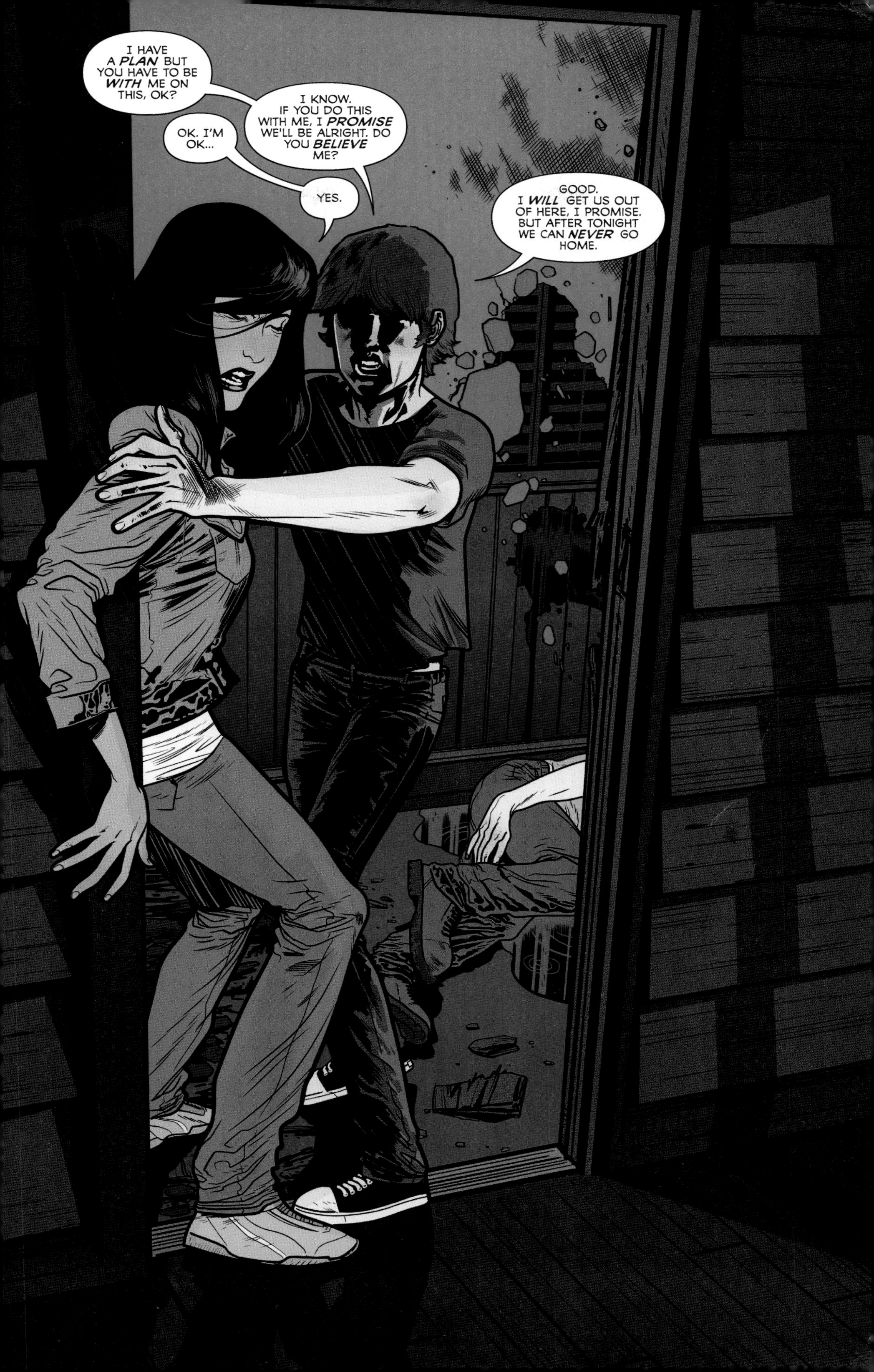
I HAVE A *PLAN* BUT YOU HAVE TO BE *WITH* ME ON THIS, OK?
OK. I'M OK...
I KNOW. IF YOU DO THIS WITH ME, I *PROMISE* WE'LL BE ALRIGHT. DO YOU *BELIEVE* ME?
YES.
GOOD. I *WILL* GET US OUT OF HERE, I PROMISE. BUT AFTER TONIGHT WE CAN *NEVER* GO HOME.

CHAPTER 2

THAT'S WHEN I REACH FOR MY REVOLVER

B 1989 IN A SMALL TOWN.

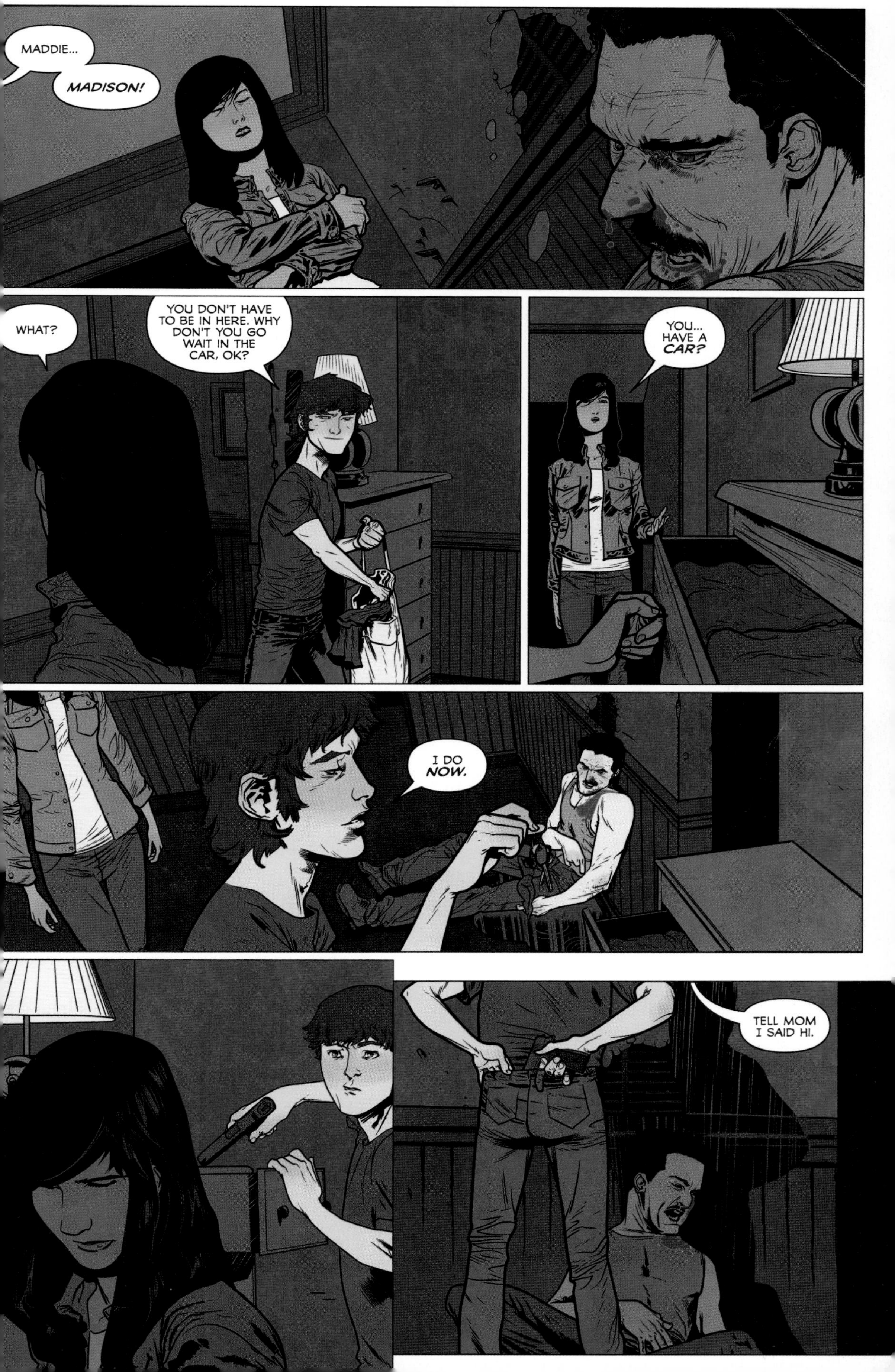
MADDIE...
MADISON!
WHAT?
YOU DON'T HAVE TO BE IN HERE. WHY DON'T YOU GO WAIT IN THE CAR, OK?
YOU... HAVE A CAR?
I DO NOW.
TELL MOM I SAID HI.

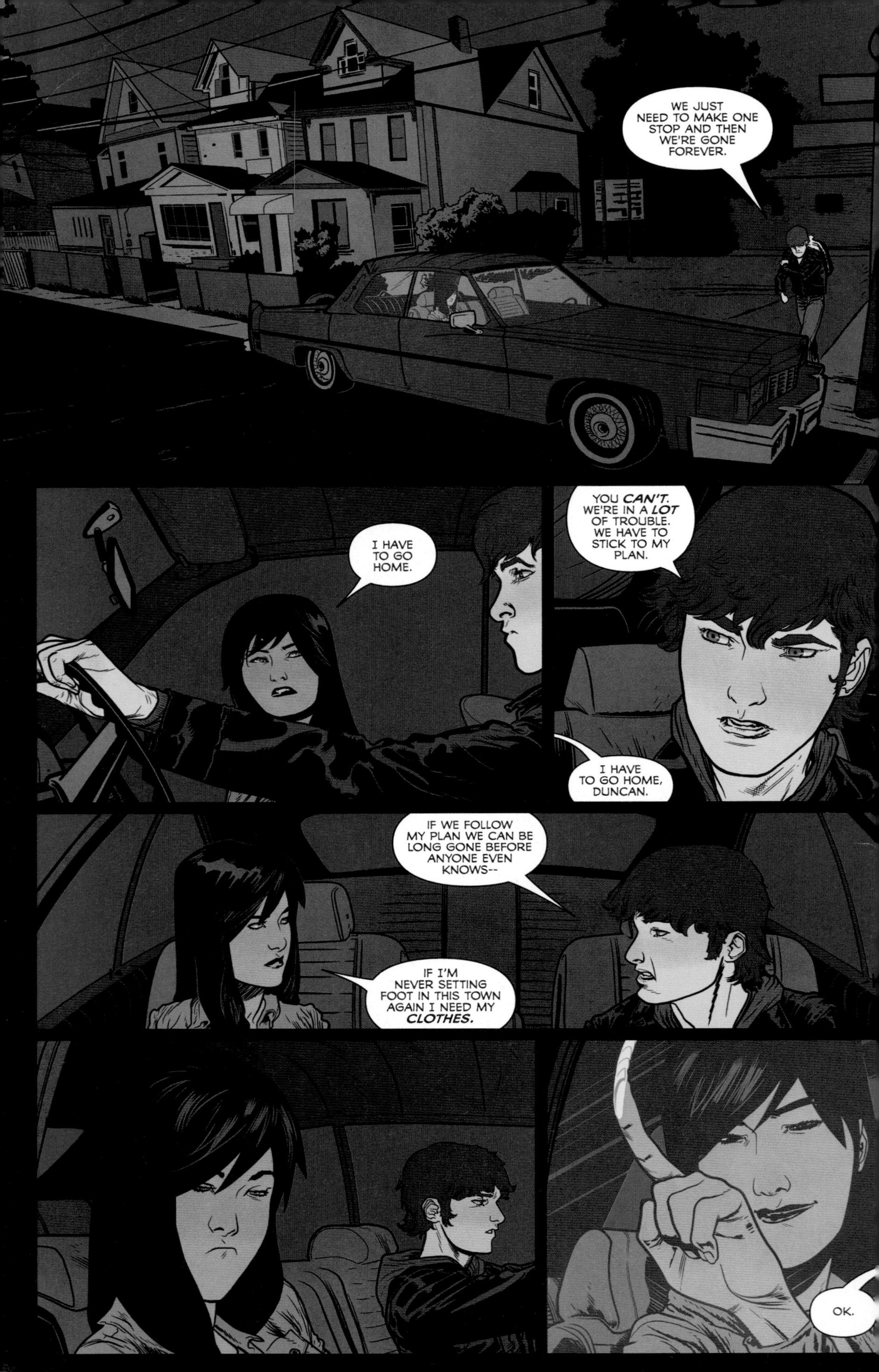
WE JUST NEED TO MAKE ONE STOP AND THEN WE'RE GONE FOREVER.
I HAVE TO GO HOME.
YOU *CAN'T*. WE'RE IN A *LOT* OF TROUBLE. WE HAVE TO STICK TO MY PLAN.
I HAVE TO GO HOME, DUNCAN.
IF WE FOLLOW MY PLAN WE CAN BE LONG GONE BEFORE ANYONE EVEN KNOWS--
IF I'M NEVER SETTING FOOT IN THIS TOWN AGAIN I NEED MY *CLOTHES.*
OK.

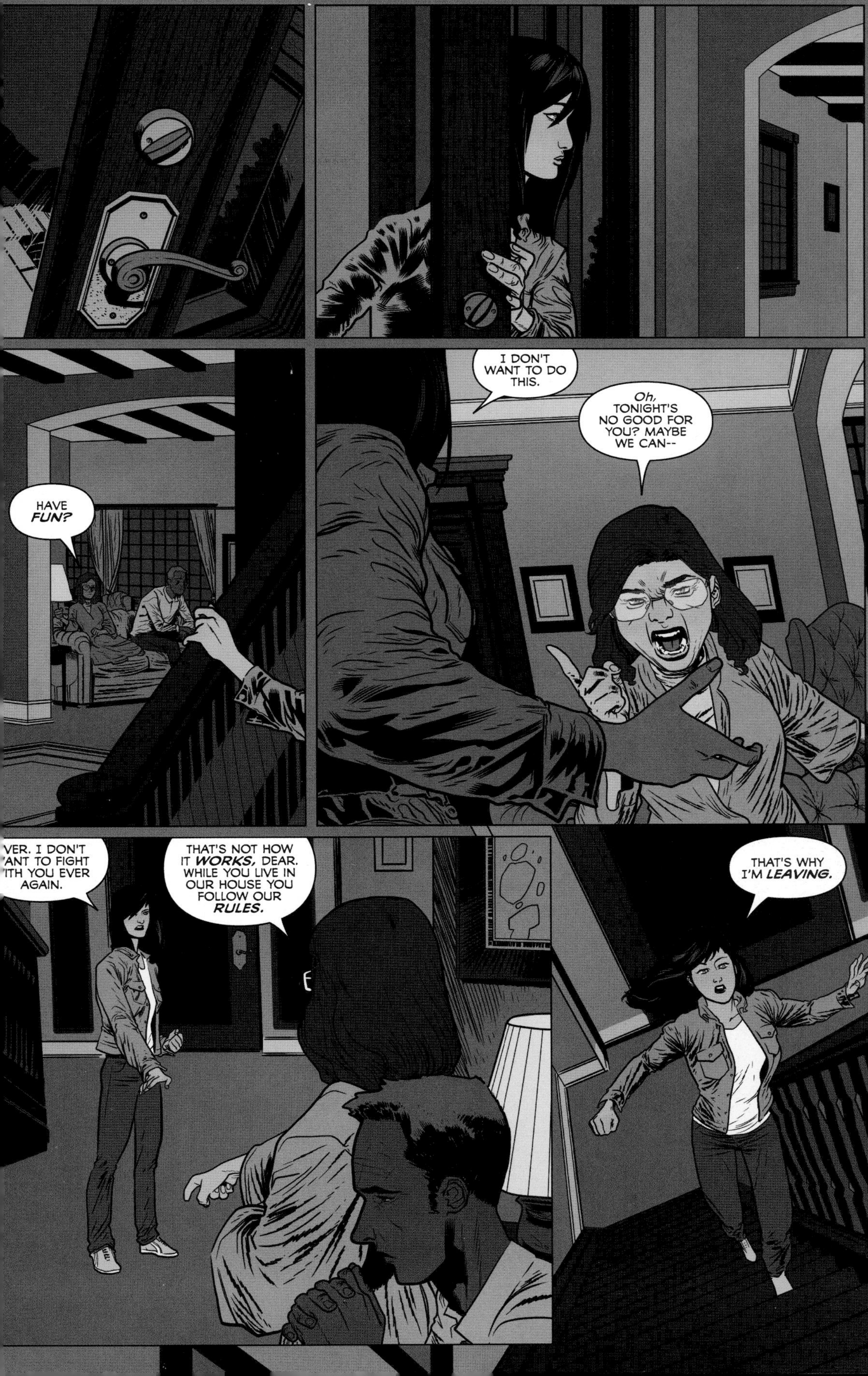
HAVE *FUN?*
I DON'T WANT TO DO THIS.
Oh, TONIGHT'S NO GOOD FOR YOU? MAYBE WE CAN--
VER. I DON'T ANT TO FIGHT ITH YOU EVER AGAIN.
THAT'S NOT HOW IT ***WORKS,*** DEAR. WHILE YOU LIVE IN OUR HOUSE YOU FOLLOW OUR ***RULES.***
THAT'S WHY I'M ***LEAVING.***

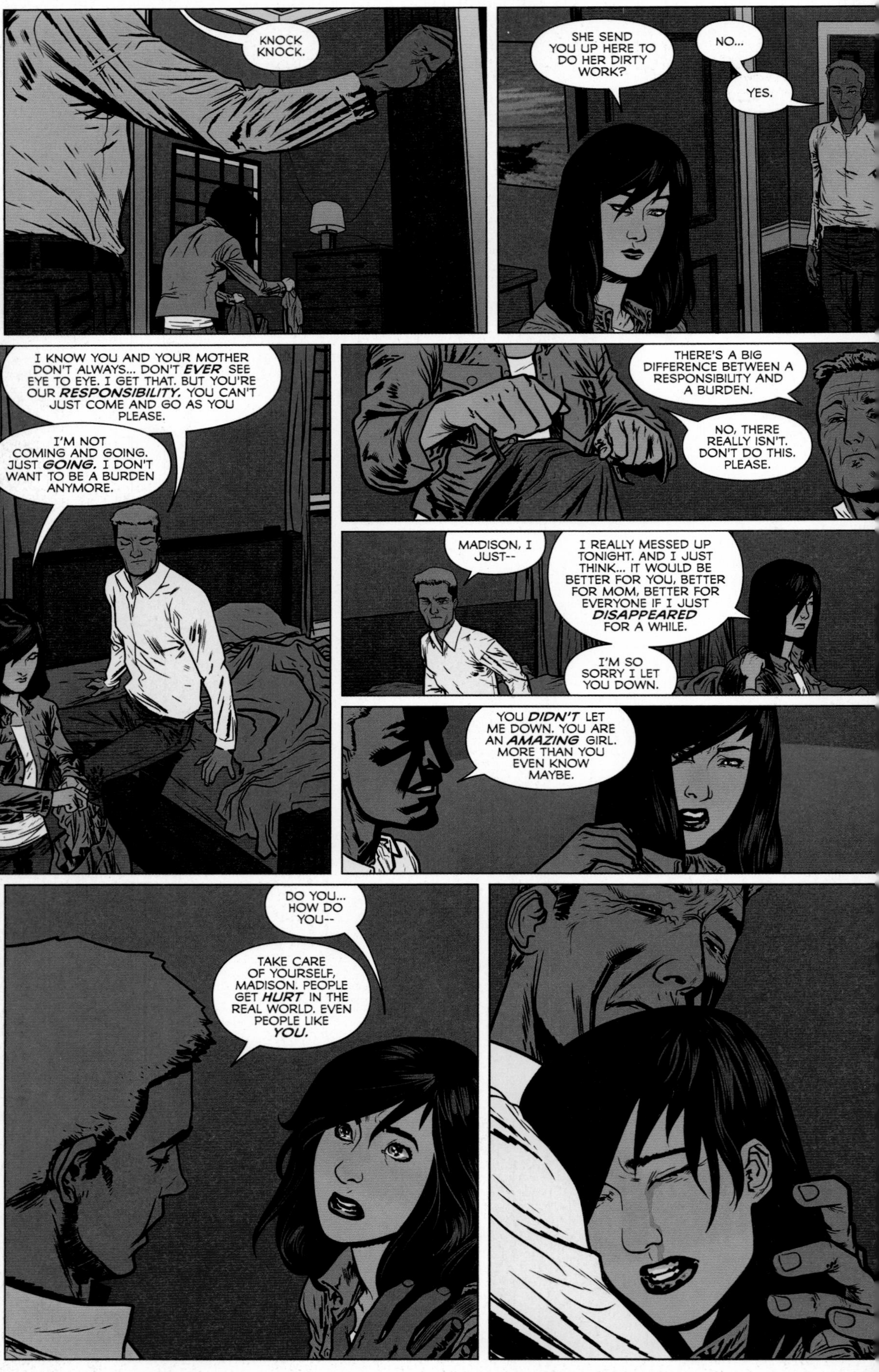
KNOCK KNOCK.
SHE SEND YOU UP HERE TO DO HER DIRTY WORK?
NO...
YES.
I KNOW YOU AND YOUR MOTHER DON'T ALWAYS... DON'T ***EVER*** SEE EYE TO EYE. I GET THAT. BUT YOU'RE OUR ***RESPONSIBILITY.*** YOU CAN'T JUST COME AND GO AS YOU PLEASE.
I'M NOT COMING AND GOING. JUST ***GOING.*** I DON'T WANT TO BE A BURDEN ANYMORE.
THERE'S A BIG DIFFERENCE BETWEEN A RESPONSIBILITY AND A BURDEN.
NO, THERE REALLY ISN'T. DON'T DO THIS. PLEASE.
MADISON, I JUST--
I REALLY MESSED UP TONIGHT. AND I JUST THINK... IT WOULD BE BETTER FOR YOU, BETTER FOR MOM, BETTER FOR EVERYONE IF I JUST ***DISAPPEARED*** FOR A WHILE.
I'M SO SORRY I LET YOU DOWN.
YOU ***DIDN'T*** LET ME DOWN. YOU ARE AN ***AMAZING*** GIRL. MORE THAN YOU EVEN KNOW MAYBE.
DO YOU... HOW DO YOU--
TAKE CARE OF YOURSELF, MADISON. PEOPLE GET ***HURT*** IN THE REAL WORLD. EVEN PEOPLE LIKE ***YOU.***

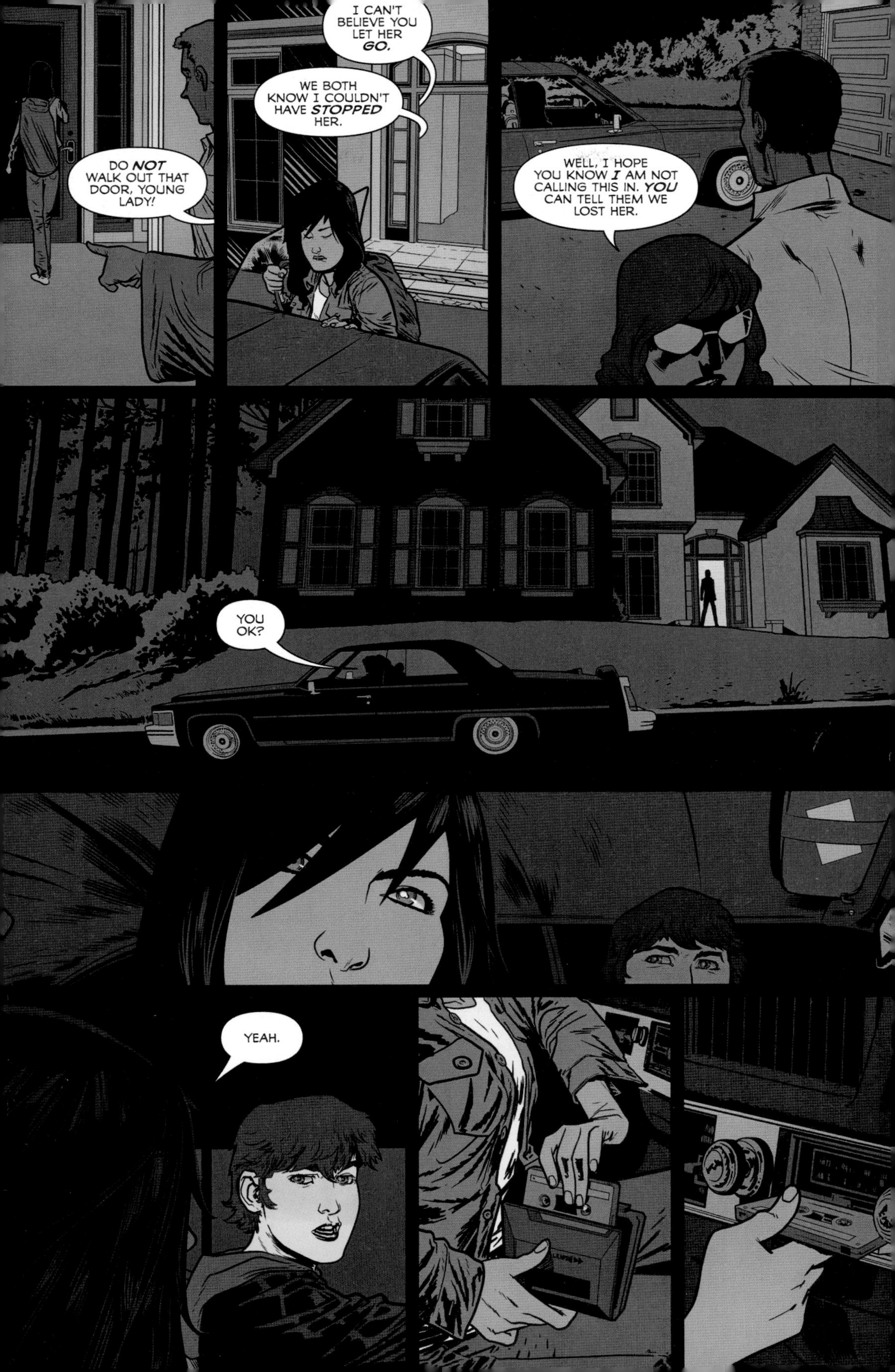
DO NOT WALK OUT THAT DOOR, YOUNG LADY!
I CAN'T BELIEVE YOU LET HER GO.
WE BOTH KNOW I COULDN'T HAVE STOPPED HER.
WELL, I HOPE YOU KNOW I AM NOT CALLING THIS IN. YOU CAN TELL THEM WE LOST HER.
YOU OK?
YEAH.

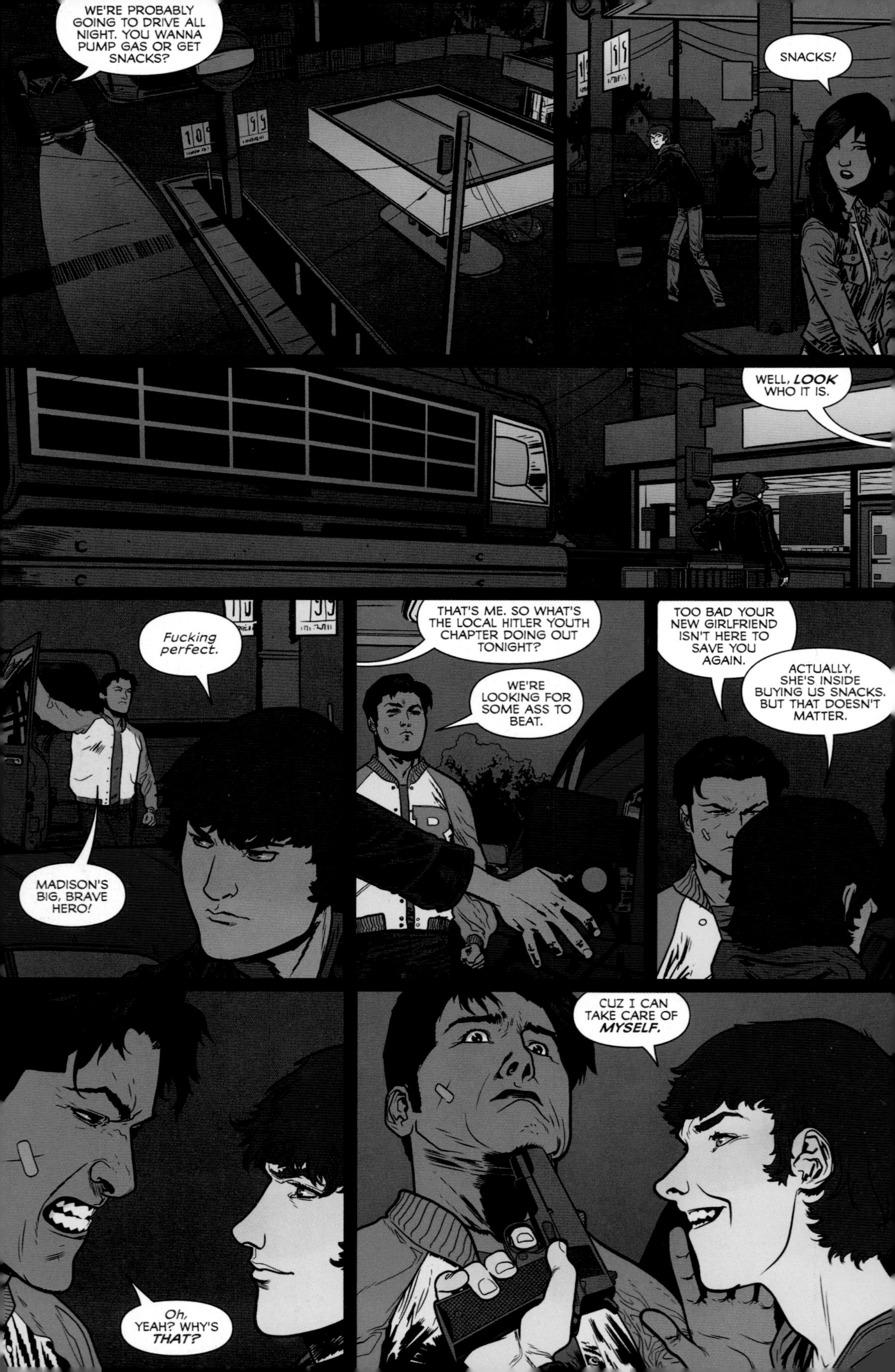
WE'RE PROBABLY GOING TO DRIVE ALL NIGHT. YOU WANNA PUMP GAS OR GET SNACKS?
SNACKS!
WELL, *LOOK* WHO IT IS.
Fucking perfect.
MADISON'S BIG, BRAVE HERO!
THAT'S ME. SO WHAT'S THE LOCAL HITLER YOUTH CHAPTER DOING OUT TONIGHT?
WE'RE LOOKING FOR SOME ASS TO BEAT.
TOO BAD YOUR NEW GIRLFRIEND ISN'T HERE TO SAVE YOU AGAIN.
ACTUALLY, SHE'S INSIDE BUYING US SNACKS. BUT THAT DOESN'T MATTER.
Oh, YEAH? WHY'S *THAT?*
CUZ I CAN TAKE CARE OF *MYSELF.*

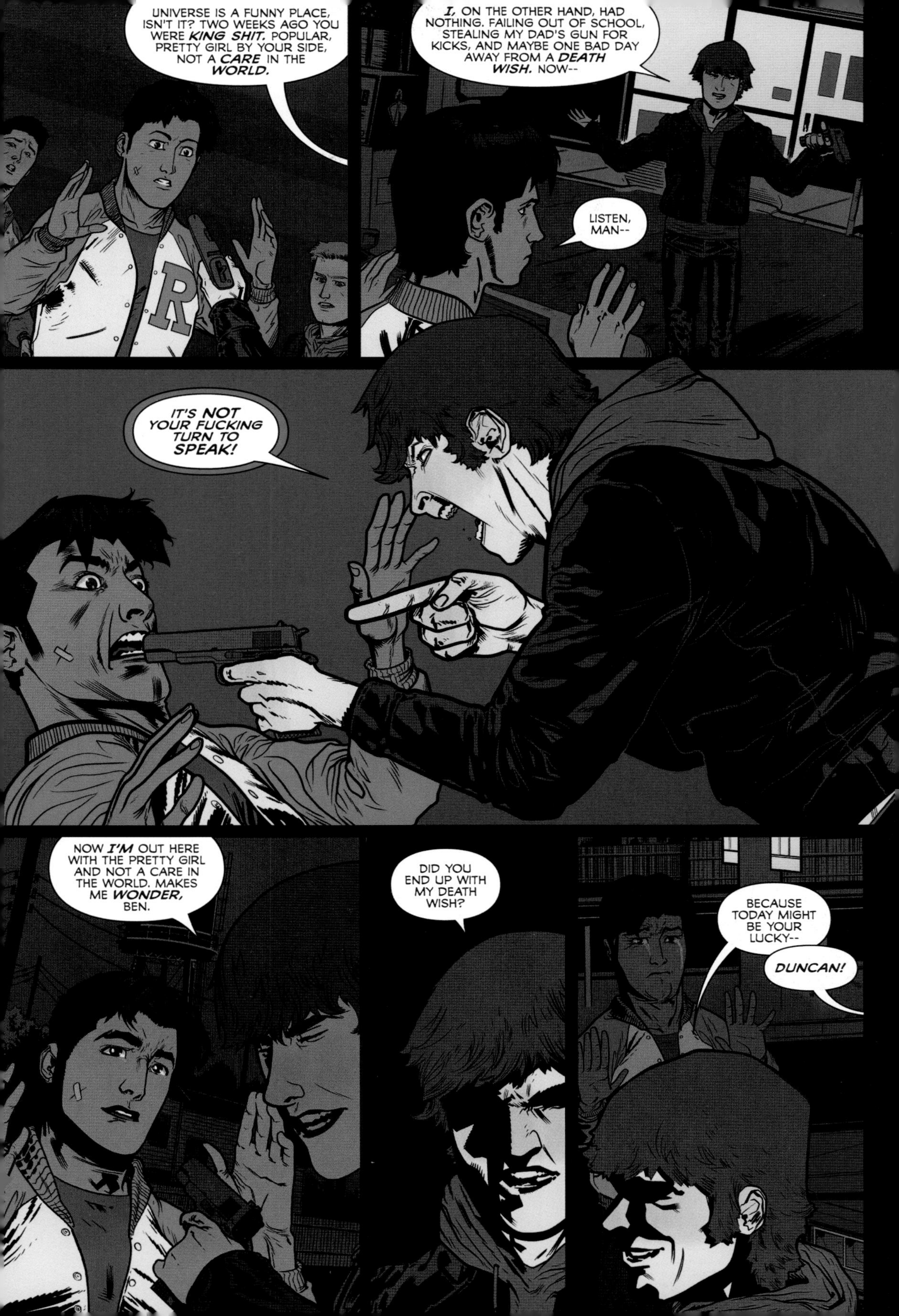
UNIVERSE IS A FUNNY PLACE, ISN'T IT? TWO WEEKS AGO YOU WERE KING SHIT. POPULAR, PRETTY GIRL BY YOUR SIDE, NOT A CARE IN THE WORLD.
I, ON THE OTHER HAND, HAD NOTHING. FAILING OUT OF SCHOOL, STEALING MY DAD'S GUN FOR KICKS, AND MAYBE ONE BAD DAY AWAY FROM A DEATH WISH. NOW--
LISTEN, MAN--
IT'S NOT YOUR FUCKING TURN TO SPEAK!
NOW I'M OUT HERE WITH THE PRETTY GIRL AND NOT A CARE IN THE WORLD. MAKES ME WONDER, BEN.
DID YOU END UP WITH MY DEATH WISH?
BECAUSE TODAY MIGHT BE YOUR LUCKY--
DUNCAN!

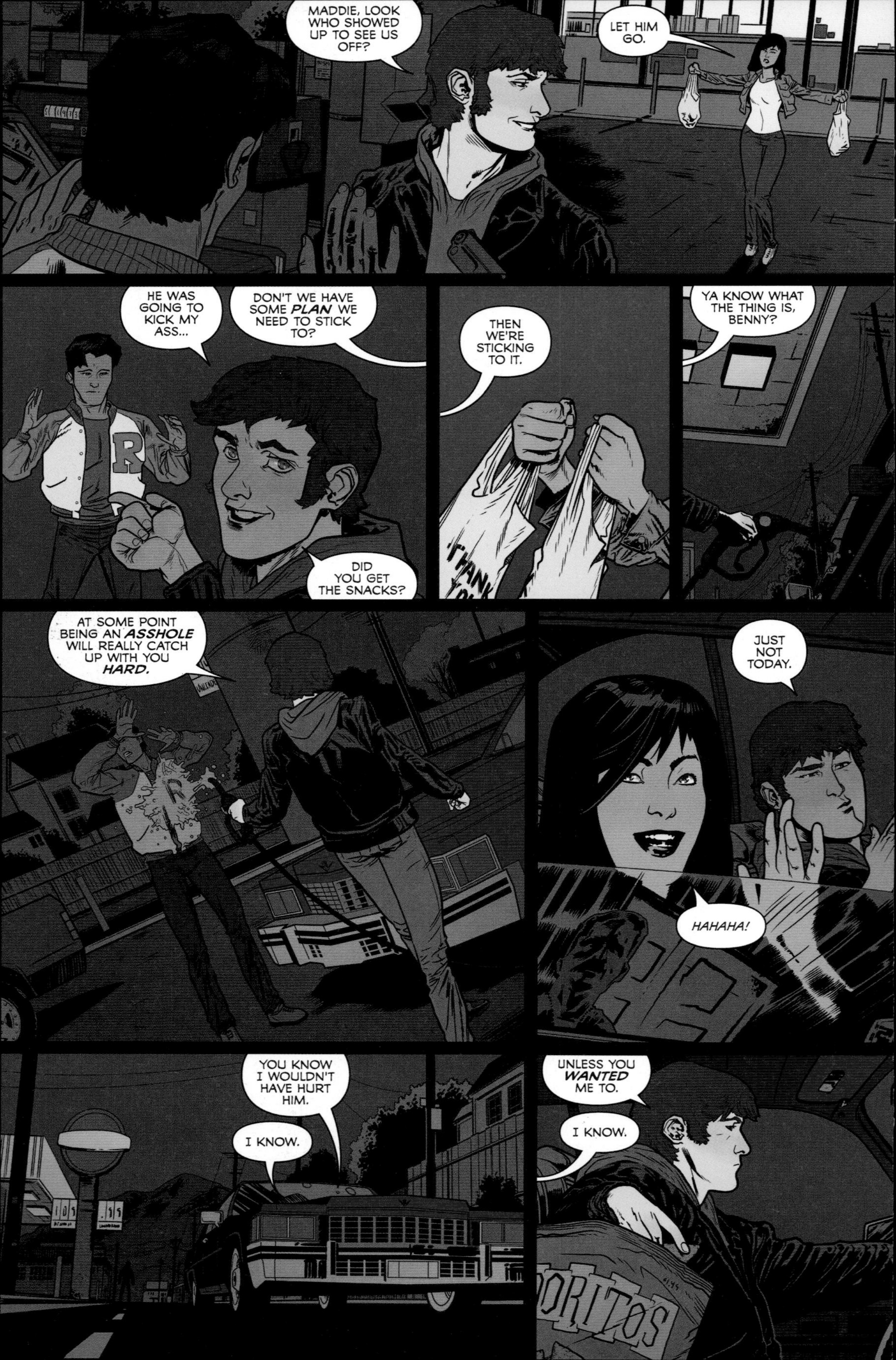
MADDIE, LOOK WHO SHOWED UP TO SEE US OFF?
LET HIM GO.
HE WAS GOING TO KICK MY ASS...
DON'T WE HAVE SOME *PLAN* WE NEED TO STICK TO?
DID YOU GET THE SNACKS?
THEN WE'RE STICKING TO IT.
YA KNOW WHAT THE THING IS, BENNY?
AT SOME POINT BEING AN *ASSHOLE* WILL REALLY CATCH UP WITH YOU *HARD.*
JUST NOT TODAY.
HAHAHA!
YOU KNOW I WOULDN'T HAVE HURT HIM.
I KNOW.
UNLESS YOU *WANTED* ME TO.
I KNOW.
DORITOS

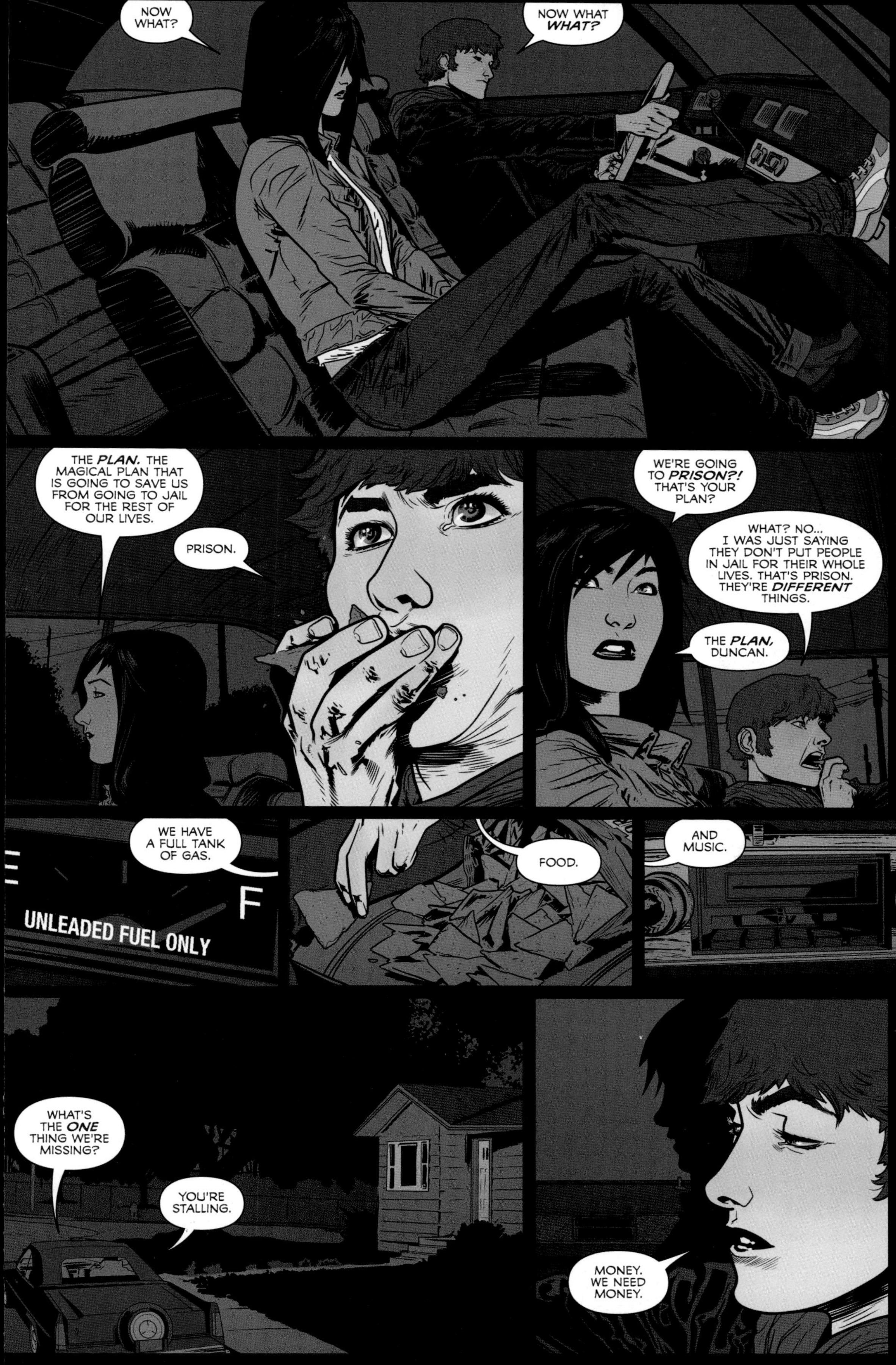
NOW WHAT?
NOW WHAT *WHAT?*
THE *PLAN.* THE MAGICAL PLAN THAT IS GOING TO SAVE US FROM GOING TO JAIL FOR THE REST OF OUR LIVES.
PRISON.
WE'RE GOING TO *PRISON?!* THAT'S YOUR PLAN?
WHAT? NO... I WAS JUST SAYING THEY DON'T PUT PEOPLE IN JAIL FOR THEIR WHOLE LIVES. THAT'S PRISON. THEY'RE *DIFFERENT* THINGS.
THE *PLAN,* DUNCAN.
WE HAVE A FULL TANK OF GAS.
E
F
UNLEADED FUEL ONLY
FOOD.
AND MUSIC.
WHAT'S THE *ONE* THING WE'RE MISSING?
YOU'RE STALLING.
MONEY. WE NEED MONEY.

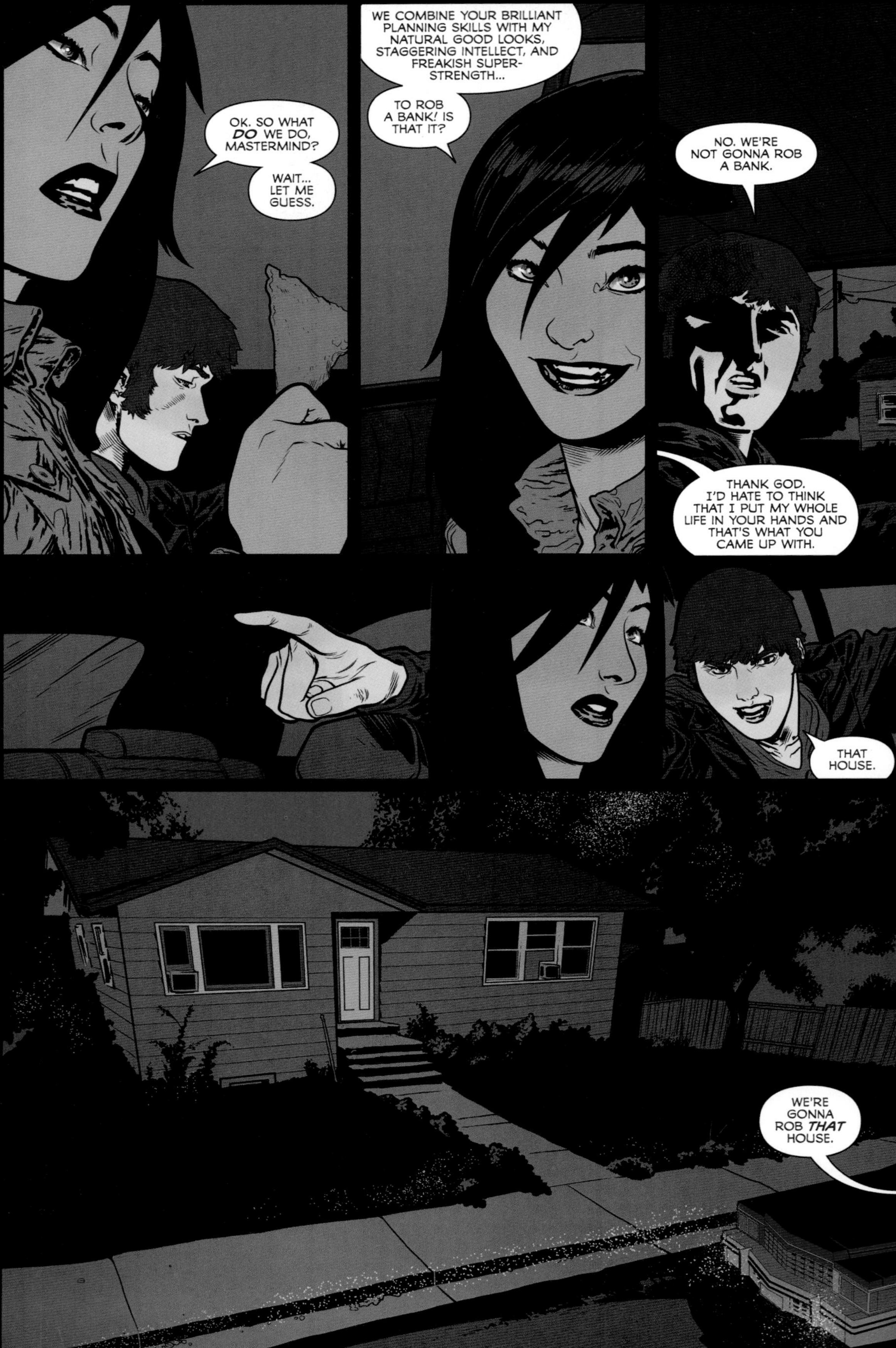
OK. SO WHAT *DO* WE DO, MASTERMIND?
WAIT... LET ME GUESS.
WE COMBINE YOUR BRILLIANT PLANNING SKILLS WITH MY NATURAL GOOD LOOKS, STAGGERING INTELLECT, AND FREAKISH SUPER-STRENGTH...
TO ROB A BANK*!* IS THAT IT?
NO. WE'RE NOT GONNA ROB A BANK.
THANK GOD. I'D HATE TO THINK THAT I PUT MY WHOLE LIFE IN YOUR HANDS AND THAT'S WHAT YOU CAME UP WITH.
THAT HOUSE.
WE'RE GONNA ROB *THAT* HOUSE.

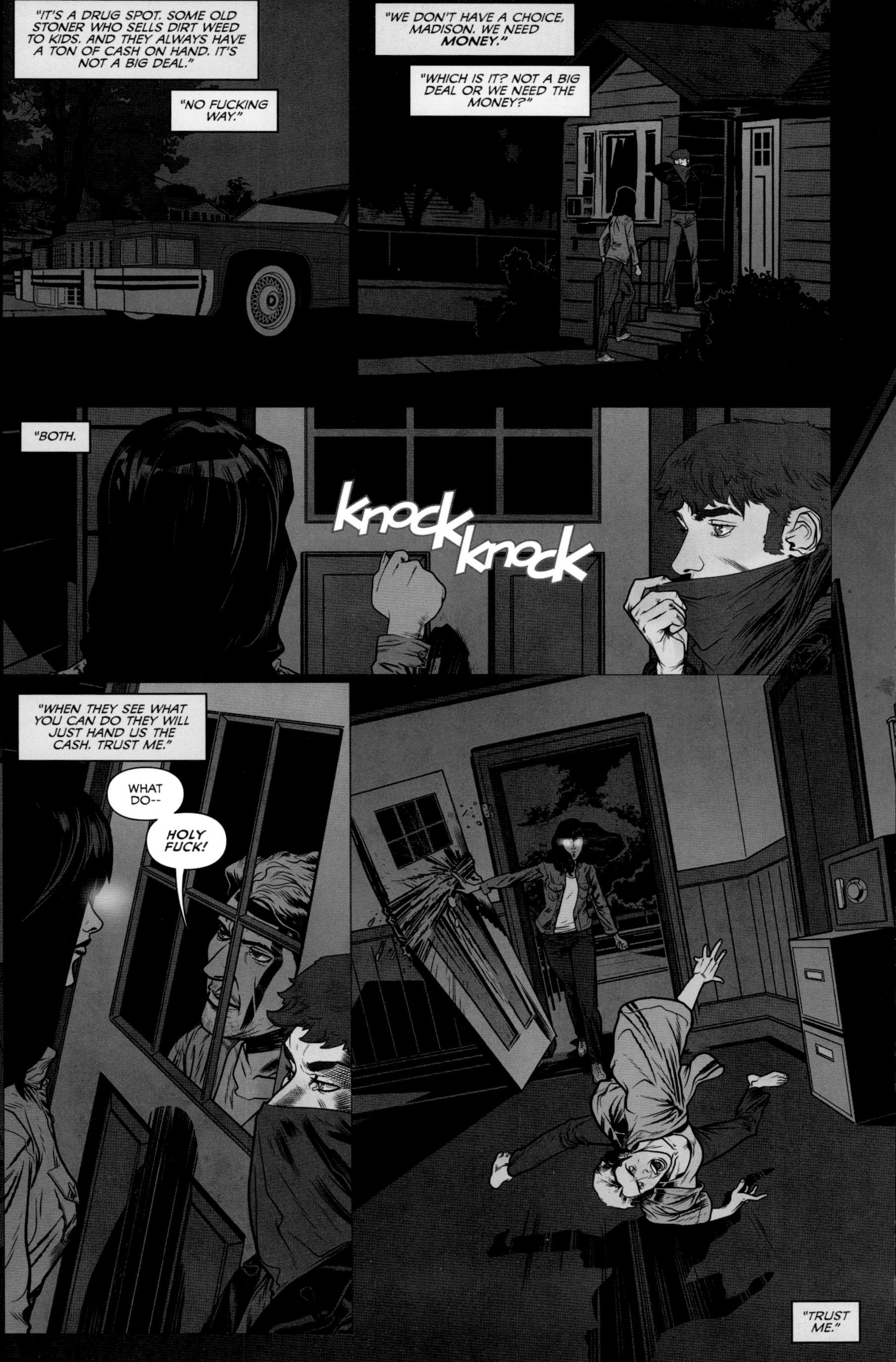
"IT'S A DRUG SPOT. SOME OLD STONER WHO SELLS DIRT WEED TO KIDS. AND THEY ALWAYS HAVE A TON OF CASH ON HAND. IT'S NOT A BIG DEAL."
"NO FUCKING WAY."
"WE DON'T HAVE A CHOICE, MADISON. WE NEED **MONEY.**"
"WHICH IS IT? NOT A BIG DEAL OR WE NEED THE MONEY?"
"BOTH.
knock knock
"WHEN THEY SEE WHAT YOU CAN DO THEY WILL JUST HAND US THE CASH. TRUST ME."
WHAT DO--
HOLY FUCK!
"TRUST ME."

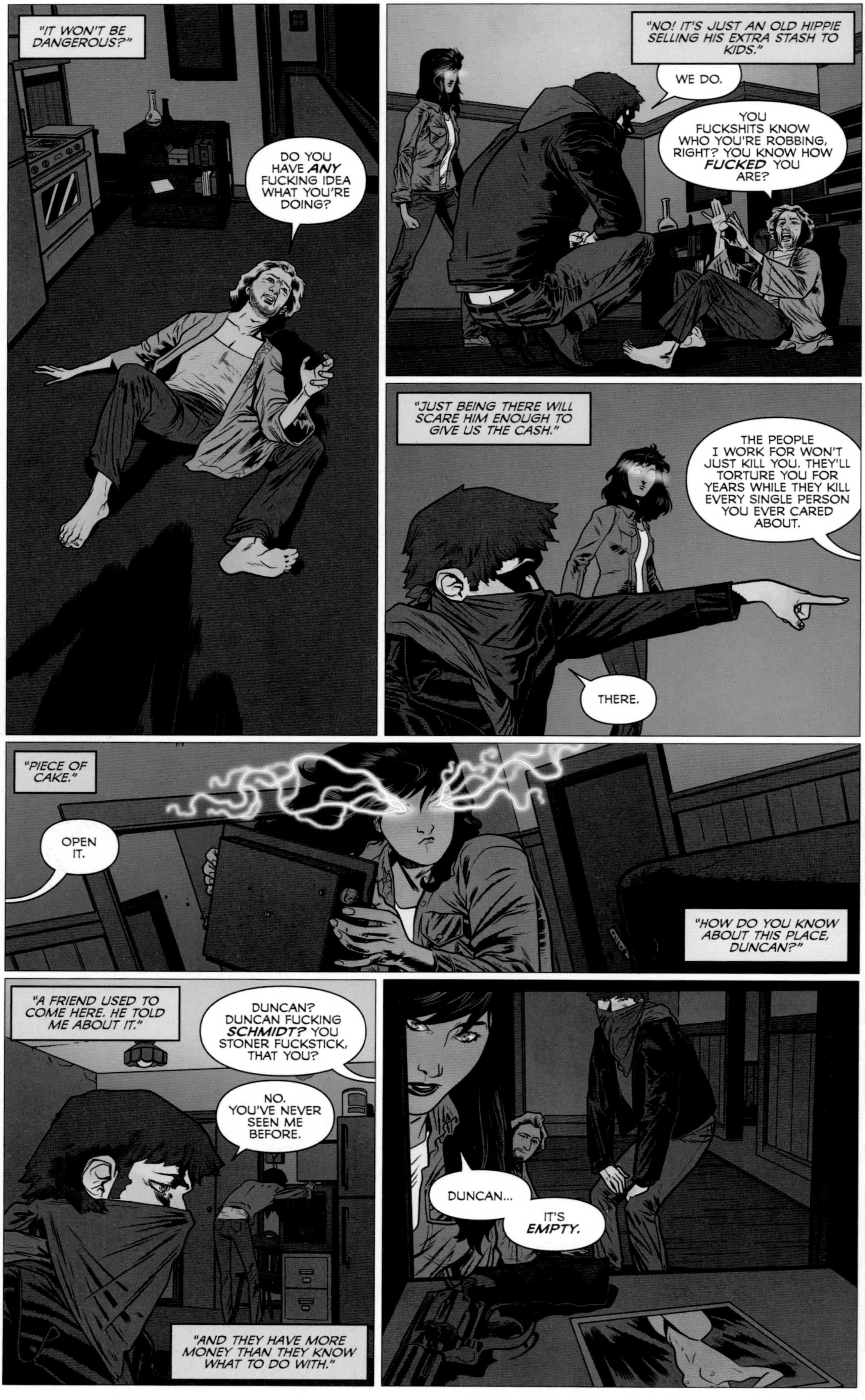
"IT WON'T BE DANGEROUS?"
DO YOU HAVE ANY FUCKING IDEA WHAT YOU'RE DOING?
"NO! IT'S JUST AN OLD HIPPIE SELLING HIS EXTRA STASH TO KIDS."
WE DO.
YOU FUCKSHITS KNOW WHO YOU'RE ROBBING, RIGHT? YOU KNOW HOW FUCKED YOU ARE?
"JUST BEING THERE WILL SCARE HIM ENOUGH TO GIVE US THE CASH."
THE PEOPLE I WORK FOR WON'T JUST KILL YOU. THEY'LL TORTURE YOU FOR YEARS WHILE THEY KILL EVERY SINGLE PERSON YOU EVER CARED ABOUT.
THERE.
"PIECE OF CAKE."
OPEN IT.
"HOW DO YOU KNOW ABOUT THIS PLACE, DUNCAN?"
"A FRIEND USED TO COME HERE. HE TOLD ME ABOUT IT."
DUNCAN? DUNCAN FUCKING SCHMIDT? YOU STONER FUCKSTICK, THAT YOU?
NO. YOU'VE NEVER SEEN ME BEFORE.
"AND THEY HAVE MORE MONEY THAN THEY KNOW WHAT TO DO WITH."
DUNCAN...
IT'S EMPTY.

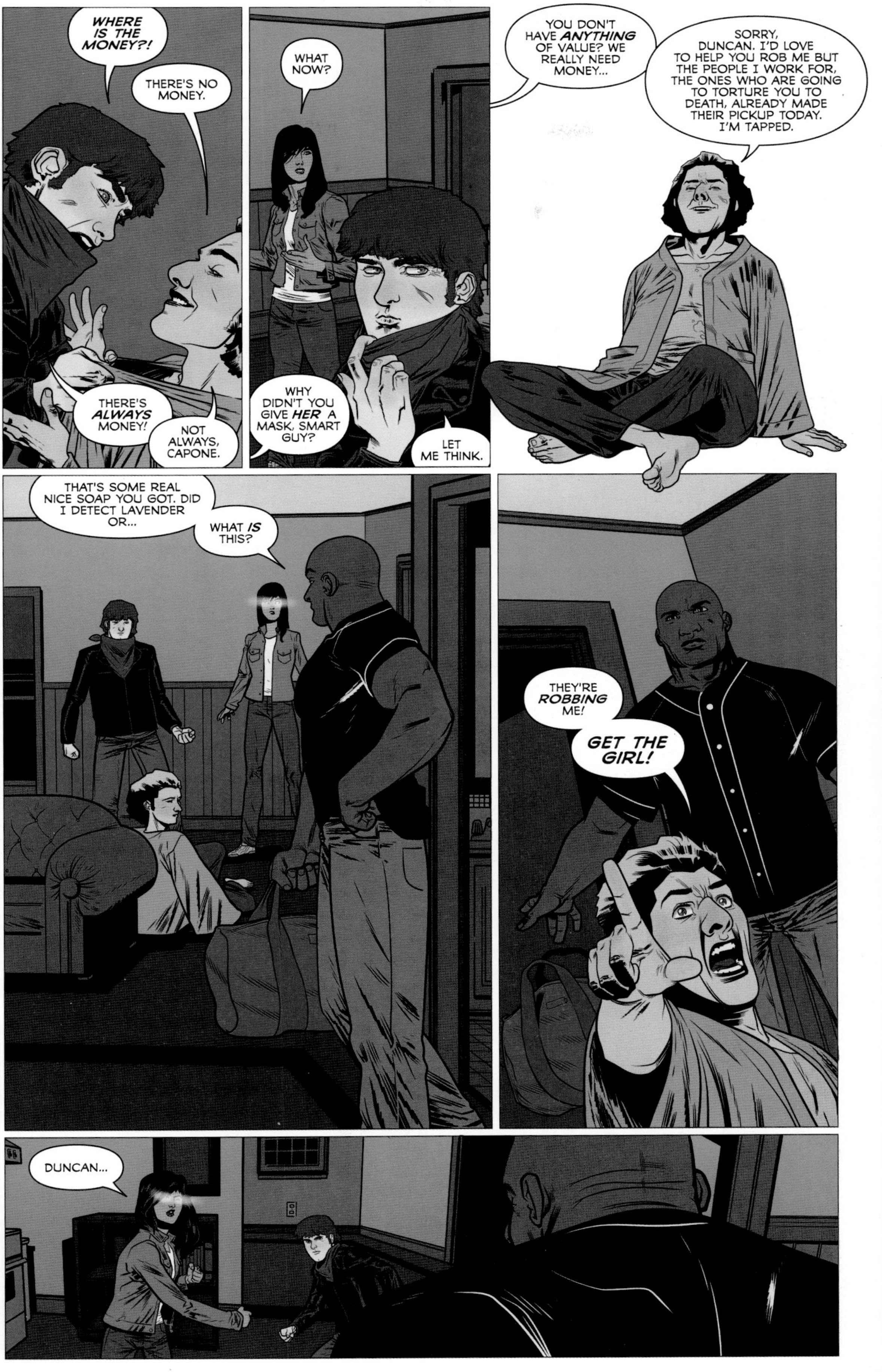
WHERE IS THE MONEY?!
THERE'S NO MONEY.
THERE'S ALWAYS MONEY!
NOT ALWAYS, CAPONE.
WHAT NOW?
WHY DIDN'T YOU GIVE HER A MASK, SMART GUY?
LET ME THINK.
YOU DON'T HAVE ANYTHING OF VALUE? WE REALLY NEED MONEY...
SORRY, DUNCAN. I'D LOVE TO HELP YOU ROB ME BUT THE PEOPLE I WORK FOR, THE ONES WHO ARE GOING TO TORTURE YOU TO DEATH, ALREADY MADE THEIR PICKUP TODAY. I'M TAPPED.
THAT'S SOME REAL NICE SOAP YOU GOT. DID I DETECT LAVENDER OR...
WHAT IS THIS?
THEY'RE ROBBING ME!
GET THE GIRL!
DUNCAN...

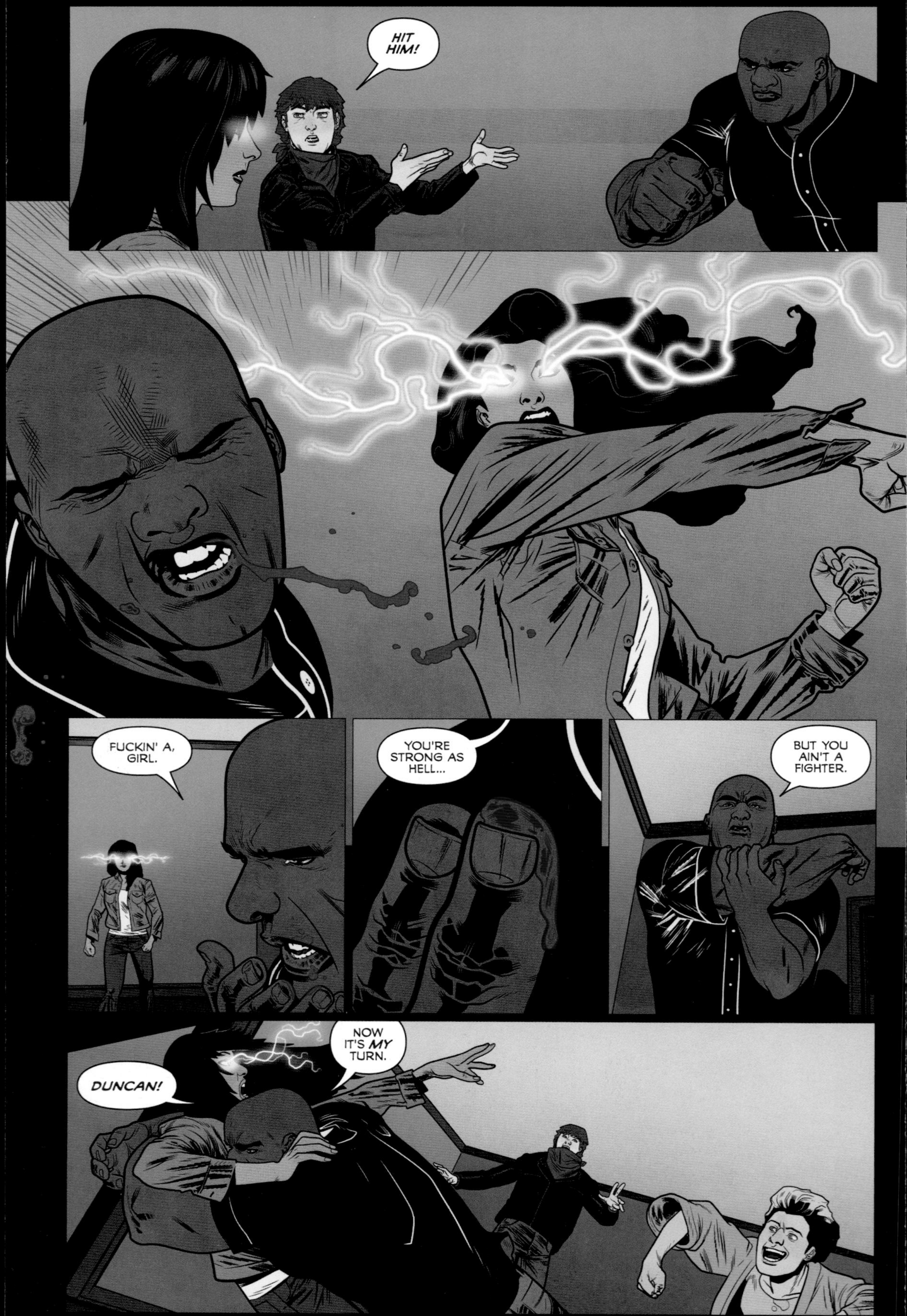
HIT HIM!
FUCKIN' A, GIRL.
YOU'RE STRONG AS HELL...
BUT YOU AIN'T A FIGHTER.
DUNCAN!
NOW IT'S *MY* TURN.

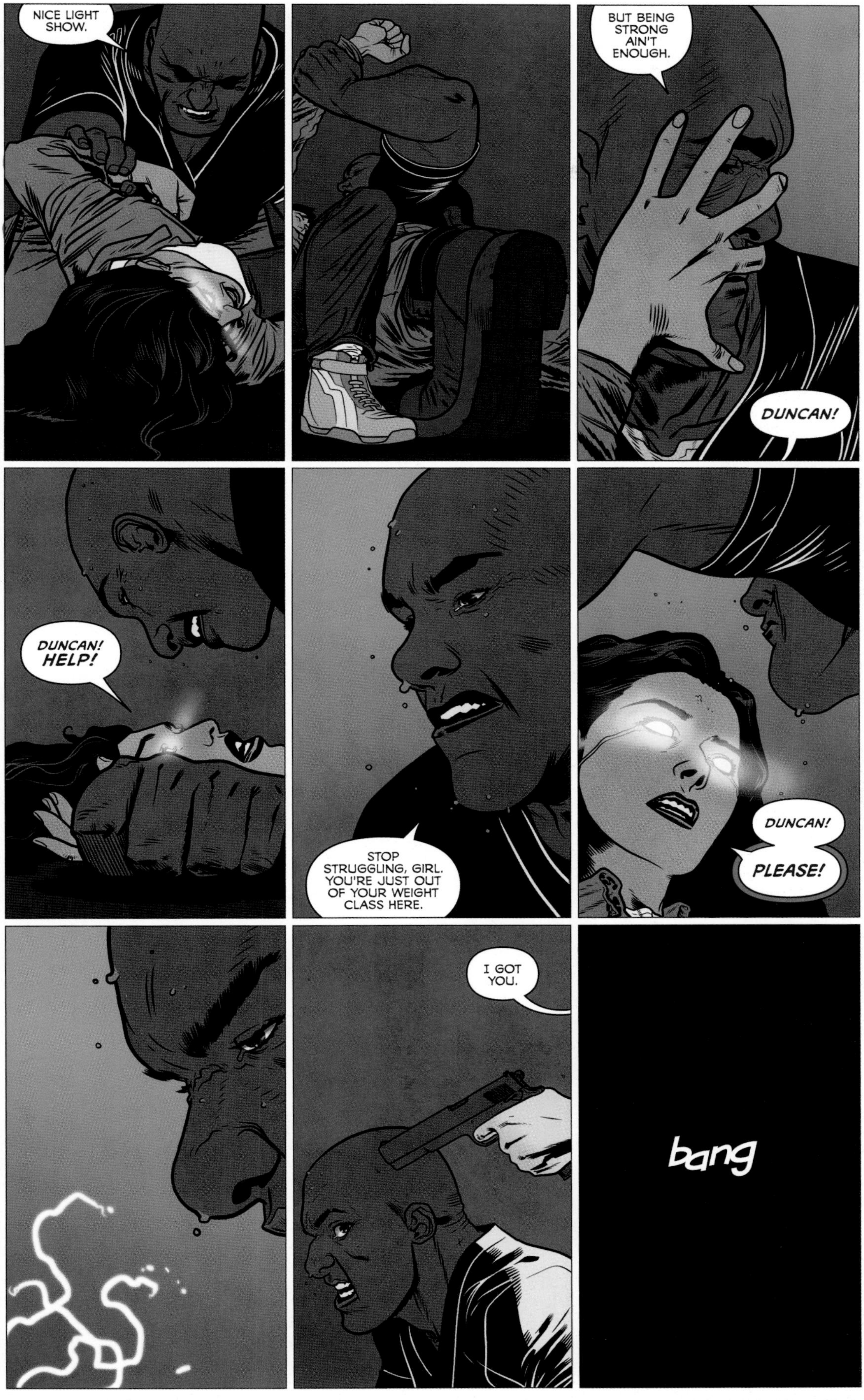
NICE LIGHT SHOW.
BUT BEING STRONG AIN'T ENOUGH.
DUNCAN!
DUNCAN! HELP!
STOP STRUGGLING, GIRL. YOU'RE JUST OUT OF YOUR WEIGHT CLASS HERE.
DUNCAN!
PLEASE!
I GOT YOU.
bang

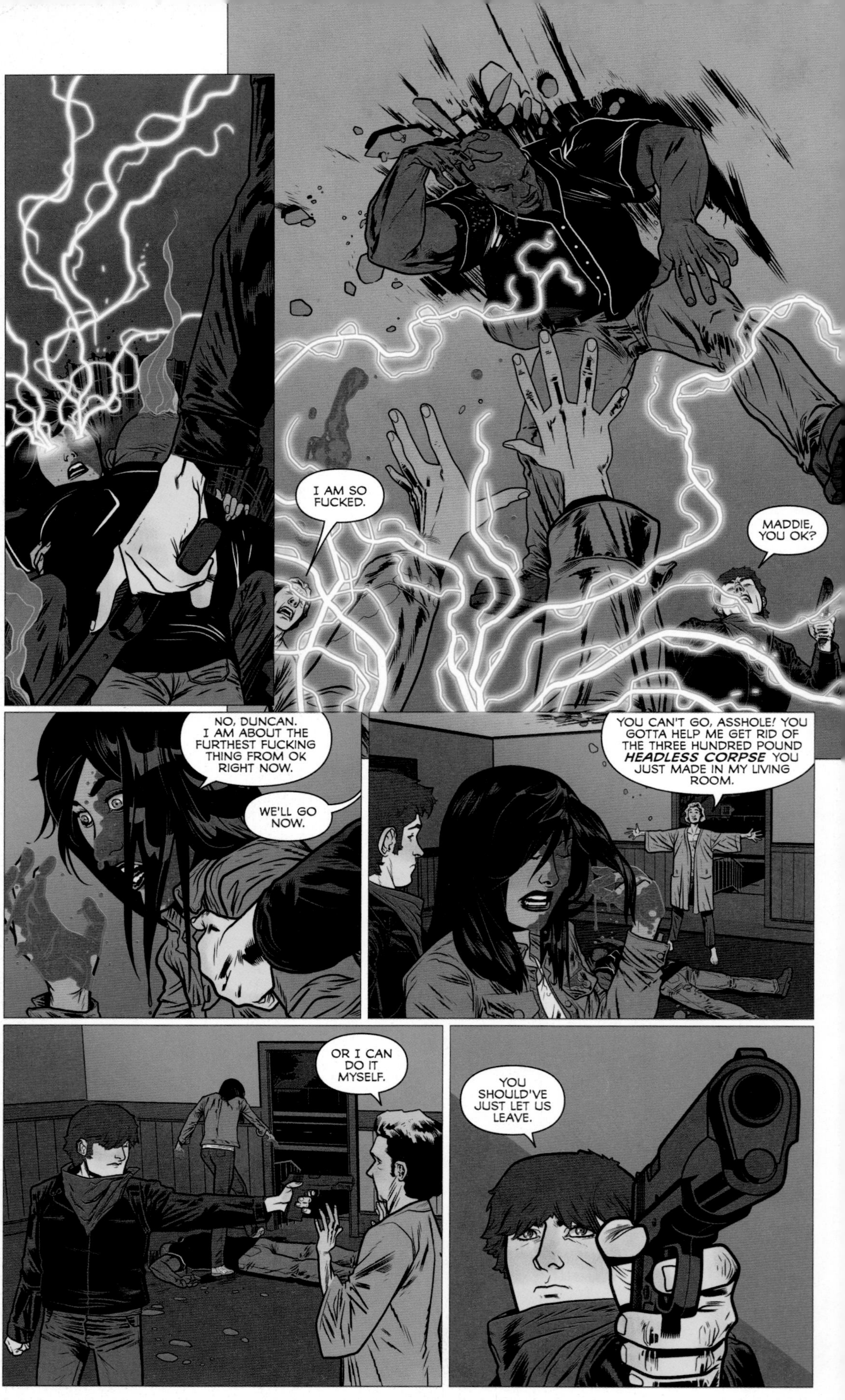
I AM SO FUCKED.
MADDIE, YOU OK?
NO, DUNCAN. I AM ABOUT THE FURTHEST FUCKING THING FROM OK RIGHT NOW.
WE'LL GO NOW.
YOU CAN'T GO, ASSHOLE! YOU GOTTA HELP ME GET RID OF THE THREE HUNDRED POUND HEADLESS CORPSE YOU JUST MADE IN MY LIVING ROOM.
OR I CAN DO IT MYSELF.
YOU SHOULD'VE JUST LET US LEAVE.

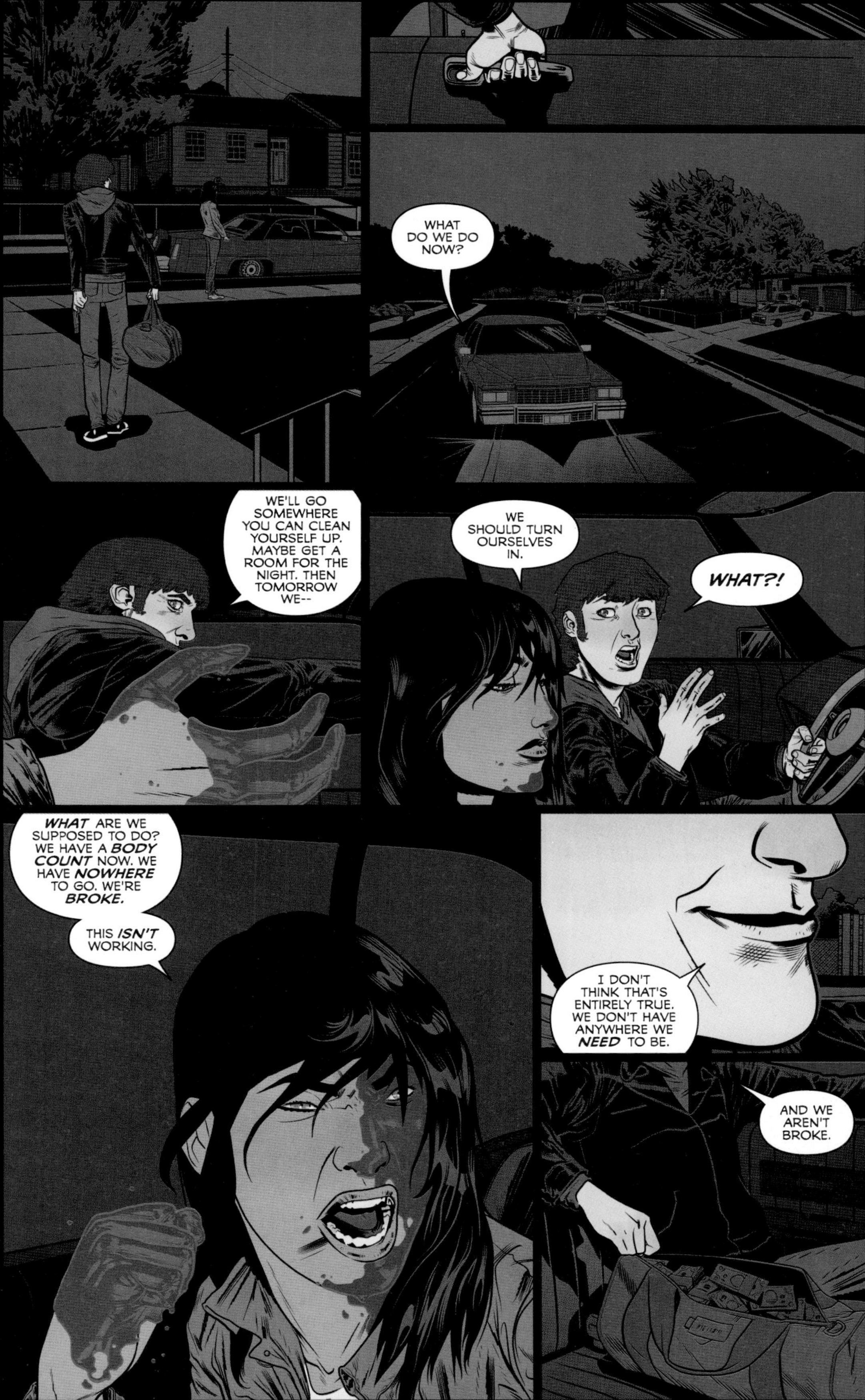
WHAT DO WE DO NOW?
WE'LL GO SOMEWHERE YOU CAN CLEAN YOURSELF UP. MAYBE GET A ROOM FOR THE NIGHT. THEN TOMORROW WE--
WE SHOULD TURN OURSELVES IN.
WHAT?!
WHAT ARE WE SUPPOSED TO DO? WE HAVE A BODY COUNT NOW. WE HAVE NOWHERE TO GO. WE'RE BROKE.
THIS ISN'T WORKING.
I DON'T THINK THAT'S ENTIRELY TRUE. WE DON'T HAVE ANYWHERE WE NEED TO BE.
AND WE AREN'T BROKE.

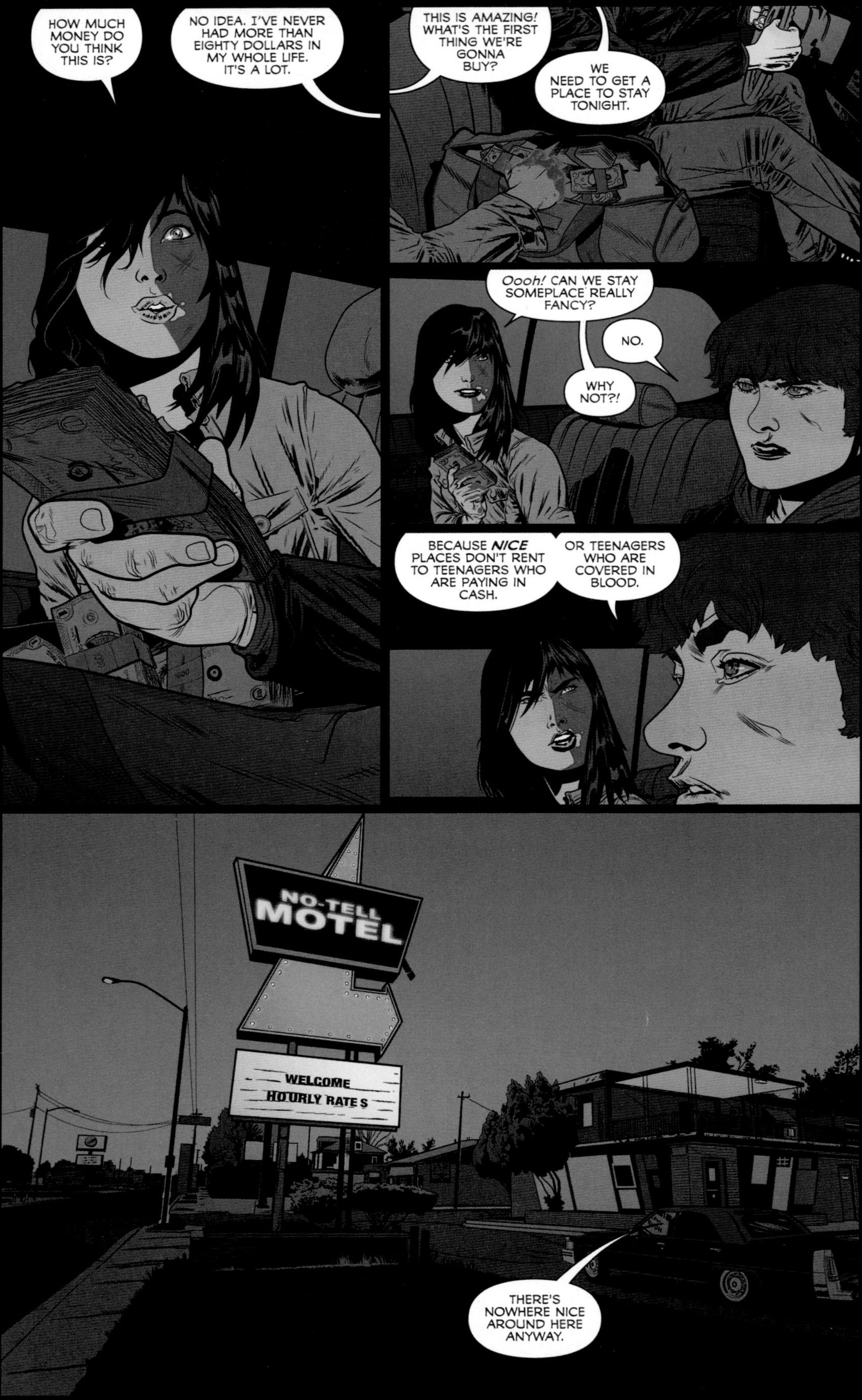
HOW MUCH MONEY DO YOU THINK THIS IS?
NO IDEA. I'VE NEVER HAD MORE THAN EIGHTY DOLLARS IN MY WHOLE LIFE. IT'S A LOT.
THIS IS AMAZING! WHAT'S THE FIRST THING WE'RE GONNA BUY?
WE NEED TO GET A PLACE TO STAY TONIGHT.
Oooh! CAN WE STAY SOMEPLACE REALLY FANCY?
NO.
WHY NOT?!
BECAUSE ***NICE*** PLACES DON'T RENT TO TEENAGERS WHO ARE PAYING IN CASH.
OR TEENAGERS WHO ARE COVERED IN BLOOD.
NO-TELL MOTEL
WELCOME
HOURLY RATE S
THERE'S NOWHERE NICE AROUND HERE ANYWAY.

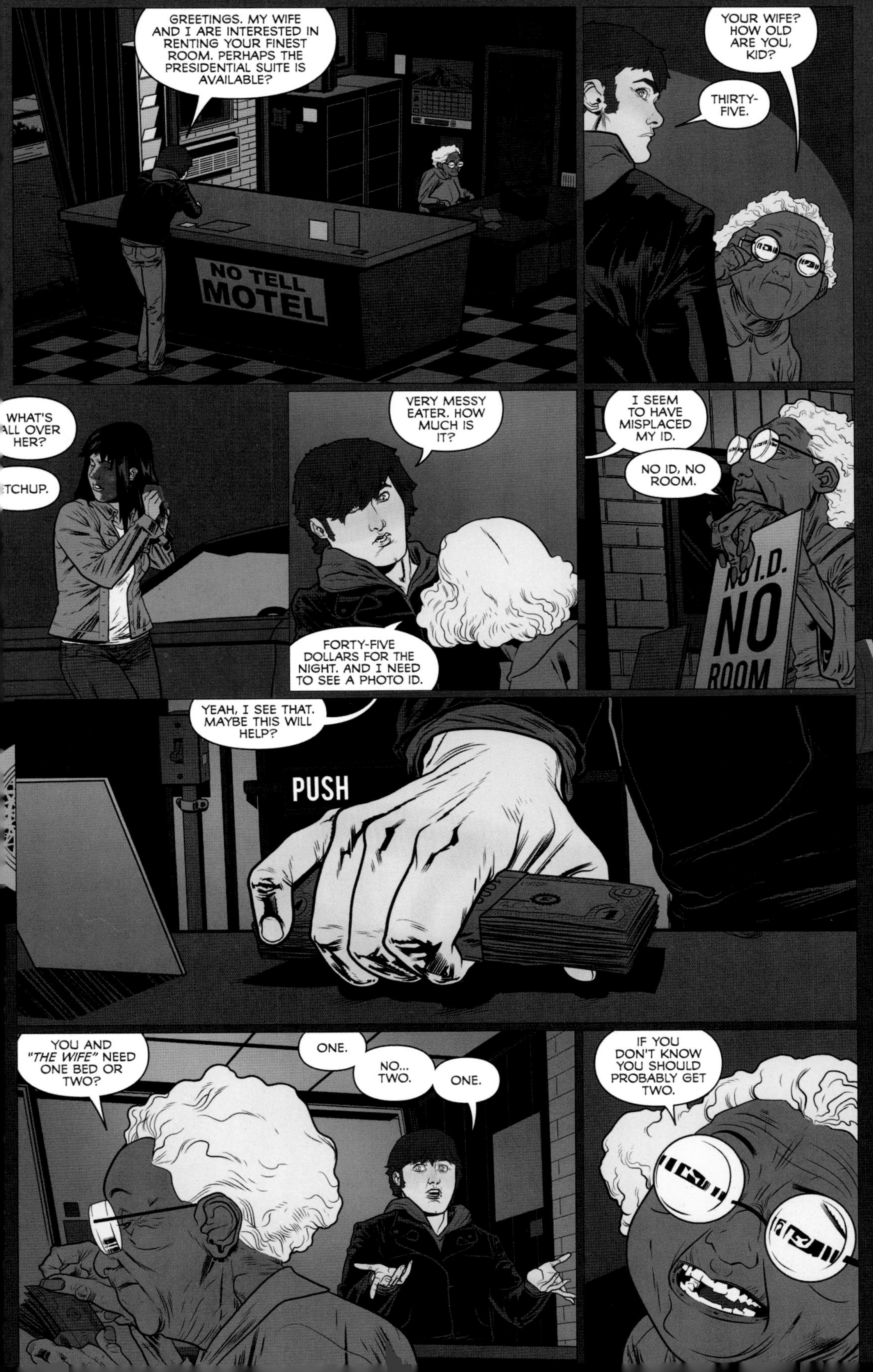
GREETINGS. MY WIFE AND I ARE INTERESTED IN RENTING YOUR FINEST ROOM. PERHAPS THE PRESIDENTIAL SUITE IS AVAILABLE?
NO TELL MOTEL
YOUR WIFE? HOW OLD ARE YOU, KID?
THIRTY-FIVE.
WHAT'S ALL OVER HER?
TCHUP.
VERY MESSY EATER. HOW MUCH IS IT?
FORTY-FIVE DOLLARS FOR THE NIGHT. AND I NEED TO SEE A PHOTO ID.
I SEEM TO HAVE MISPLACED MY ID.
NO ID, NO ROOM.
I.D. NO ROOM
YEAH, I SEE THAT. MAYBE THIS WILL HELP?
PUSH
YOU AND *"THE WIFE"* NEED ONE BED OR TWO?
ONE.
NO... TWO.
ONE.
IF YOU DON'T KNOW YOU SHOULD PROBABLY GET TWO.

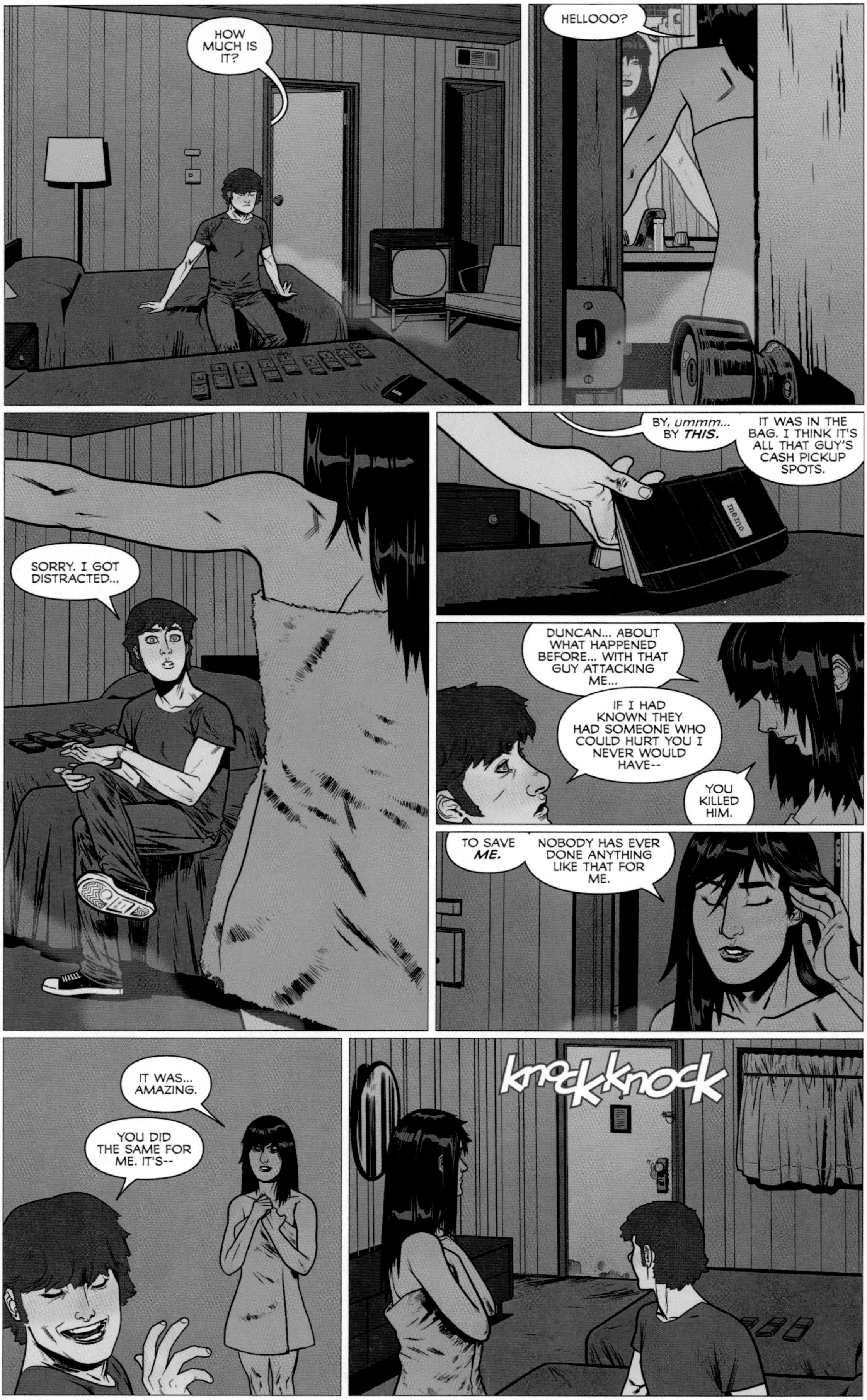
HOW MUCH IS IT?
HELLOOO?
SORRY. I GOT DISTRACTED...
BY, *ummm...* BY ***THIS.***
IT WAS IN THE BAG. I THINK IT'S ALL THAT GUY'S CASH PICKUP SPOTS.
memo
DUNCAN... ABOUT WHAT HAPPENED BEFORE... WITH THAT GUY ATTACKING ME...
IF I HAD KNOWN THEY HAD SOMEONE WHO COULD HURT YOU I NEVER WOULD HAVE--
YOU KILLED HIM.
TO SAVE ***ME.***
NOBODY HAS EVER DONE ANYTHING LIKE THAT FOR ME.
IT WAS... AMAZING.
YOU DID THE SAME FOR ME. IT'S--
knock knock

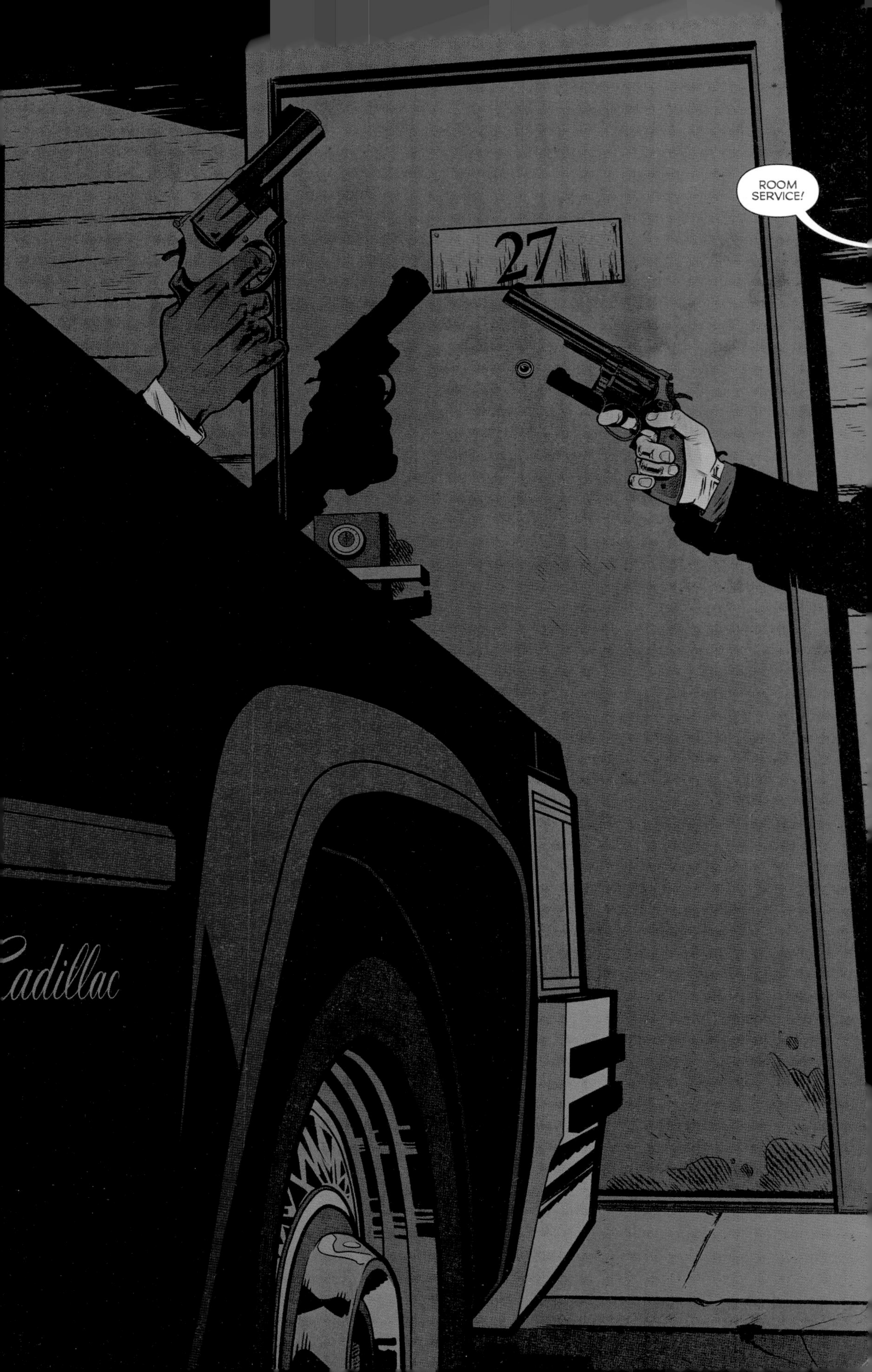
ROOM SERVICE!
27
Cadillac

CHAPTER 3

BIGMOUTH STRIKES AGAIN

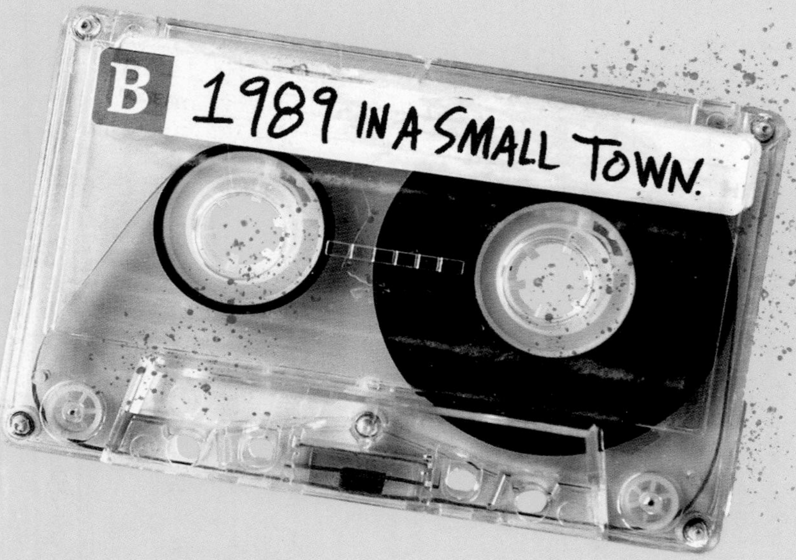
B
1989 IN A SMALL TOWN.

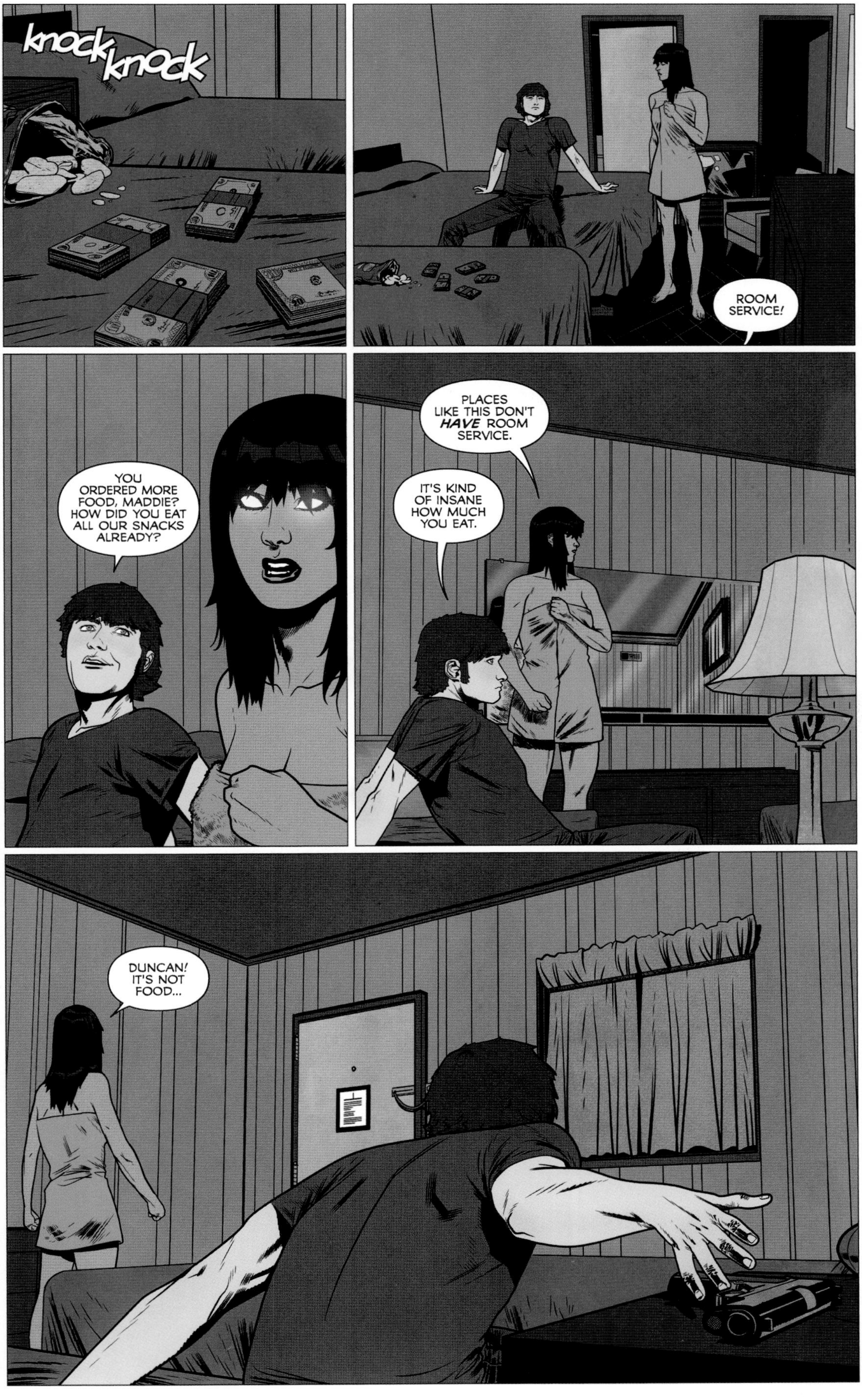
knock knock
ROOM SERVICE!
YOU ORDERED MORE FOOD, MADDIE? HOW DID YOU EAT ALL OUR SNACKS ALREADY?
PLACES LIKE THIS DON'T *HAVE* ROOM SERVICE.
IT'S KIND OF INSANE HOW MUCH YOU EAT.
DUNCAN! IT'S NOT FOOD...

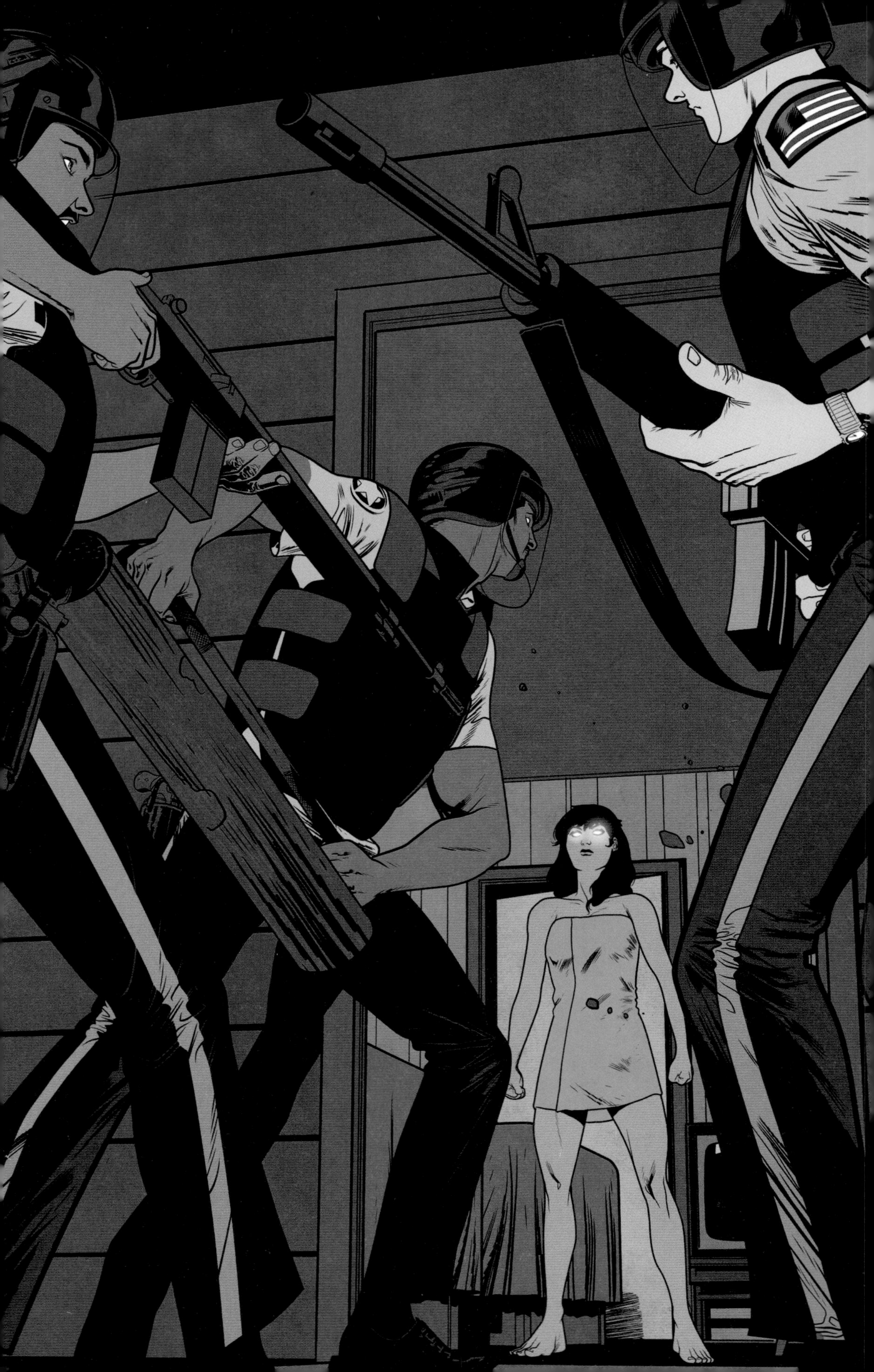

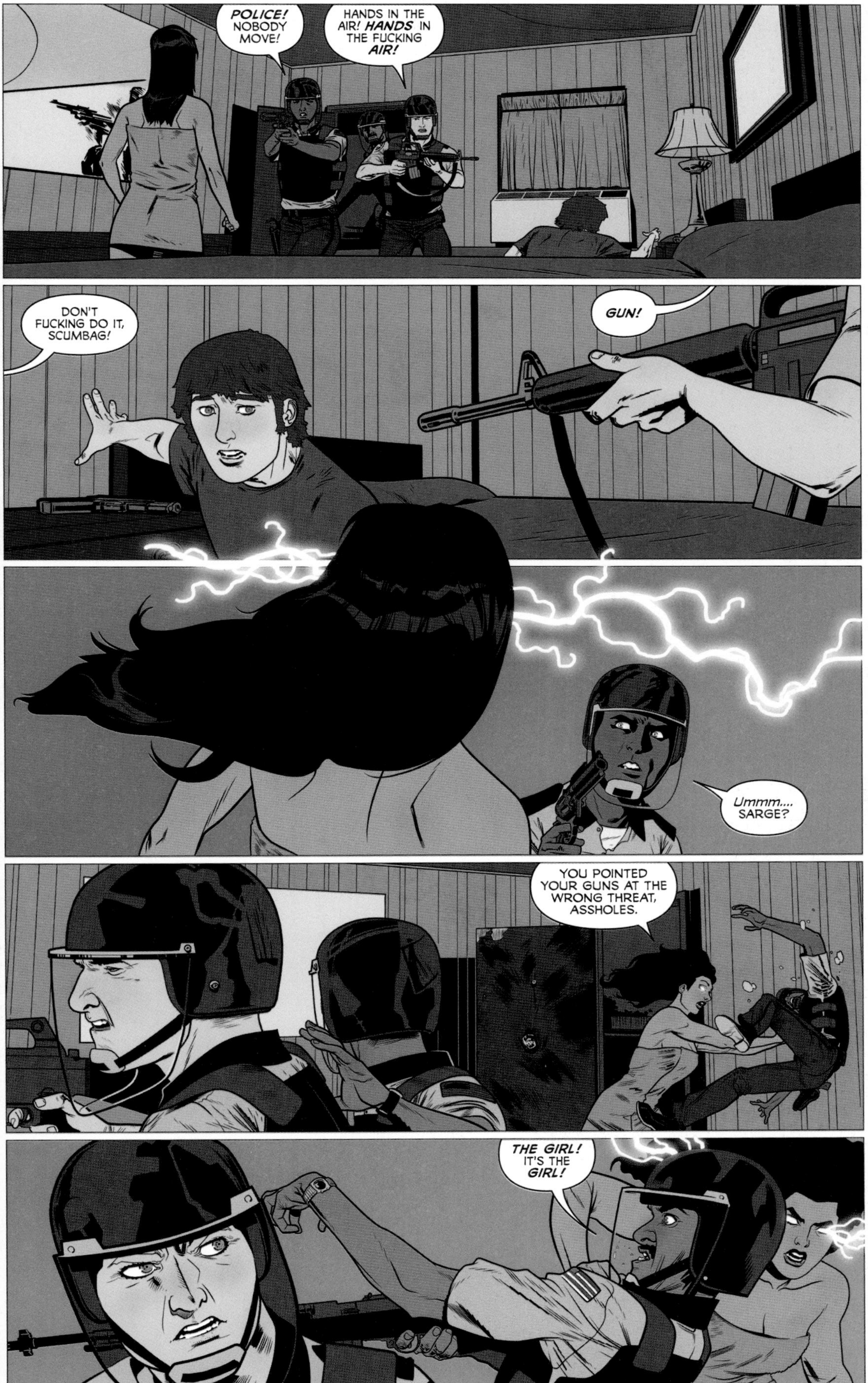
POLICE! NOBODY MOVE!
HANDS IN THE AIR! ***HANDS*** IN THE FUCKING ***AIR!***
DON'T FUCKING DO IT, SCUMBAG!
GUN!
Ummm.... SARGE?
YOU POINTED YOUR GUNS AT THE WRONG THREAT, ASSHOLES.
THE GIRL! IT'S THE ***GIRL!***

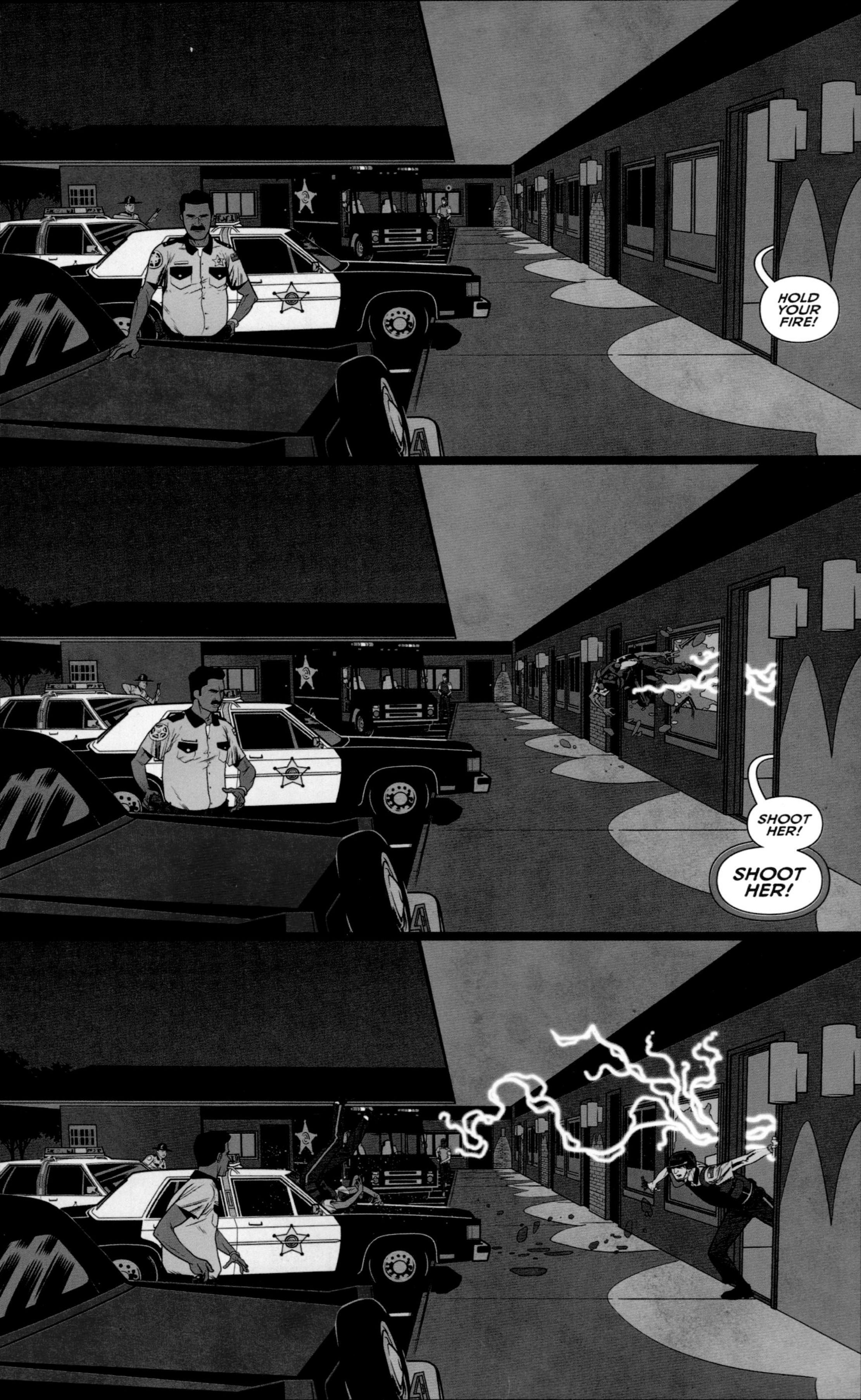
HOLD YOUR FIRE!
SHOOT HER!
SHOOT HER!

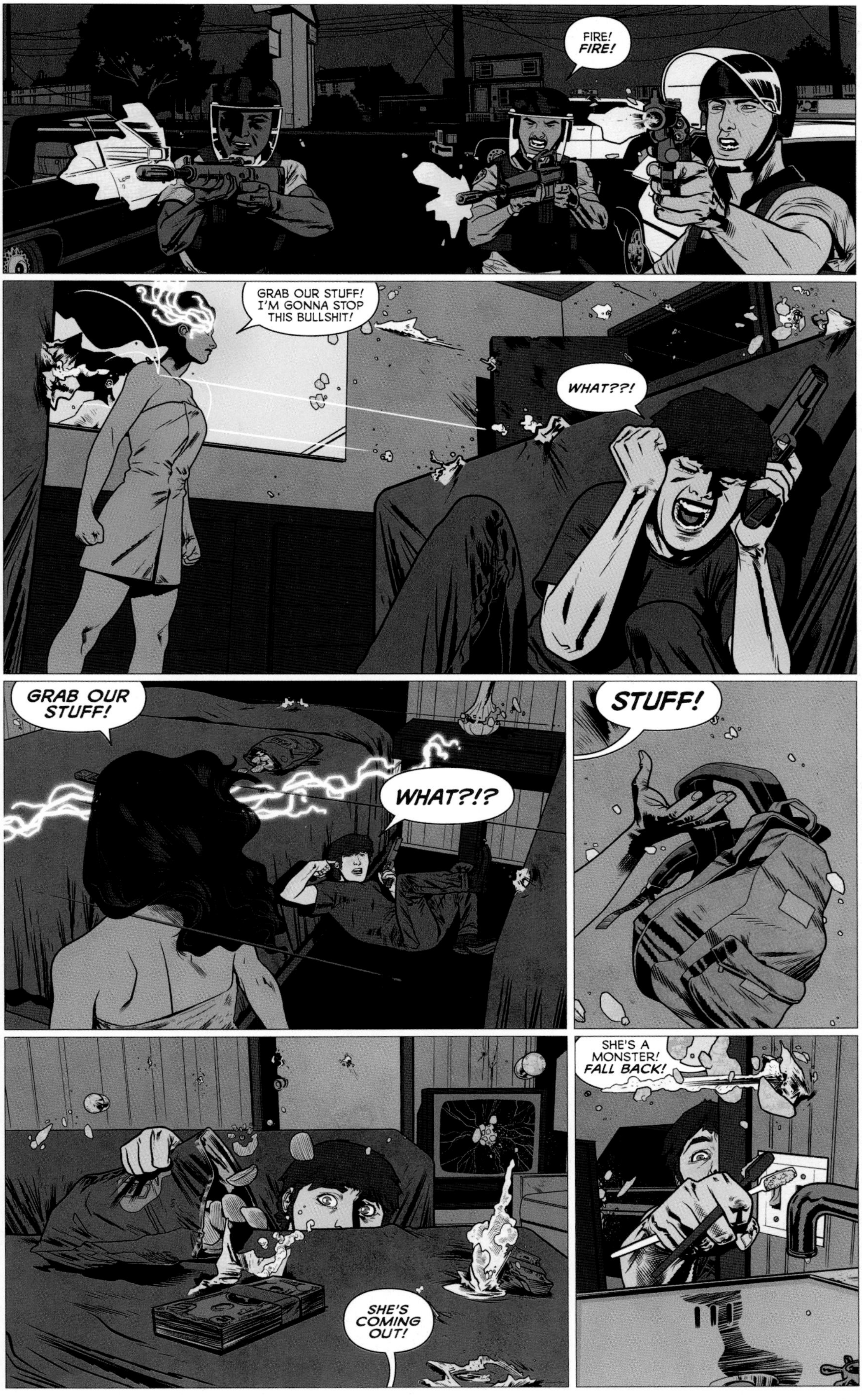
FIRE! FIRE!
GRAB OUR STUFF! I'M GONNA STOP THIS BULLSHIT!
WHAT??!
GRAB OUR STUFF!
WHAT?!?
STUFF!
SHE'S COMING OUT!
SHE'S A MONSTER! FALL BACK!

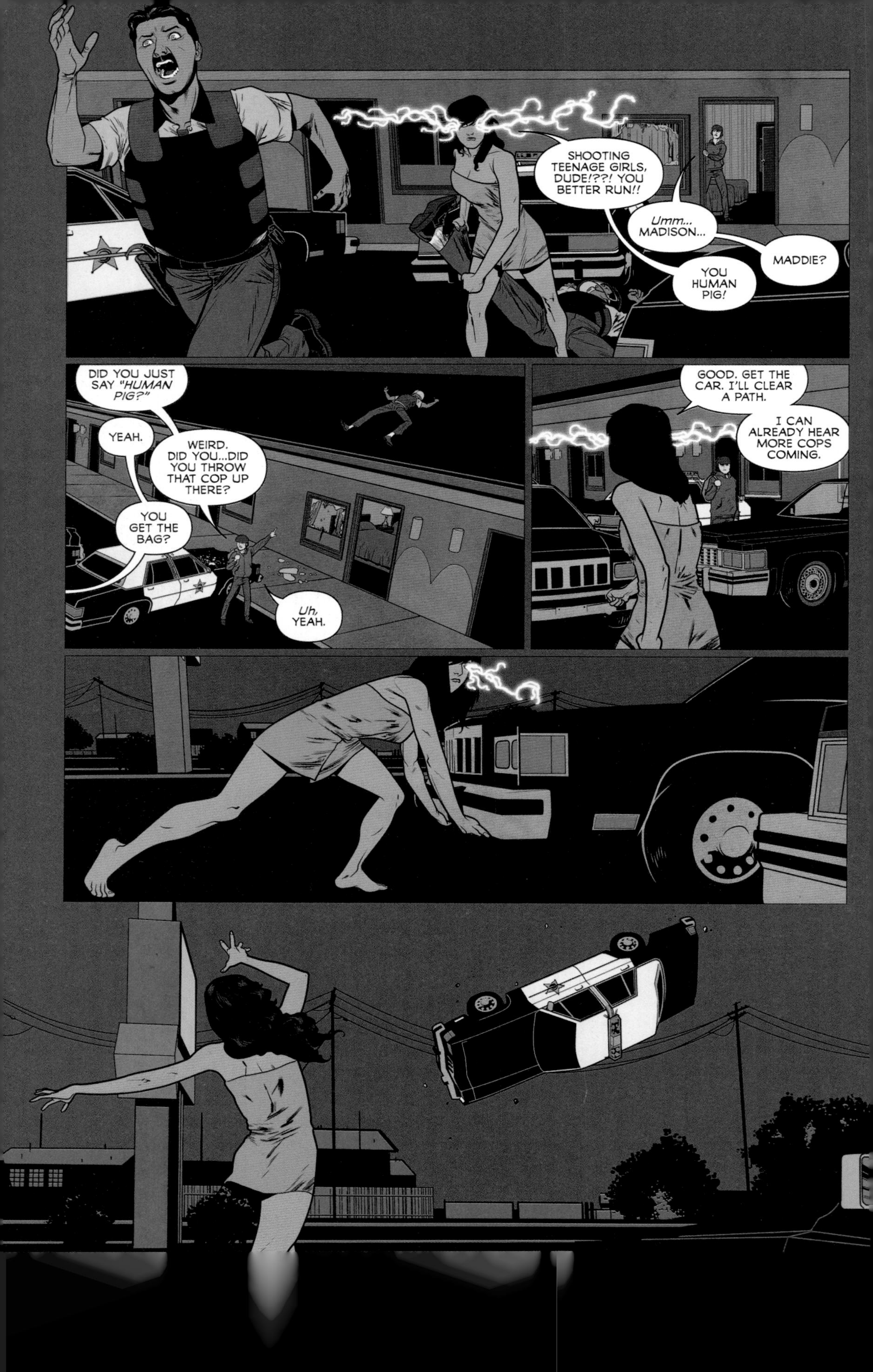
SHOOTING TEENAGE GIRLS, DUDE!??! YOU BETTER RUN!!
Umm... MADISON...
MADDIE?
YOU HUMAN PIG!
DID YOU JUST SAY "HUMAN PIG?"
YEAH.
WEIRD. DID YOU...DID YOU THROW THAT COP UP THERE?
YOU GET THE BAG?
Uh, YEAH.
GOOD. GET THE CAR. I'LL CLEAR A PATH.
I CAN ALREADY HEAR MORE COPS COMING.

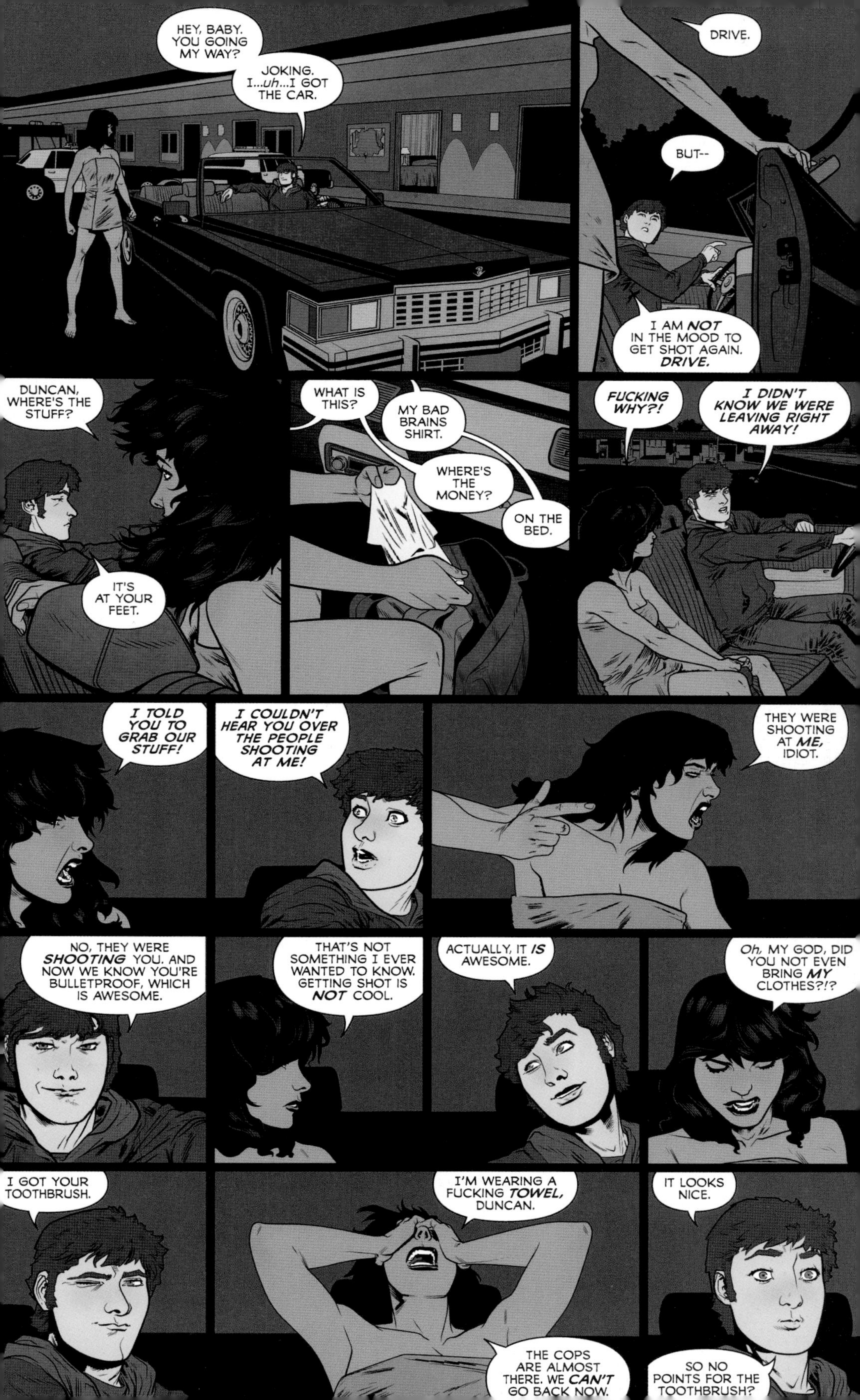
HEY, BABY. YOU GOING MY WAY?
JOKING. I...*uh*...I GOT THE CAR.
DRIVE.
BUT--
I AM **NOT** IN THE MOOD TO GET SHOT AGAIN. **DRIVE.**
DUNCAN, WHERE'S THE STUFF?
IT'S AT YOUR FEET.
WHAT IS THIS?
MY BAD BRAINS SHIRT.
WHERE'S THE MONEY?
ON THE BED.
FUCKING WHY?!
I DIDN'T KNOW WE WERE LEAVING RIGHT AWAY!
I TOLD YOU TO GRAB OUR STUFF!
I COULDN'T HEAR YOU OVER THE PEOPLE SHOOTING AT ME!
THEY WERE SHOOTING AT *ME,* IDIOT.
NO, THEY WERE *SHOOTING* YOU. AND NOW WE KNOW YOU'RE BULLETPROOF, WHICH IS AWESOME.
THAT'S NOT SOMETHING I EVER WANTED TO KNOW. GETTING SHOT IS *NOT* COOL.
ACTUALLY, IT *IS* AWESOME.
Oh, MY GOD, DID YOU NOT EVEN BRING *MY* CLOTHES?!?
I GOT YOUR TOOTHBRUSH.
I'M WEARING A FUCKING *TOWEL,* DUNCAN.
THE COPS ARE ALMOST THERE. WE *CAN'T* GO BACK NOW.
IT LOOKS NICE.
SO NO POINTS FOR THE TOOTHBRUSH?

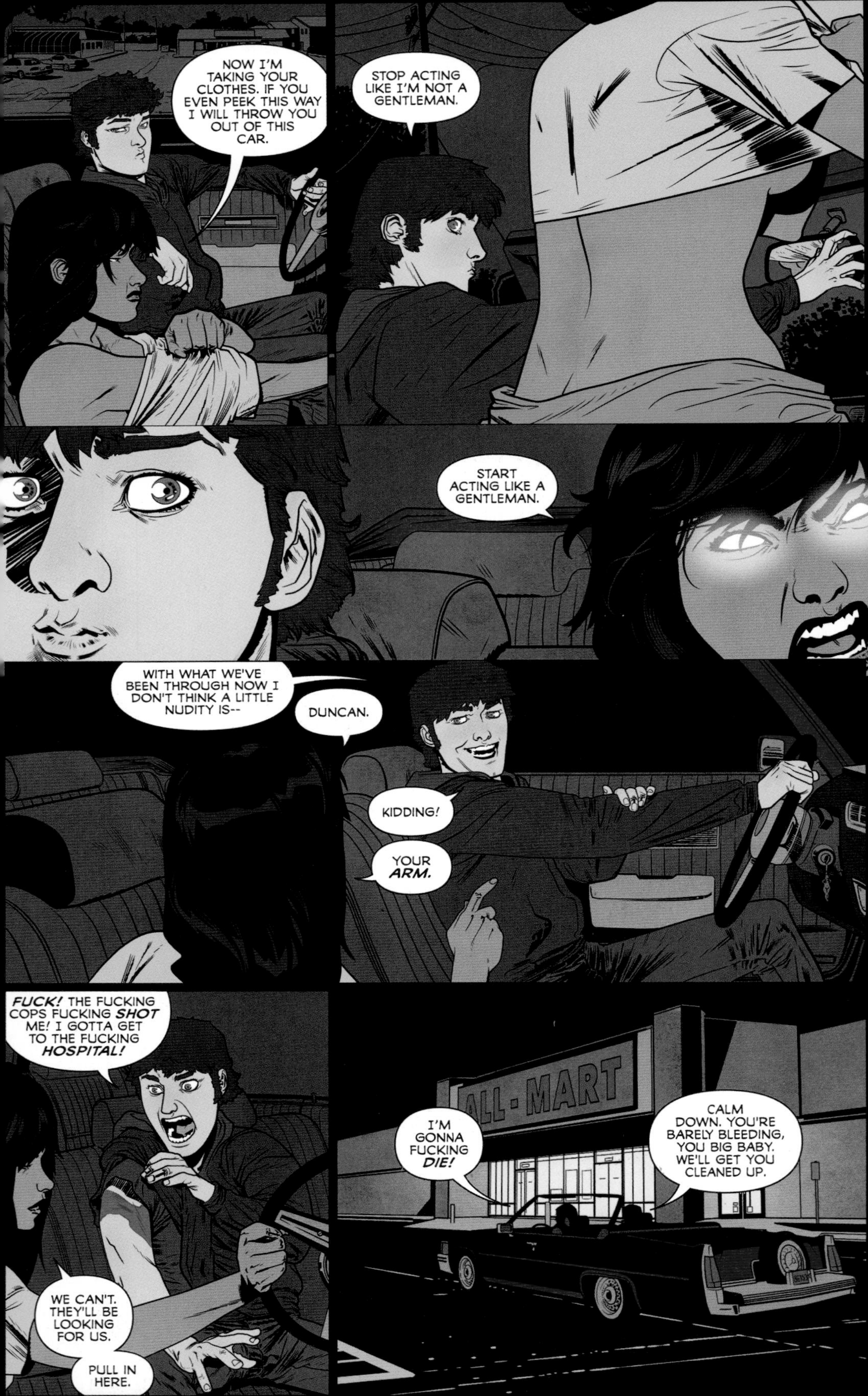
NOW I'M TAKING YOUR CLOTHES. IF YOU EVEN PEEK THIS WAY I WILL THROW YOU OUT OF THIS CAR.
STOP ACTING LIKE I'M NOT A GENTLEMAN.
START ACTING LIKE A GENTLEMAN.
WITH WHAT WE'VE BEEN THROUGH NOW I DON'T THINK A LITTLE NUDITY IS--
DUNCAN.
KIDDING!
YOUR *ARM.*
FUCK! THE FUCKING COPS FUCKING *SHOT* ME! I GOTTA GET TO THE FUCKING *HOSPITAL!*
WE CAN'T. THEY'LL BE LOOKING FOR US.
PULL IN HERE.
ALL-MART
I'M GONNA FUCKING *DIE!*
CALM DOWN. YOU'RE BARELY BLEEDING, YOU BIG BABY. WE'LL GET YOU CLEANED UP.

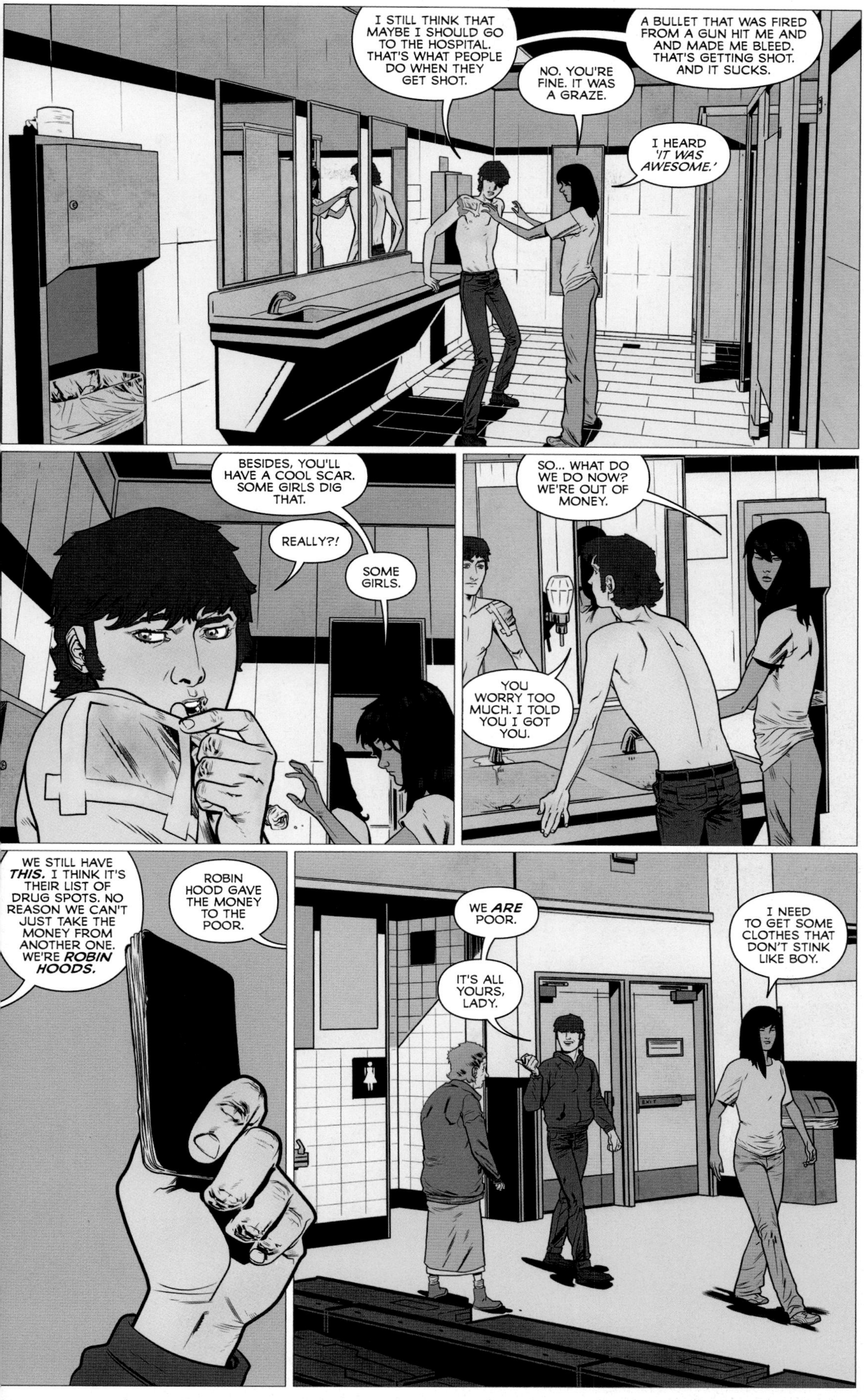
I STILL THINK THAT MAYBE I SHOULD GO TO THE HOSPITAL. THAT'S WHAT PEOPLE DO WHEN THEY GET SHOT.
NO. YOU'RE FINE. IT WAS A GRAZE.
A BULLET THAT WAS FIRED FROM A GUN HIT ME AND AND MADE ME BLEED. THAT'S GETTING SHOT. AND IT SUCKS.
I HEARD *'IT WAS AWESOME.'*
BESIDES, YOU'LL HAVE A COOL SCAR. SOME GIRLS DIG THAT.
REALLY?!
SOME GIRLS.
SO... WHAT DO WE DO NOW? WE'RE OUT OF MONEY.
YOU WORRY TOO MUCH. I TOLD YOU I GOT YOU.
WE STILL HAVE ***THIS.*** I THINK IT'S THEIR LIST OF DRUG SPOTS. NO REASON WE CAN'T JUST TAKE THE MONEY FROM ANOTHER ONE. WE'RE ***ROBIN HOODS.***
ROBIN HOOD GAVE THE MONEY TO THE POOR.
WE ***ARE*** POOR.
IT'S ALL YOURS, LADY.
I NEED TO GET SOME CLOTHES THAT DON'T STINK LIKE BOY.

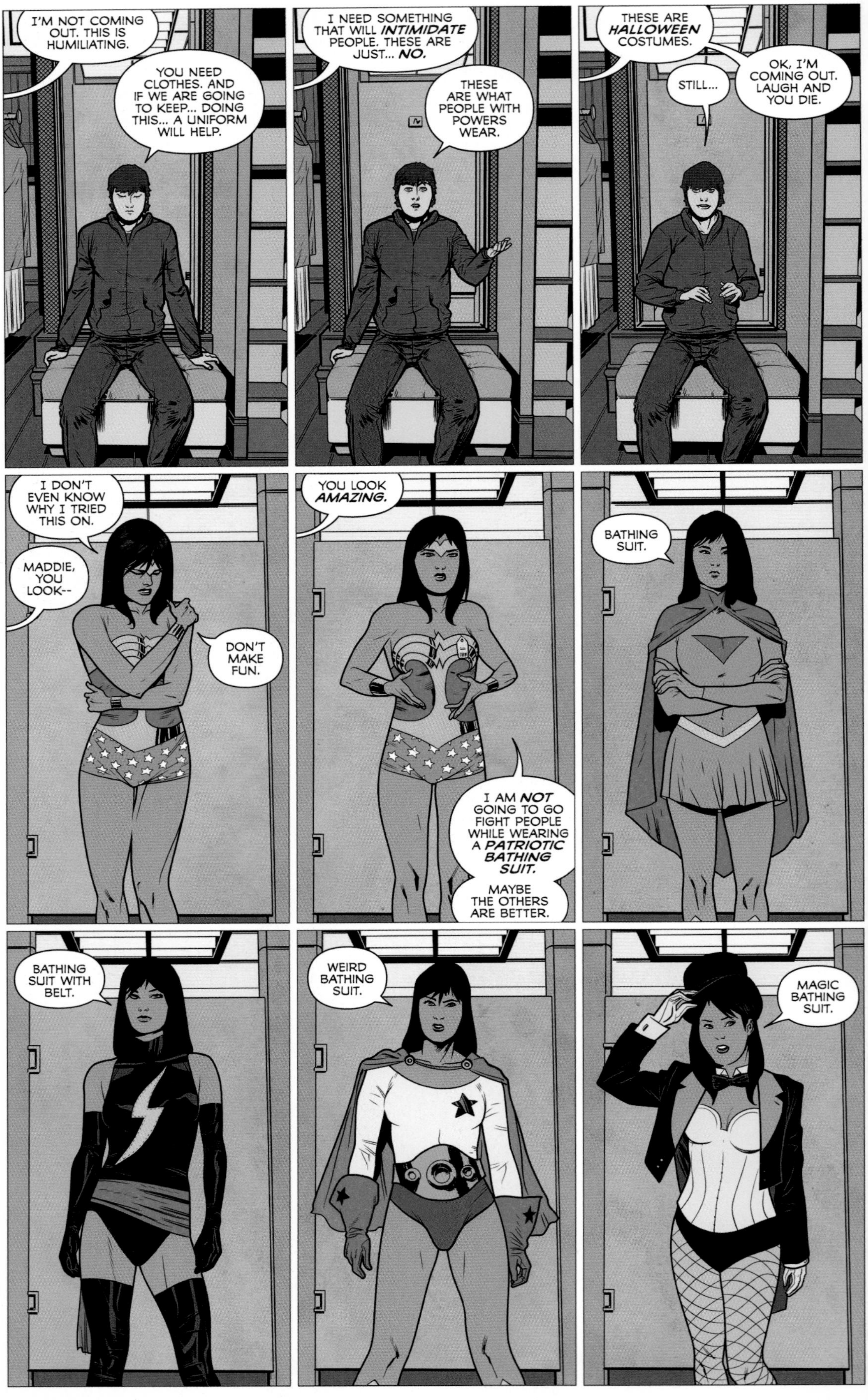
I'M NOT COMING OUT. THIS IS HUMILIATING.
YOU NEED CLOTHES. AND IF WE ARE GOING TO KEEP... DOING THIS... A UNIFORM WILL HELP.
I NEED SOMETHING THAT WILL *INTIMIDATE* PEOPLE. THESE ARE JUST... *NO.*
THESE ARE WHAT PEOPLE WITH POWERS WEAR.
THESE ARE *HALLOWEEN* COSTUMES.
STILL...
OK, I'M COMING OUT. LAUGH AND YOU DIE.
I DON'T EVEN KNOW WHY I TRIED THIS ON.
MADDIE, YOU LOOK--
DON'T MAKE FUN.
YOU LOOK *AMAZING.*
I AM *NOT* GOING TO GO FIGHT PEOPLE WHILE WEARING A *PATRIOTIC BATHING SUIT.*
MAYBE THE OTHERS ARE BETTER.
BATHING SUIT.
BATHING SUIT WITH BELT.
WEIRD BATHING SUIT.
MAGIC BATHING SUIT.

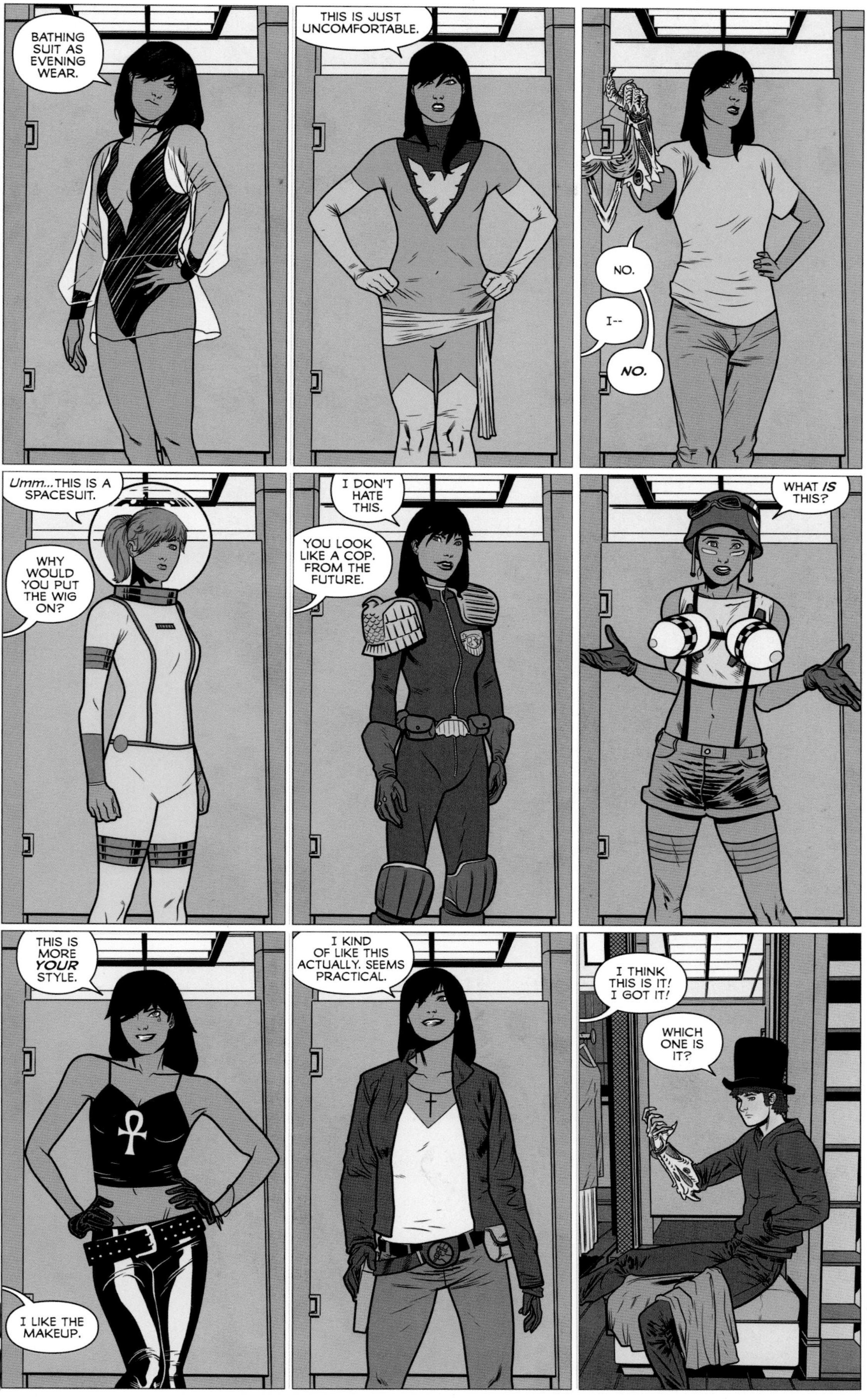
BATHING SUIT AS EVENING WEAR.
THIS IS JUST UNCOMFORTABLE.
NO.
I--
NO.
Umm... THIS IS A SPACESUIT.
WHY WOULD YOU PUT THE WIG ON?
I DON'T HATE THIS.
YOU LOOK LIKE A COP. FROM THE FUTURE.
WHAT ***IS*** THIS?
THIS IS MORE ***YOUR*** STYLE.
I LIKE THE MAKEUP.
I KIND OF LIKE THIS ACTUALLY. SEEMS PRACTICAL.
I THINK THIS IS IT! I GOT IT!
WHICH ONE IS IT?

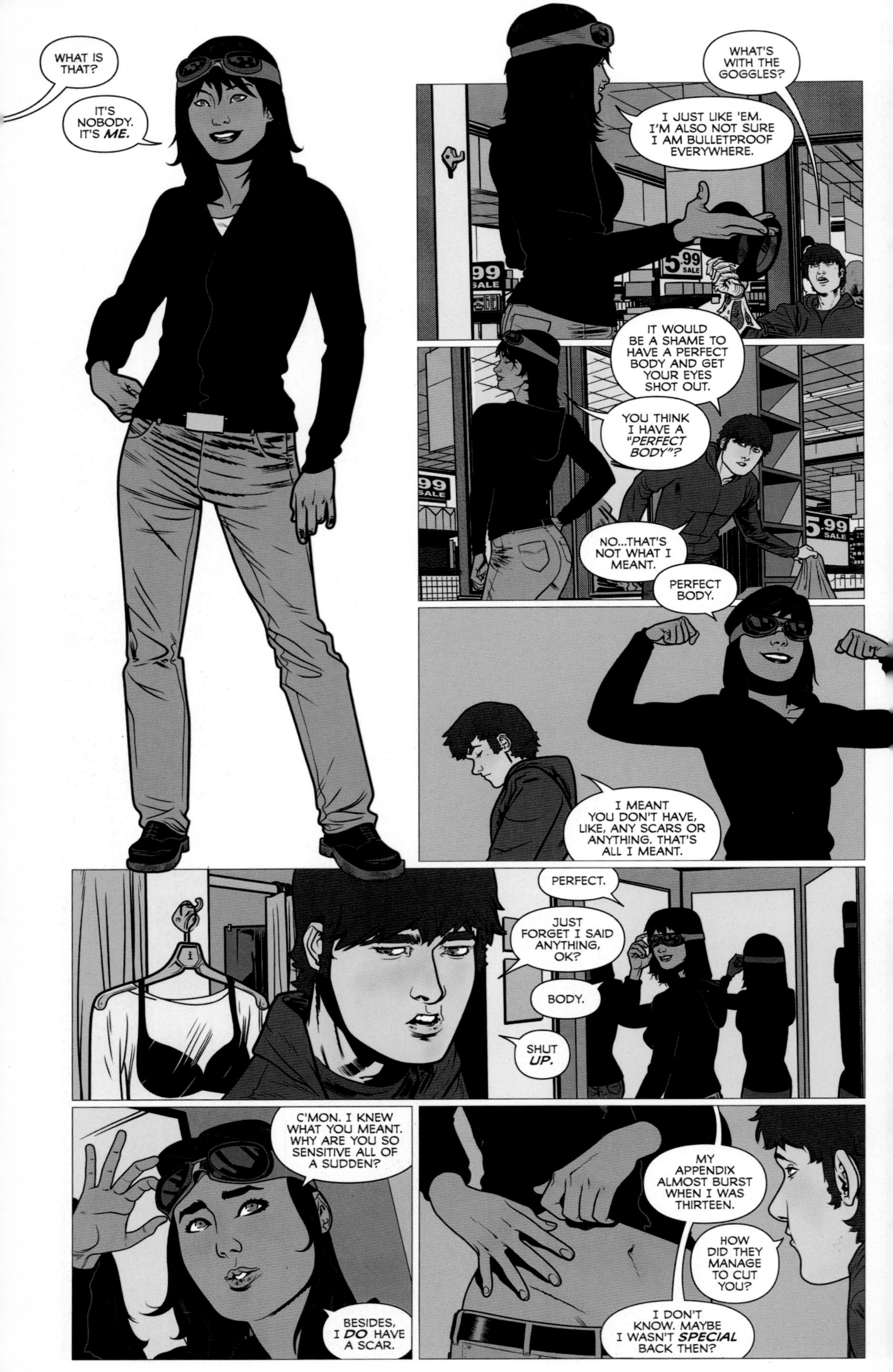
WHAT IS THAT?
IT'S NOBODY. IT'S *ME.*
WHAT'S WITH THE GOGGLES?
I JUST LIKE 'EM. I'M ALSO NOT SURE I AM BULLETPROOF EVERYWHERE.
5.99 SALE
IT WOULD BE A SHAME TO HAVE A PERFECT BODY AND GET YOUR EYES SHOT OUT.
YOU THINK I HAVE A *"PERFECT BODY"?*
NO...THAT'S NOT WHAT I MEANT.
PERFECT BODY.
I MEANT YOU DON'T HAVE, LIKE, ANY SCARS OR ANYTHING. THAT'S ALL I MEANT.
PERFECT.
JUST FORGET I SAID ANYTHING, OK?
BODY.
SHUT *UP.*
C'MON. I KNEW WHAT YOU MEANT. WHY ARE YOU SO SENSITIVE ALL OF A SUDDEN?
BESIDES, I *DO* HAVE A SCAR.
MY APPENDIX ALMOST BURST WHEN I WAS THIRTEEN.
HOW DID THEY MANAGE TO CUT YOU?
I DON'T KNOW. MAYBE I WASN'T *SPECIAL* BACK THEN?

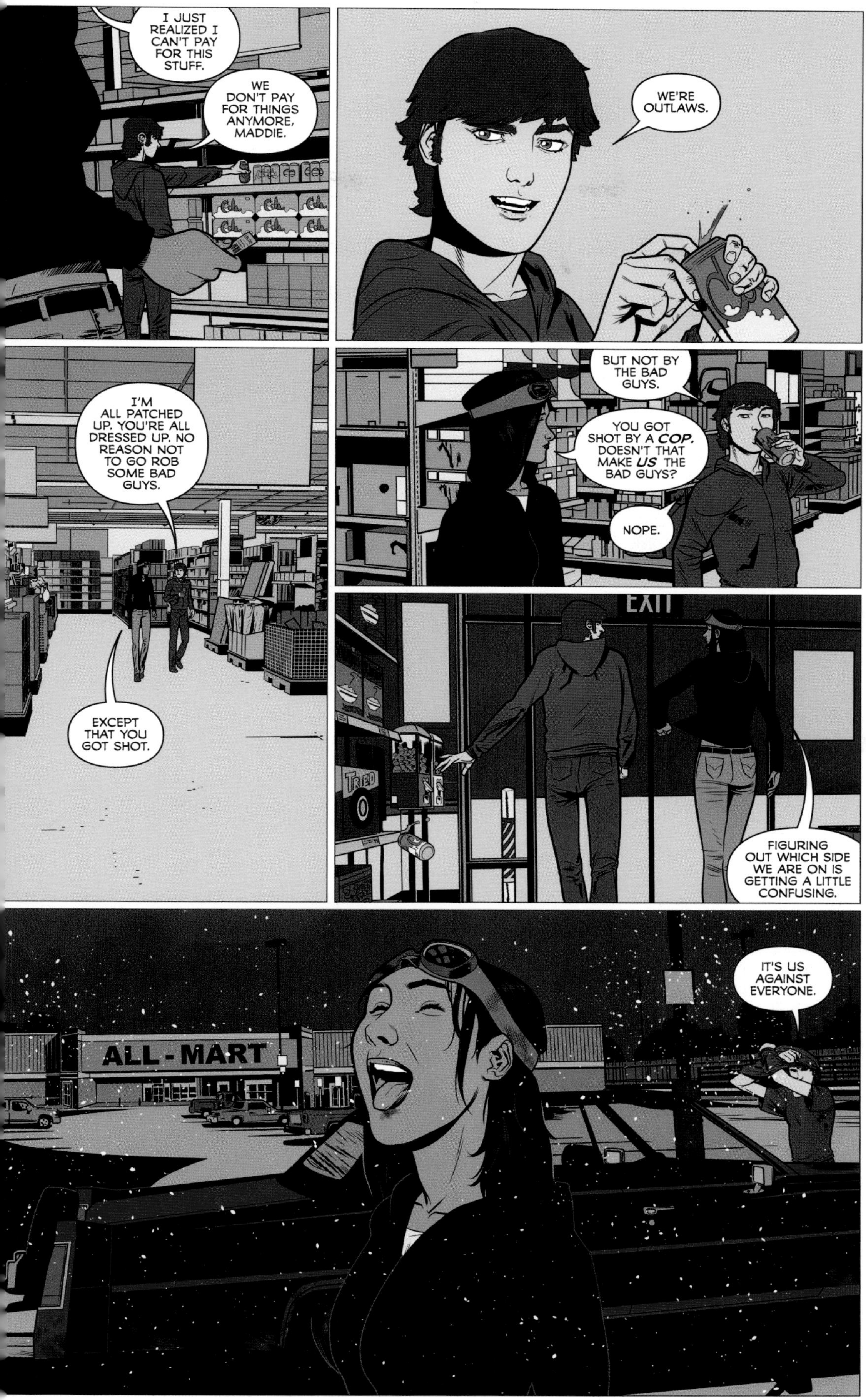
I JUST REALIZED I CAN'T PAY FOR THIS STUFF.
WE DON'T PAY FOR THINGS ANYMORE, MADDIE.
WE'RE OUTLAWS.
I'M ALL PATCHED UP. YOU'RE ALL DRESSED UP. NO REASON NOT TO GO ROB SOME BAD GUYS.
EXCEPT THAT YOU GOT SHOT.
BUT NOT BY THE BAD GUYS.
YOU GOT SHOT BY A *COP.* DOESN'T THAT MAKE *US* THE BAD GUYS?
NOPE.
EXIT
FIGURING OUT WHICH SIDE WE ARE ON IS GETTING A LITTLE CONFUSING.
ALL-MART
IT'S US AGAINST EVERYONE.

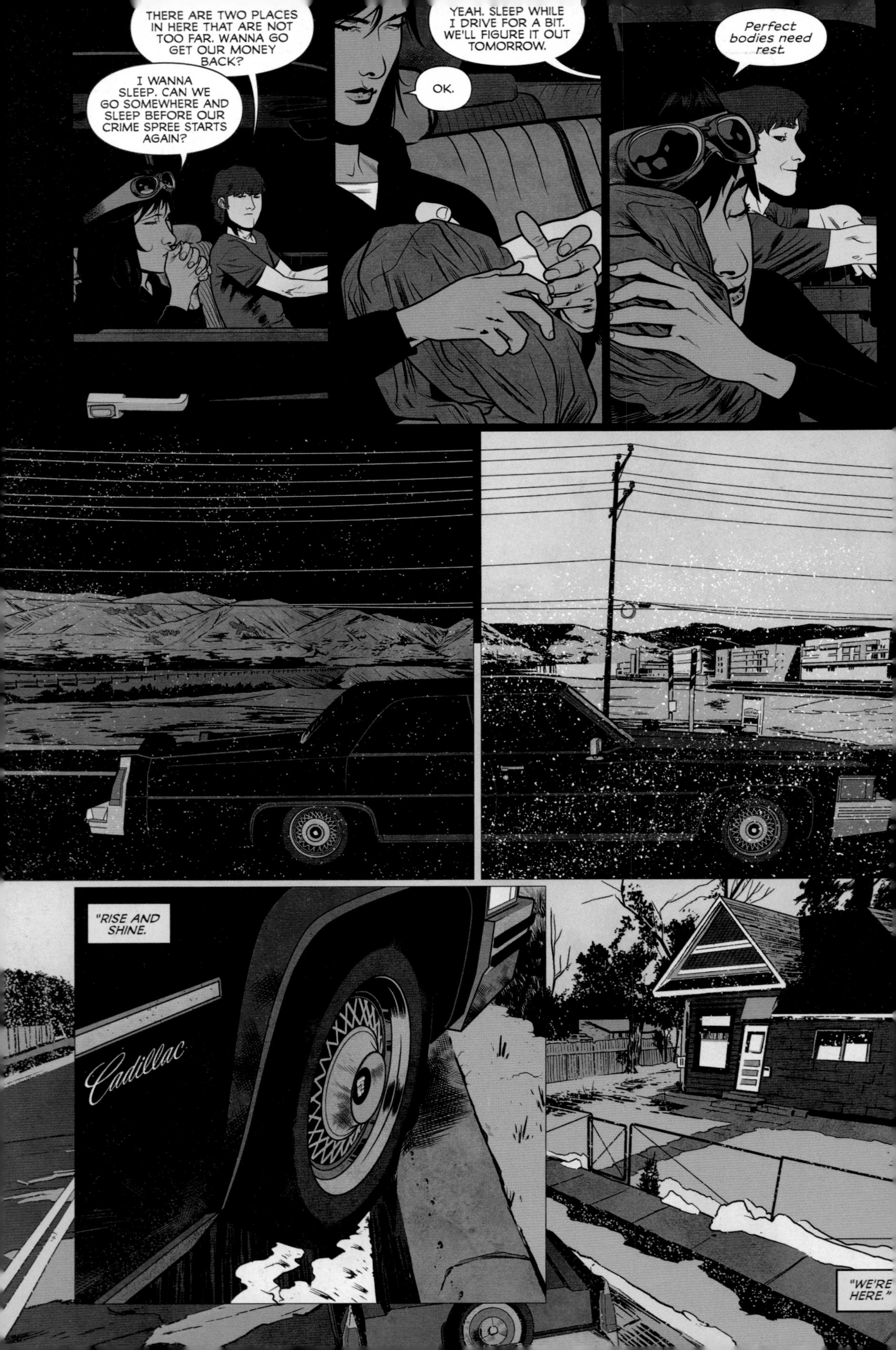
THERE ARE TWO PLACES IN HERE THAT ARE NOT TOO FAR. WANNA GO GET OUR MONEY BACK?
I WANNA SLEEP. CAN WE GO SOMEWHERE AND SLEEP BEFORE OUR CRIME SPREE STARTS AGAIN?
YEAH. SLEEP WHILE I DRIVE FOR A BIT. WE'LL FIGURE IT OUT TOMORROW.
OK.
Perfect bodies need rest.
"RISE AND SHINE.
Cadillac
"WE'RE HERE."

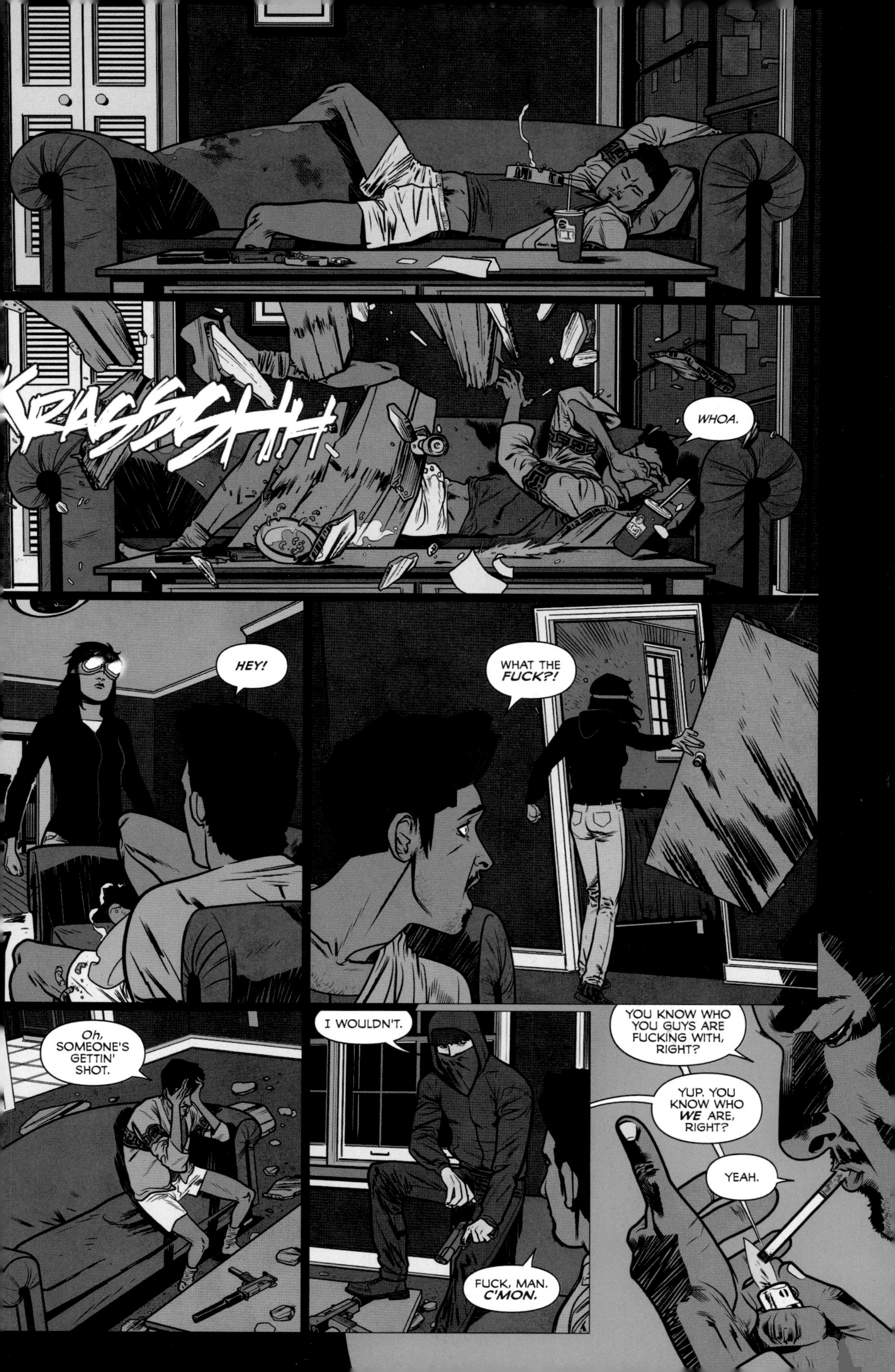
KRASSSHH
WHOA.
HEY!
WHAT THE FUCK?!
Oh, SOMEONE'S GETTIN' SHOT.
I WOULDN'T.
FUCK, MAN. C'MON.
YOU KNOW WHO YOU GUYS ARE FUCKING WITH, RIGHT?
YUP. YOU KNOW WHO WE ARE, RIGHT?
YEAH.

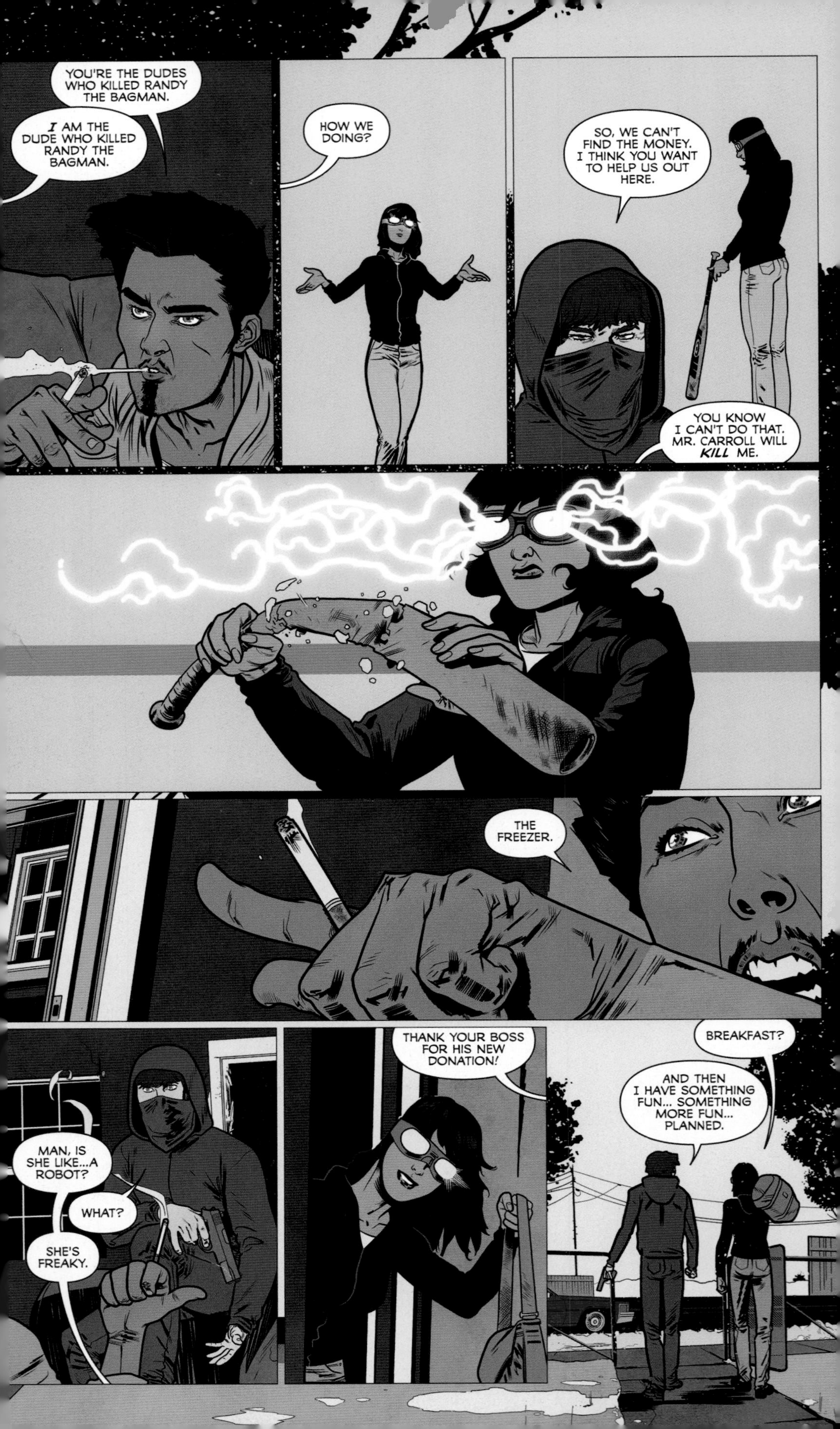
YOU'RE THE DUDES WHO KILLED RANDY THE BAGMAN.
I AM THE DUDE WHO KILLED RANDY THE BAGMAN.
HOW WE DOING?
SO, WE CAN'T FIND THE MONEY. I THINK YOU WANT TO HELP US OUT HERE.
YOU KNOW I CAN'T DO THAT. MR. CARROLL WILL KILL ME.
THE FREEZER.
MAN, IS SHE LIKE...A ROBOT?
WHAT?
SHE'S FREAKY.
THANK YOUR BOSS FOR HIS NEW DONATION!
BREAKFAST?
AND THEN I HAVE SOMETHING FUN... SOMETHING MORE FUN... PLANNED.

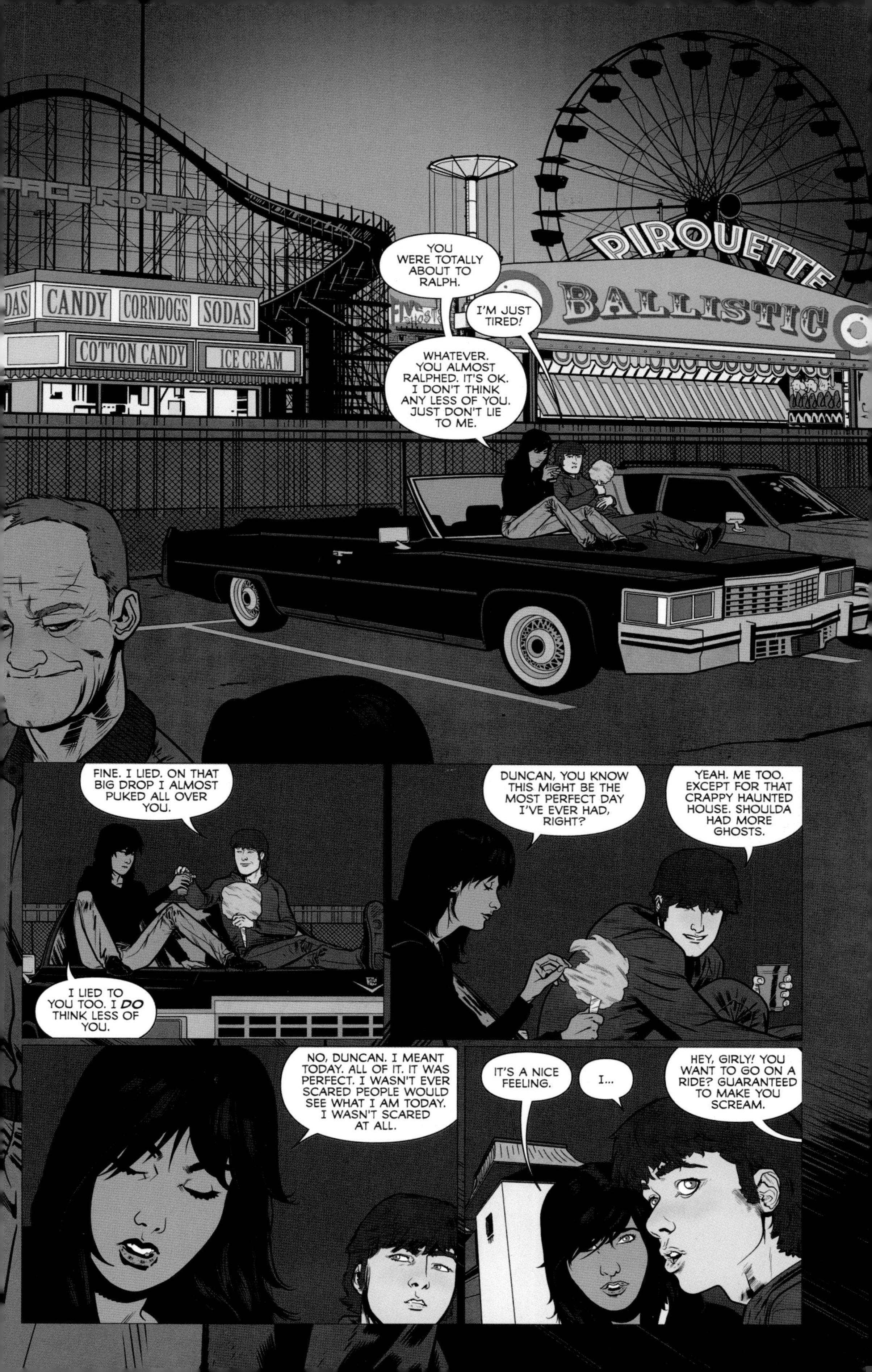
CANDY
CORNDOGS
SODAS
COTTON CANDY
ICE CREAM
PIROUETTE
BALLISTIC
YOU WERE TOTALLY ABOUT TO RALPH.
I'M JUST TIRED!
WHATEVER. YOU ALMOST RALPHED. IT'S OK. I DON'T THINK ANY LESS OF YOU. JUST DON'T LIE TO ME.
FINE. I LIED. ON THAT BIG DROP I ALMOST PUKED ALL OVER YOU.
I LIED TO YOU TOO. I *DO* THINK LESS OF YOU.
DUNCAN, YOU KNOW THIS MIGHT BE THE MOST PERFECT DAY I'VE EVER HAD, RIGHT?
YEAH. ME TOO. EXCEPT FOR THAT CRAPPY HAUNTED HOUSE. SHOULDA HAD MORE GHOSTS.
NO, DUNCAN. I MEANT TODAY. ALL OF IT. IT WAS PERFECT. I WASN'T EVER SCARED PEOPLE WOULD SEE WHAT I AM TODAY. I WASN'T SCARED AT ALL.
IT'S A NICE FEELING.
I...
HEY, GIRLY! YOU WANT TO GO ON A RIDE? GUARANTEED TO MAKE YOU SCREAM.

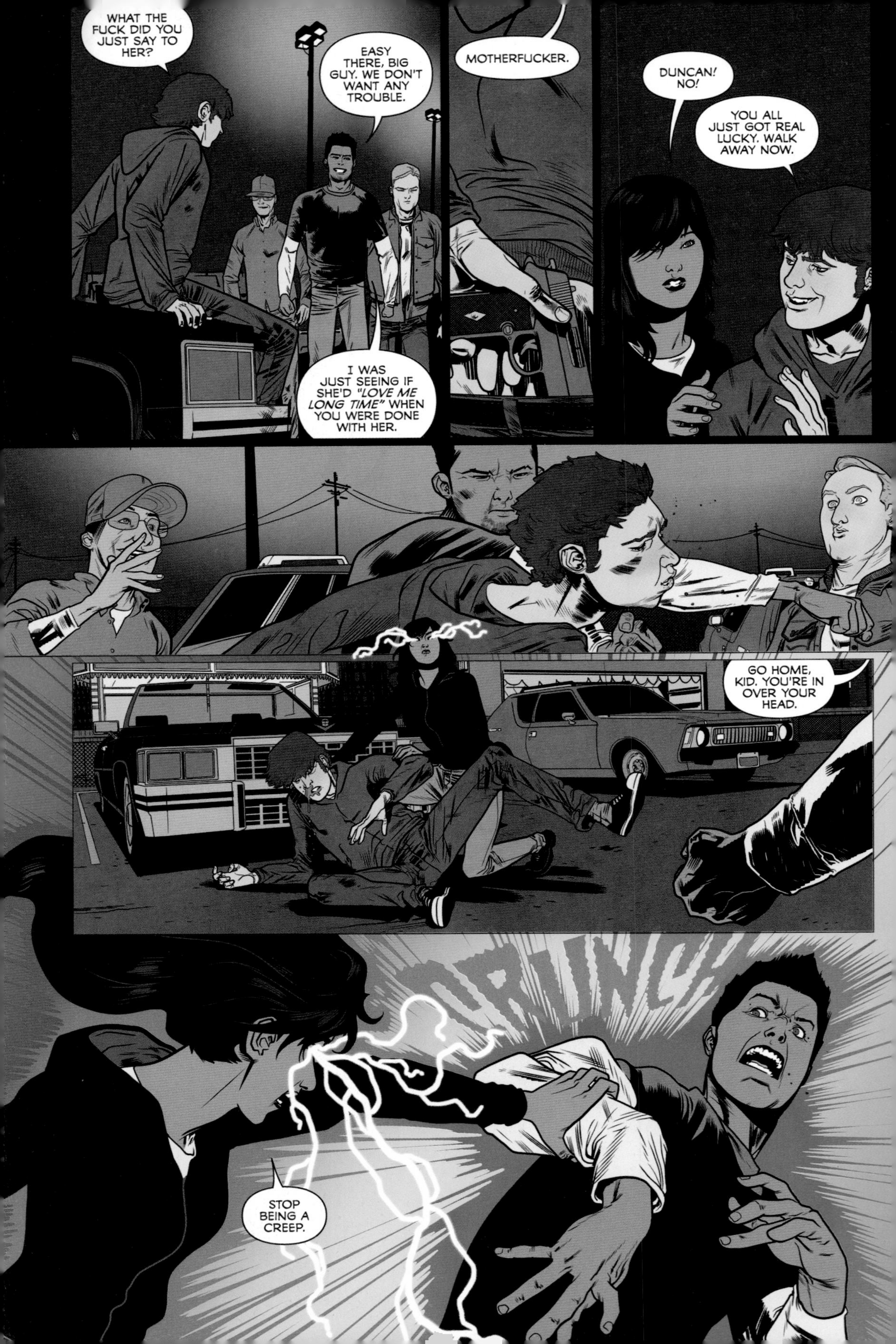
WHAT THE FUCK DID YOU JUST SAY TO HER?
EASY THERE, BIG GUY. WE DON'T WANT ANY TROUBLE.
I WAS JUST SEEING IF SHE'D *"LOVE ME LONG TIME"* WHEN YOU WERE DONE WITH HER.
MOTHERFUCKER.
DUNCAN! NO!
YOU ALL JUST GOT REAL LUCKY. WALK AWAY NOW.
GO HOME, KID. YOU'RE IN OVER YOUR HEAD.
STOP BEING A CREEP.

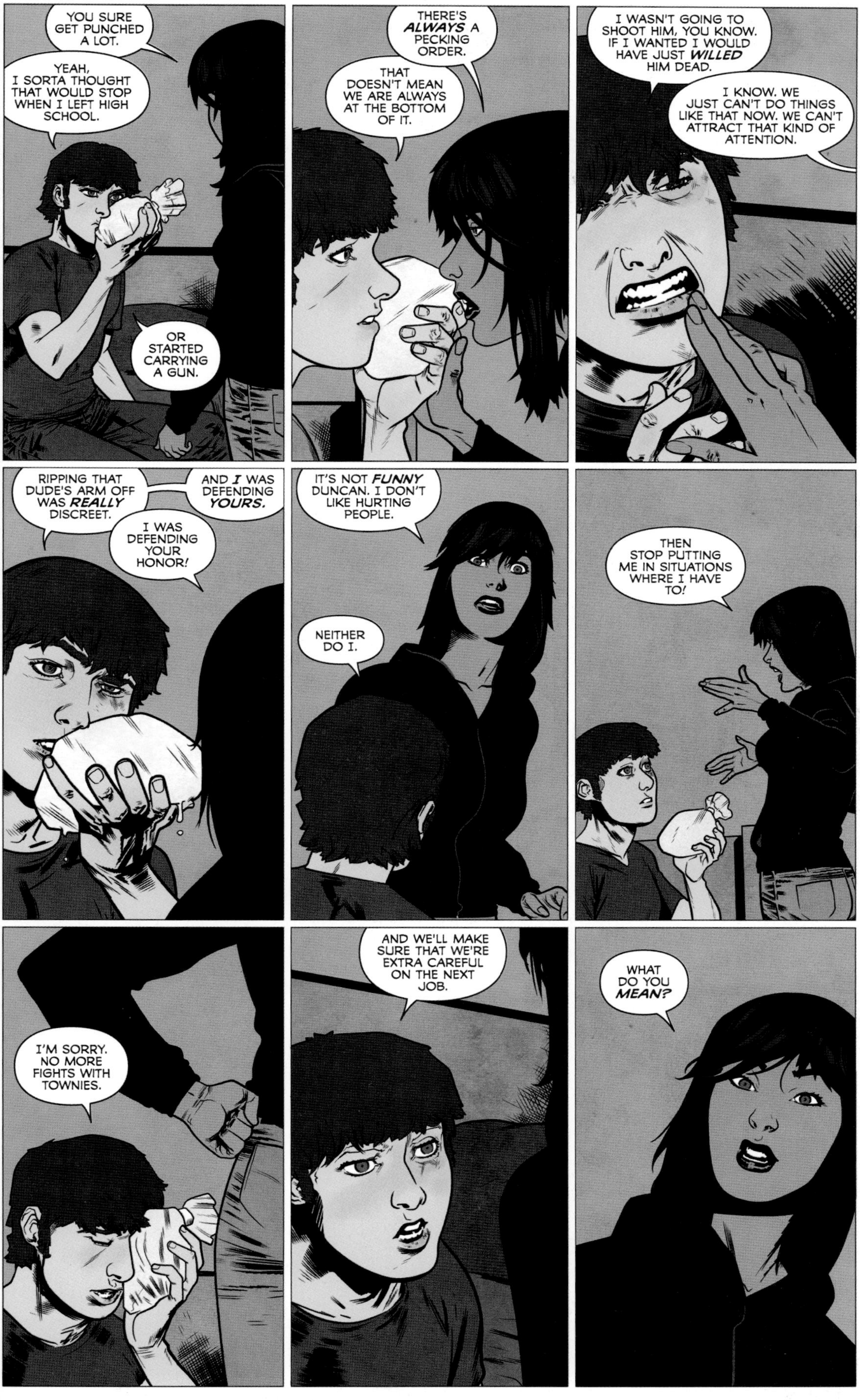
YOU SURE GET PUNCHED A LOT.
YEAH, I SORTA THOUGHT THAT WOULD STOP WHEN I LEFT HIGH SCHOOL.
OR STARTED CARRYING A GUN.
THERE'S *ALWAYS* A PECKING ORDER.
THAT DOESN'T MEAN WE ARE ALWAYS AT THE BOTTOM OF IT.
I WASN'T GOING TO SHOOT HIM, YOU KNOW. IF I WANTED I WOULD HAVE JUST *WILLED* HIM DEAD.
I KNOW. WE JUST CAN'T DO THINGS LIKE THAT NOW. WE CAN'T ATTRACT THAT KIND OF ATTENTION.
RIPPING THAT DUDE'S ARM OFF WAS *REALLY* DISCREET.
I WAS DEFENDING YOUR HONOR!
AND *I* WAS DEFENDING *YOURS.*
IT'S NOT *FUNNY* DUNCAN. I DON'T LIKE HURTING PEOPLE.
NEITHER DO I.
THEN STOP PUTTING ME IN SITUATIONS WHERE I HAVE TO!
I'M SORRY. NO MORE FIGHTS WITH TOWNIES.
AND WE'LL MAKE SURE THAT WE'RE EXTRA CAREFUL ON THE NEXT JOB.
WHAT DO YOU *MEAN?*

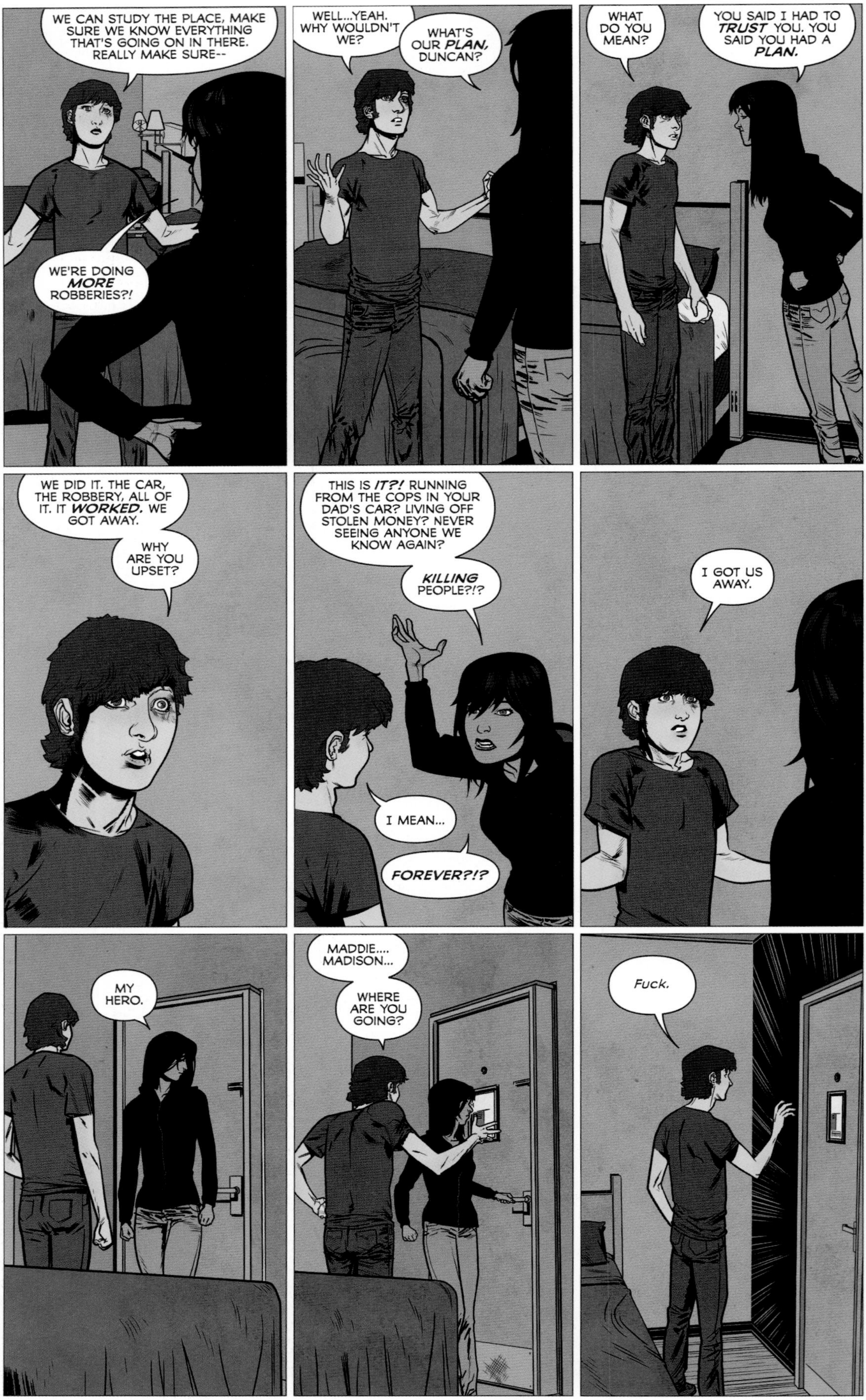
WE CAN STUDY THE PLACE, MAKE SURE WE KNOW EVERYTHING THAT'S GOING ON IN THERE. REALLY MAKE SURE--
WE'RE DOING *MORE* ROBBERIES?!
WELL...YEAH. WHY WOULDN'T WE?
WHAT'S OUR *PLAN,* DUNCAN?
WHAT DO YOU MEAN?
YOU SAID I HAD TO *TRUST* YOU. YOU SAID YOU HAD A *PLAN.*
WE DID IT. THE CAR, THE ROBBERY, ALL OF IT. IT *WORKED.* WE GOT AWAY.
WHY ARE YOU UPSET?
THIS IS *IT?!* RUNNING FROM THE COPS IN YOUR DAD'S CAR? LIVING OFF STOLEN MONEY? NEVER SEEING ANYONE WE KNOW AGAIN?
KILLING PEOPLE?!?
I MEAN...
FOREVER?!?
I GOT US AWAY.
MY HERO.
MADDIE.... MADISON...
WHERE ARE YOU GOING?
Fuck.

IF IT WEREN'T FOR ME, YOU'D BE IN A FUCKING JAIL SOMEWHERE. OR MAYBE IN A LAB. SO, YES, I *DO* THINK AN APOLOGY IS IN ORDER.

I'M SORRY, MADDIE. I AM. YOU SAVED ME AND I WANTED TO SAVE YOU. BIG TIME. YOUR KNIGHT IN SHINY ARMOR.

"I KNOW, DUNCAN. YOU'RE THE BEST."

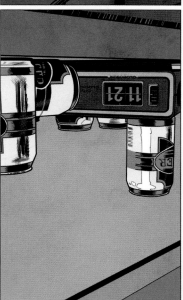

GIRL LIKE ME AND A GUY LIKE YOU, MADISON? IT DOESN'T EVEN MAKES ANY SENSE AT ALL, RIGHT? S'CRAZY. I--

knock knock

Ooof. WHO IS IT?

YOU CAME BACK.

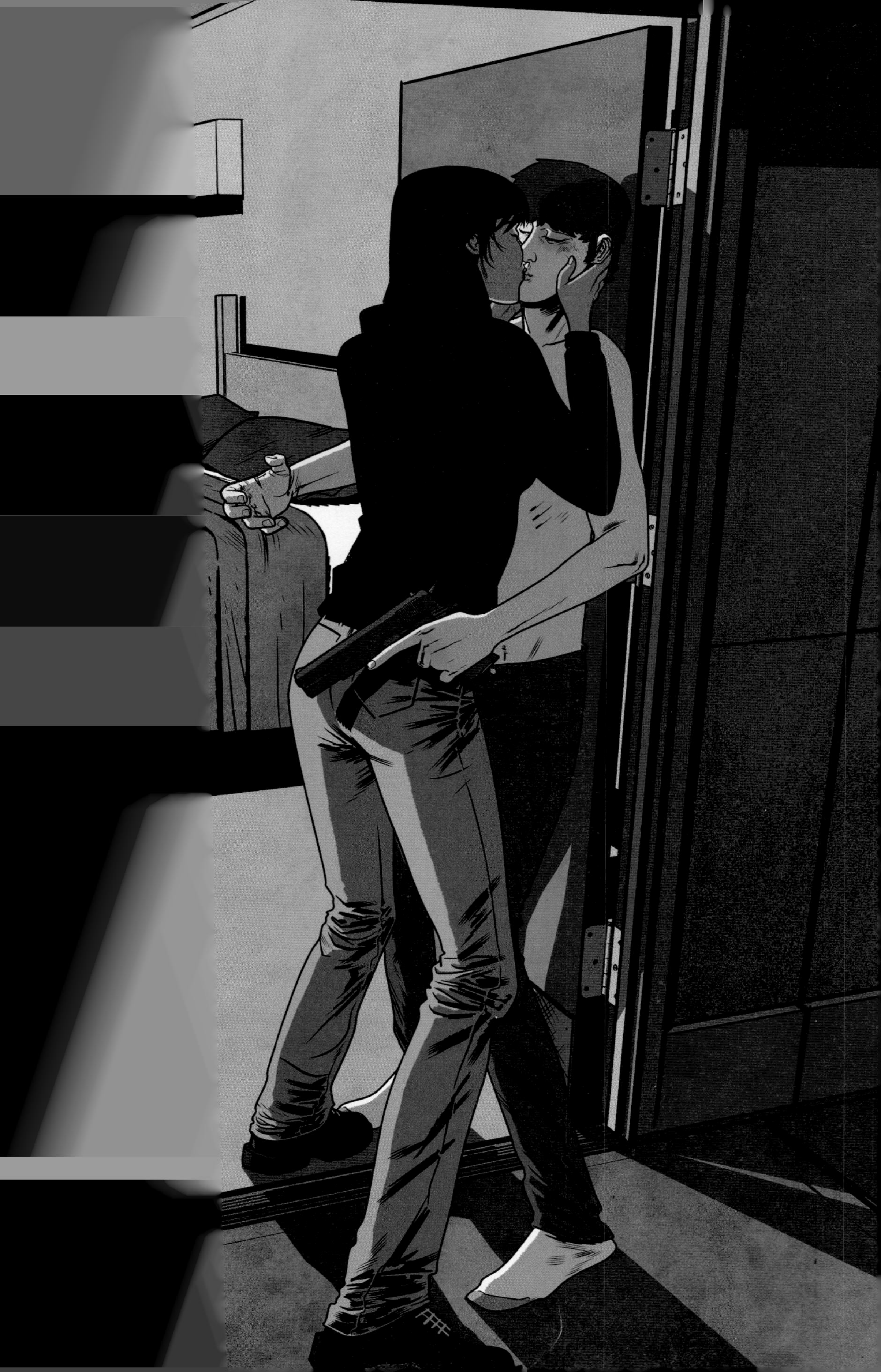

CHAPTER 4

HELP SAVE THE YOUTH OF AMERICA

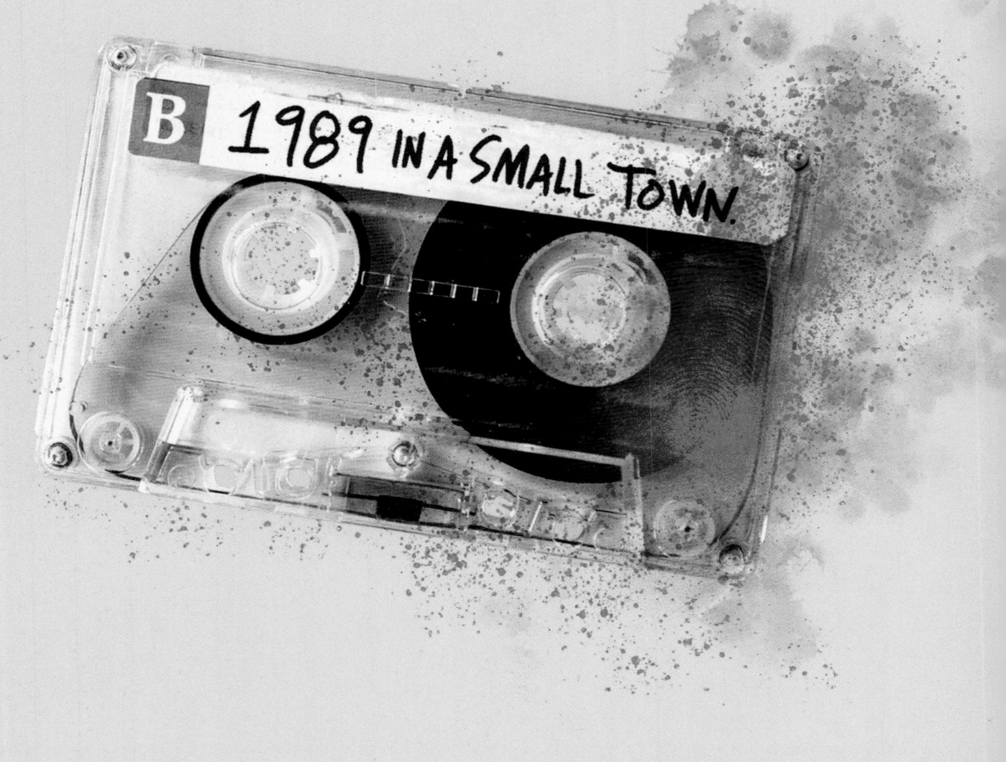
B
1989 IN A SMALL TOWN.

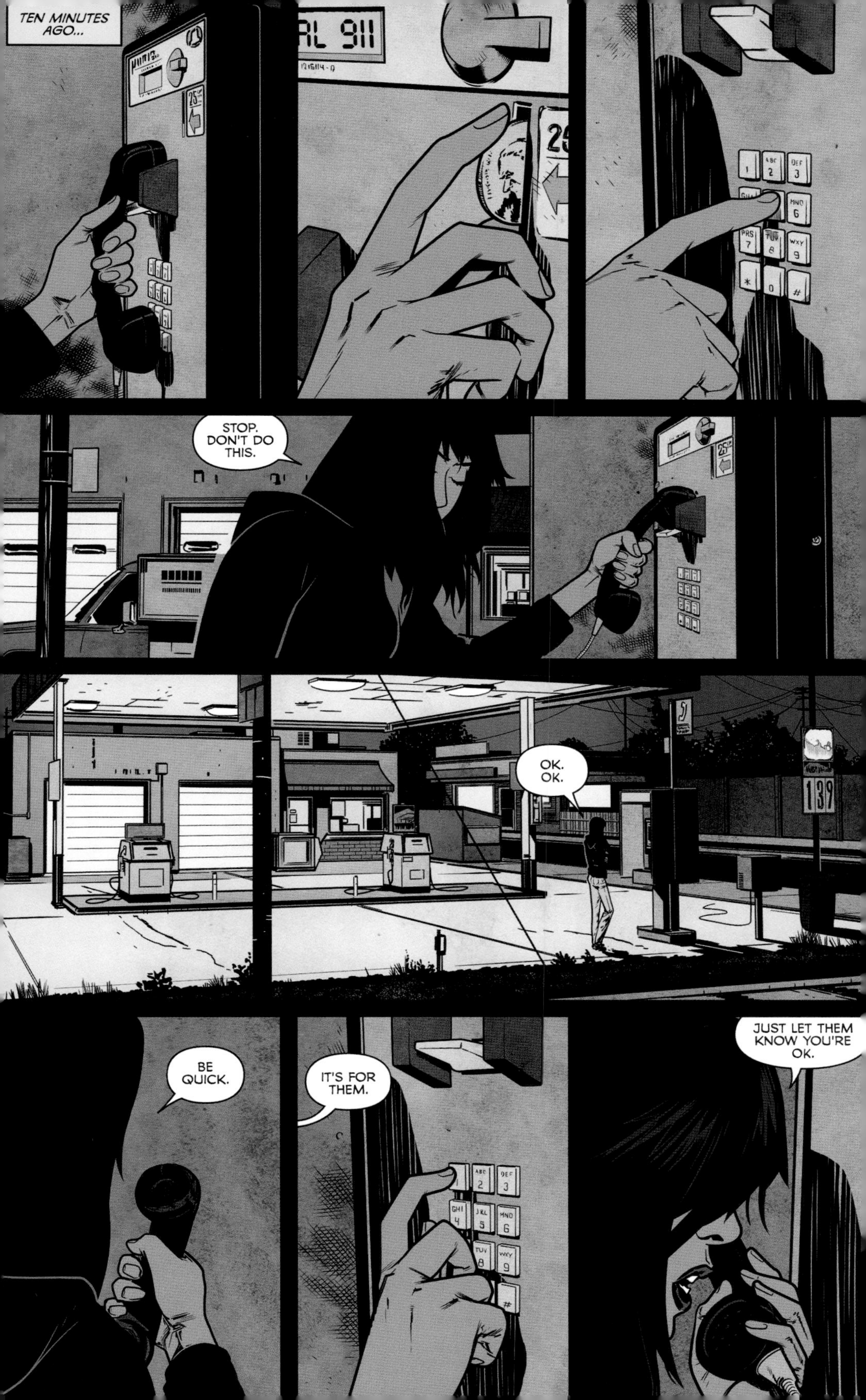
TEN MINUTES AGO...
STOP. DON'T DO THIS.
OK. OK.
BE QUICK.
IT'S FOR THEM.
JUST LET THEM KNOW YOU'RE OK.

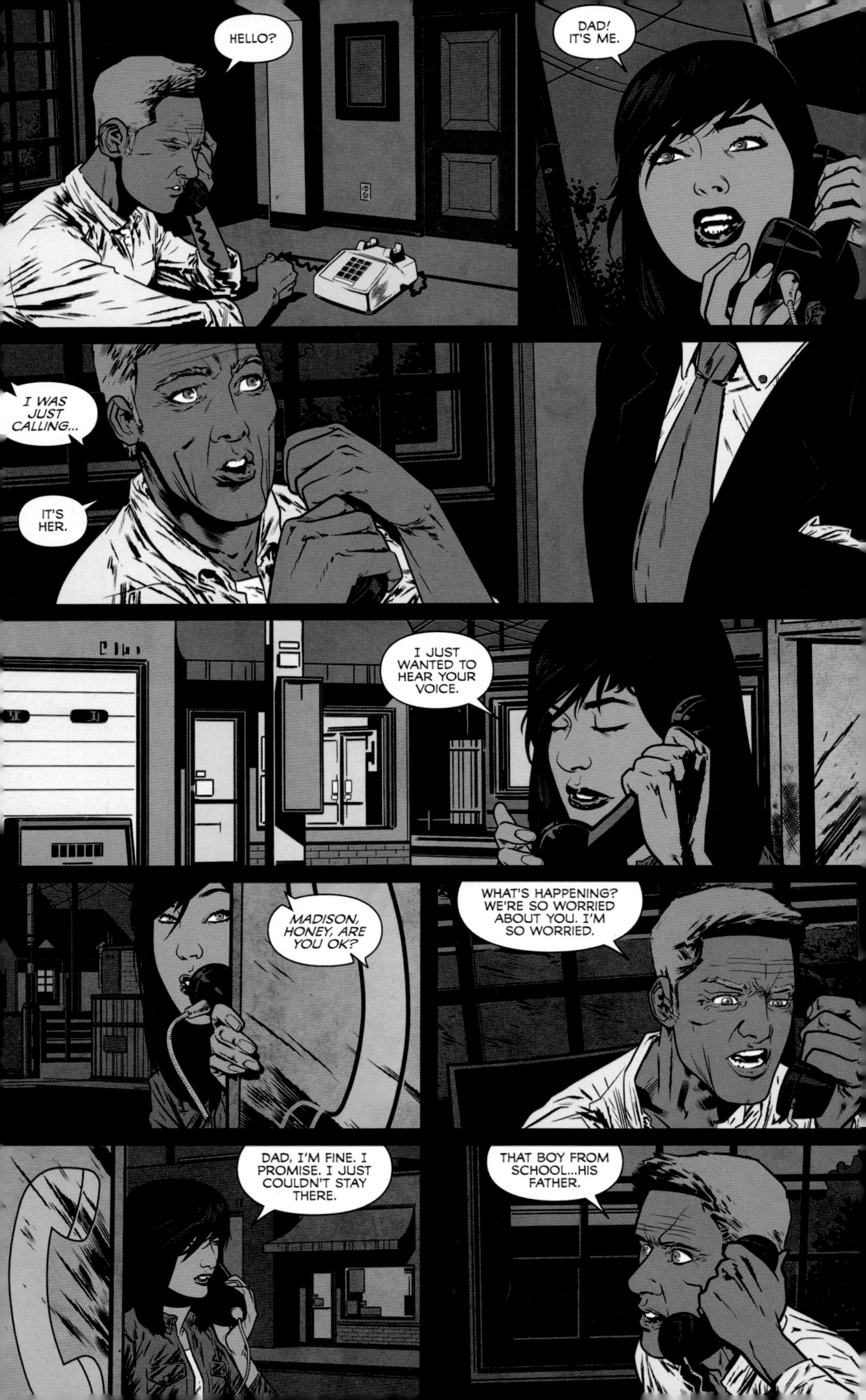
HELLO?
DAD! IT'S ME.
I WAS JUST CALLING...
IT'S HER.
I JUST WANTED TO HEAR YOUR VOICE.
MADISON, HONEY, ARE YOU OK?
WHAT'S HAPPENING? WE'RE SO WORRIED ABOUT YOU. I'M SO WORRIED.
DAD, I'M FINE. I PROMISE. I JUST COULDN'T STAY THERE.
THAT BOY FROM SCHOOL...HIS FATHER.

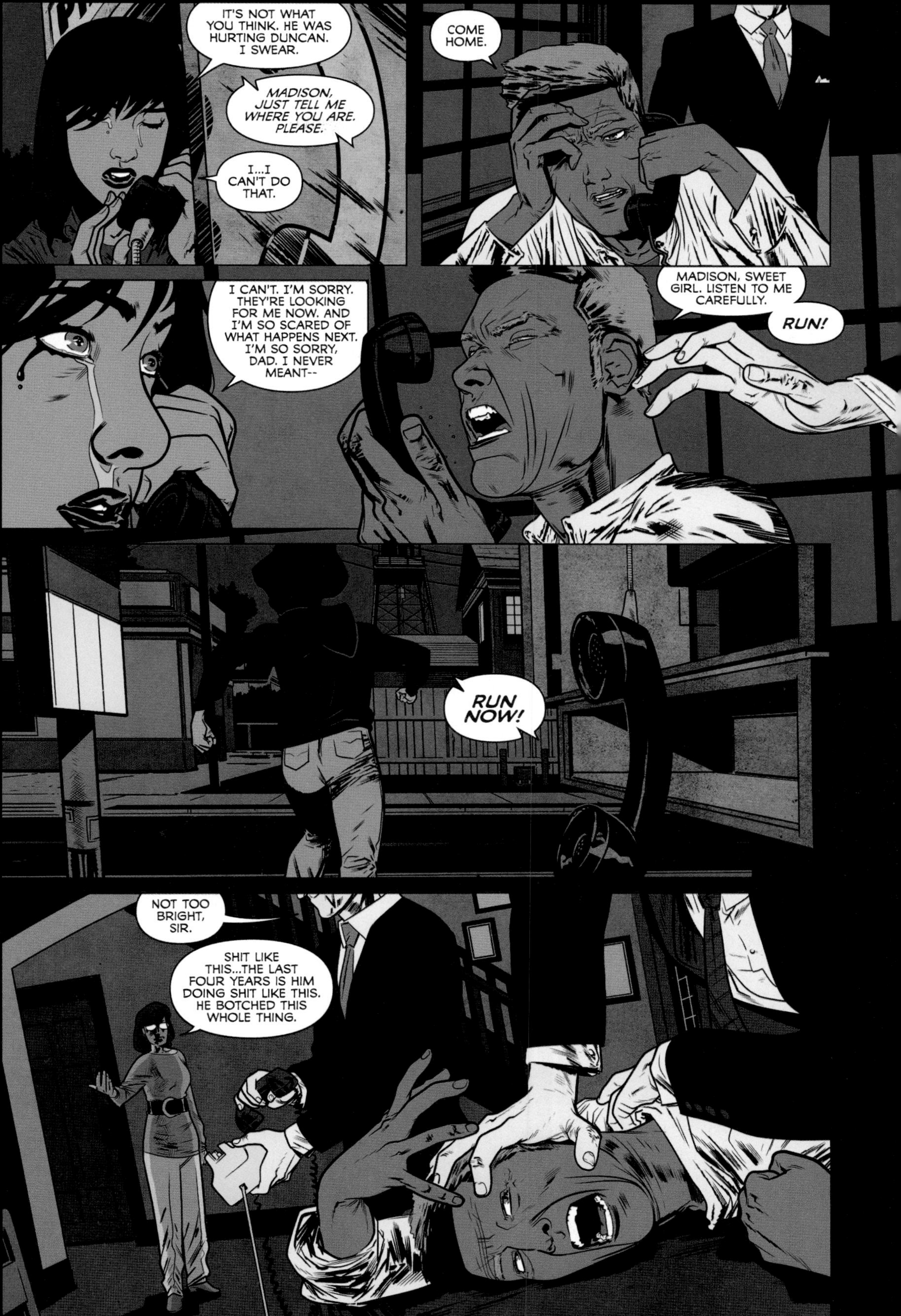
IT'S NOT WHAT YOU THINK. HE WAS HURTING DUNCAN. I SWEAR.
MADISON, JUST TELL ME WHERE YOU ARE. PLEASE.
I...I CAN'T DO THAT.
COME HOME.
I CAN'T. I'M SORRY. THEY'RE LOOKING FOR ME NOW. AND I'M SO SCARED OF WHAT HAPPENS NEXT. I'M SO SORRY, DAD. I NEVER MEANT--
MADISON, SWEET GIRL. LISTEN TO ME CAREFULLY.
RUN!
RUN NOW!
NOT TOO BRIGHT, SIR.
SHIT LIKE THIS...THE LAST FOUR YEARS IS HIM DOING SHIT LIKE THIS. HE BOTCHED THIS WHOLE THING.

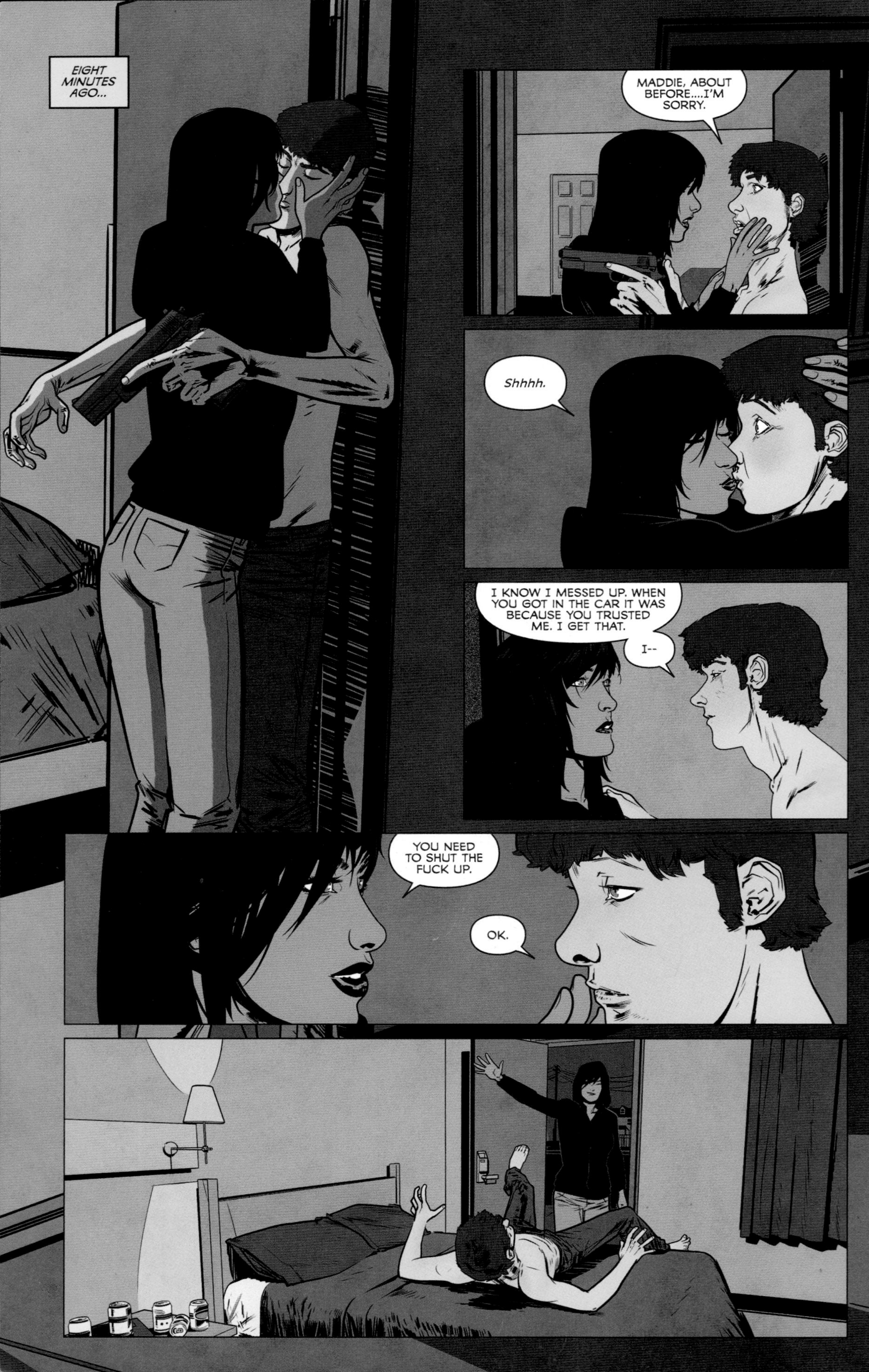
EIGHT MINUTES AGO...
MADDIE, ABOUT BEFORE....I'M SORRY.
Shhhh.
I KNOW I MESSED UP. WHEN YOU GOT IN THE CAR IT WAS BECAUSE YOU TRUSTED ME. I GET THAT.
I--
YOU NEED TO SHUT THE FUCK UP.
OK.

YOU ARE SO BEAUTIFUL.

I KNOW.

Oh GOD.

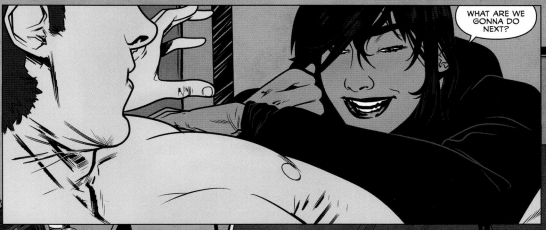

WHAT ARE WE GONNA DO NEXT?

I WAS REALLY HOPING YOU WOULD KEEP DOING WHAT YOU WERE DOING.

YOU EIGHTEEN YEAR OLD BOYS ARE ALL THE SAME.

I'M SEVENTEEN.

WOW. I MEANT WHERE DO WE GO FROM HERE?

WHERE EVER.

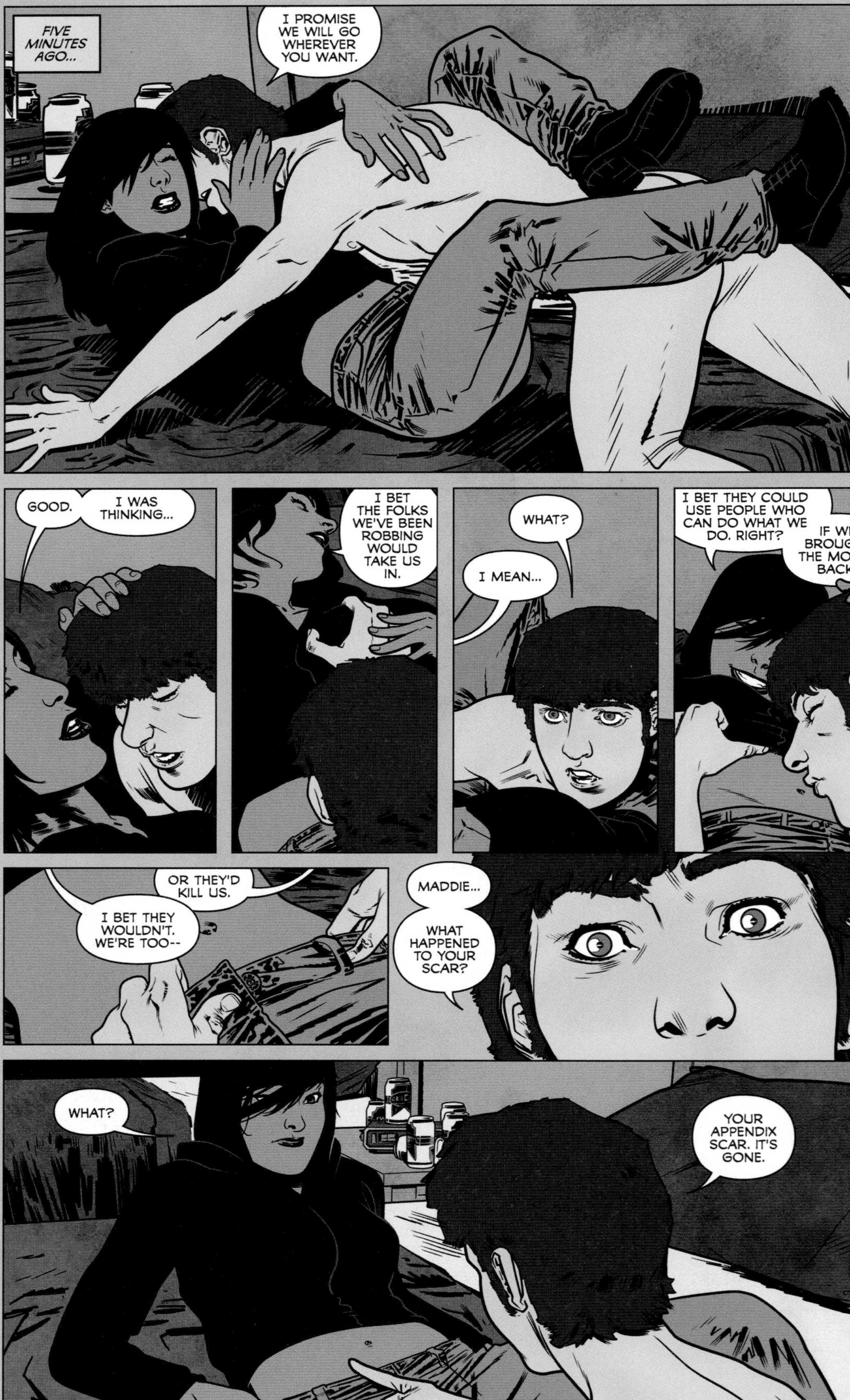
FIVE MINUTES AGO...
I PROMISE WE WILL GO WHEREVER YOU WANT.
GOOD.
I WAS THINKING...
I BET THE FOLKS WE'VE BEEN ROBBING WOULD TAKE US IN.
WHAT?
I MEAN...
I BET THEY COULD USE PEOPLE WHO CAN DO WHAT WE DO. RIGHT?
IF WE BROUGHT THE MONEY BACK.
OR THEY'D KILL US.
I BET THEY WOULDN'T. WE'RE TOO--
MADDIE...
WHAT HAPPENED TO YOUR SCAR?
WHAT?
YOUR APPENDIX SCAR. IT'S GONE.

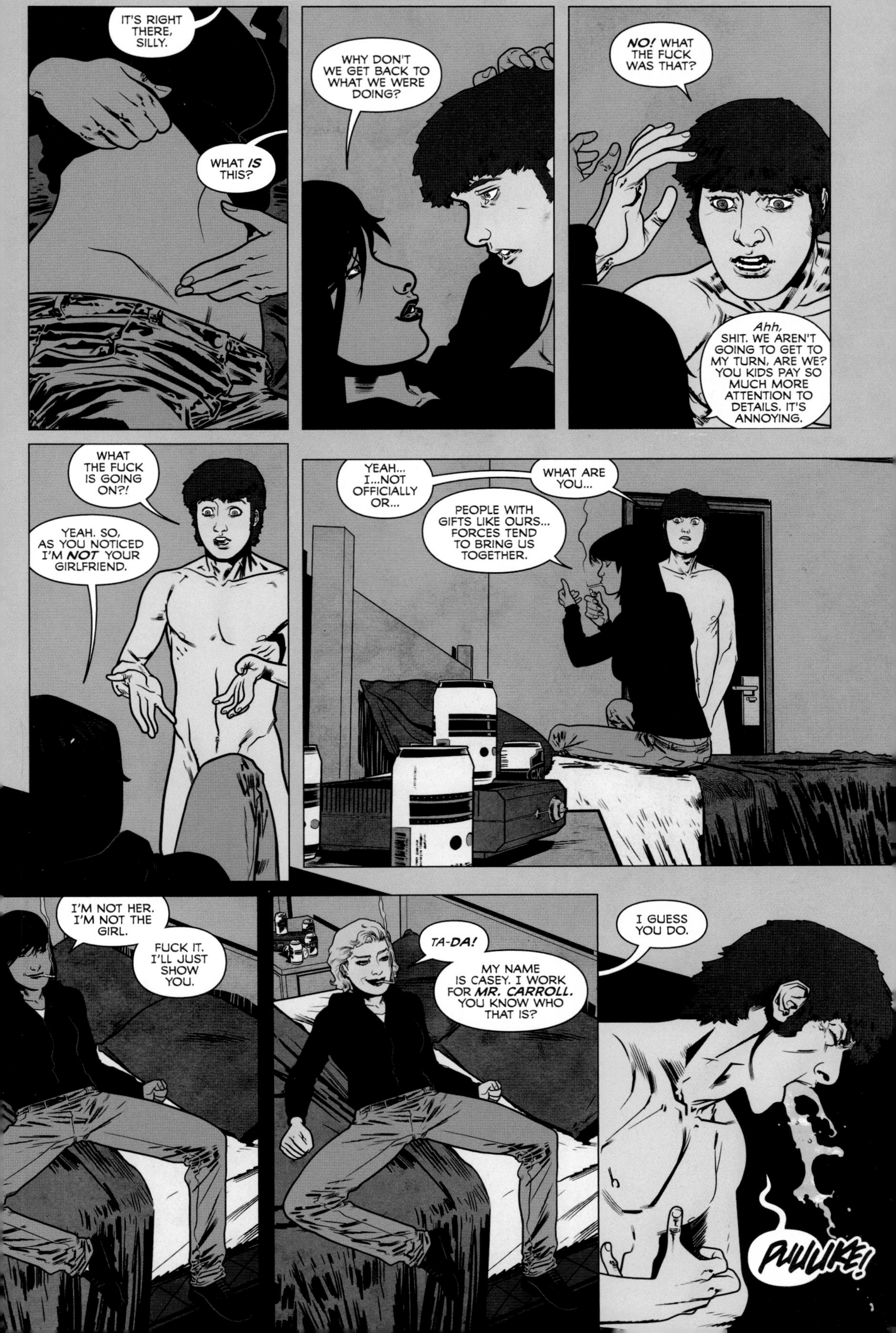
IT'S RIGHT THERE, SILLY.
WHAT *IS* THIS?
WHY DON'T WE GET BACK TO WHAT WE WERE DOING?
NO! WHAT THE FUCK WAS THAT?
Ahh, SHIT. WE AREN'T GOING TO GET TO MY TURN, ARE WE? YOU KIDS PAY SO MUCH MORE ATTENTION TO DETAILS. IT'S ANNOYING.
WHAT THE FUCK IS GOING ON?!
YEAH. SO, AS YOU NOTICED I'M ***NOT*** YOUR GIRLFRIEND.
WHAT ARE YOU...
YEAH... I...NOT OFFICIALLY OR...
PEOPLE WITH GIFTS LIKE OURS... FORCES TEND TO BRING US TOGETHER.
I'M NOT HER. I'M NOT THE GIRL.
FUCK IT. I'LL JUST SHOW YOU.
*TA-**DA!***
MY NAME IS CASEY. I WORK FOR ***MR. CARROLL.*** YOU KNOW WHO THAT IS?
I GUESS YOU DO.
PUUUKE!

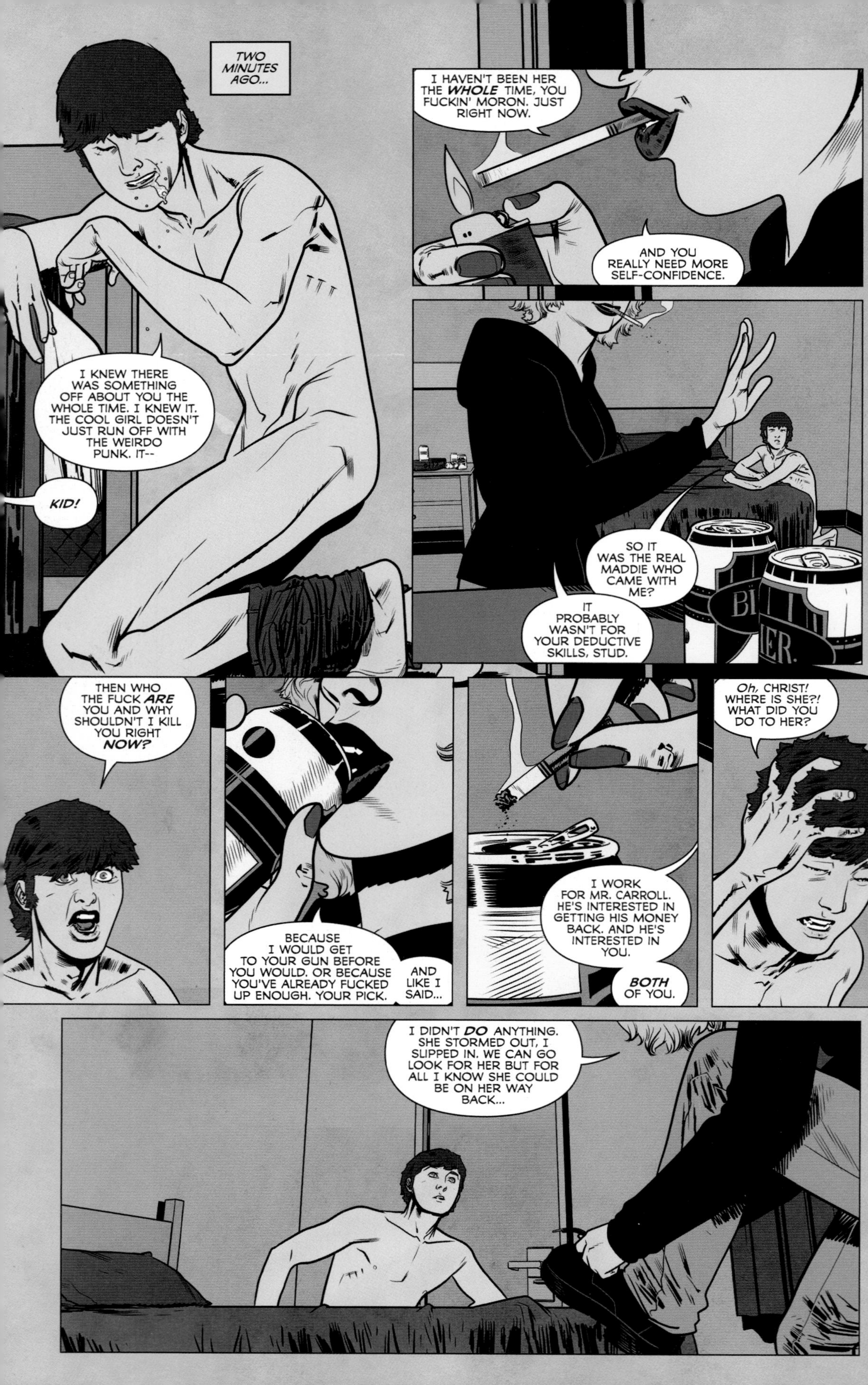
TWO MINUTES AGO...
I KNEW THERE WAS SOMETHING OFF ABOUT YOU THE WHOLE TIME. I KNEW IT. THE COOL GIRL DOESN'T JUST RUN OFF WITH THE WEIRDO PUNK. IT--
KID!
I HAVEN'T BEEN HER THE WHOLE TIME, YOU FUCKIN' MORON. JUST RIGHT NOW.
AND YOU REALLY NEED MORE SELF-CONFIDENCE.
SO IT WAS THE REAL MADDIE WHO CAME WITH ME?
IT PROBABLY WASN'T FOR YOUR DEDUCTIVE SKILLS, STUD.
THEN WHO THE FUCK ARE YOU AND WHY SHOULDN'T I KILL YOU RIGHT NOW?
BECAUSE I WOULD GET TO YOUR GUN BEFORE YOU WOULD. OR BECAUSE YOU'VE ALREADY FUCKED UP ENOUGH. YOUR PICK.
AND LIKE I SAID...
I WORK FOR MR. CARROLL. HE'S INTERESTED IN GETTING HIS MONEY BACK. AND HE'S INTERESTED IN YOU.
BOTH OF YOU.
Oh, CHRIST! WHERE IS SHE?! WHAT DID YOU DO TO HER?
I DIDN'T DO ANYTHING. SHE STORMED OUT, I SLIPPED IN. WE CAN GO LOOK FOR HER BUT FOR ALL I KNOW SHE COULD BE ON HER WAY BACK...

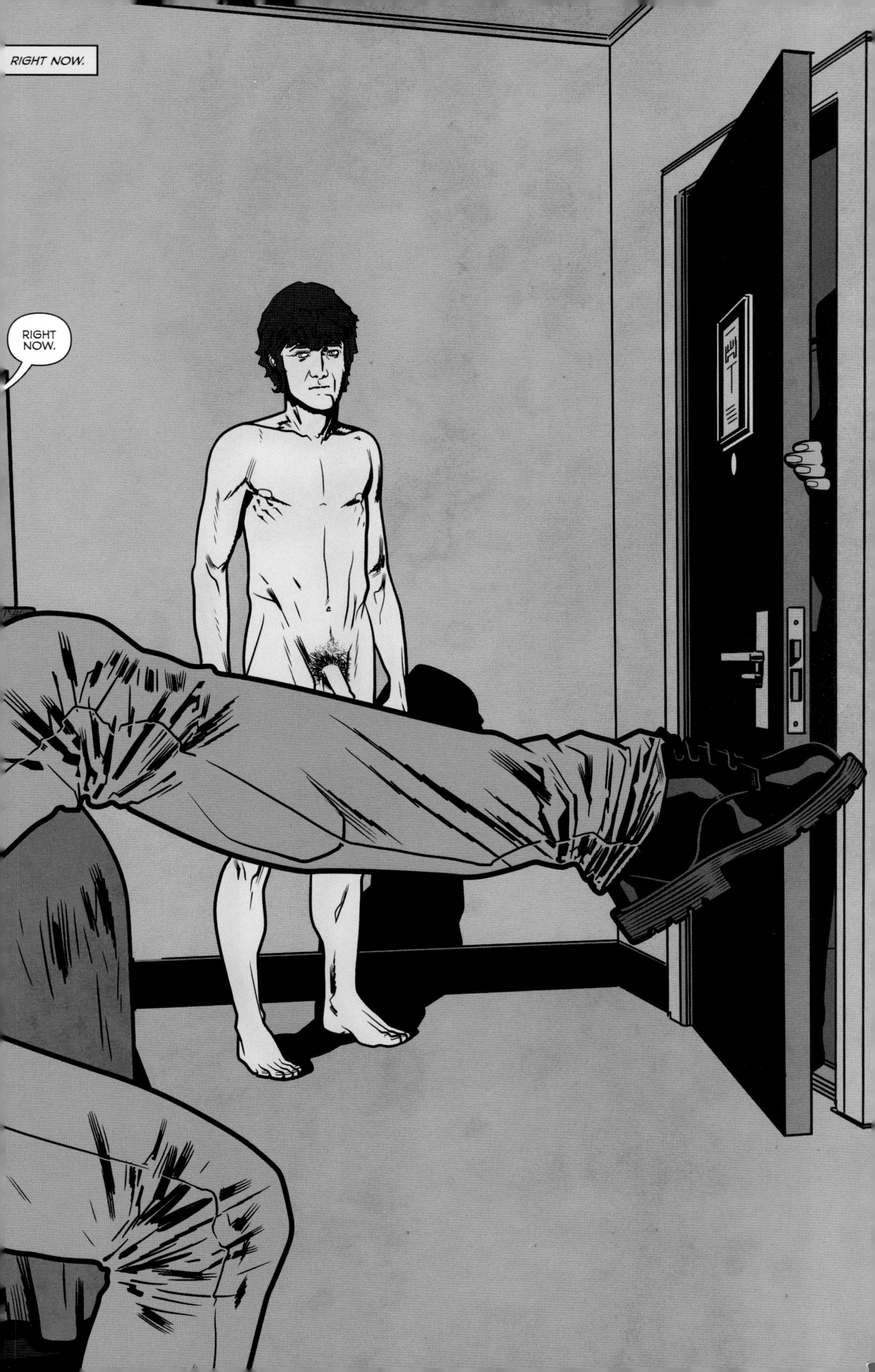
RIGHT NOW.
RIGHT NOW.

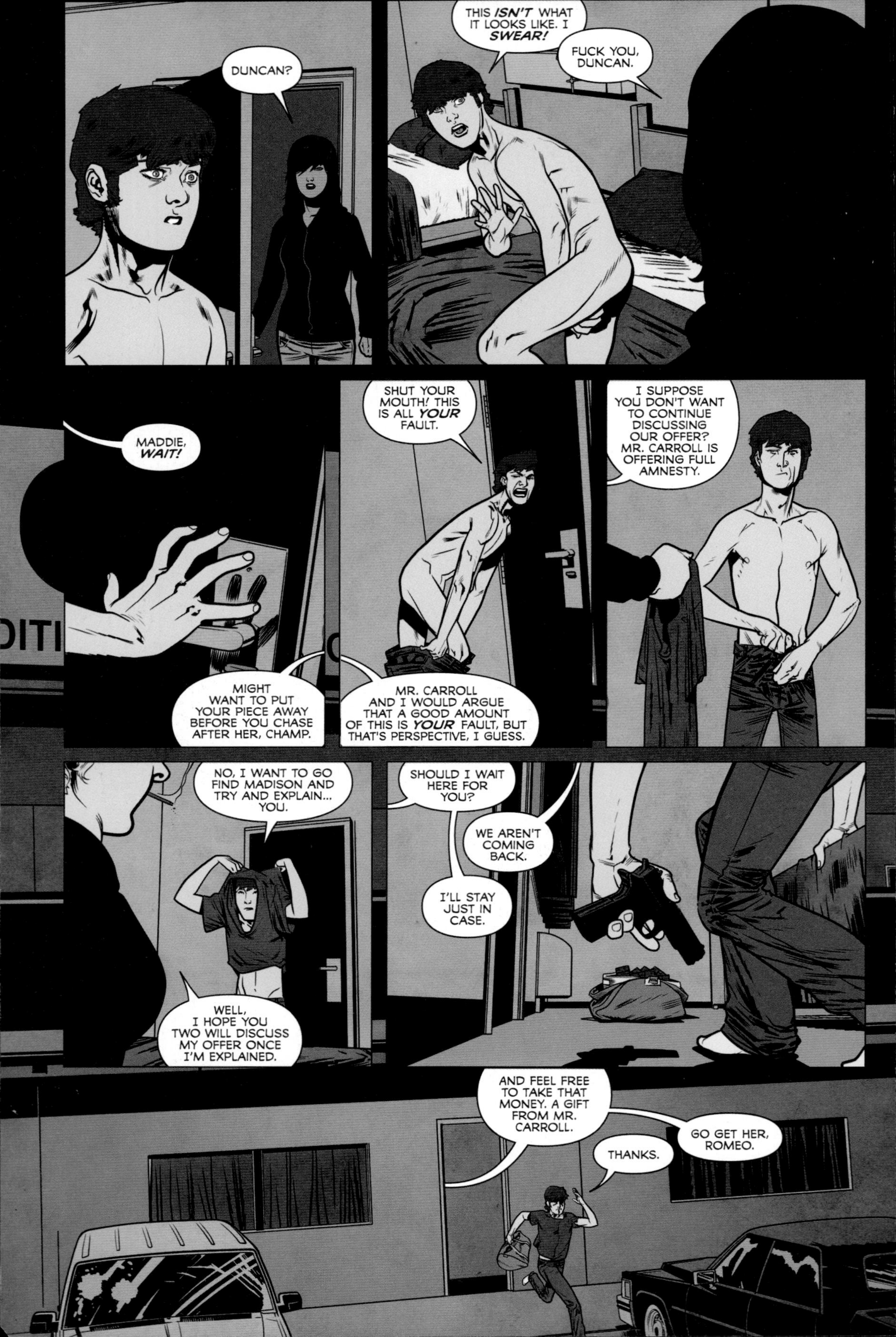
DUNCAN?
THIS *ISN'T* WHAT IT LOOKS LIKE. I *SWEAR!*
FUCK YOU, DUNCAN.
MADDIE, *WAIT!*
DITI
MIGHT WANT TO PUT YOUR PIECE AWAY BEFORE YOU CHASE AFTER HER, CHAMP.
SHUT YOUR MOUTH! THIS IS ALL *YOUR* FAULT.
MR. CARROLL AND I WOULD ARGUE THAT A GOOD AMOUNT OF THIS IS *YOUR* FAULT, BUT THAT'S PERSPECTIVE, I GUESS.
I SUPPOSE YOU DON'T WANT TO CONTINUE DISCUSSING OUR OFFER? MR. CARROLL IS OFFERING FULL AMNESTY.
NO, I WANT TO GO FIND MADISON AND TRY AND EXPLAIN... YOU.
WELL, I HOPE YOU TWO WILL DISCUSS MY OFFER ONCE I'M EXPLAINED.
SHOULD I WAIT HERE FOR YOU?
WE AREN'T COMING BACK.
I'LL STAY JUST IN CASE.
AND FEEL FREE TO TAKE THAT MONEY. A GIFT FROM MR. CARROLL.
GO GET HER, ROMEO.
THANKS.

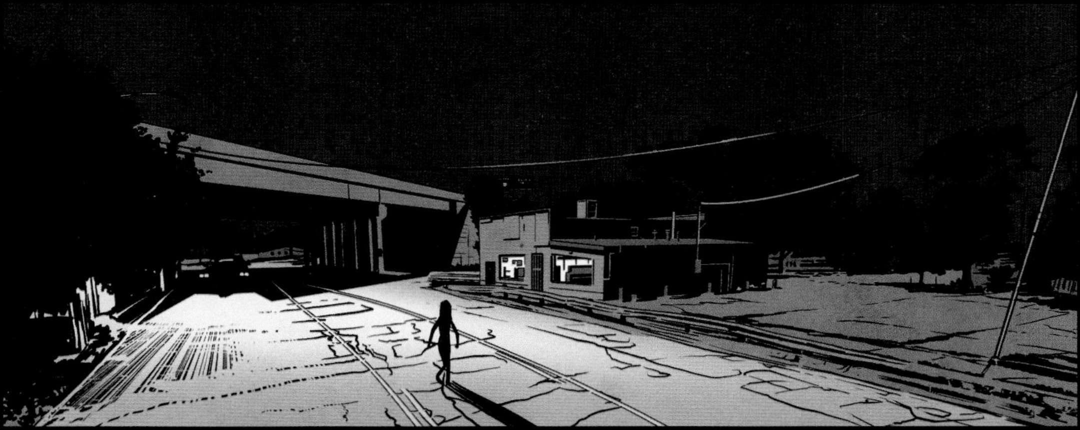
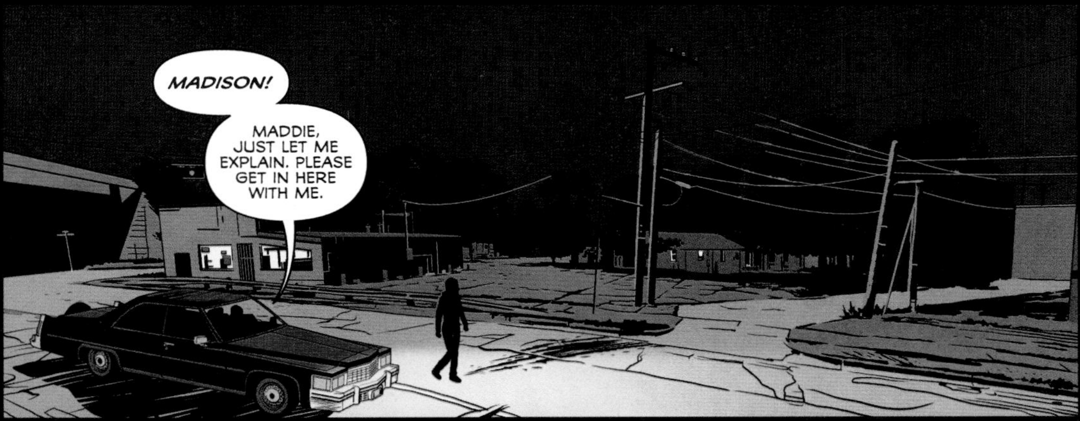
MADISON!
MADDIE, JUST LET ME EXPLAIN. PLEASE GET IN HERE WITH ME.
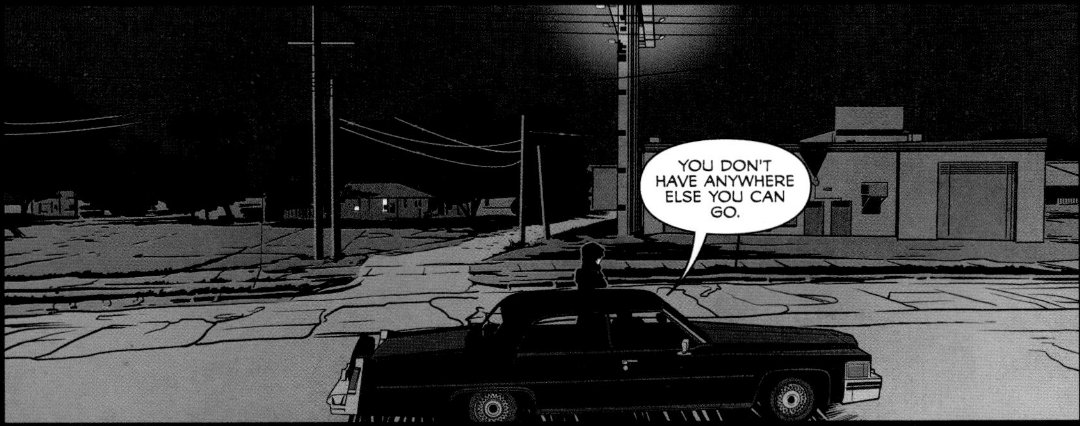
YOU DON'T HAVE ANYWHERE ELSE YOU CAN GO.
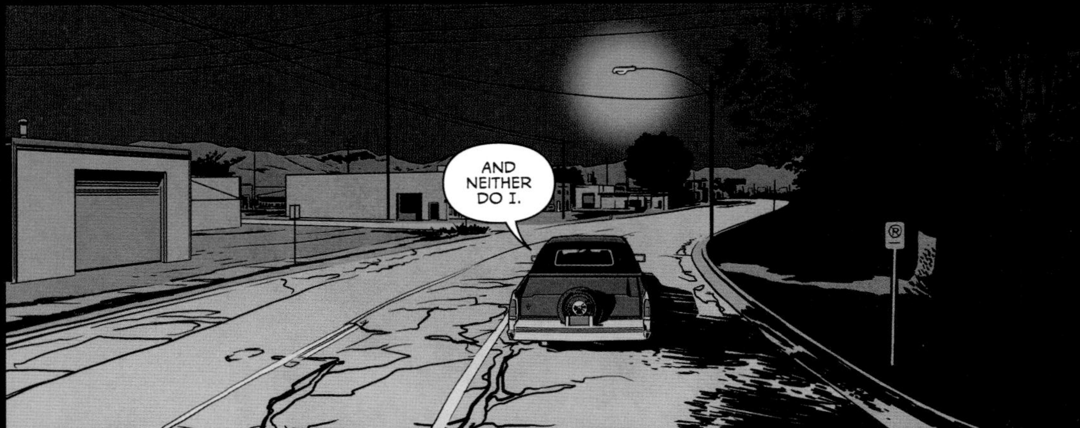
AND NEITHER DO I.

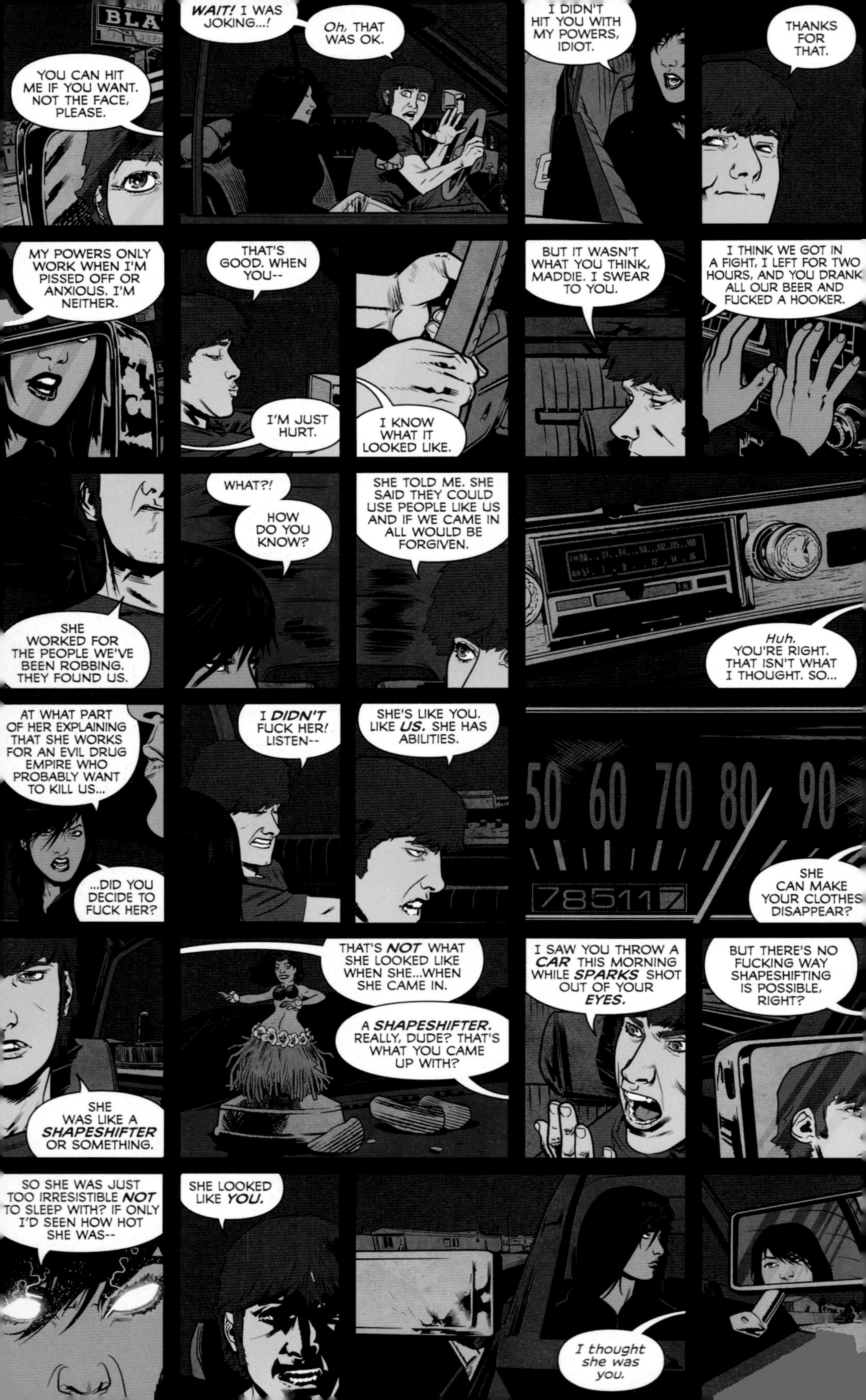

YOU CAN HIT ME IF YOU WANT. NOT THE FACE, PLEASE.
WAIT! I WAS JOKING...!
Oh, THAT WAS OK.
I DIDN'T HIT YOU WITH MY POWERS, IDIOT.
THANKS FOR THAT.
MY POWERS ONLY WORK WHEN I'M PISSED OFF OR ANXIOUS. I'M NEITHER.
THAT'S GOOD. WHEN YOU--
I'M JUST HURT.
I KNOW WHAT IT LOOKED LIKE.
BUT IT WASN'T WHAT YOU THINK, MADDIE. I SWEAR TO YOU.
I THINK WE GOT IN A FIGHT, I LEFT FOR TWO HOURS, AND YOU DRANK ALL OUR BEER AND FUCKED A HOOKER.
SHE WORKED FOR THE PEOPLE WE'VE BEEN ROBBING. THEY FOUND US.
WHAT?!
HOW DO YOU KNOW?
SHE TOLD ME. SHE SAID THEY COULD USE PEOPLE LIKE US AND IF WE CAME IN ALL WOULD BE FORGIVEN.
Huh. YOU'RE RIGHT. THAT ISN'T WHAT I THOUGHT. SO...
AT WHAT PART OF HER EXPLAINING THAT SHE WORKS FOR AN EVIL DRUG EMPIRE WHO PROBABLY WANT TO KILL US...
...DID YOU DECIDE TO FUCK HER?
I DIDN'T FUCK HER! LISTEN--
SHE'S LIKE YOU. LIKE US. SHE HAS ABILITIES.
SHE CAN MAKE YOUR CLOTHES DISAPPEAR?
SHE WAS LIKE A SHAPESHIFTER OR SOMETHING.
THAT'S NOT WHAT SHE LOOKED LIKE WHEN SHE...WHEN SHE CAME IN.
A SHAPESHIFTER. REALLY, DUDE? THAT'S WHAT YOU CAME UP WITH?
I SAW YOU THROW A CAR THIS MORNING WHILE SPARKS SHOT OUT OF YOUR EYES.
BUT THERE'S NO FUCKING WAY SHAPESHIFTING IS POSSIBLE, RIGHT?
SO SHE WAS JUST TOO IRRESISTIBLE NOT TO SLEEP WITH? IF ONLY I'D SEEN HOW HOT SHE WAS--
SHE LOOKED LIKE YOU.
I thought she was you.

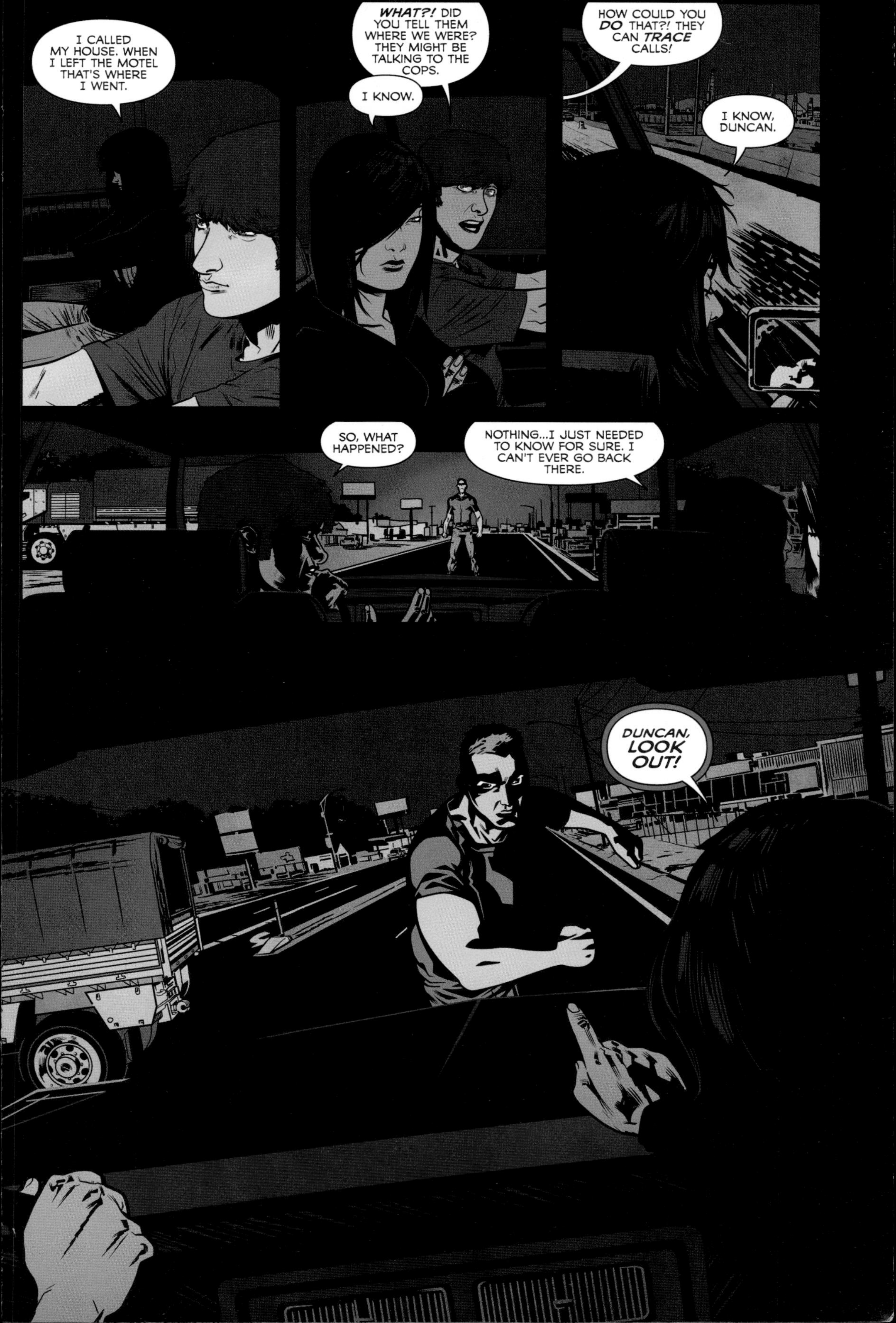
I CALLED MY HOUSE. WHEN I LEFT THE MOTEL THAT'S WHERE I WENT.
WHAT?! DID YOU TELL THEM WHERE WE WERE? THEY MIGHT BE TALKING TO THE COPS.
I KNOW.
HOW COULD YOU DO THAT?! THEY CAN TRACE CALLS!
I KNOW, DUNCAN.
SO, WHAT HAPPENED?
NOTHING...I JUST NEEDED TO KNOW FOR SURE. I CAN'T EVER GO BACK THERE.
DUNCAN, LOOK OUT!

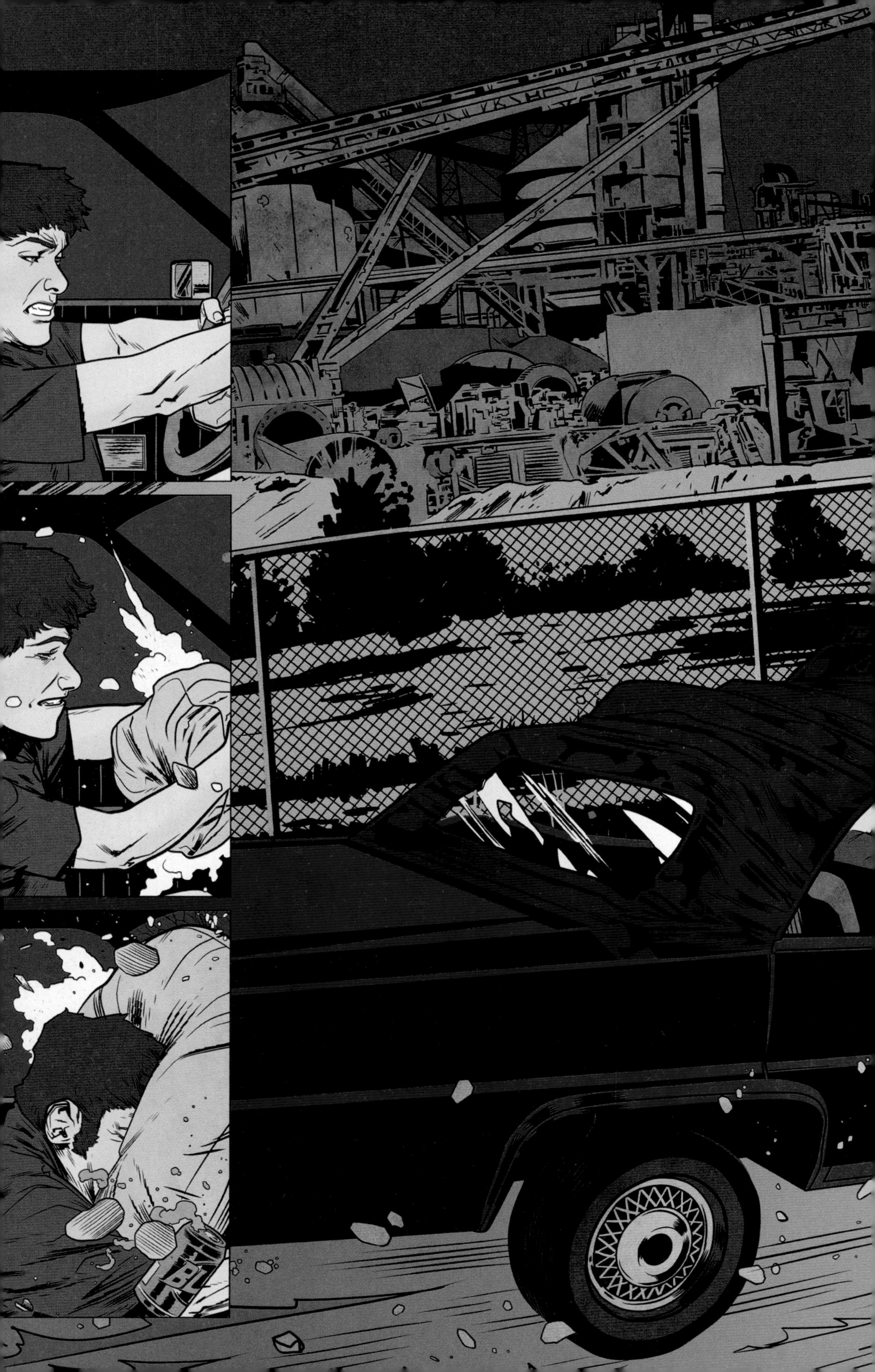

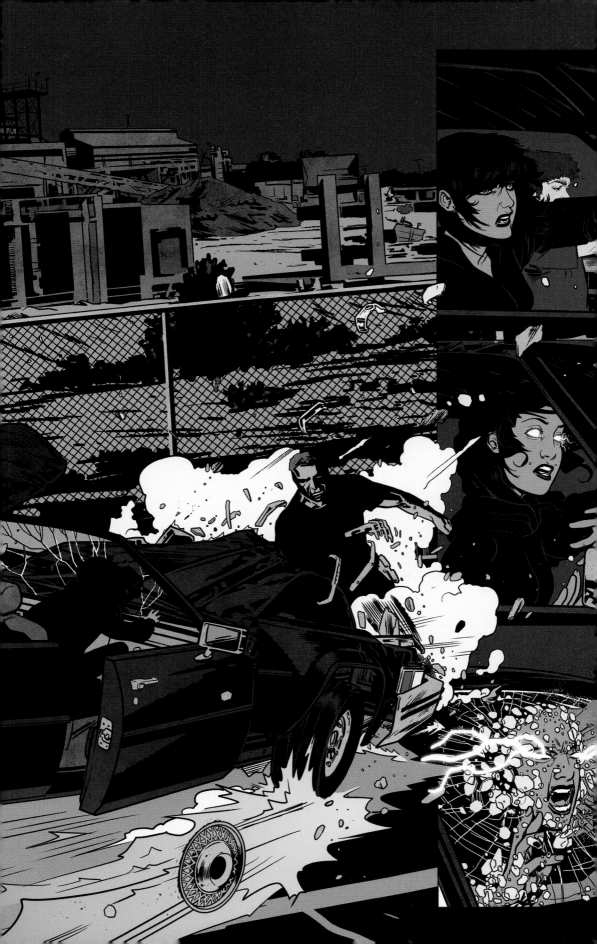

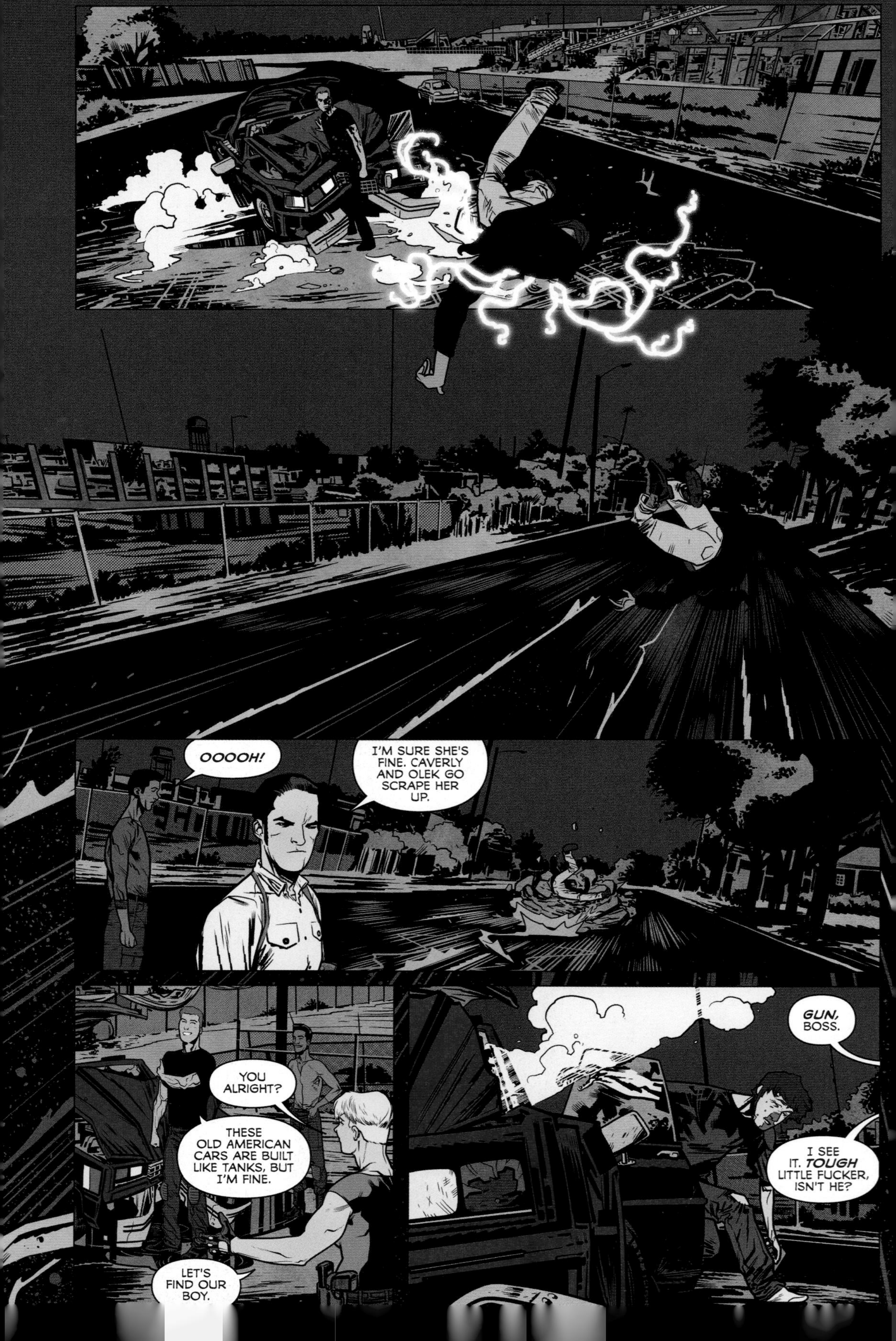
OOOOH!
I'M SURE SHE'S FINE. CAVERLY AND OLEK GO SCRAPE HER UP.
YOU ALRIGHT?
THESE OLD AMERICAN CARS ARE BUILT LIKE TANKS, BUT I'M FINE.
LET'S FIND OUR BOY.
GUN, BOSS.
I SEE IT. TOUGH LITTLE FUCKER, ISN'T HE?

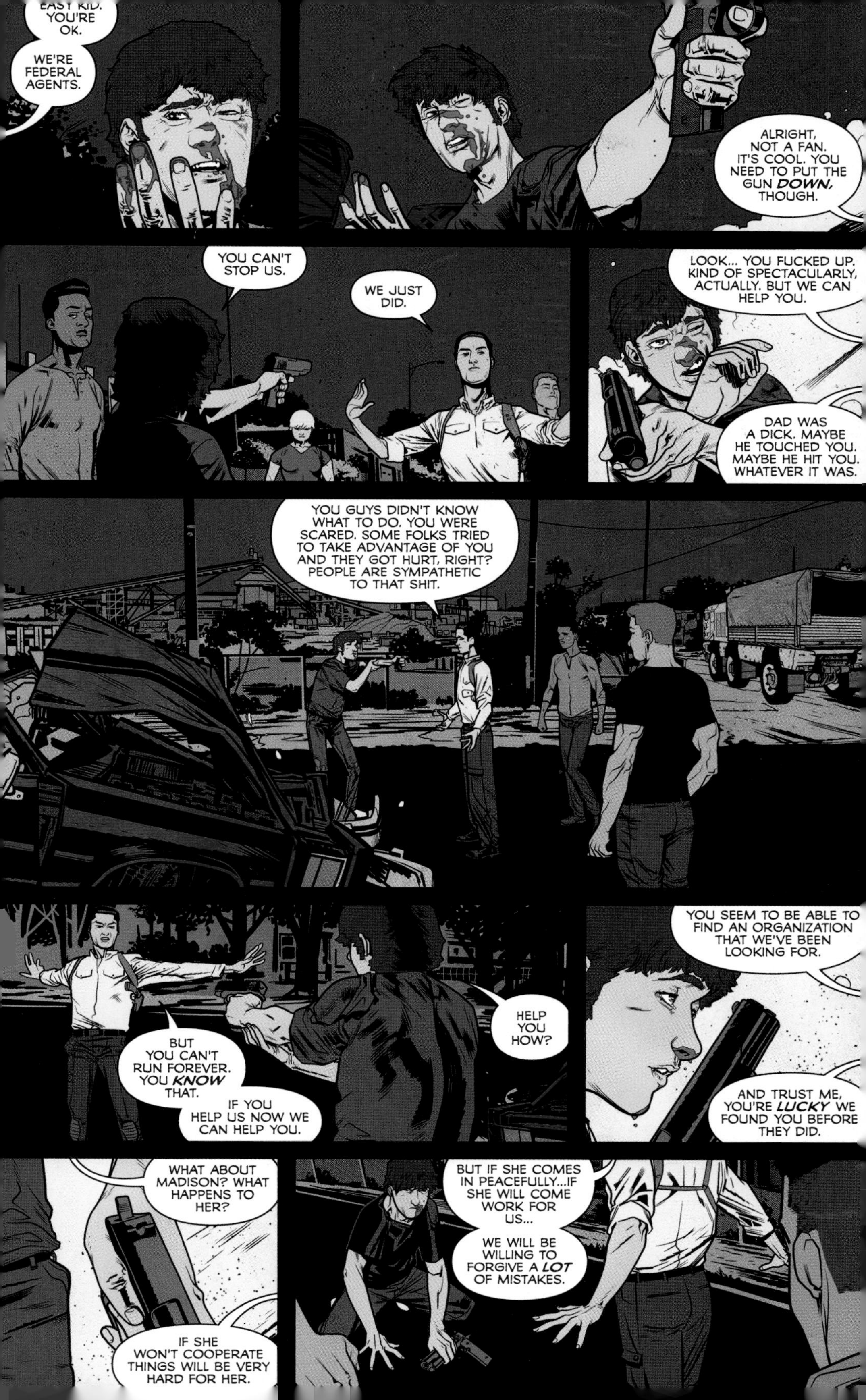
EASY KID. YOU'RE OK.
WE'RE FEDERAL AGENTS.
ALRIGHT, NOT A FAN. IT'S COOL. YOU NEED TO PUT THE GUN *DOWN,* THOUGH.
YOU CAN'T STOP US.
WE JUST DID.
LOOK... YOU FUCKED UP. KIND OF SPECTACULARLY, ACTUALLY. BUT WE CAN HELP YOU.
DAD WAS A DICK. MAYBE HE TOUCHED YOU. MAYBE HE HIT YOU. WHATEVER IT WAS.
YOU GUYS DIDN'T KNOW WHAT TO DO. YOU WERE SCARED. SOME FOLKS TRIED TO TAKE ADVANTAGE OF YOU AND THEY GOT HURT, RIGHT? PEOPLE ARE SYMPATHETIC TO THAT SHIT.
BUT YOU CAN'T RUN FOREVER. YOU *KNOW* THAT.
IF YOU HELP US NOW WE CAN HELP YOU.
HELP YOU HOW?
YOU SEEM TO BE ABLE TO FIND AN ORGANIZATION THAT WE'VE BEEN LOOKING FOR.
AND TRUST ME, YOU'RE *LUCKY* WE FOUND YOU BEFORE THEY DID.
WHAT ABOUT MADISON? WHAT HAPPENS TO HER?
IF SHE WON'T COOPERATE THINGS WILL BE VERY HARD FOR HER.
BUT IF SHE COMES IN PEACEFULLY...IF SHE WILL COME WORK FOR US...
WE WILL BE WILLING TO FORGIVE A *LOT* OF MISTAKES.

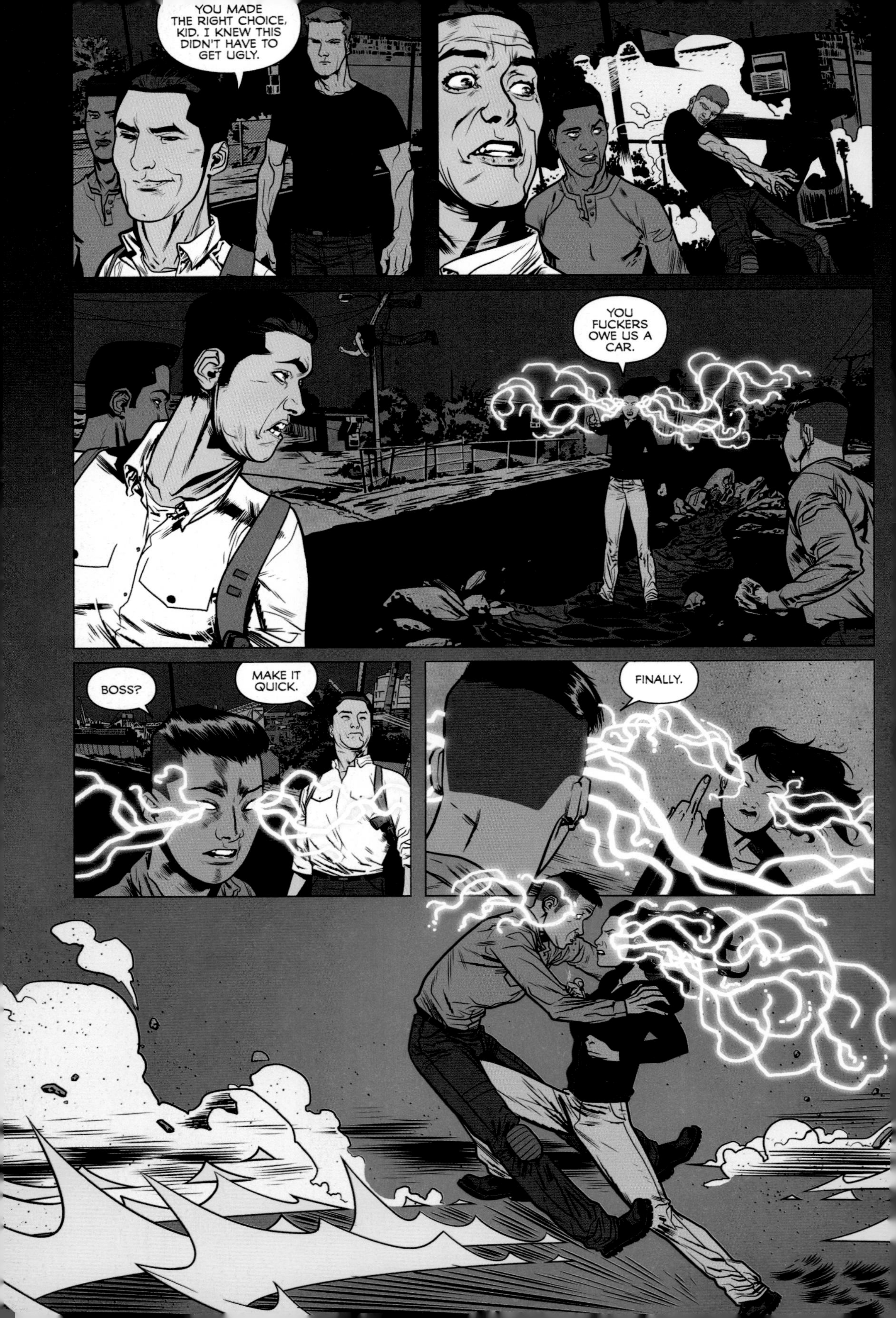
YOU MADE THE RIGHT CHOICE, KID. I KNEW THIS DIDN'T HAVE TO GET UGLY.
YOU FUCKERS OWE US A CAR.
BOSS?
MAKE IT QUICK.
FINALLY.

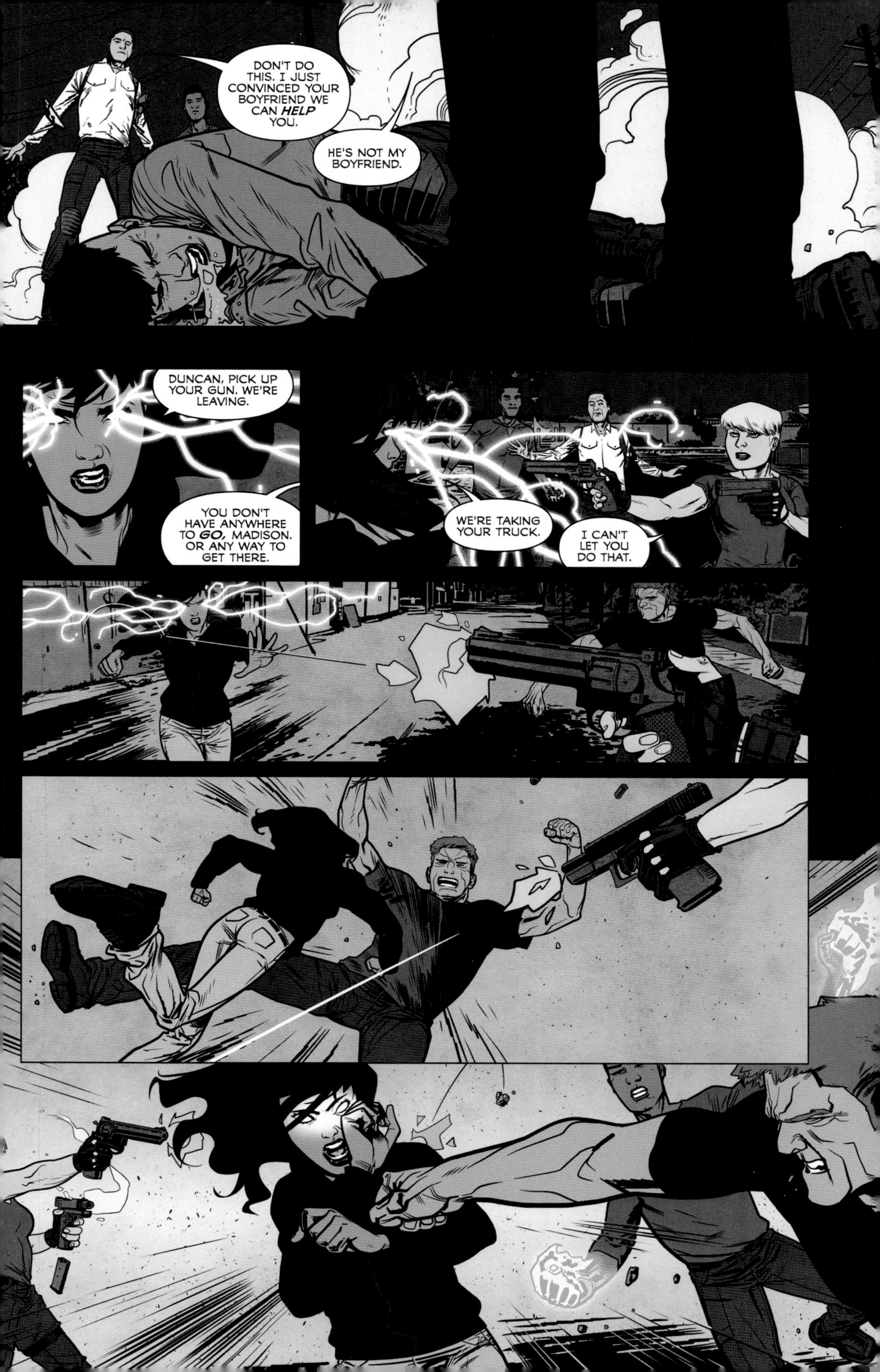
DON'T DO THIS. I JUST CONVINCED YOUR BOYFRIEND WE CAN *HELP* YOU.
HE'S NOT MY BOYFRIEND.
DUNCAN, PICK UP YOUR GUN. WE'RE LEAVING.
YOU DON'T HAVE ANYWHERE TO *GO,* MADISON. OR ANY WAY TO GET THERE.
WE'RE TAKING YOUR TRUCK.
I CAN'T LET YOU DO THAT.

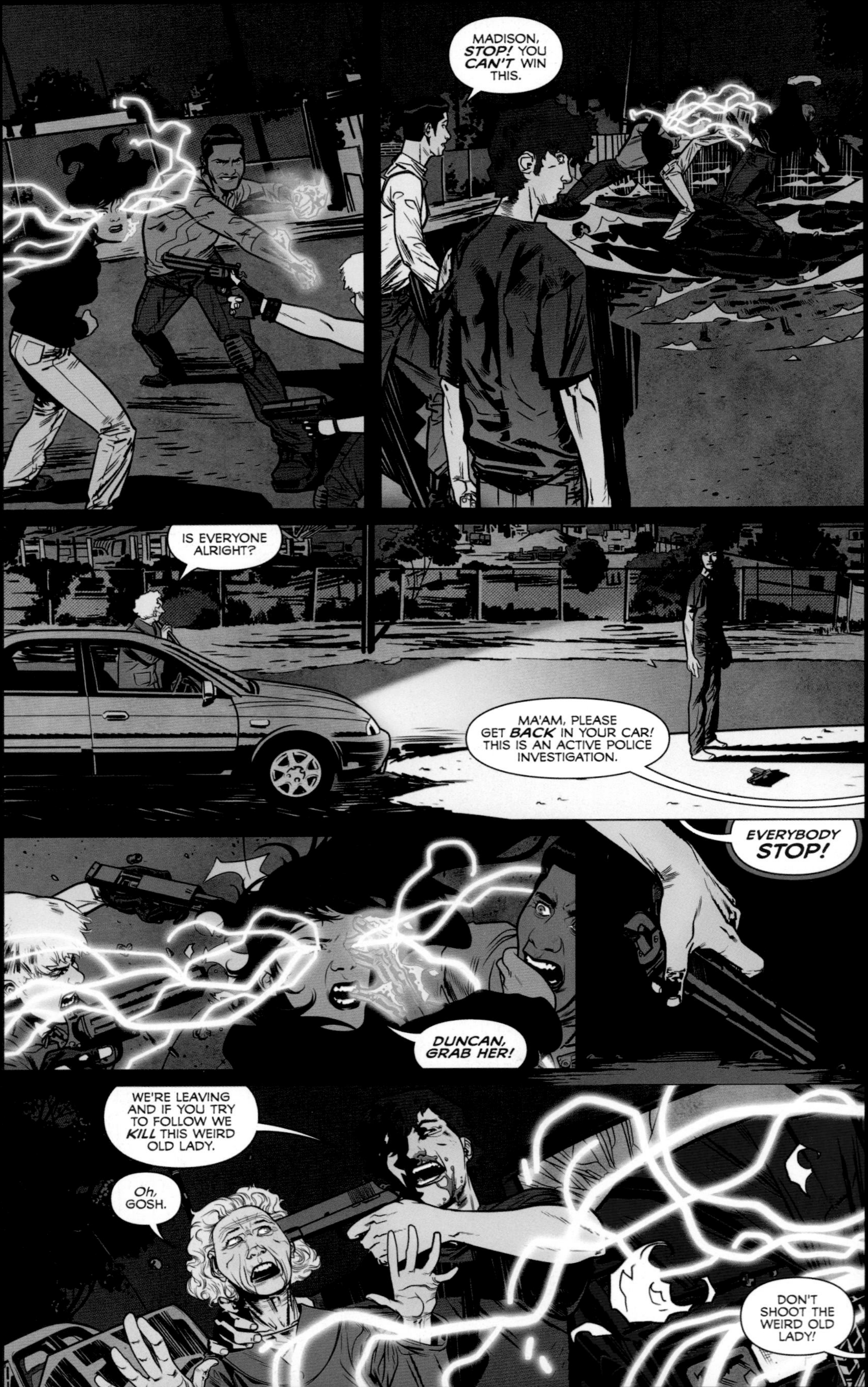
MADISON, STOP! YOU CAN'T WIN THIS.
IS EVERYONE ALRIGHT?
MA'AM, PLEASE GET BACK IN YOUR CAR! THIS IS AN ACTIVE POLICE INVESTIGATION.
DUNCAN, GRAB HER!
EVERYBODY STOP!
WE'RE LEAVING AND IF YOU TRY TO FOLLOW WE KILL THIS WEIRD OLD LADY.
Oh, GOSH.
DON'T SHOOT THE WEIRD OLD LADY!

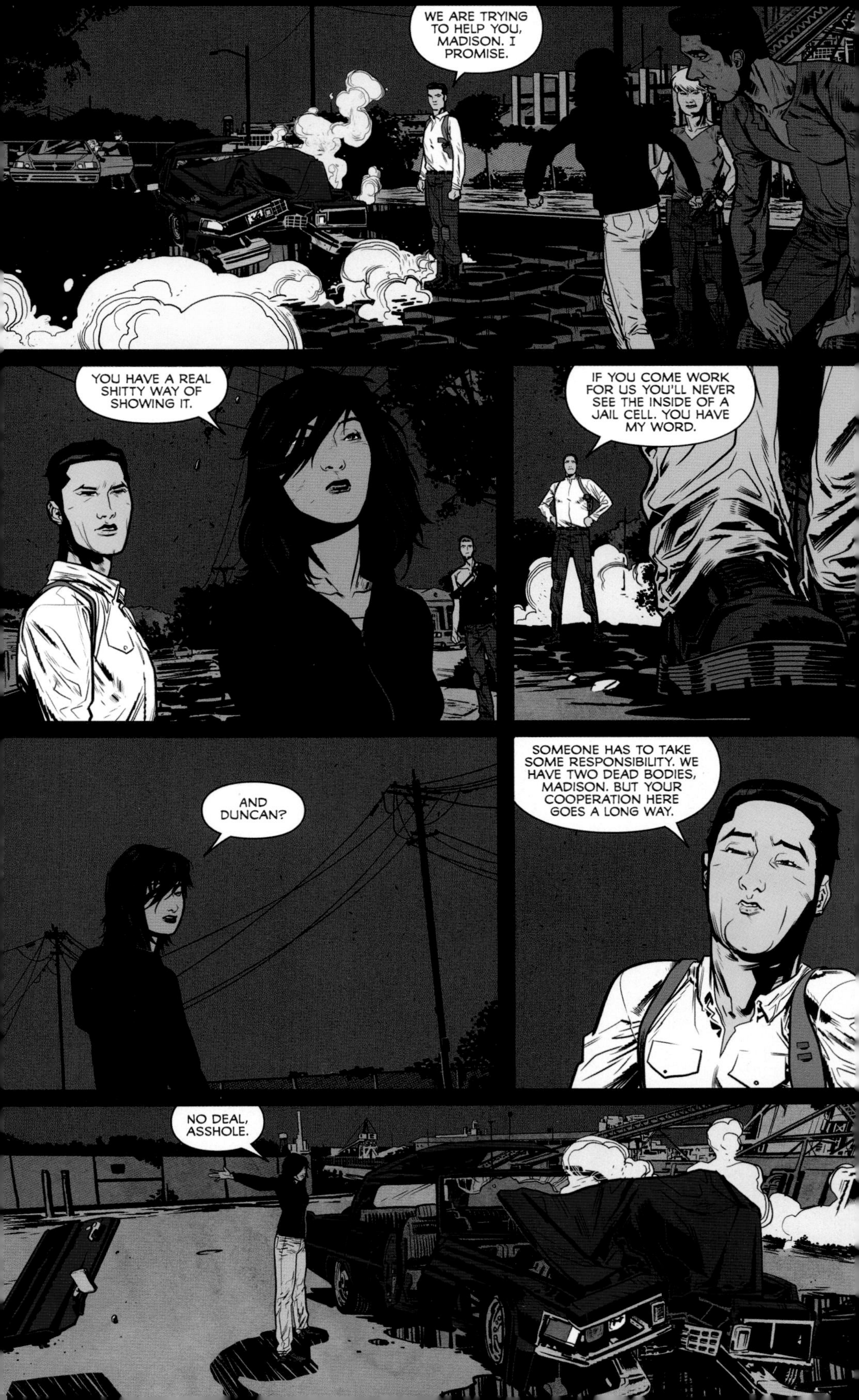
WE ARE TRYING TO HELP YOU, MADISON. I PROMISE.
YOU HAVE A REAL SHITTY WAY OF SHOWING IT.
IF YOU COME WORK FOR US YOU'LL NEVER SEE THE INSIDE OF A JAIL CELL. YOU HAVE MY WORD.
AND DUNCAN?
SOMEONE HAS TO TAKE SOME RESPONSIBILITY. WE HAVE TWO DEAD BODIES, MADISON. BUT YOUR COOPERATION HERE GOES A LONG WAY.
NO DEAL, ASSHOLE.

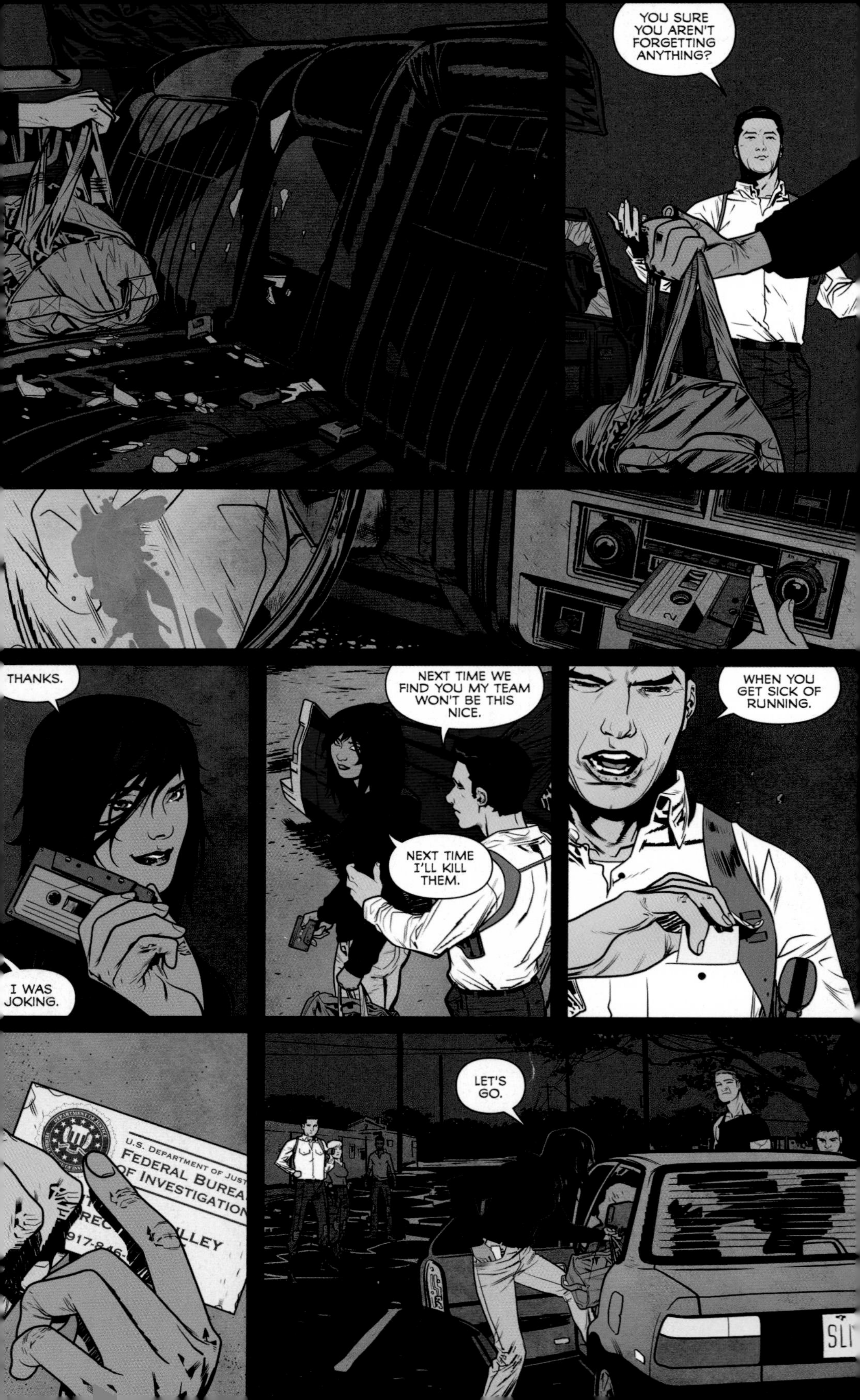

YOU SURE YOU AREN'T FORGETTING ANYTHING?
THANKS.
I WAS JOKING.
NEXT TIME WE FIND YOU MY TEAM WON'T BE THIS NICE.
NEXT TIME I'LL KILL THEM.
WHEN YOU GET SICK OF RUNNING.
U.S. DEPARTMENT OF JUST
FEDERAL BUREA
OF INVESTIGATION
917-846-
LET'S GO.

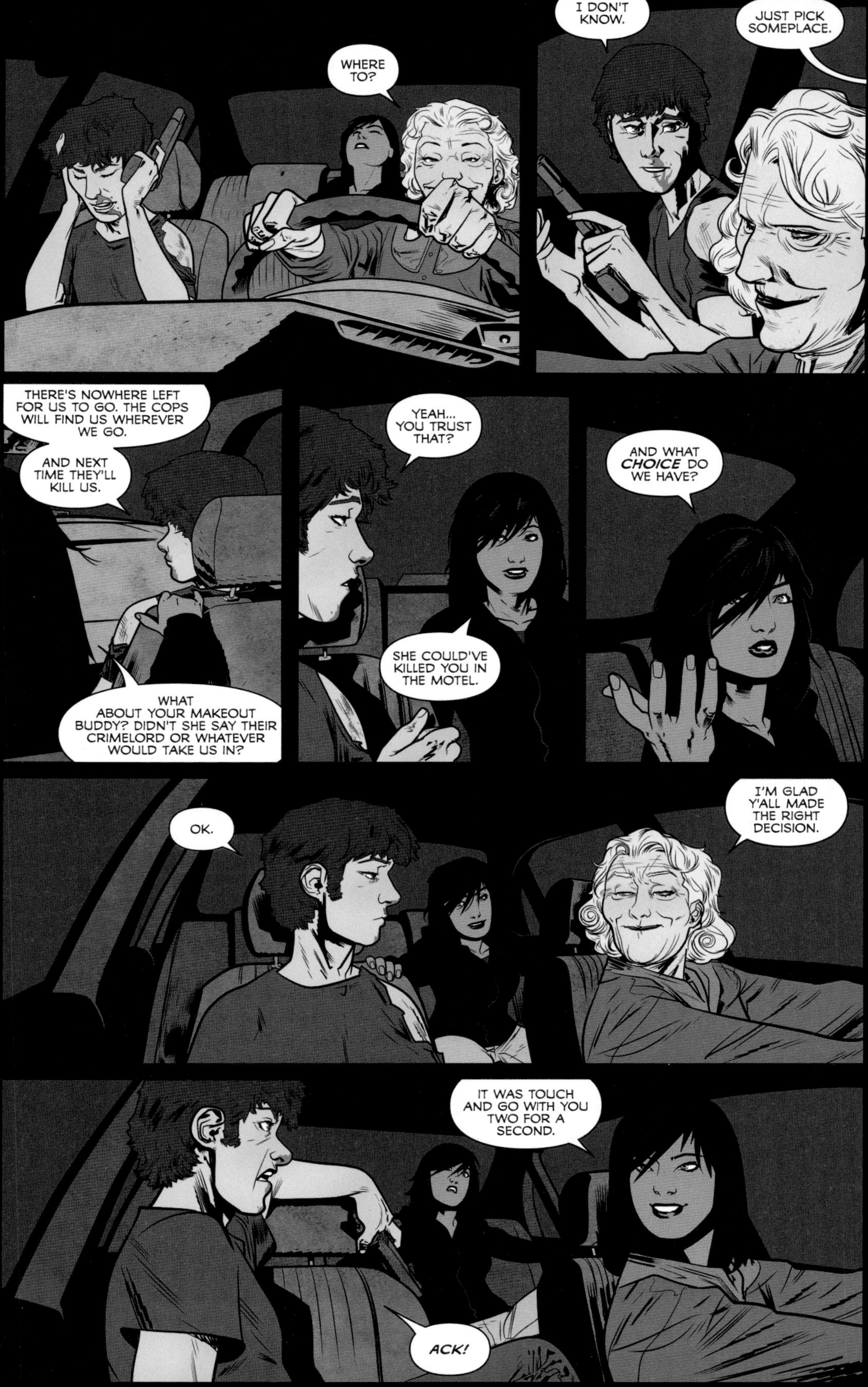
WHERE TO?
I DON'T KNOW.
JUST PICK SOMEPLACE.
THERE'S NOWHERE LEFT FOR US TO GO. THE COPS WILL FIND US WHEREVER WE GO.
AND NEXT TIME THEY'LL KILL US.
WHAT ABOUT YOUR MAKEOUT BUDDY? DIDN'T SHE SAY THEIR CRIMELORD OR WHATEVER WOULD TAKE US IN?
YEAH... YOU TRUST THAT?
SHE COULD'VE KILLED YOU IN THE MOTEL.
AND WHAT *CHOICE* DO WE HAVE?
OK.
I'M GLAD Y'ALL MADE THE RIGHT DECISION.
IT WAS TOUCH AND GO WITH YOU TWO FOR A SECOND.
ACK!

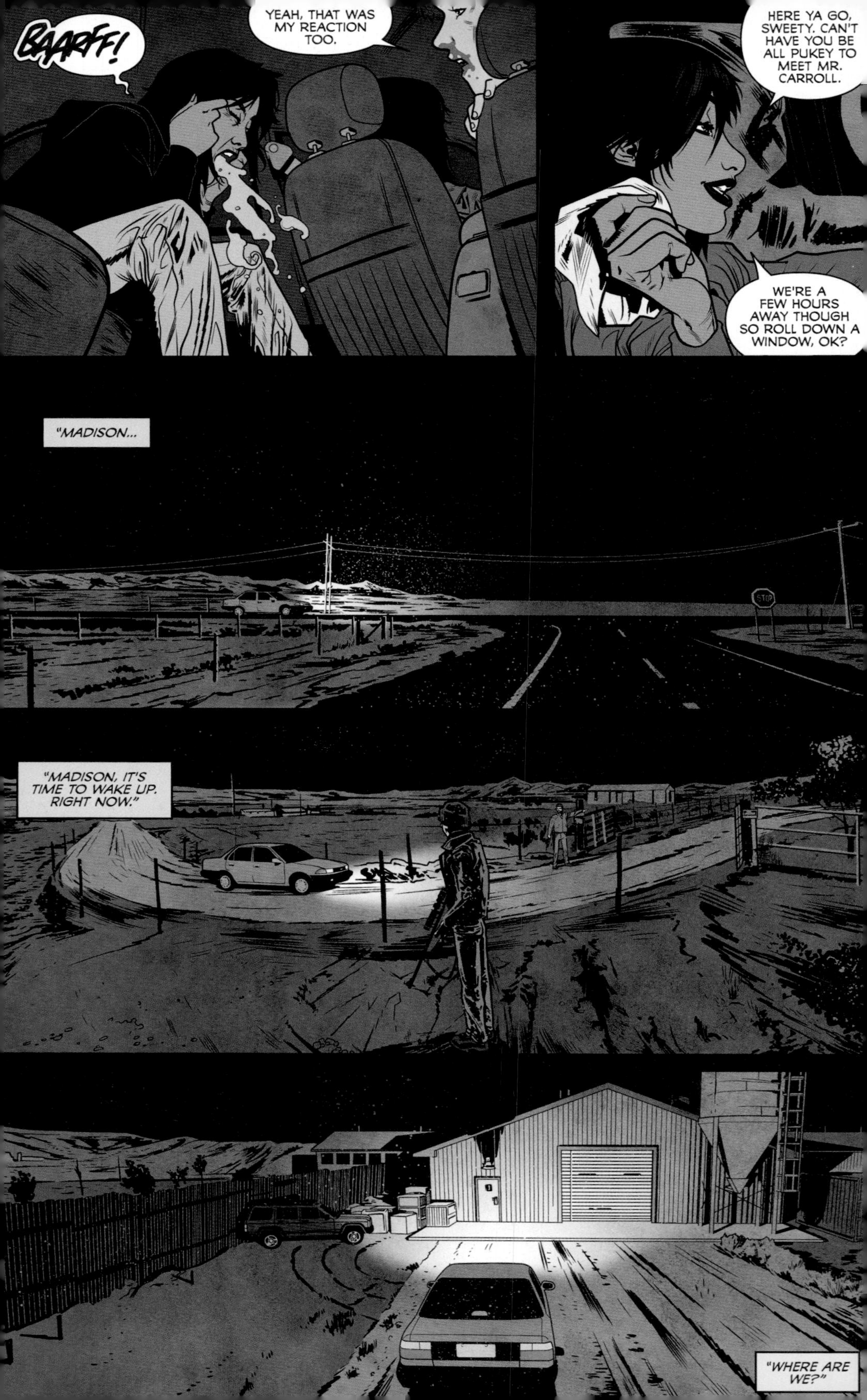
BAARFF!
YEAH, THAT WAS MY REACTION TOO.
HERE YA GO, SWEETY. CAN'T HAVE YOU BE ALL PUKEY TO MEET MR. CARROLL.
WE'RE A FEW HOURS AWAY THOUGH SO ROLL DOWN A WINDOW, OK?
"MADISON...
STOP
"MADISON, IT'S TIME TO WAKE UP. RIGHT NOW."
"WHERE ARE WE?"

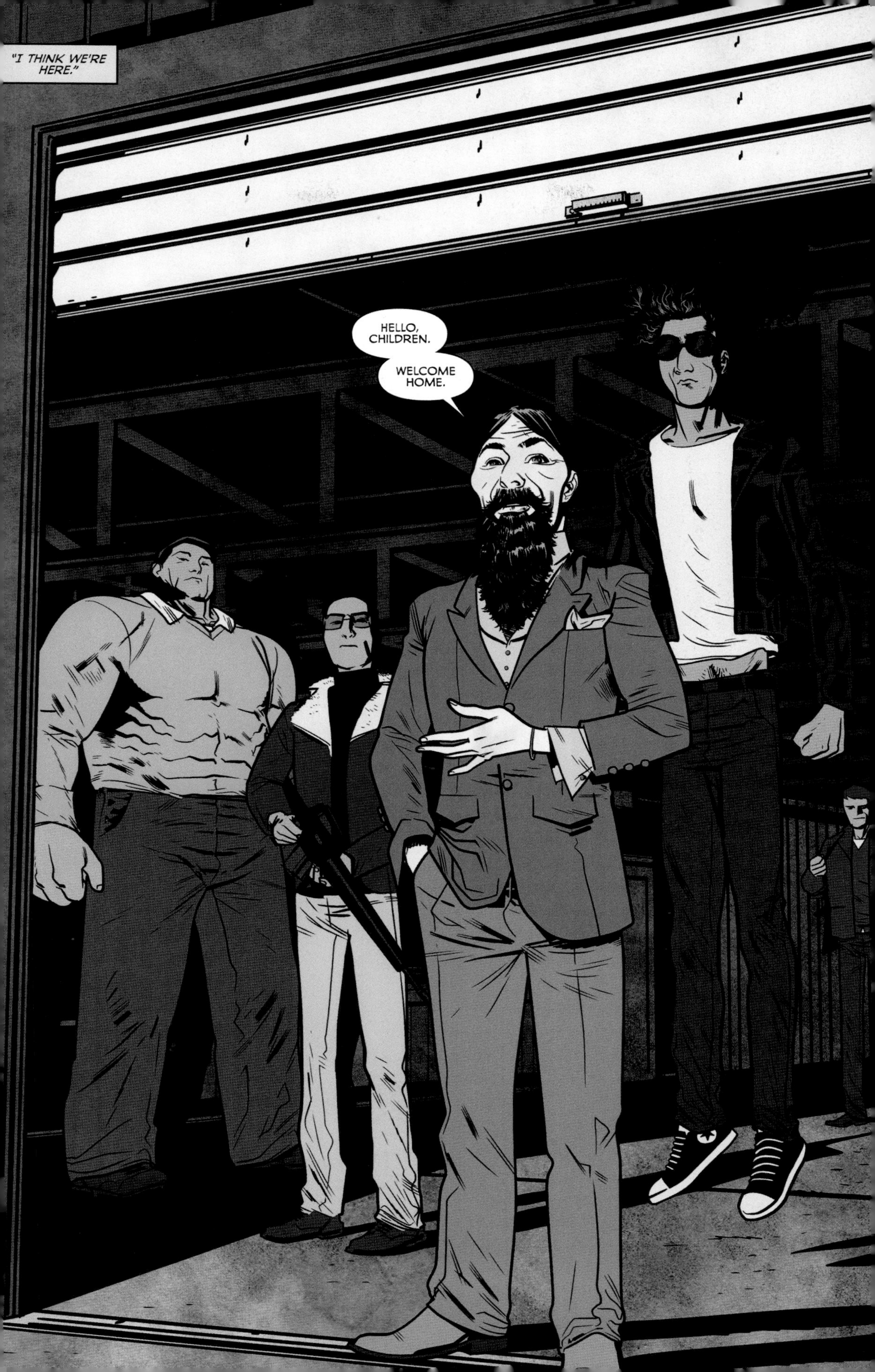
"I THINK WE'RE HERE."
HELLO, CHILDREN.
WELCOME HOME.

CHAPTER 5

DEATH OR GLORY

B 1989 IN A SMALL TOWN.

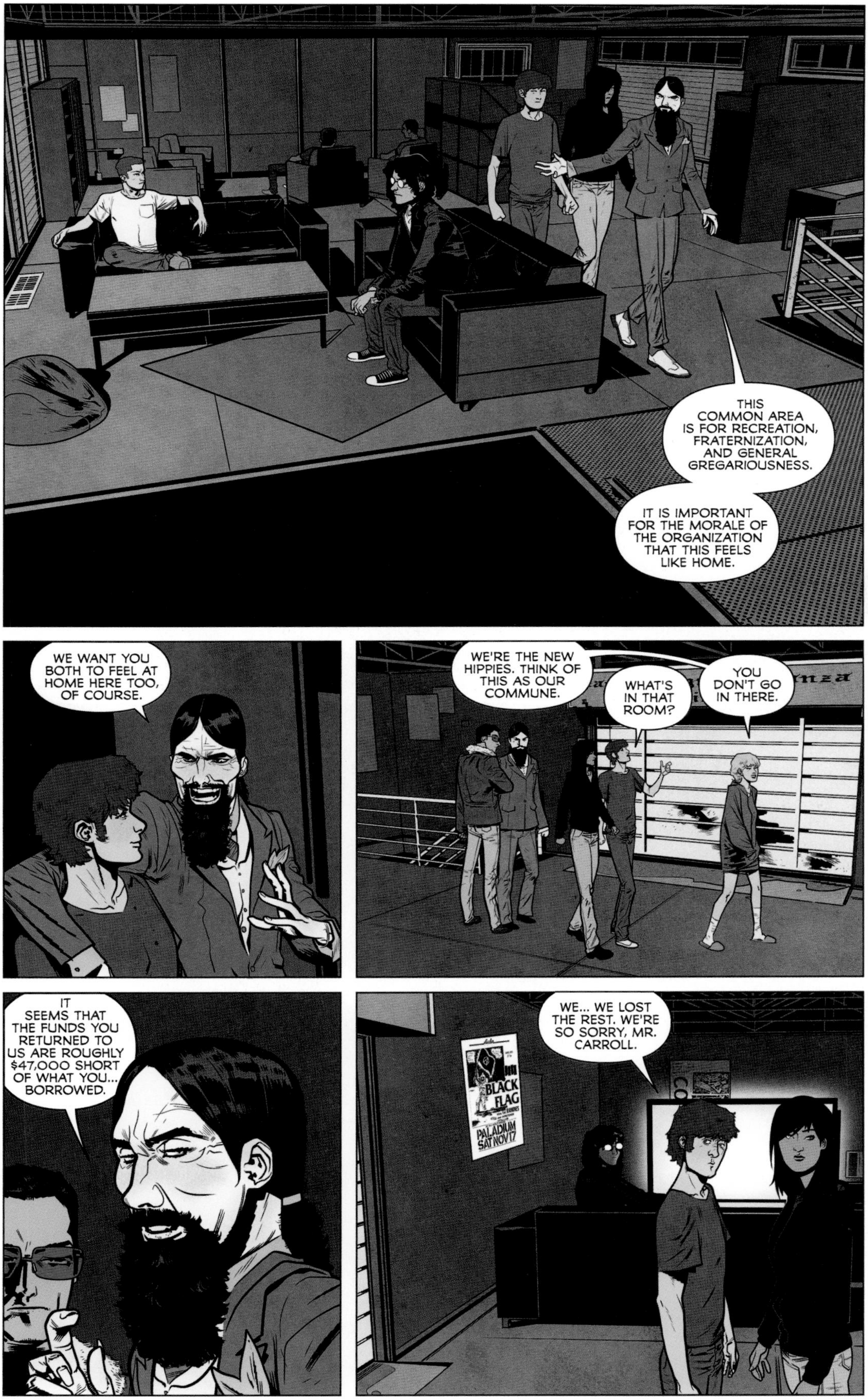
THIS COMMON AREA IS FOR RECREATION, FRATERNIZATION, AND GENERAL GREGARIOUSNESS.
IT IS IMPORTANT FOR THE MORALE OF THE ORGANIZATION THAT THIS FEELS LIKE HOME.
WE WANT YOU BOTH TO FEEL AT HOME HERE TOO, OF COURSE.
WE'RE THE NEW HIPPIES. THINK OF THIS AS OUR COMMUNE.
WHAT'S IN THAT ROOM?
YOU DON'T GO IN THERE.
IT SEEMS THAT THE FUNDS YOU RETURNED TO US ARE ROUGHLY $47,000 SHORT OF WHAT YOU... BORROWED.
WE... WE LOST THE REST. WE'RE SO SORRY, MR. CARROLL.
BLACK FLAG
PALADIUM SAT NOV 17

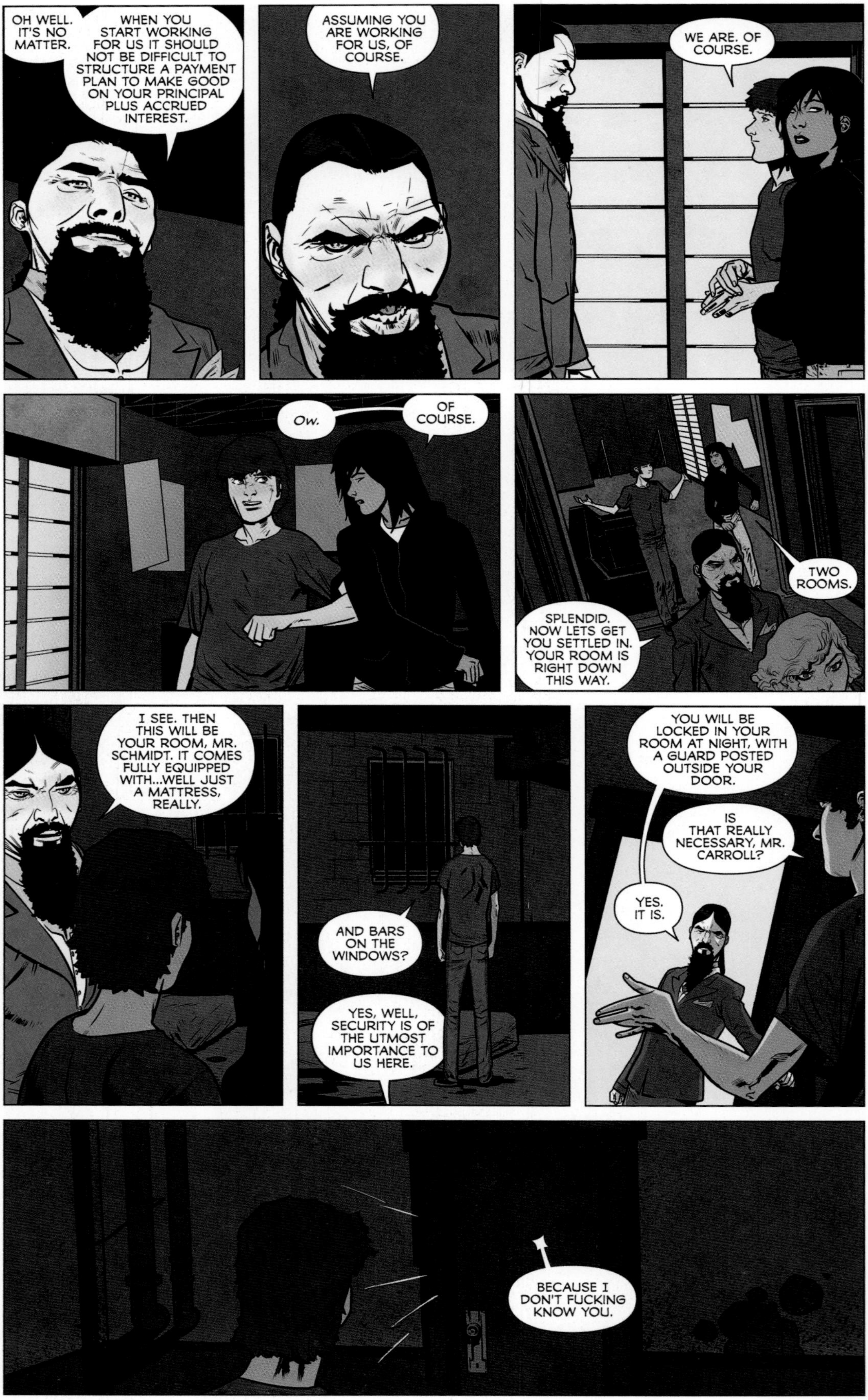
OH WELL. IT'S NO MATTER.
WHEN YOU START WORKING FOR US IT SHOULD NOT BE DIFFICULT TO STRUCTURE A PAYMENT PLAN TO MAKE GOOD ON YOUR PRINCIPAL PLUS ACCRUED INTEREST.
ASSUMING YOU ARE WORKING FOR US, OF COURSE.
WE ARE. OF COURSE.
Ow.
OF COURSE.
TWO ROOMS.
SPLENDID. NOW LETS GET YOU SETTLED IN. YOUR ROOM IS RIGHT DOWN THIS WAY.
I SEE. THEN THIS WILL BE YOUR ROOM, MR. SCHMIDT. IT COMES FULLY EQUIPPED WITH...WELL JUST A MATTRESS, REALLY.
AND BARS ON THE WINDOWS?
YES, WELL, SECURITY IS OF THE UTMOST IMPORTANCE TO US HERE.
YOU WILL BE LOCKED IN YOUR ROOM AT NIGHT, WITH A GUARD POSTED OUTSIDE YOUR DOOR.
IS THAT REALLY NECESSARY, MR. CARROLL?
YES. IT IS.
BECAUSE I DON'T FUCKING KNOW YOU.

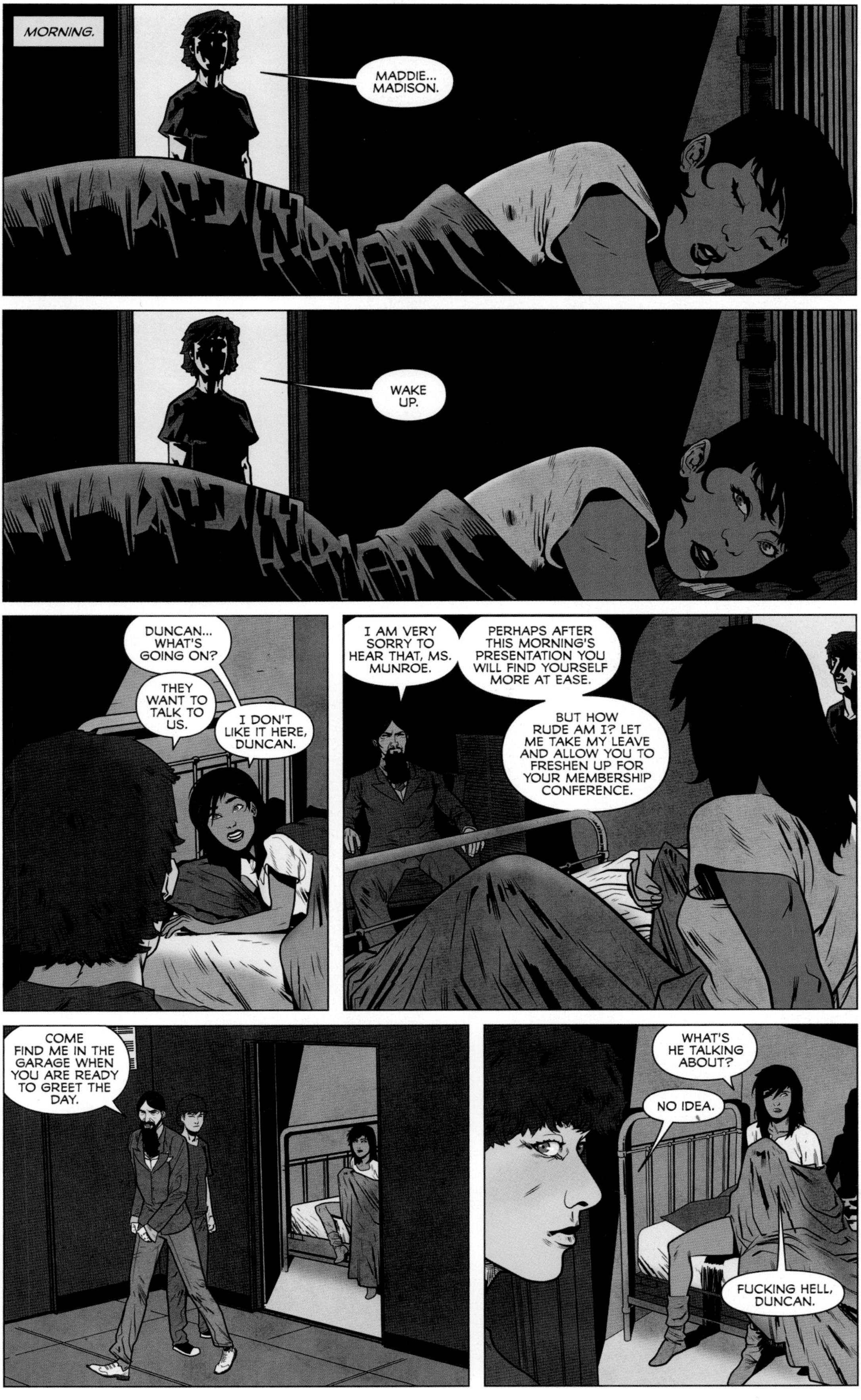
MORNING.
MADDIE... MADISON.
WAKE UP.
DUNCAN... WHAT'S GOING ON?
THEY WANT TO TALK TO US.
I DON'T LIKE IT HERE, DUNCAN.
I AM VERY SORRY TO HEAR THAT, MS. MUNROE.
PERHAPS AFTER THIS MORNING'S PRESENTATION YOU WILL FIND YOURSELF MORE AT EASE.
BUT HOW RUDE AM I? LET ME TAKE MY LEAVE AND ALLOW YOU TO FRESHEN UP FOR YOUR MEMBERSHIP CONFERENCE.
COME FIND ME IN THE GARAGE WHEN YOU ARE READY TO GREET THE DAY.
WHAT'S HE TALKING ABOUT?
NO IDEA.
FUCKING HELL, DUNCAN.

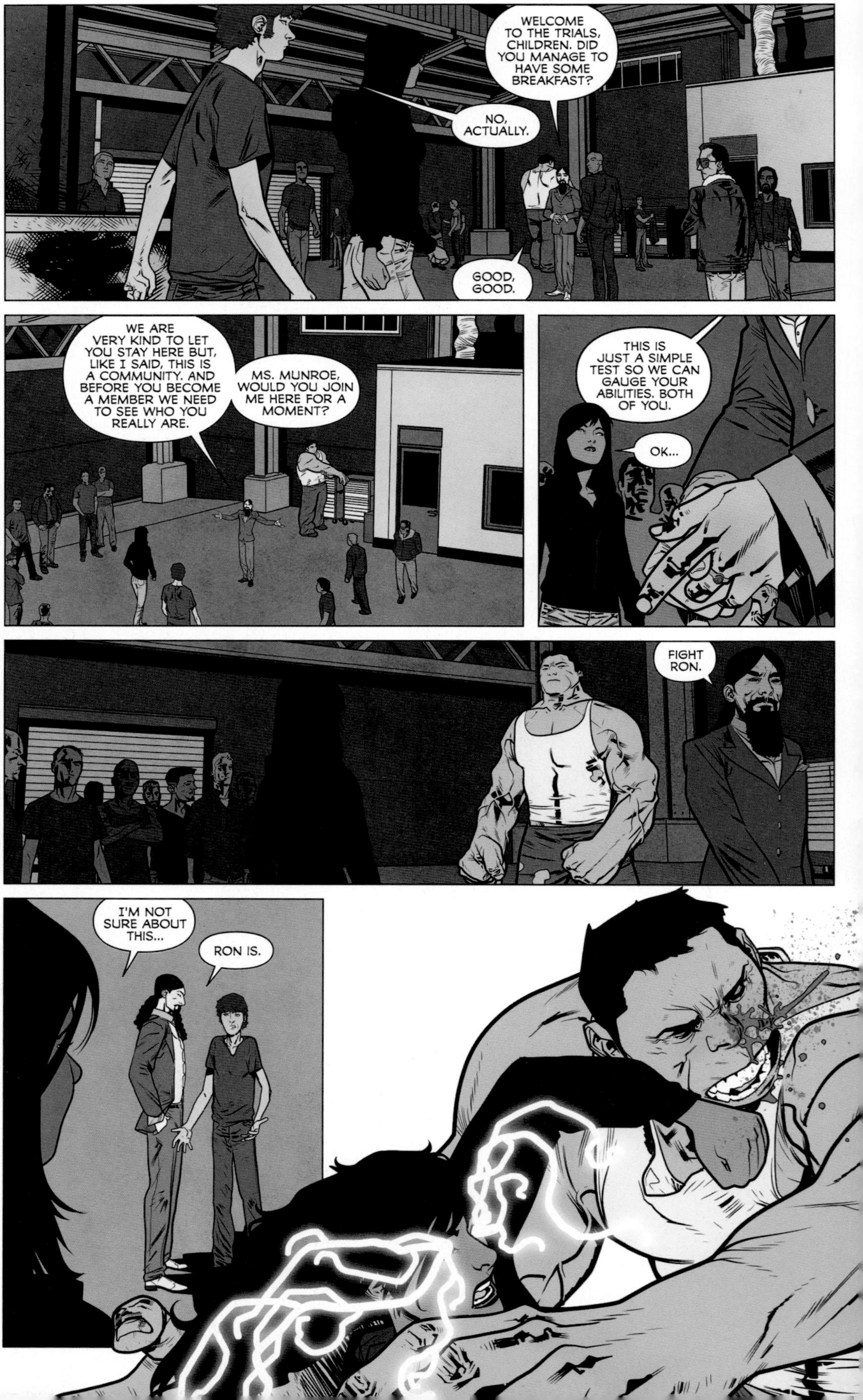
WELCOME TO THE TRIALS, CHILDREN. DID YOU MANAGE TO HAVE SOME BREAKFAST?
NO, ACTUALLY.
GOOD, GOOD.
WE ARE VERY KIND TO LET YOU STAY HERE BUT, LIKE I SAID, THIS IS A COMMUNITY. AND BEFORE YOU BECOME A MEMBER WE NEED TO SEE WHO YOU REALLY ARE.
MS. MUNROE, WOULD YOU JOIN ME HERE FOR A MOMENT?
THIS IS JUST A SIMPLE TEST SO WE CAN GAUGE YOUR ABILITIES. BOTH OF YOU.
OK...
FIGHT RON.
I'M NOT SURE ABOUT THIS...
RON IS.

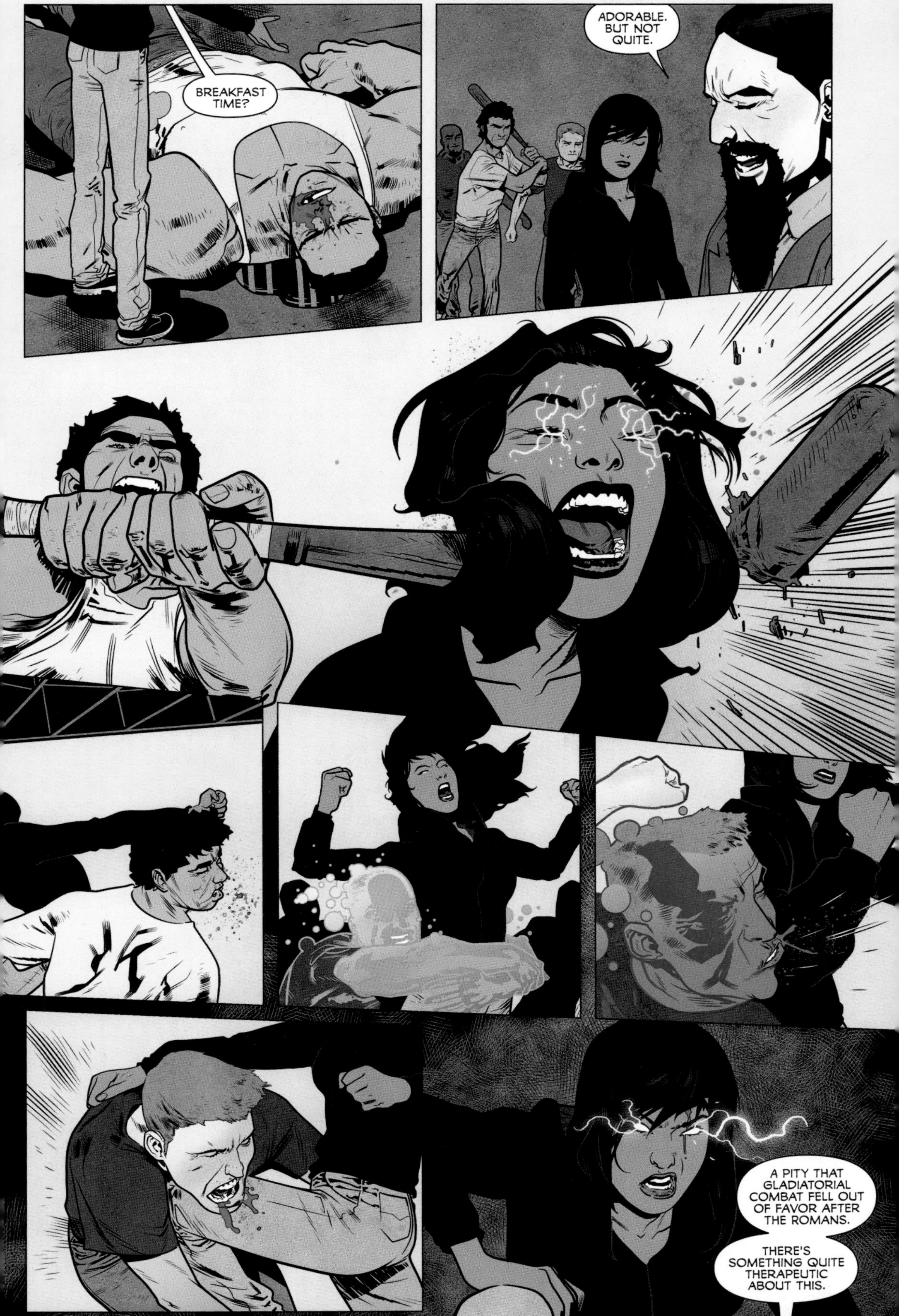
BREAKFAST TIME?
ADORABLE. BUT NOT QUITE.
A PITY THAT GLADIATORIAL COMBAT FELL OUT OF FAVOR AFTER THE ROMANS.
THERE'S SOMETHING QUITE THERAPEUTIC ABOUT THIS.

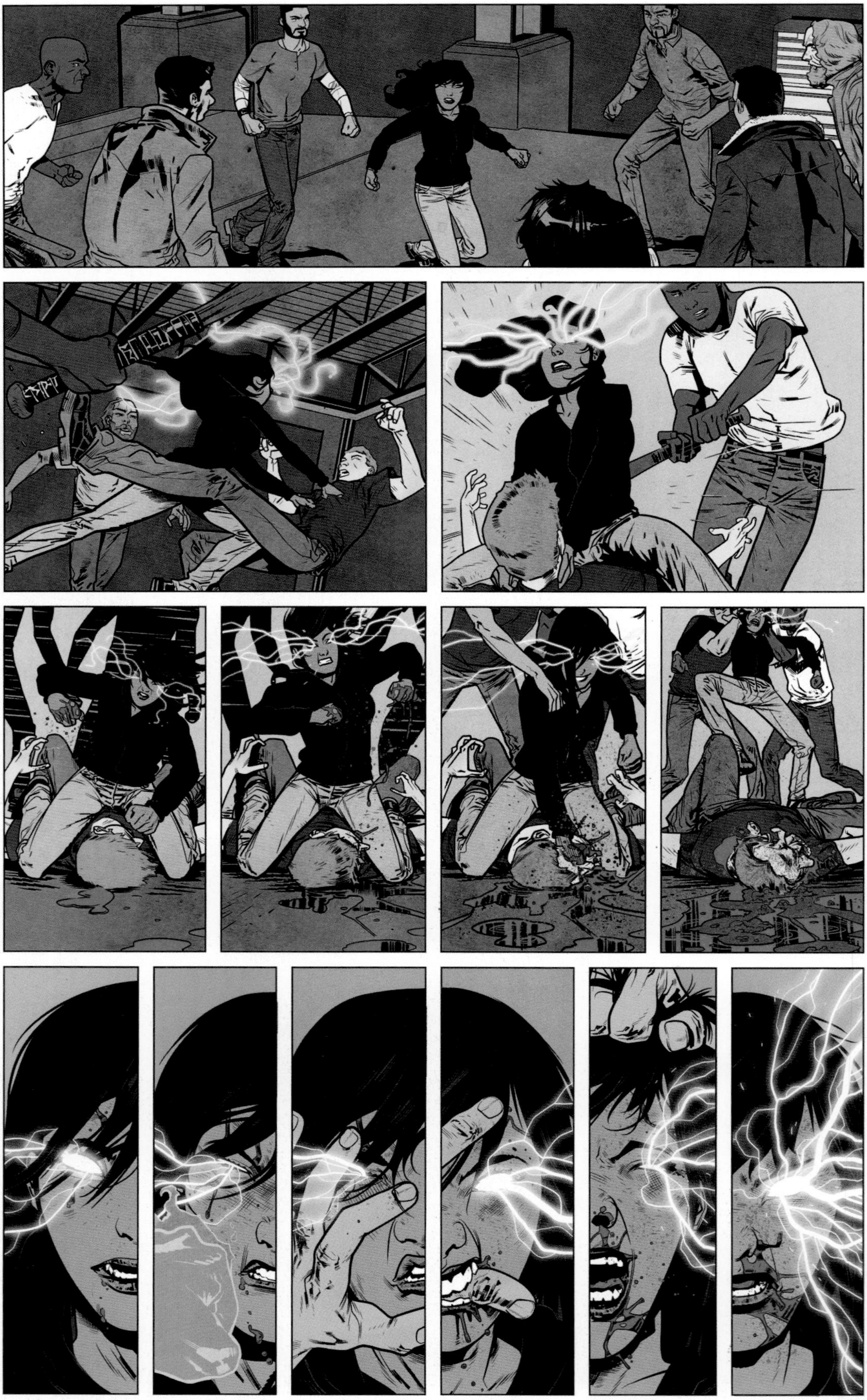

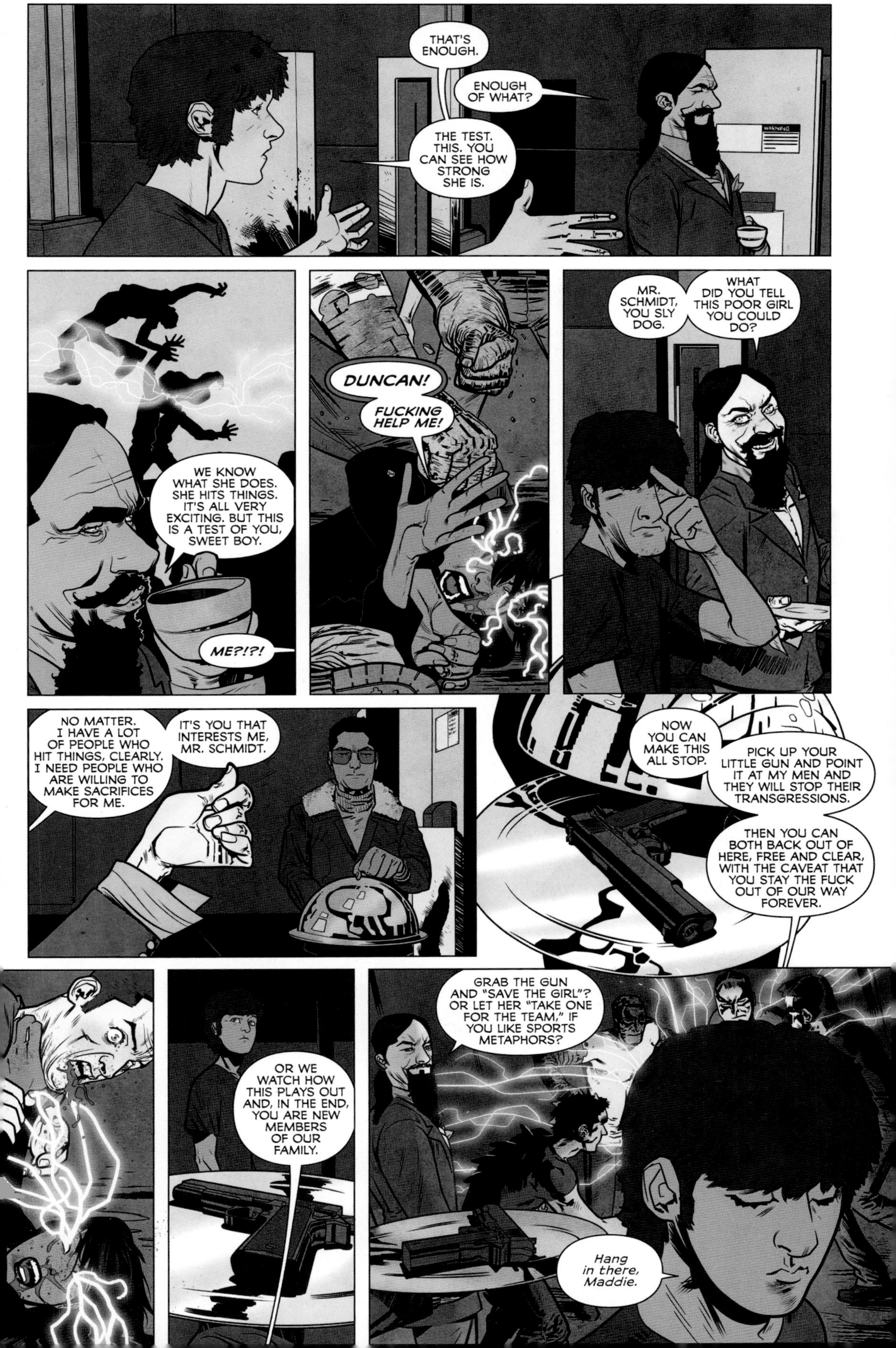

THAT'S ENOUGH.
ENOUGH OF WHAT?
THE TEST. THIS. YOU CAN SEE HOW STRONG SHE IS.
WE KNOW WHAT SHE DOES. SHE HITS THINGS. IT'S ALL VERY EXCITING. BUT THIS IS A TEST OF YOU, SWEET BOY.
ME?!?!
DUNCAN!
FUCKING HELP ME!
MR. SCHMIDT, YOU SLY DOG.
WHAT DID YOU TELL THIS POOR GIRL YOU COULD DO?
NO MATTER. I HAVE A LOT OF PEOPLE WHO HIT THINGS, CLEARLY. I NEED PEOPLE WHO ARE WILLING TO MAKE SACRIFICES FOR ME.
IT'S YOU THAT INTERESTS ME, MR. SCHMIDT.
NOW YOU CAN MAKE THIS ALL STOP.
PICK UP YOUR LITTLE GUN AND POINT IT AT MY MEN AND THEY WILL STOP THEIR TRANSGRESSIONS.
THEN YOU CAN BOTH BACK OUT OF HERE, FREE AND CLEAR, WITH THE CAVEAT THAT YOU STAY THE FUCK OUT OF OUR WAY FOREVER.
OR WE WATCH HOW THIS PLAYS OUT AND, IN THE END, YOU ARE NEW MEMBERS OF OUR FAMILY.
GRAB THE GUN AND "SAVE THE GIRL"? OR LET HER "TAKE ONE FOR THE TEAM," IF YOU LIKE SPORTS METAPHORS?
Hang in there, Maddie.

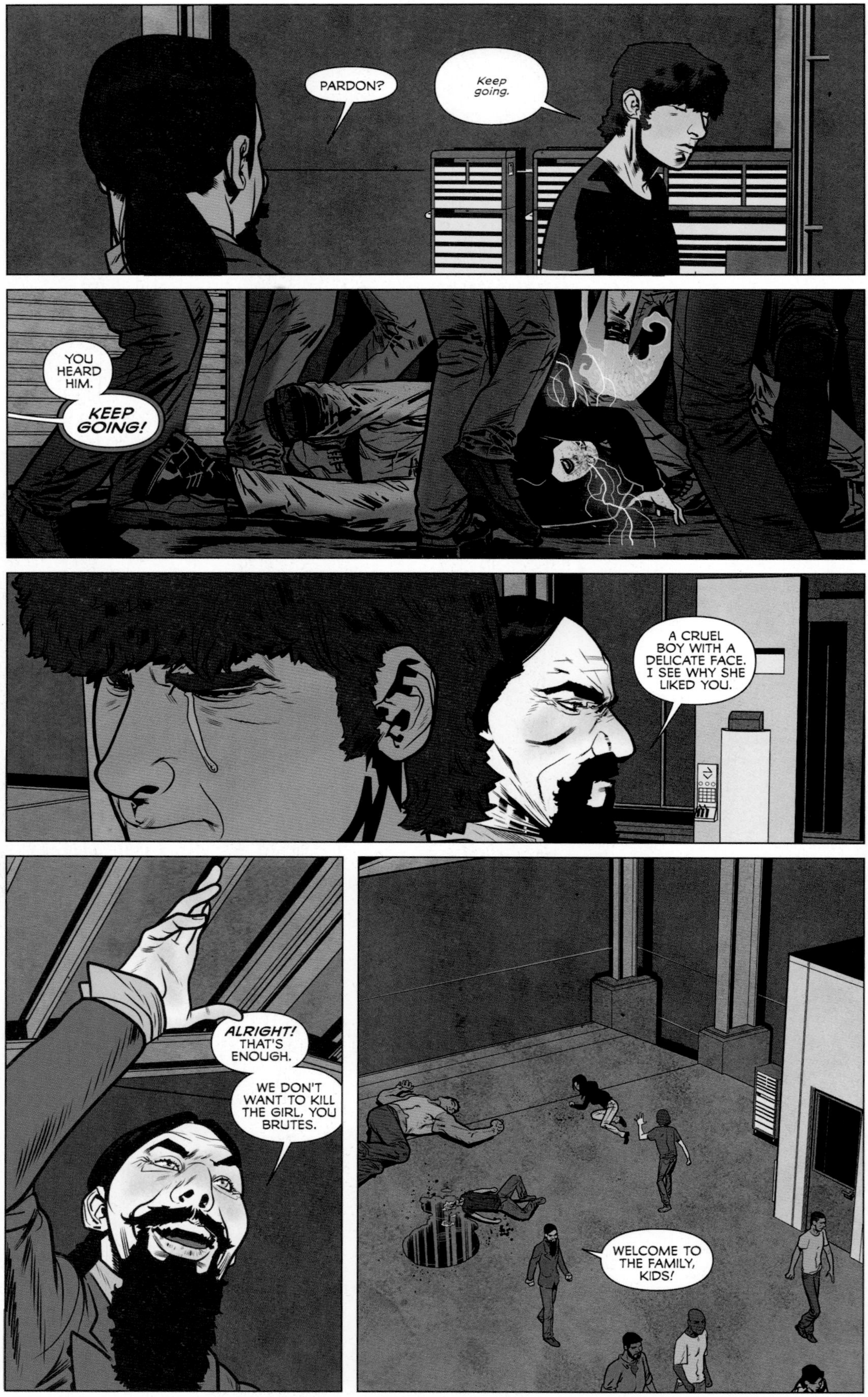
PARDON?
Keep going.
YOU HEARD HIM.
KEEP GOING!
A CRUEL BOY WITH A DELICATE FACE. I SEE WHY SHE LIKED YOU.
ALRIGHT! THAT'S ENOUGH.
WE DON'T WANT TO KILL THE GIRL, YOU BRUTES.
WELCOME TO THE FAMILY, KIDS!

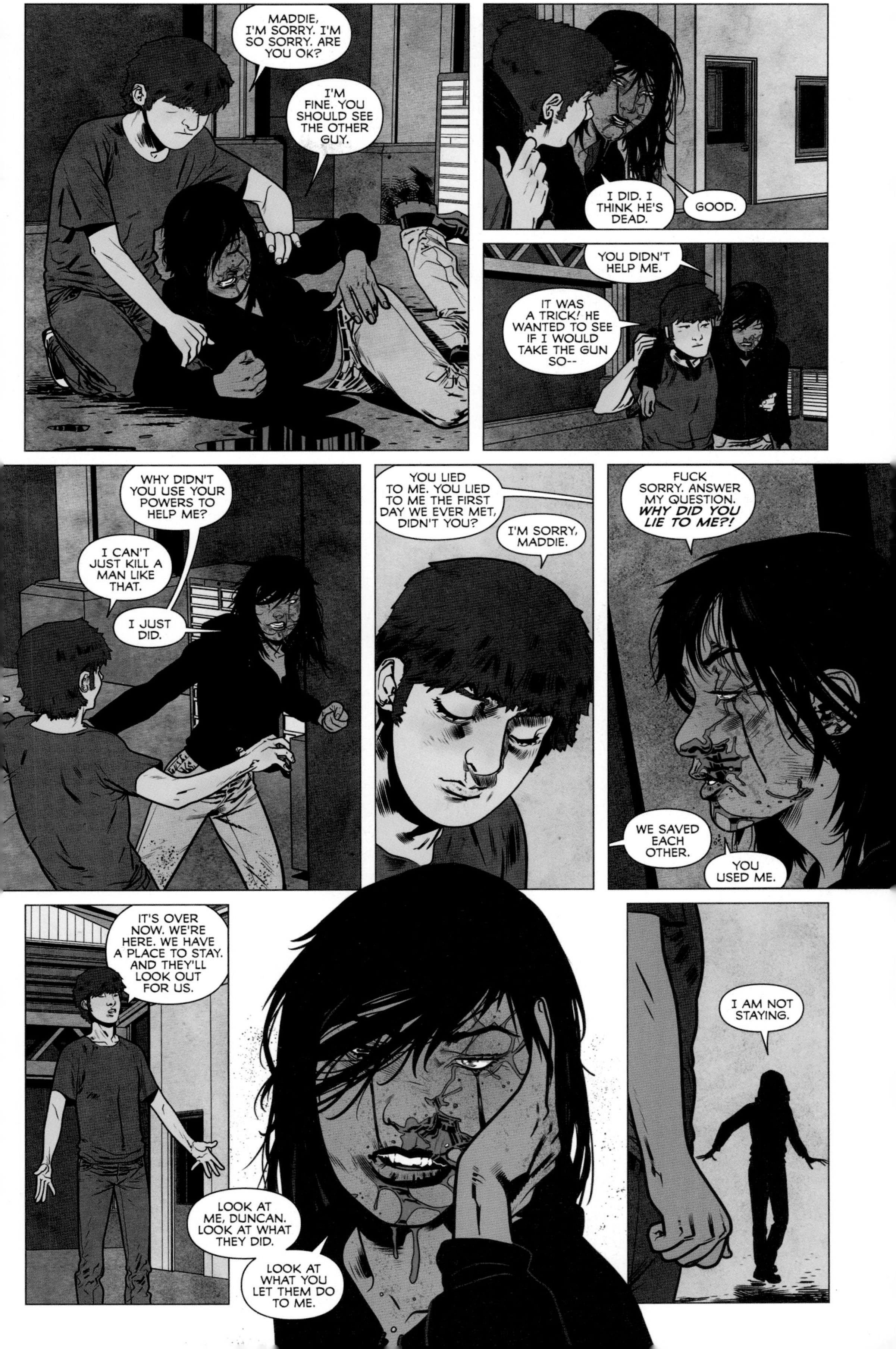
MADDIE, I'M SORRY. I'M SO SORRY. ARE YOU OK?
I'M FINE. YOU SHOULD SEE THE OTHER GUY.
I DID. I THINK HE'S DEAD.
GOOD.
YOU DIDN'T HELP ME.
IT WAS A TRICK! HE WANTED TO SEE IF I WOULD TAKE THE GUN SO--
WHY DIDN'T YOU USE YOUR POWERS TO HELP ME?
I CAN'T JUST KILL A MAN LIKE THAT.
I JUST DID.
YOU LIED TO ME. YOU LIED TO ME THE FIRST DAY WE EVER MET, DIDN'T YOU?
I'M SORRY, MADDIE.
FUCK SORRY. ANSWER MY QUESTION. ***WHY DID YOU LIE TO ME?!***
WE SAVED EACH OTHER.
YOU USED ME.
IT'S OVER NOW. WE'RE HERE. WE HAVE A PLACE TO STAY. AND THEY'LL LOOK OUT FOR US.
LOOK AT ME, DUNCAN. LOOK AT WHAT THEY DID.
LOOK AT WHAT YOU LET THEM DO TO ME.
I AM NOT STAYING.

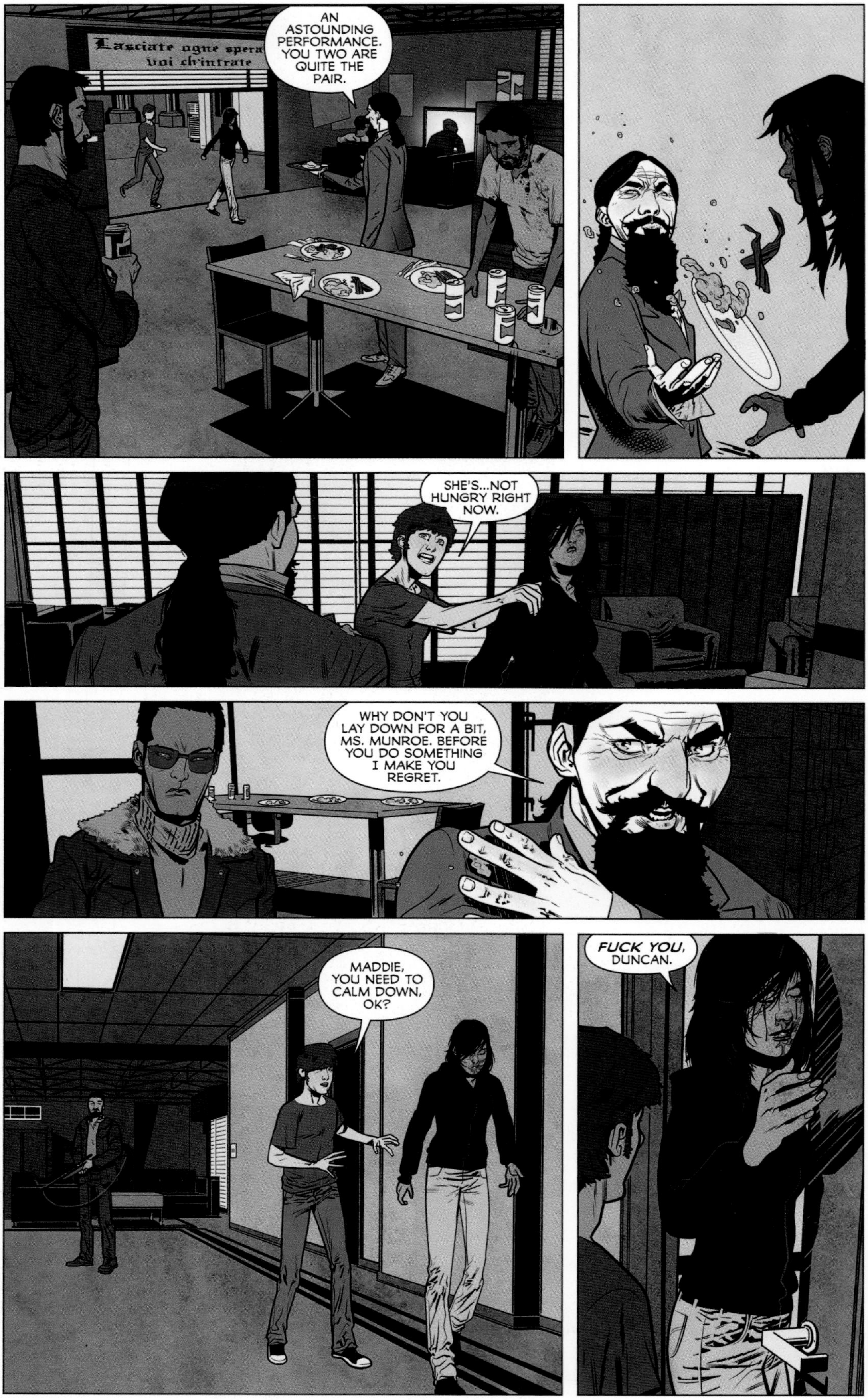
Lasciate ogne spera
voi ch'intrate
AN ASTOUNDING PERFORMANCE. YOU TWO ARE QUITE THE PAIR.
SHE'S...NOT HUNGRY RIGHT NOW.
WHY DON'T YOU LAY DOWN FOR A BIT, MS. MUNROE. BEFORE YOU DO SOMETHING I MAKE YOU REGRET.
MADDIE, YOU NEED TO CALM DOWN, OK?
FUCK YOU, DUNCAN.

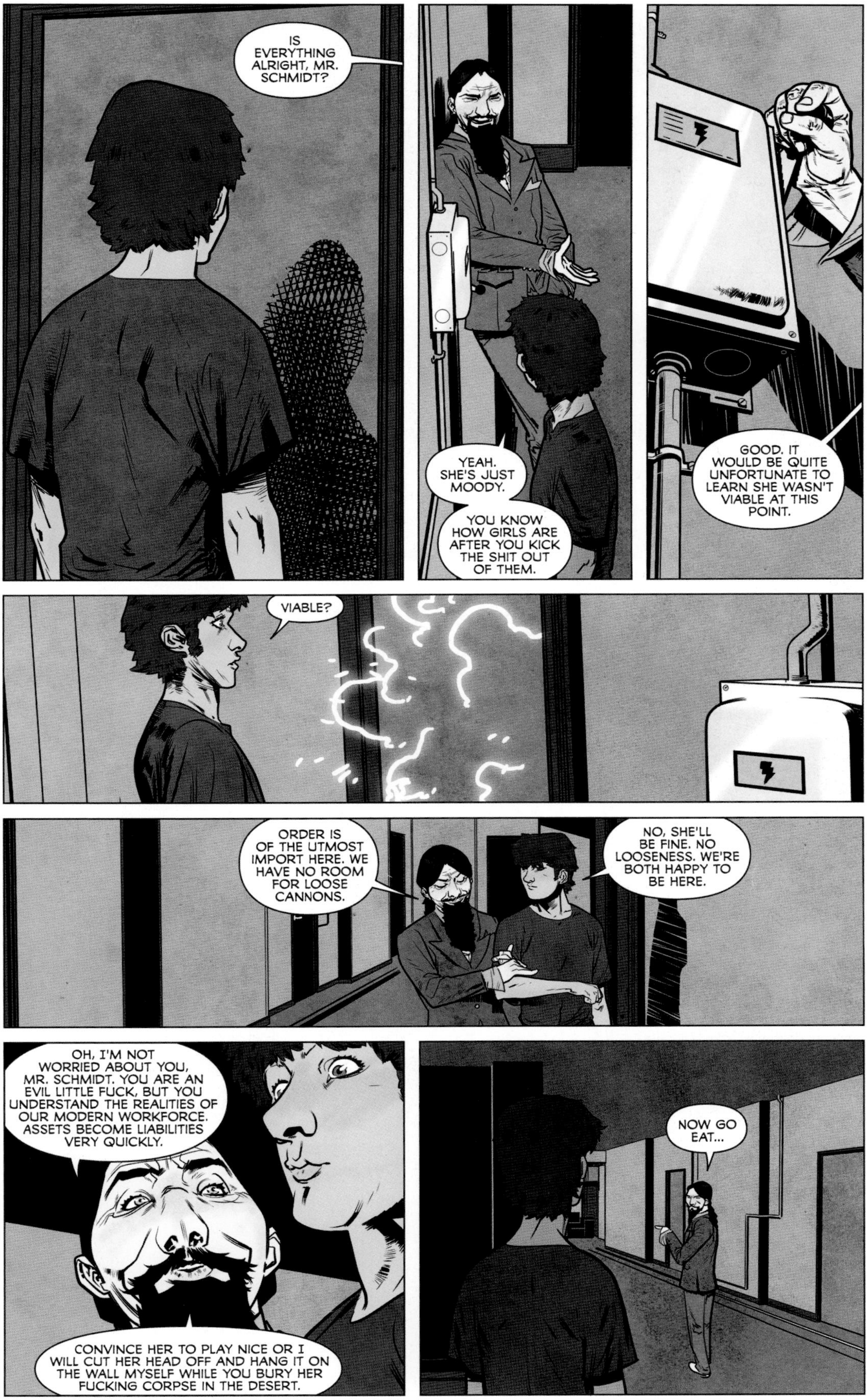
IS EVERYTHING ALRIGHT, MR. SCHMIDT?
YEAH. SHE'S JUST MOODY.
YOU KNOW HOW GIRLS ARE AFTER YOU KICK THE SHIT OUT OF THEM.
GOOD. IT WOULD BE QUITE UNFORTUNATE TO LEARN SHE WASN'T VIABLE AT THIS POINT.
VIABLE?
ORDER IS OF THE UTMOST IMPORT HERE. WE HAVE NO ROOM FOR LOOSE CANNONS.
NO, SHE'LL BE FINE. NO LOOSENESS. WE'RE BOTH HAPPY TO BE HERE.
OH, I'M NOT WORRIED ABOUT YOU, MR. SCHMIDT. YOU ARE AN EVIL LITTLE FUCK, BUT YOU UNDERSTAND THE REALITIES OF OUR MODERN WORKFORCE. ASSETS BECOME LIABILITIES VERY QUICKLY.
CONVINCE HER TO PLAY NICE OR I WILL CUT HER HEAD OFF AND HANG IT ON THE WALL MYSELF WHILE YOU BURY HER FUCKING CORPSE IN THE DESERT.
NOW GO EAT...

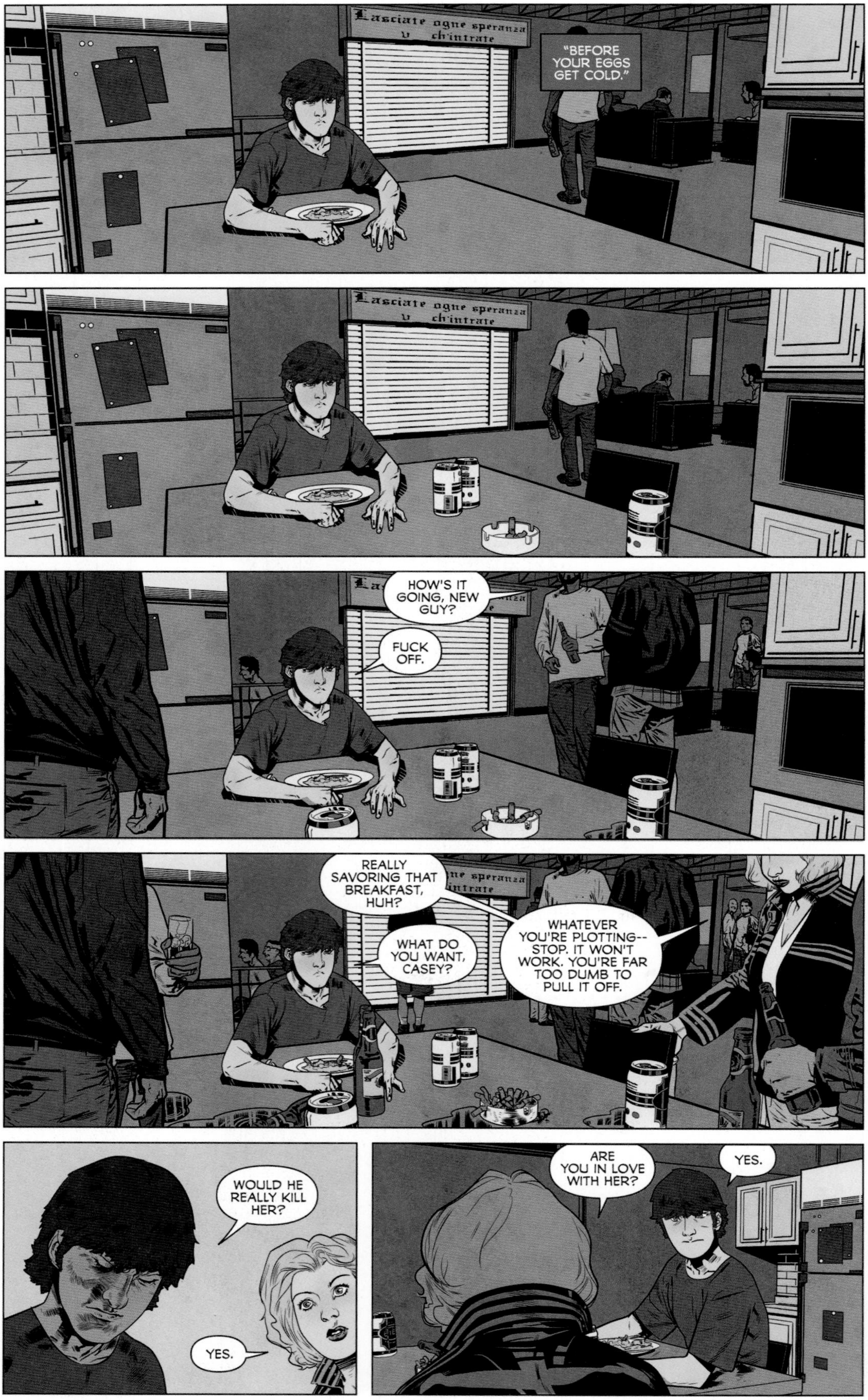
Lasciate ogne speranza voi ch'intrate
"BEFORE YOUR EGGS GET COLD."
Lasciate ogne speranza voi ch'intrate
HOW'S IT GOING, NEW GUY?
FUCK OFF.
REALLY SAVORING THAT BREAKFAST, HUH?
WHAT DO YOU WANT, CASEY?
WHATEVER YOU'RE PLOTTING-- STOP. IT WON'T WORK. YOU'RE FAR TOO DUMB TO PULL IT OFF.
WOULD HE REALLY KILL HER?
YES.
ARE YOU IN LOVE WITH HER?
YES.

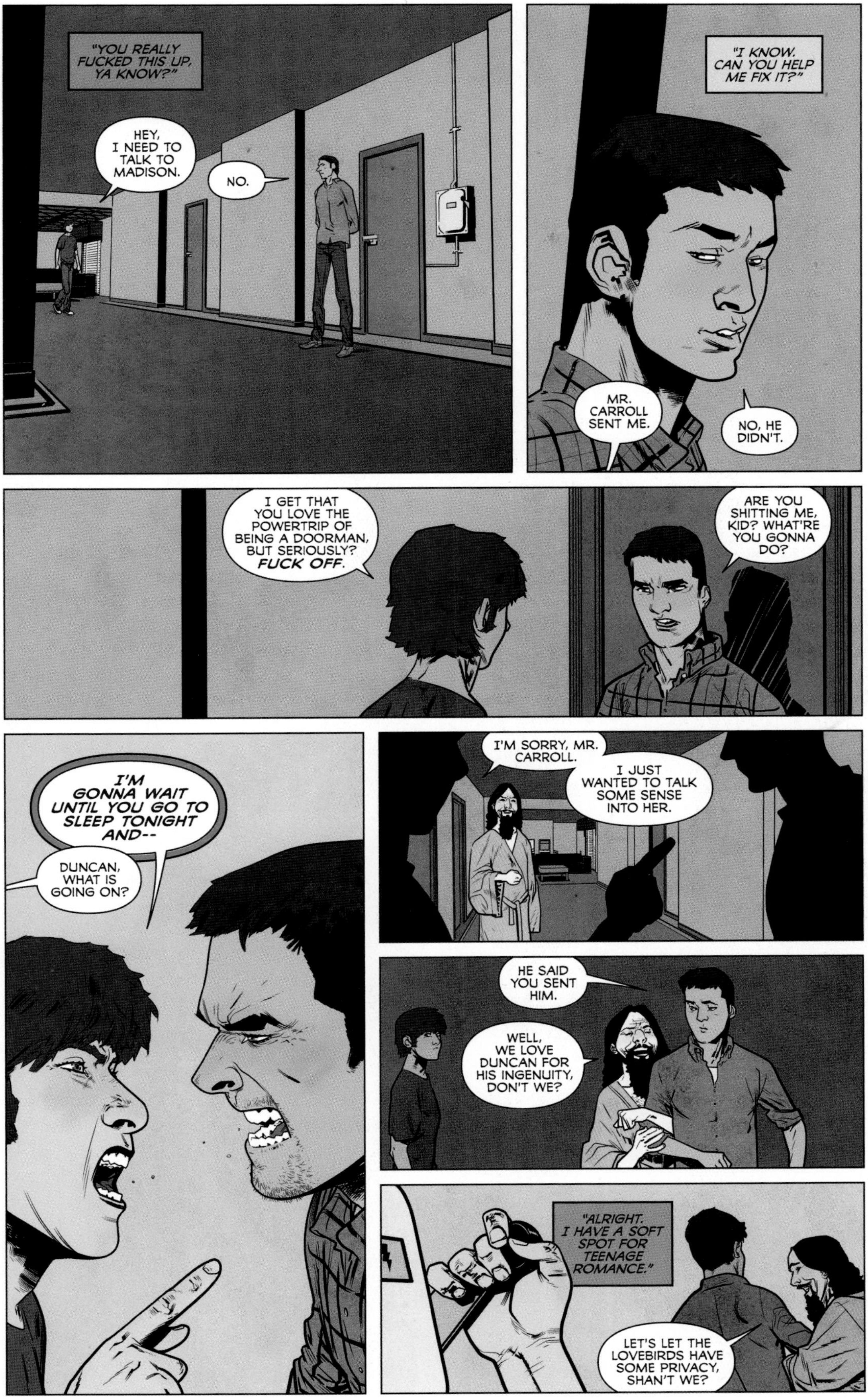
"YOU REALLY FUCKED THIS UP, YA KNOW?"
HEY, I NEED TO TALK TO MADISON.
NO.
"I KNOW. CAN YOU HELP ME FIX IT?"
MR. CARROLL SENT ME.
NO, HE DIDN'T.
I GET THAT YOU LOVE THE POWERTRIP OF BEING A DOORMAN, BUT SERIOUSLY? FUCK OFF.
ARE YOU SHITTING ME, KID? WHAT'RE YOU GONNA DO?
I'M GONNA WAIT UNTIL YOU GO TO SLEEP TONIGHT AND--
DUNCAN, WHAT IS GOING ON?
I'M SORRY, MR. CARROLL.
I JUST WANTED TO TALK SOME SENSE INTO HER.
HE SAID YOU SENT HIM.
WELL, WE LOVE DUNCAN FOR HIS INGENUITY, DON'T WE?
"ALRIGHT. I HAVE A SOFT SPOT FOR TEENAGE ROMANCE."
LET'S LET THE LOVEBIRDS HAVE SOME PRIVACY, SHAN'T WE?

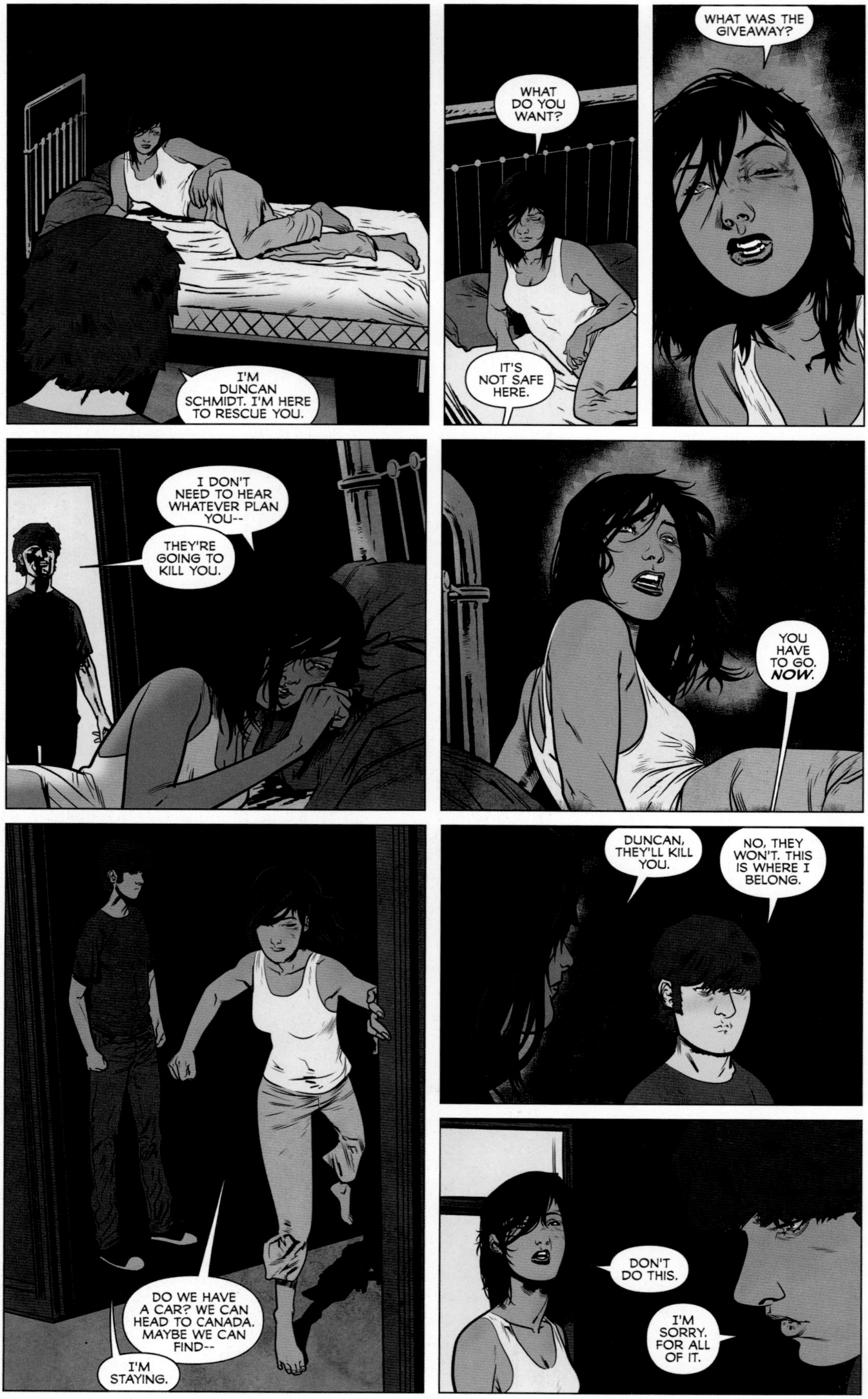
I'M DUNCAN SCHMIDT. I'M HERE TO RESCUE YOU.
WHAT DO YOU WANT?
IT'S NOT SAFE HERE.
WHAT WAS THE GIVEAWAY?
I DON'T NEED TO HEAR WHATEVER PLAN YOU--
THEY'RE GOING TO KILL YOU.
YOU HAVE TO GO. ***NOW***.
DO WE HAVE A CAR? WE CAN HEAD TO CANADA. MAYBE WE CAN FIND--
I'M STAYING.
DUNCAN, THEY'LL KILL YOU.
NO, THEY WON'T. THIS IS WHERE I BELONG.
DON'T DO THIS.
I'M SORRY. FOR ALL OF IT.

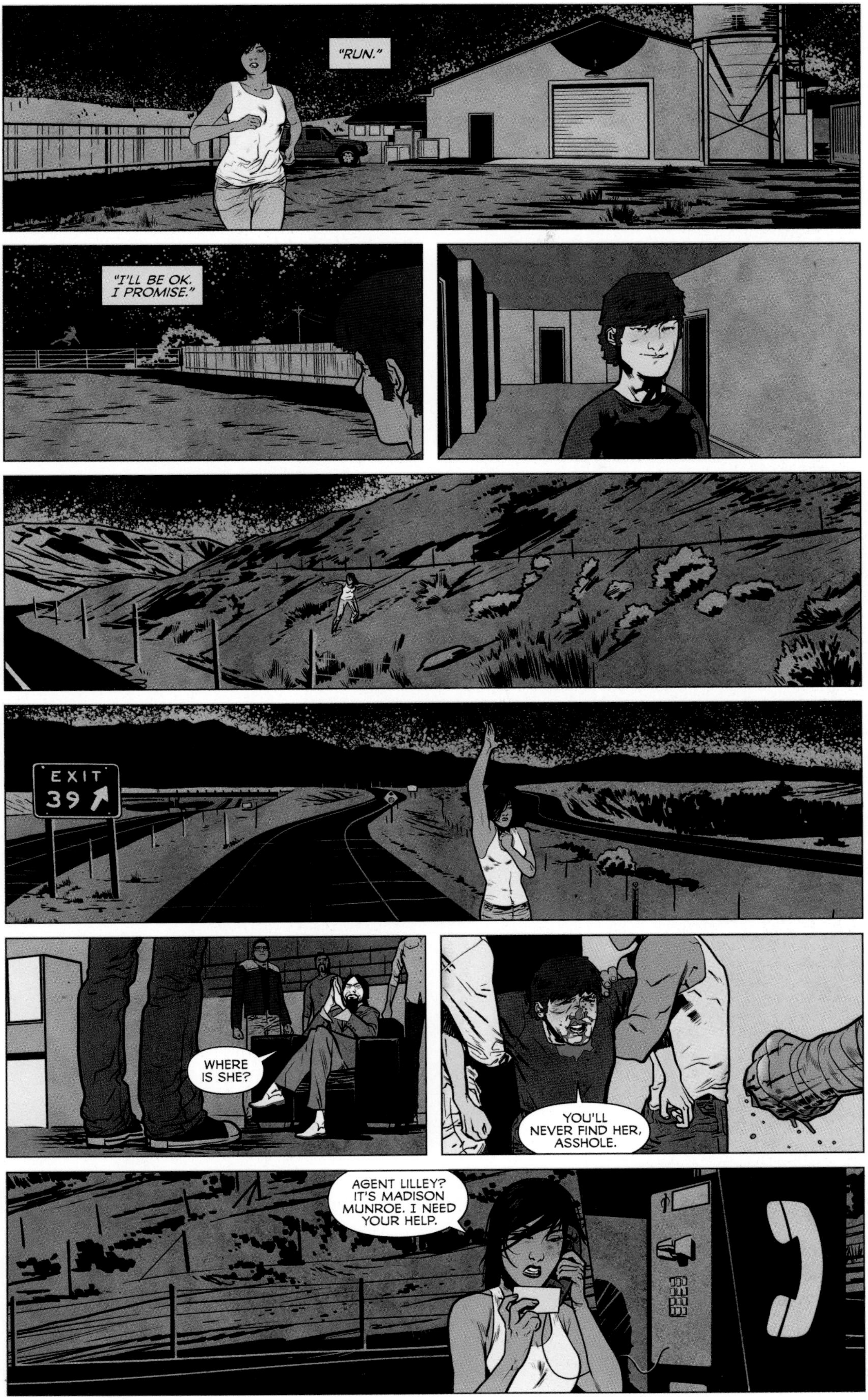
"RUN."
"I'LL BE OK. I PROMISE."
EXIT 39
WHERE IS SHE?
YOU'LL NEVER FIND HER, ASSHOLE.
AGENT LILLEY? IT'S MADISON MUNROE. I NEED YOUR HELP.

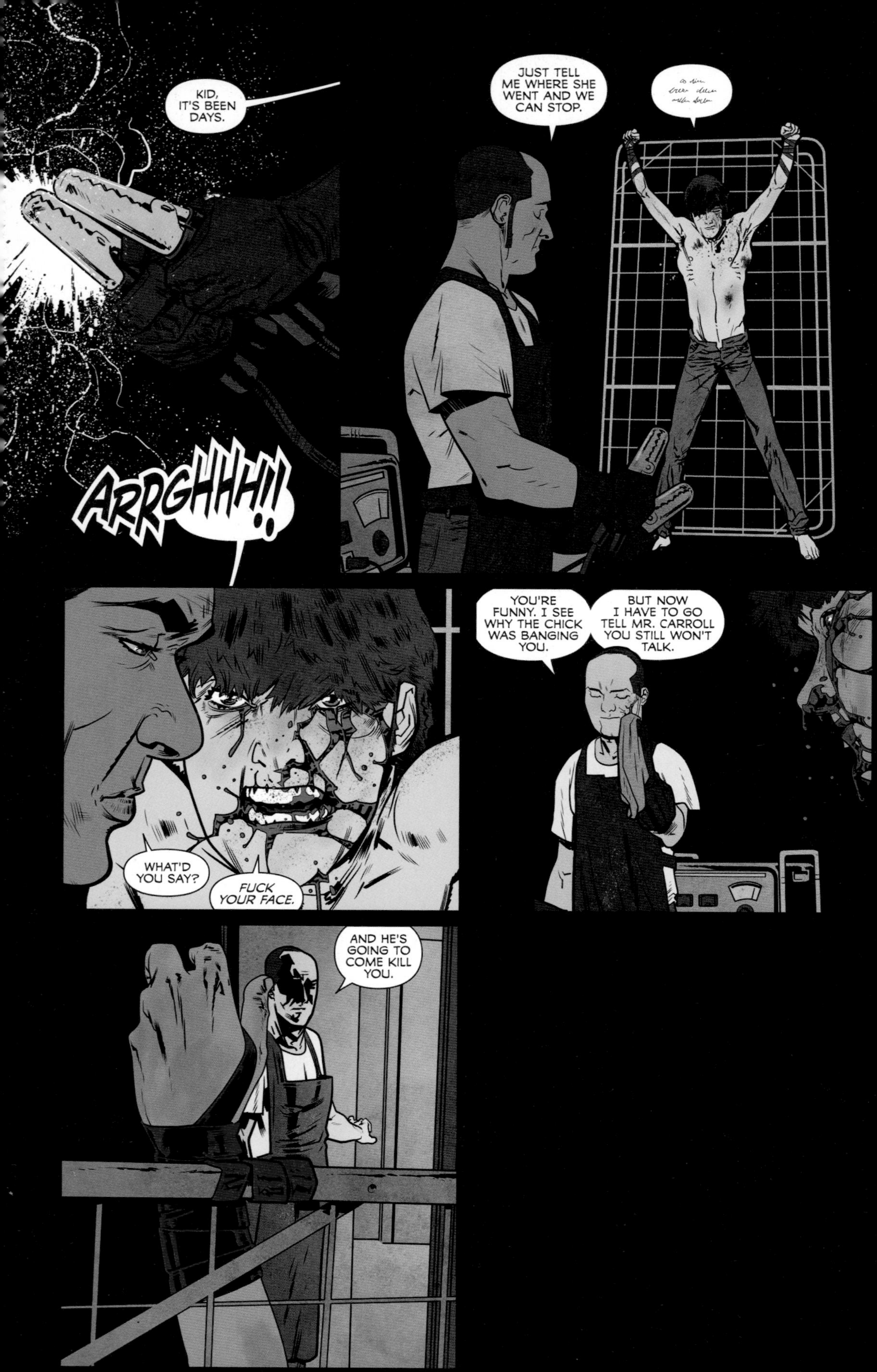
KID, IT'S BEEN DAYS.
ARRGHHH!!
JUST TELL ME WHERE SHE WENT AND WE CAN STOP.
WHAT'D YOU SAY?
FUCK YOUR FACE.
YOU'RE FUNNY. I SEE WHY THE CHICK WAS BANGING YOU.
BUT NOW I HAVE TO GO TELL MR. CARROLL YOU STILL WON'T TALK.
AND HE'S GOING TO COME KILL YOU.

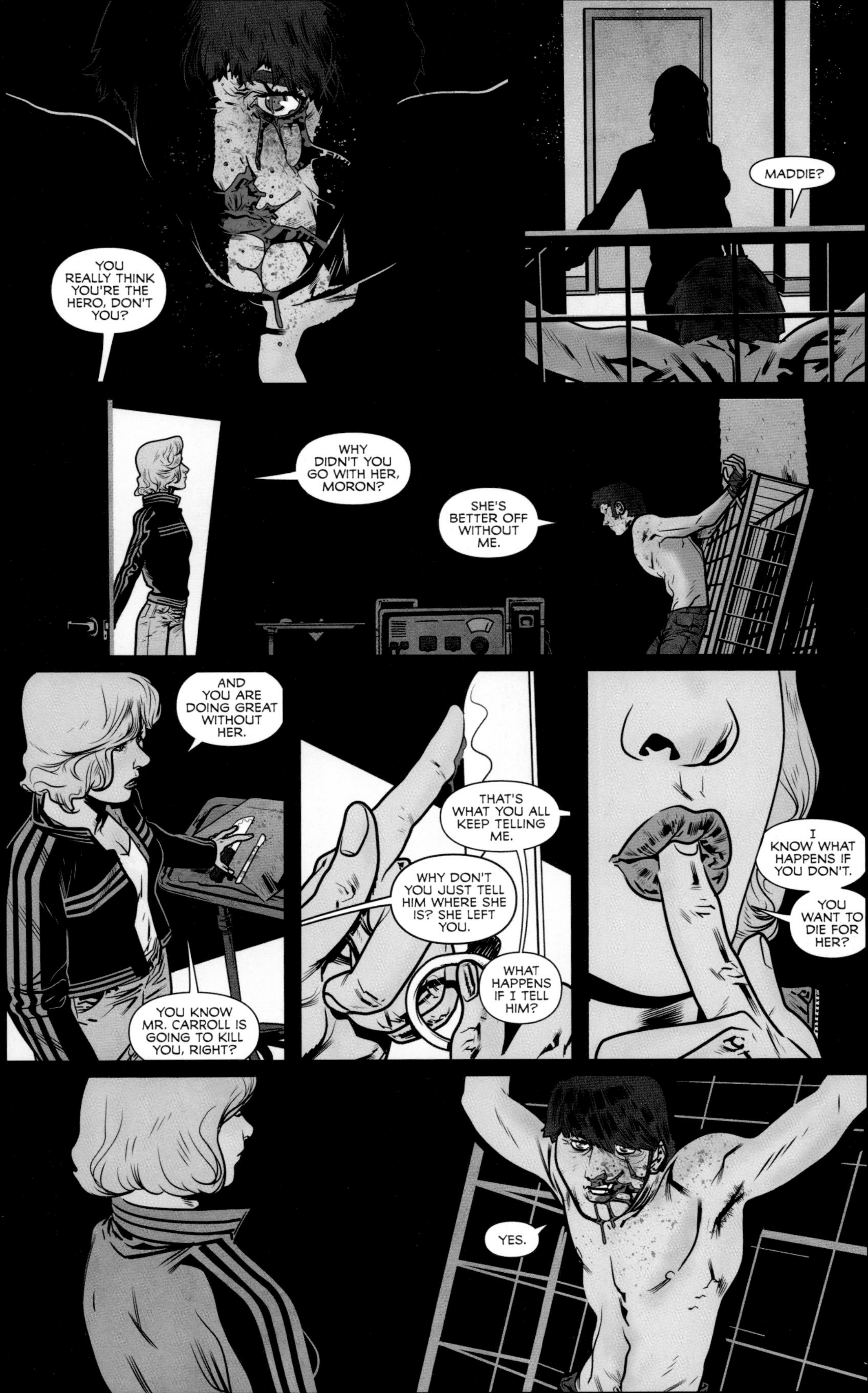
YOU REALLY THINK YOU'RE THE HERO, DON'T YOU?
MADDIE?
WHY DIDN'T YOU GO WITH HER, MORON?
SHE'S BETTER OFF WITHOUT ME.
AND YOU ARE DOING GREAT WITHOUT HER.
YOU KNOW MR. CARROLL IS GOING TO KILL YOU, RIGHT?
THAT'S WHAT YOU ALL KEEP TELLING ME.
WHY DON'T YOU JUST TELL HIM WHERE SHE IS? SHE LEFT YOU.
WHAT HAPPENS IF I TELL HIM?
I KNOW WHAT HAPPENS IF YOU DON'T.
YOU WANT TO DIE FOR HER?
YES.

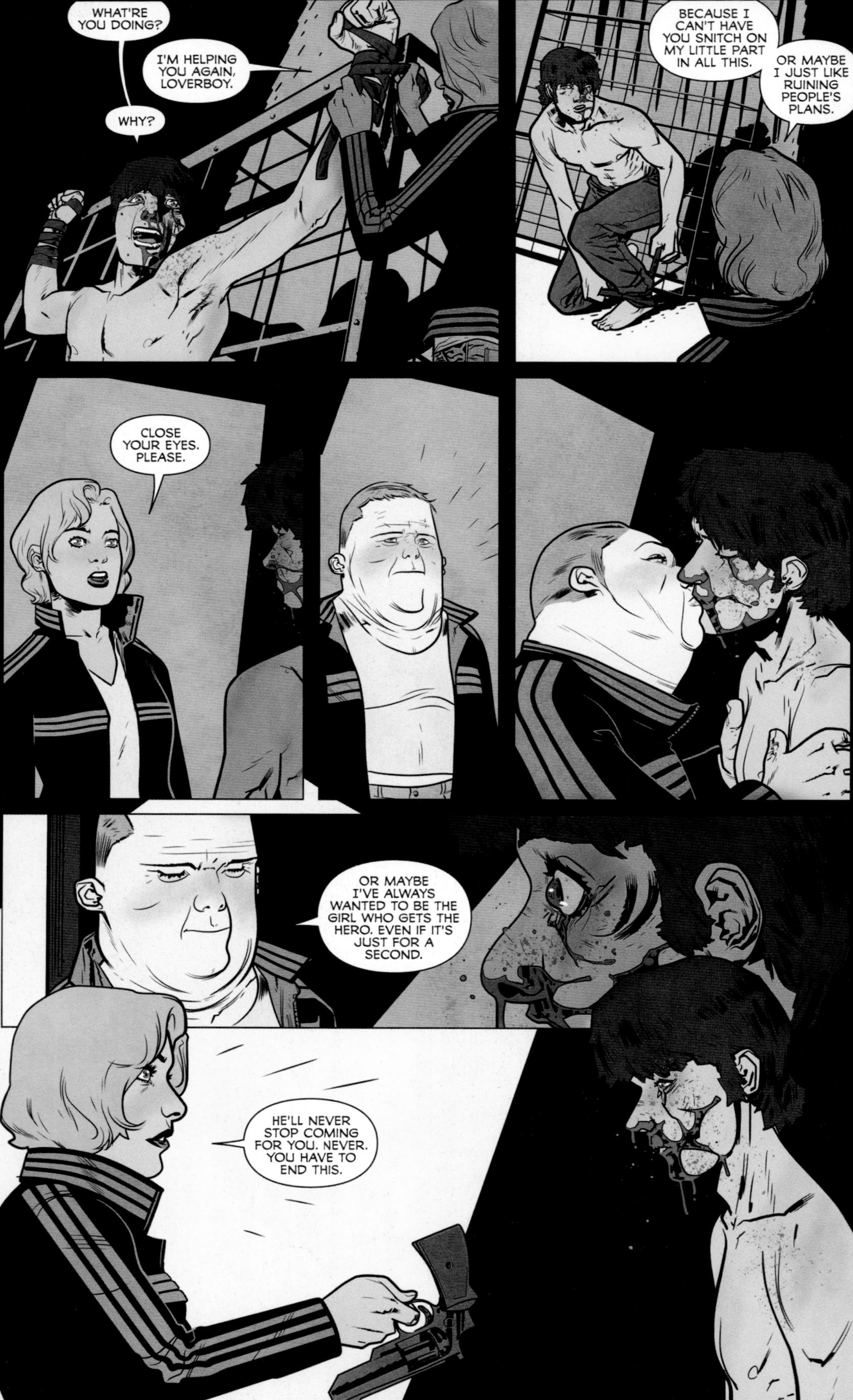
WHAT'RE YOU DOING?
I'M HELPING YOU AGAIN, LOVERBOY.
WHY?
BECAUSE I CAN'T HAVE YOU SNITCH ON MY LITTLE PART IN ALL THIS.
OR MAYBE I JUST LIKE RUINING PEOPLE'S PLANS.
CLOSE YOUR EYES. PLEASE.
OR MAYBE I'VE ALWAYS WANTED TO BE THE GIRL WHO GETS THE HERO. EVEN IF IT'S JUST FOR A SECOND.
HE'LL NEVER STOP COMING FOR YOU. NEVER. YOU HAVE TO END THIS.

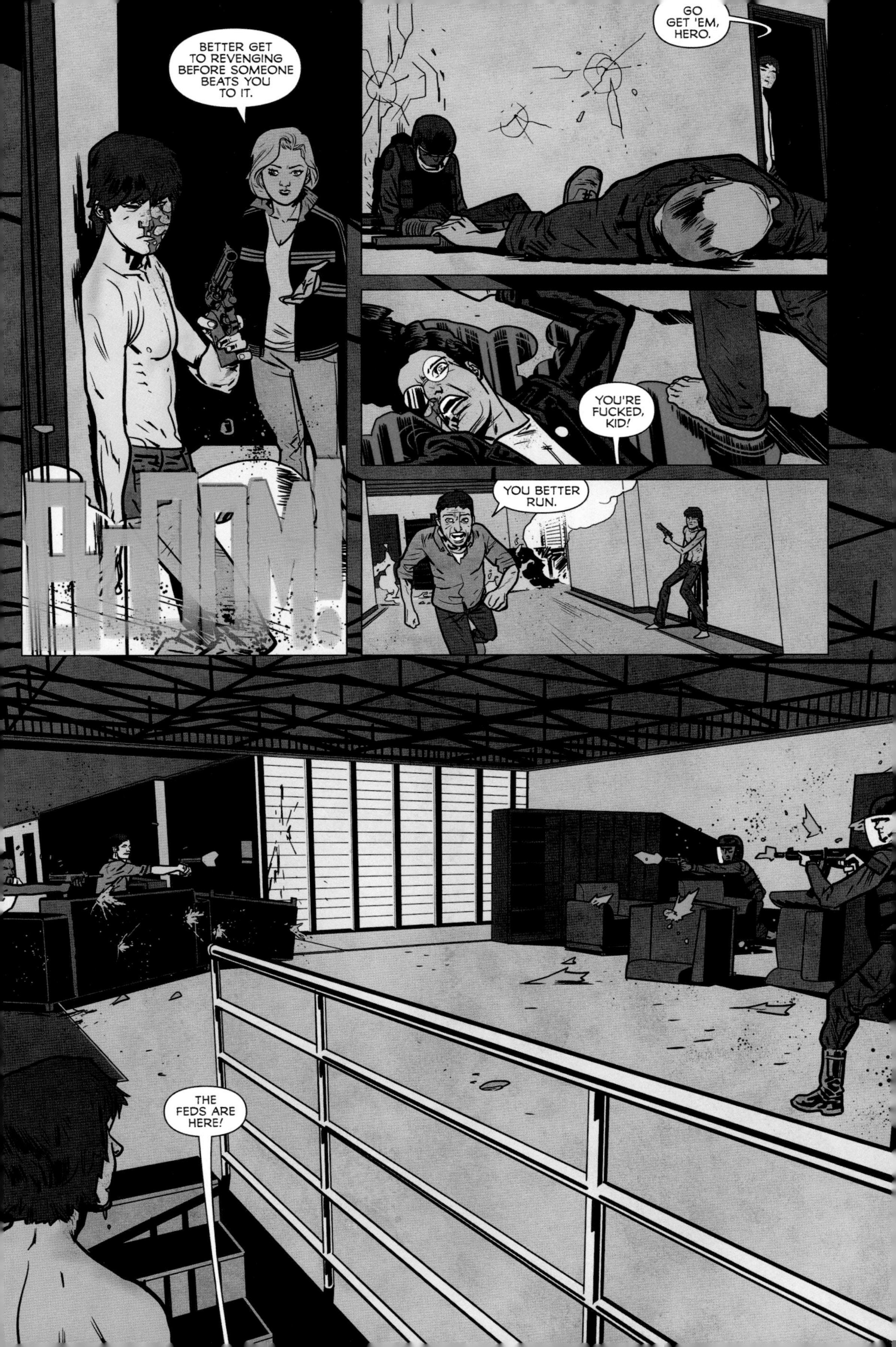
BETTER GET TO REVENGING BEFORE SOMEONE BEATS YOU TO IT.
GO GET 'EM, HERO.
YOU'RE FUCKED, KID!
YOU BETTER RUN.
THE FEDS ARE HERE!

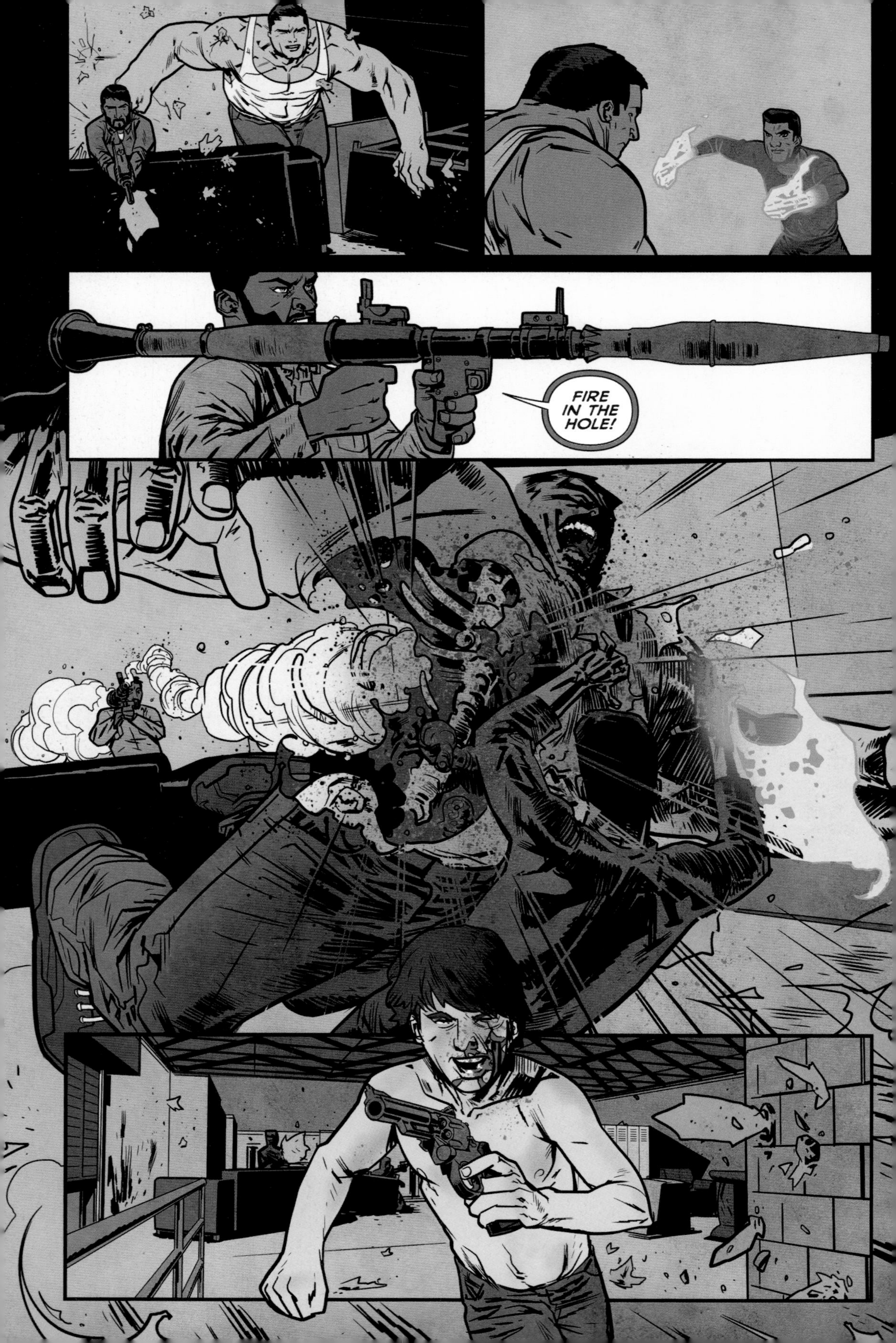
FIRE IN THE HOLE!

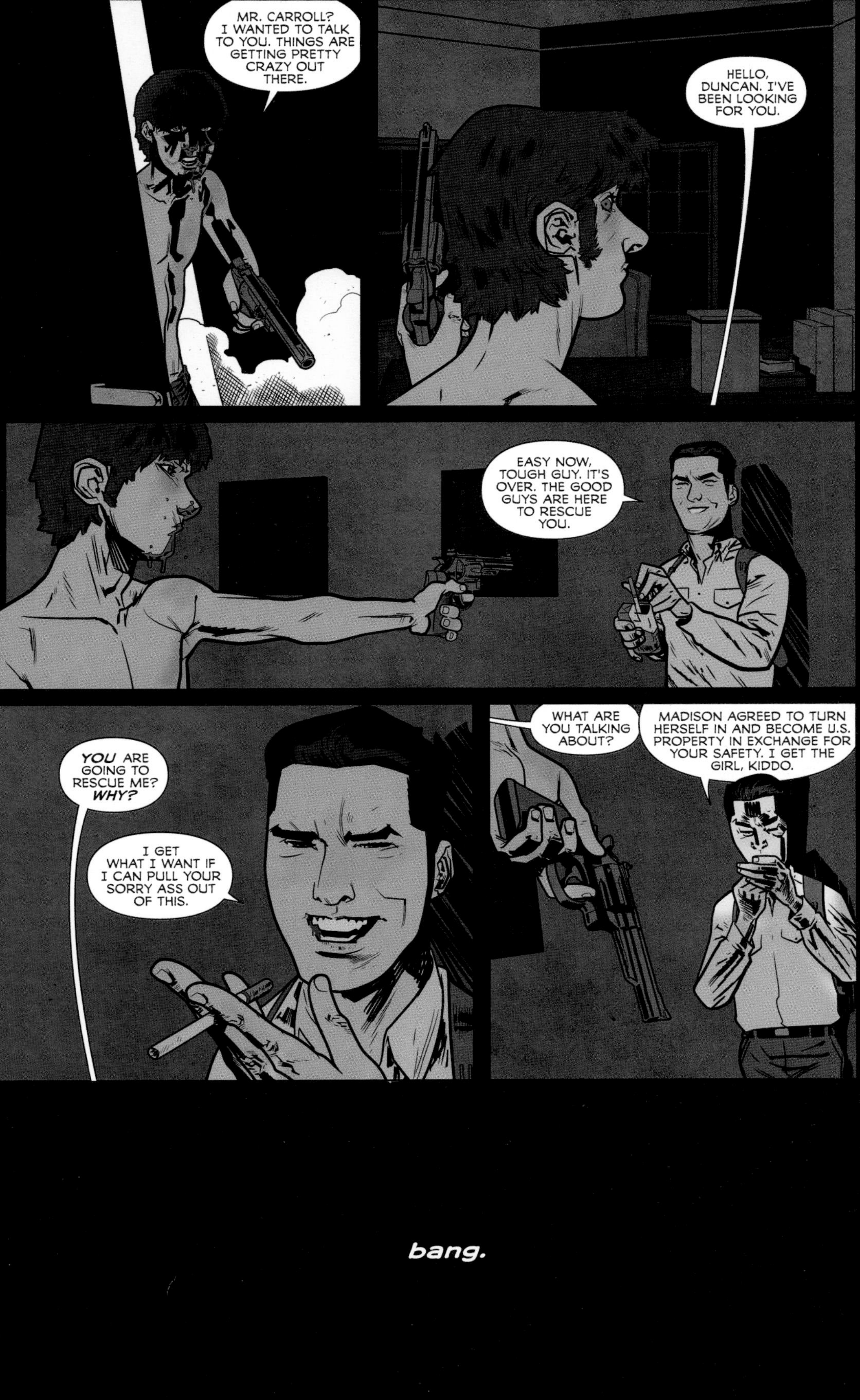
MR. CARROLL? I WANTED TO TALK TO YOU. THINGS ARE GETTING PRETTY CRAZY OUT THERE.
HELLO, DUNCAN. I'VE BEEN LOOKING FOR YOU.
EASY NOW, TOUGH GUY. IT'S OVER. THE GOOD GUYS ARE HERE TO RESCUE YOU.
YOU ARE GOING TO RESCUE ME? *WHY?*
I GET WHAT I WANT IF I CAN PULL YOUR SORRY ASS OUT OF THIS.
WHAT ARE YOU TALKING ABOUT?
MADISON AGREED TO TURN HERSELF IN AND BECOME U.S. PROPERTY IN EXCHANGE FOR YOUR SAFETY. I GET THE GIRL, KIDDO.
bang.

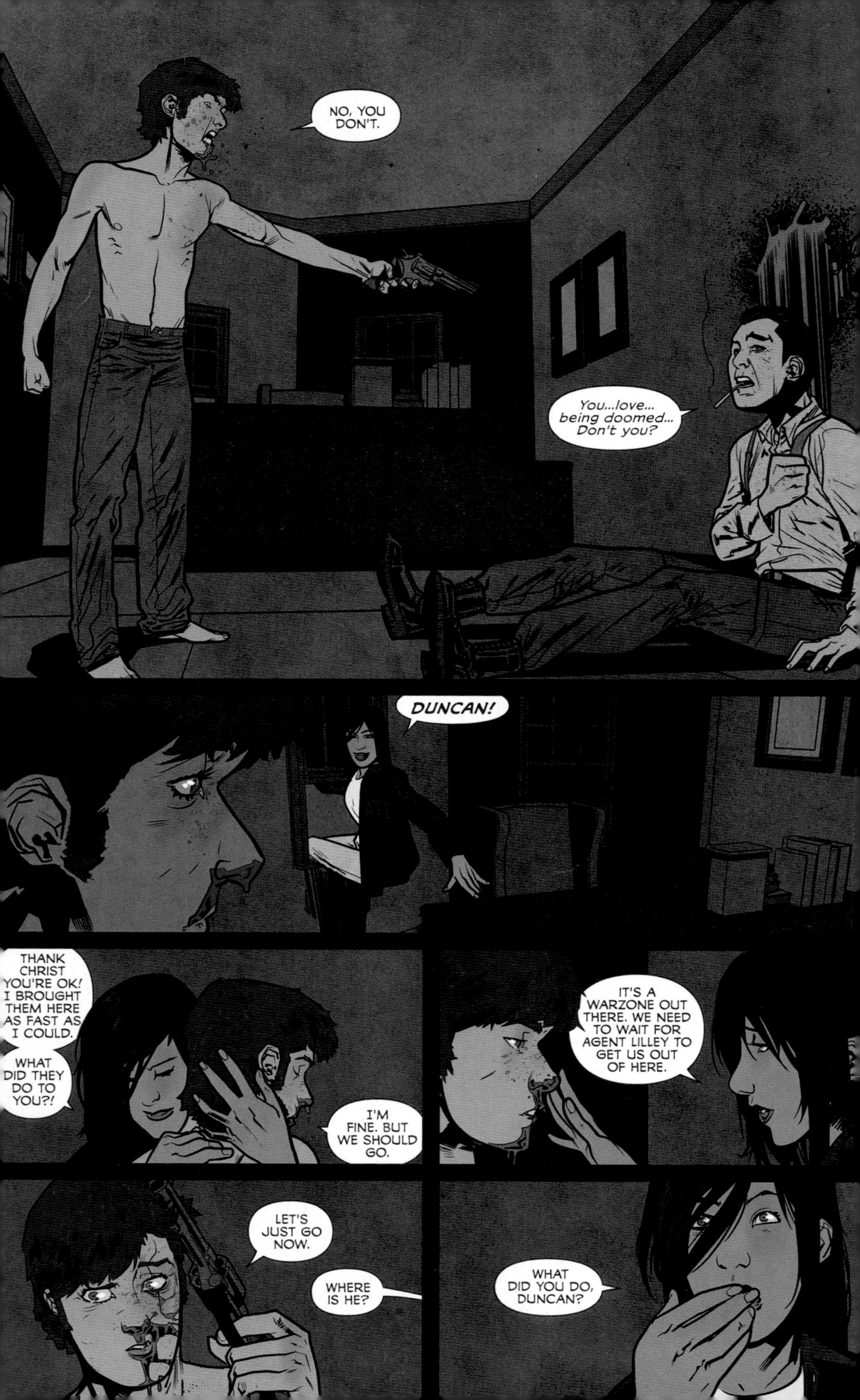
NO, YOU DON'T.
You...love... being doomed... Don't you?
DUNCAN!
THANK CHRIST YOU'RE OK! I BROUGHT THEM HERE AS FAST AS I COULD.
WHAT DID THEY DO TO YOU?!
I'M FINE. BUT WE SHOULD GO.
IT'S A WARZONE OUT THERE. WE NEED TO WAIT FOR AGENT LILLEY TO GET US OUT OF HERE.
LET'S JUST GO NOW.
WHERE IS HE?
WHAT DID YOU DO, DUNCAN?

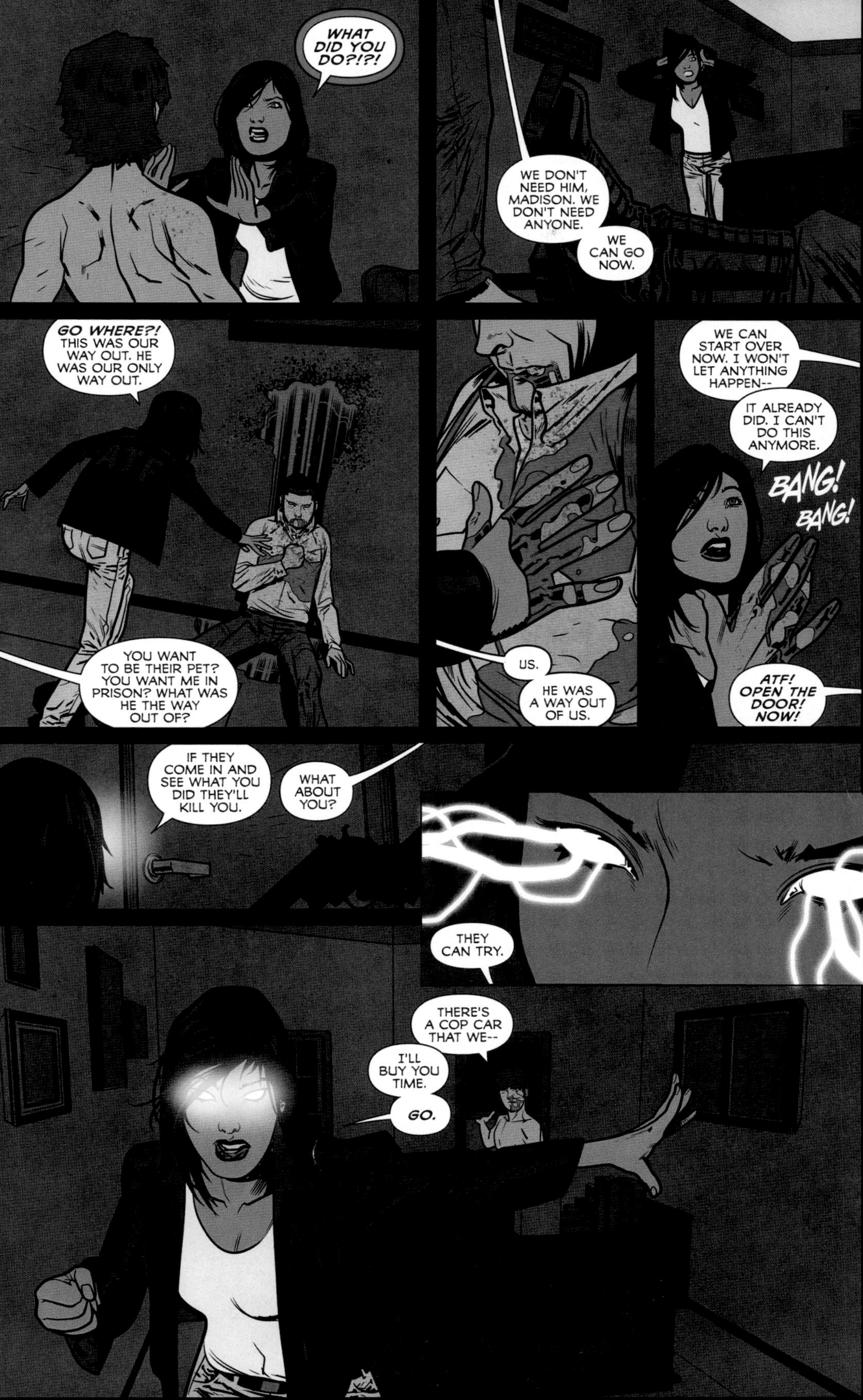
WHAT DID YOU DO?!?!
WE DON'T NEED HIM, MADISON. WE DON'T NEED ANYONE.
WE CAN GO NOW.
GO WHERE?! THIS WAS OUR WAY OUT. HE WAS OUR ONLY WAY OUT.
YOU WANT TO BE THEIR PET? YOU WANT ME IN PRISON? WHAT WAS HE THE WAY OUT OF?
US.
HE WAS A WAY OUT OF US.
WE CAN START OVER NOW. I WON'T LET ANYTHING HAPPEN--
IT ALREADY DID. I CAN'T DO THIS ANYMORE.
BANG!
BANG!
ATF! OPEN THE DOOR! NOW!
IF THEY COME IN AND SEE WHAT YOU DID THEY'LL KILL YOU.
WHAT ABOUT YOU?
THEY CAN TRY.
THERE'S A COP CAR THAT WE--
I'LL BUY YOU TIME.
GO.

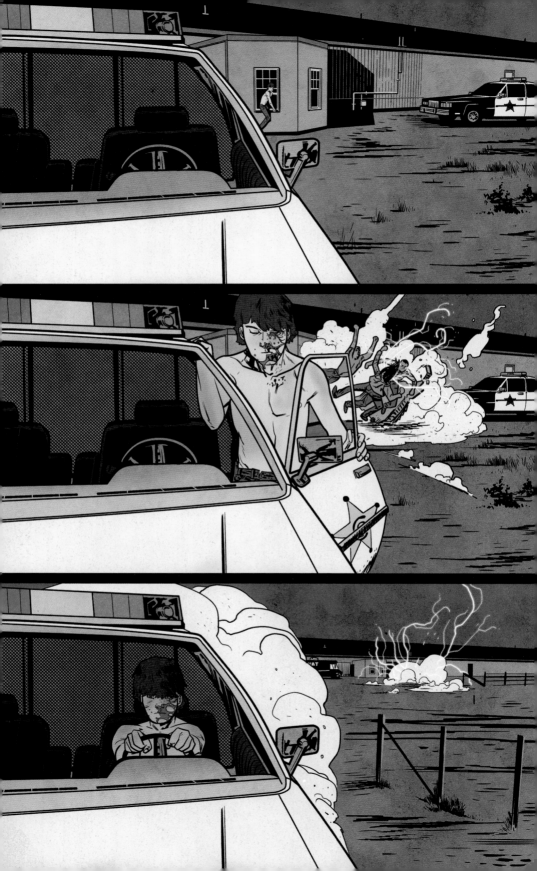

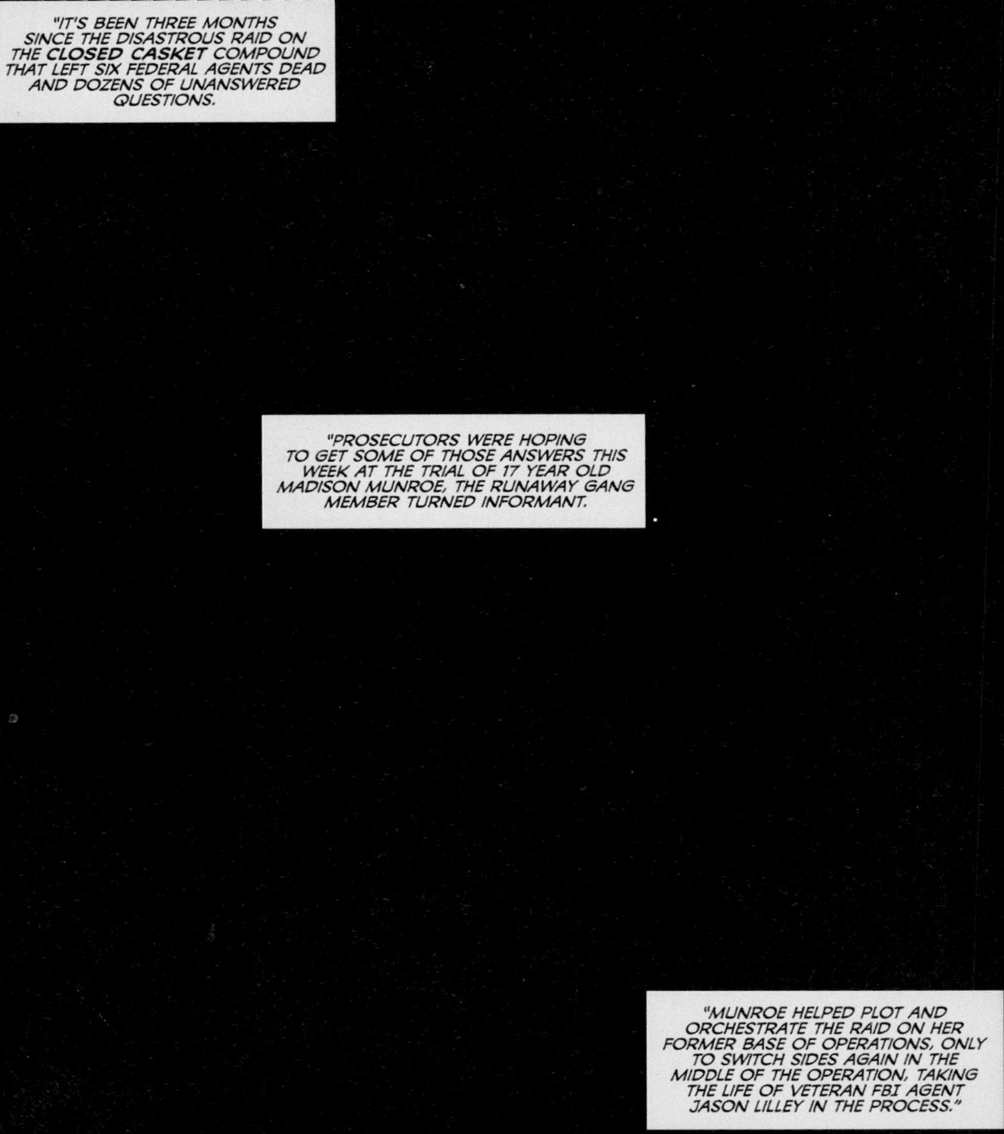
"IT'S BEEN THREE MONTHS SINCE THE DISASTROUS RAID ON THE **CLOSED CASKET** COMPOUND THAT LEFT SIX FEDERAL AGENTS DEAD AND DOZENS OF UNANSWERED QUESTIONS.
"PROSECUTORS WERE HOPING TO GET SOME OF THOSE ANSWERS THIS WEEK AT THE TRIAL OF 17 YEAR OLD MADISON MUNROE, THE RUNAWAY GANG MEMBER TURNED INFORMANT.
"MUNROE HELPED PLOT AND ORCHESTRATE THE RAID ON HER FORMER BASE OF OPERATIONS, ONLY TO SWITCH SIDES AGAIN IN THE MIDDLE OF THE OPERATION, TAKING THE LIFE OF VETERAN FBI AGENT JASON LILLEY IN THE PROCESS."

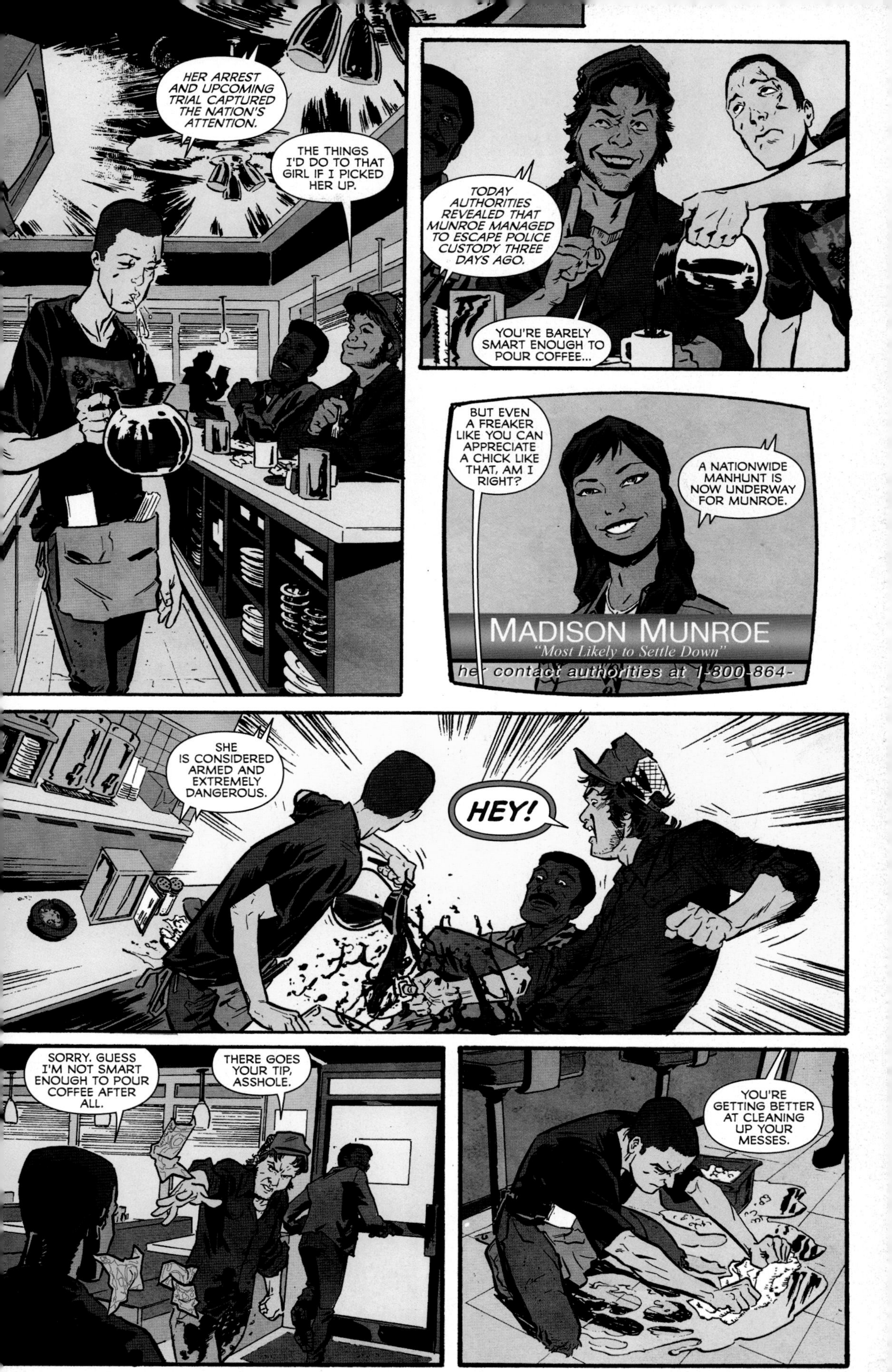
HER ARREST AND UPCOMING TRIAL CAPTURED THE NATION'S ATTENTION.
THE THINGS I'D DO TO THAT GIRL IF I PICKED HER UP.
TODAY AUTHORITIES REVEALED THAT MUNROE MANAGED TO ESCAPE POLICE CUSTODY THREE DAYS AGO.
YOU'RE BARELY SMART ENOUGH TO POUR COFFEE...
BUT EVEN A FREAKER LIKE YOU CAN APPRECIATE A CHICK LIKE THAT, AM I RIGHT?
A NATIONWIDE MANHUNT IS NOW UNDERWAY FOR MUNROE.
MADISON MUNROE
"Most Likely to Settle Down"
contact authorities at 1-800-864-
SHE IS CONSIDERED ARMED AND EXTREMELY DANGEROUS.
HEY!
SORRY. GUESS I'M NOT SMART ENOUGH TO POUR COFFEE AFTER ALL.
THERE GOES YOUR TIP, ASSHOLE.
YOU'RE GETTING BETTER AT CLEANING UP YOUR MESSES.

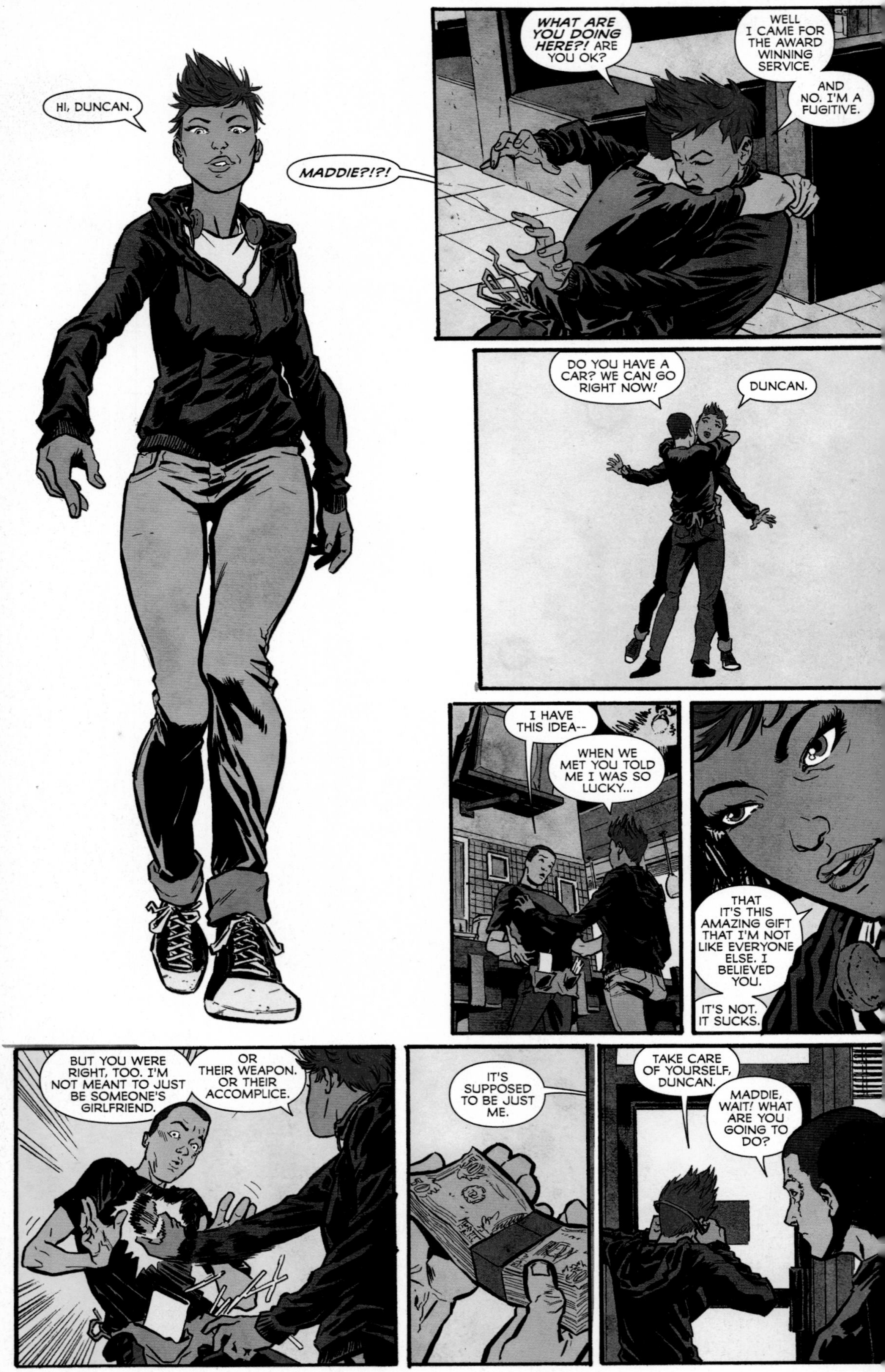
HI, DUNCAN.
MADDIE?!?!
WHAT ARE YOU DOING HERE?! ARE YOU OK?
WELL I CAME FOR THE AWARD WINNING SERVICE.
AND NO. I'M A FUGITIVE.
DO YOU HAVE A CAR? WE CAN GO RIGHT NOW!
DUNCAN.
I HAVE THIS IDEA--
WHEN WE MET YOU TOLD ME I WAS SO LUCKY...
THAT IT'S THIS AMAZING GIFT THAT I'M NOT LIKE EVERYONE ELSE. I BELIEVED YOU.
IT'S NOT. IT SUCKS.
BUT YOU WERE RIGHT, TOO. I'M NOT MEANT TO JUST BE SOMEONE'S GIRLFRIEND.
OR THEIR WEAPON. OR THEIR ACCOMPLICE.
IT'S SUPPOSED TO BE JUST ME.
TAKE CARE OF YOURSELF, DUNCAN.
MADDIE, WAIT! WHAT ARE YOU GOING TO DO?

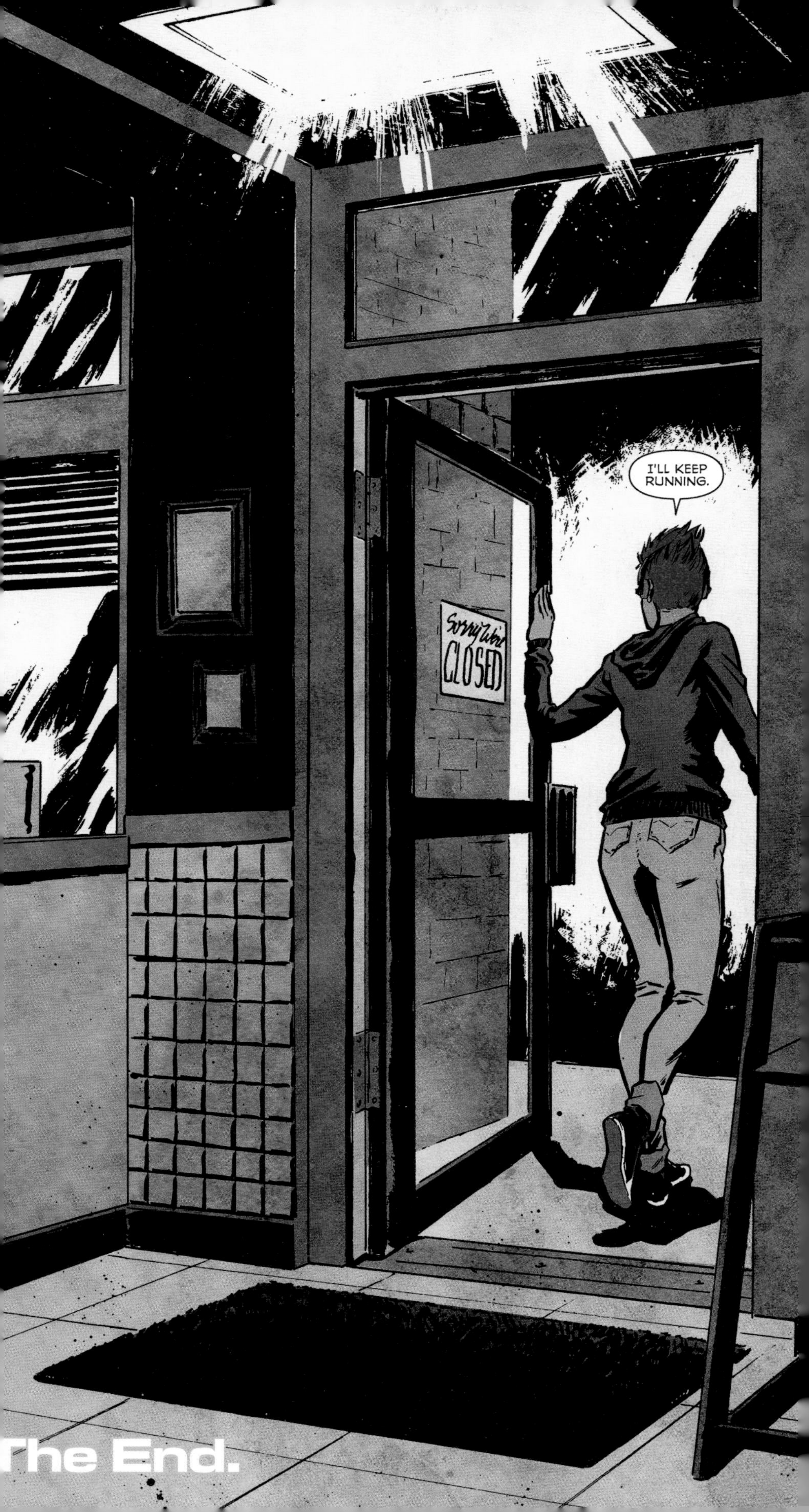
I'LL KEEP RUNNING.
CLOSED
The End.

Well...

That was kind of a bummer. But you sort of knew it would be, didn't you? Thanks for sticking with us up to here. Or, if you just skipped ahead, thanks for being an impatient weirdo. The world needs those too. You should probably go back and read the actual story at some point though.

When we started putting this collection together we thought it would be a good idea to write something at the end to address you, the reader, directly. We wanted to discuss some of the heavy ideas in this book, and we will later. But, separate from that, we wanted to talk about the making of the book you are holding in your hands. Not in terms of writing or art, but in terms of where a book like this actually comes from. It is far more than just the people listed on the credits page. This is our very long "thank you" section.

To start, we would all be dead long ago without the love and support of our families and loved ones. Thanks for keeping us alive through this process.

A huge thank you to the comic shop owners and staff who supported us and this book. For any shop or staff to look at the wall of amazing comics that comes out each week and find our book worth supporting means a great deal to us all. The same goes for book shops and librar- ies now too. Did you get this book out of a library? That's so fucking cool. Please thank your librarian for us.

Thanks also go to the many press folks, critics, bloggers, podcasters, and message board posters who have supported this book. In many ways it's a very small book and we definitely would not have been able to find our audience without your support.

We wouldn't be doing this without the comics community, so thanks to all of the comic artists, writers, inkers, colorists, flatters, letterers, designers, and editors who make work that inspires and excites us. We're proud to be a part of this with you.

We keep saying this book would not exist without various people but that is especially true of Black Mask Studios. Our heartfelt thanks to Brett, Steve, Matt, and everyone at Black Mask for their support. They consistently went above and beyond for us. Sorry we were so difficult and wanted to do so much stupid shit.

And finally you- the readers. We worked really hard to make something that was personal to us, to tell a story we wanted to tell. The fact that our weird, misfit, coming of age story con- nected with any of you is amazing. You took the time to find our book, tell your friends about it, ask your local shop for it, or post about it online. That's more than any of us could have hoped. We are humbled and overwhelmed by all of you who cosplay our characters, draw fan art, make mixtapes, collect multiple covers, or just simply like reading it. Thank you.

-We Can Never Go Home was Tyler Boss, Jim Campbell, Matt Harding, Josh Hood, David C. Hopkins, Patrick Kindlon, Vincent Kukua, Brian Level, Matthew Rosenberg, Amanda Scurti, Philip W. Smith II, Dylan Todd, Michael Walsh, Taylor Cabaniss, Ryan Ferrier, Amancay Nahuel- pan, Hana Nakamura, Orlando Perez, Ramon Villalobos, & Alexis Ziritt. Fuck Rex Banner.

TABLE OF CONTENTS

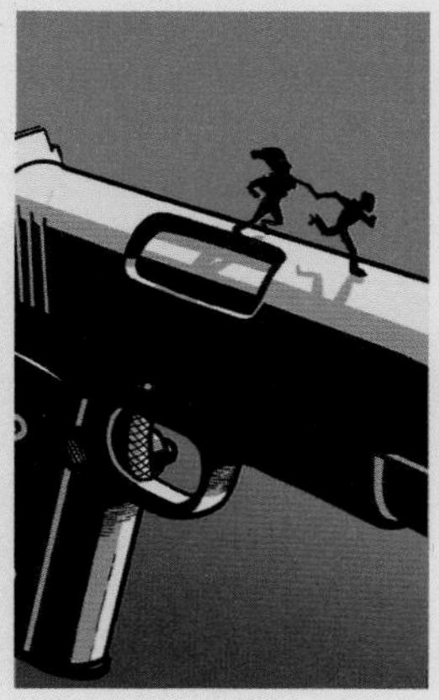

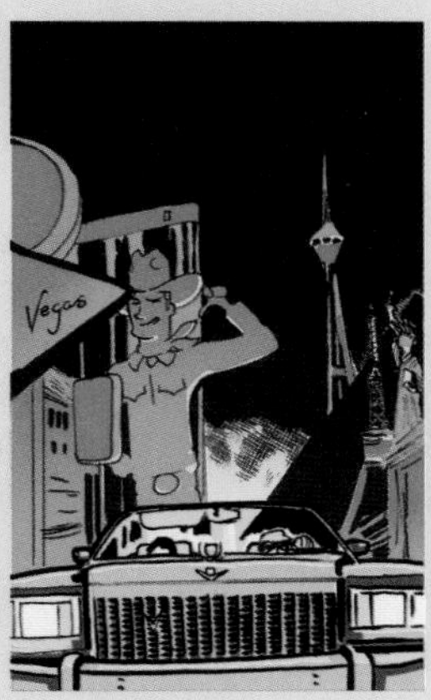
Vegas

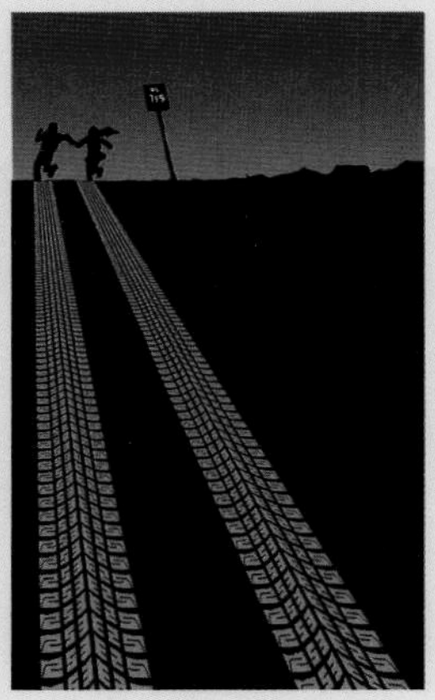

SOME THOUGHTS ON SELLING VIOLENCE AS ENTERTAINMENT.

The book in your hands is about violence. It is about other things as well-- friendship, adolescent fantasies, love, aimlessness, growing up, fitting in, bullying, betrayal, finding the right costumes, and mixtapes-- but violence is a key component. We try to handle violence and its repercussions in a thoughtful manner that conveys both its randomness and its destructiveness. That doesn't change the fact that we are telling a story where our main characters are both victims and perpetrators of violence. That should be a heavy burden. The problem is, too often, it isn't.

So many stories use violence in ways that I find distastefully casual. They make it seem fun, or easy, or unimportant. I am sure some people will feel that's true of this book, too. With We Can Never Go Home I really wanted to make it clear how this violence affects Duncan and Madison. It is brutal, intense, sudden, and life ruining. Every punch thrown and every pulled trigger has ramifications. Even with that I wonder if we did enough. That is the difficulty, isn't it?

Making art of any kind is really just starting a conversation and then walking away from it. We put our characters and ideas into the world but we don't raise them. We don't get to defend them or explain them... But now I'm going to try to do that anyway. Maybe it's my conscience. Maybe it's self doubt. But I need this to be clear. Madison and Duncan do not make good choices. It does not go well. This book is not a celebration of them.

Every time we put out a new issue of this book, it became harder and harder to talk about our "fun little story" about kids and guns, because real people in the real world were shot for real. People are shot all the time-- by criminals, by cops, by soldiers, by the mentally ill, by bigots, by zealots, by strangers, by boyfriends and husbands, and by themselves. It can be overwhelming to think about for more than a moment, but please do it. Right now. I'll wait.

Want some facts? Too bad.

-An average of 87 Americans are killed by gun violence every day.*

-Since the Sandy Hook massacre on 12/14/2012, there have been 153 shootings on school campuses in the U.S.**

-Since 9/11/2001, 76 Americans have been killed by terrorists in this country.*** Meanwhile, from 2001 to 2013 (the last year data was available), 406,496 Americans have died from gun violence in this country.****

-As many as 10,000,000 children in the U.S. witness domestic violence in their homes every year.*****

-There are approximately 1,700,000 homeless youth in America in any given year. 46% of homeless youth escaped a home where they suffered physical abuse.******

By the time this book sees print, these numbers will be tragically out of date.

So what can I (or you) do about all this? I write books with pictures in them. I have no idea what you do. Lucky for us there are people on the frontlines, fighting to stop gun violence, fighting to stop domestic violence, trying to help the homeless, trying to help victims of violent crime. Throughout the production of this book, we have donated some money from sales to various organizations that work on these causes. I urge you to check out some of the organizations listed below and see if you can donate some dollars or some hours to help them as well. But those are just some of the groups that I like. Please do research and find your own if that interests you.

Thank you so much for reading this.
-Matthew

-The Coalition To Stop Gun Violence is a non-profit that attempts to end gun violence through research, strategic engagement, and effective policy advocacy.
CSGV.org

-Incite! is a national activist organization of radical feminists of color advancing a movement to end violence against women of color and our communities.
incite-national.org

-National Coalition Against Domestic Violence believes that violence against women and children results from the abuse of power on all scales, from intimate relationships to societal issues like sexism, racism, and homophobia. NCADV advocates for societal changes to eliminate both personal and social violence for all people.
NCADV.org

-The Ali Forney Center's mission is to protect LGBTQ youths from the harms of homelessness and empower them with the tools needed to live independently. Aliforneycenter.org

*csgv.org
**Everytownsearch.org
***NewAmerica.net
****CDC.gov
*****thecenteronline.org
******Safe HorSafeHorizon.org

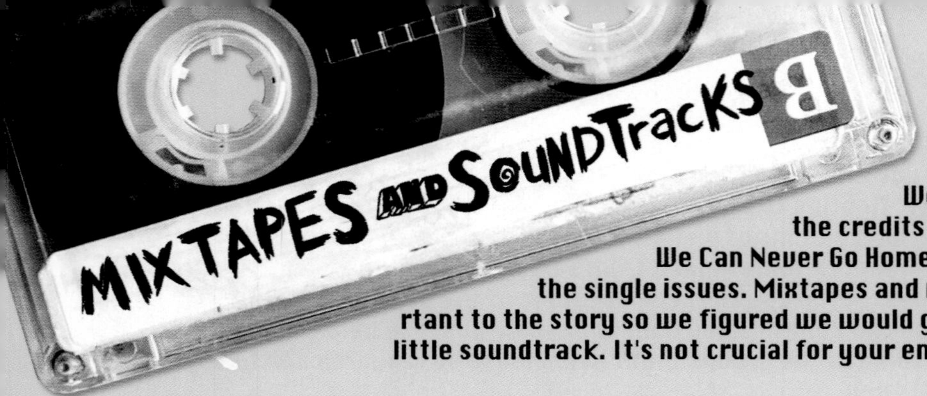
MIXTAPES AND SOUNDTracKS
B

We hid a small playlist in the credits page of every issue of We Can Never Go Home for those folks buying the single issues. Mixtapes and music are pretty important to the story so we figured we would give each issue its own little soundtrack. It's not crucial for your enjoyment of the books, but it can't hurt.

You can listen to them all on Spotify (if that still exists when you read this)
https://open.spotify.com/user/ashcanpress

Or you can go out and buy the records from all these awesome bands, give them some money, and make the mixtapes yourself. That's the best option. Support good music.

Below are the playlists for all 5 issues.

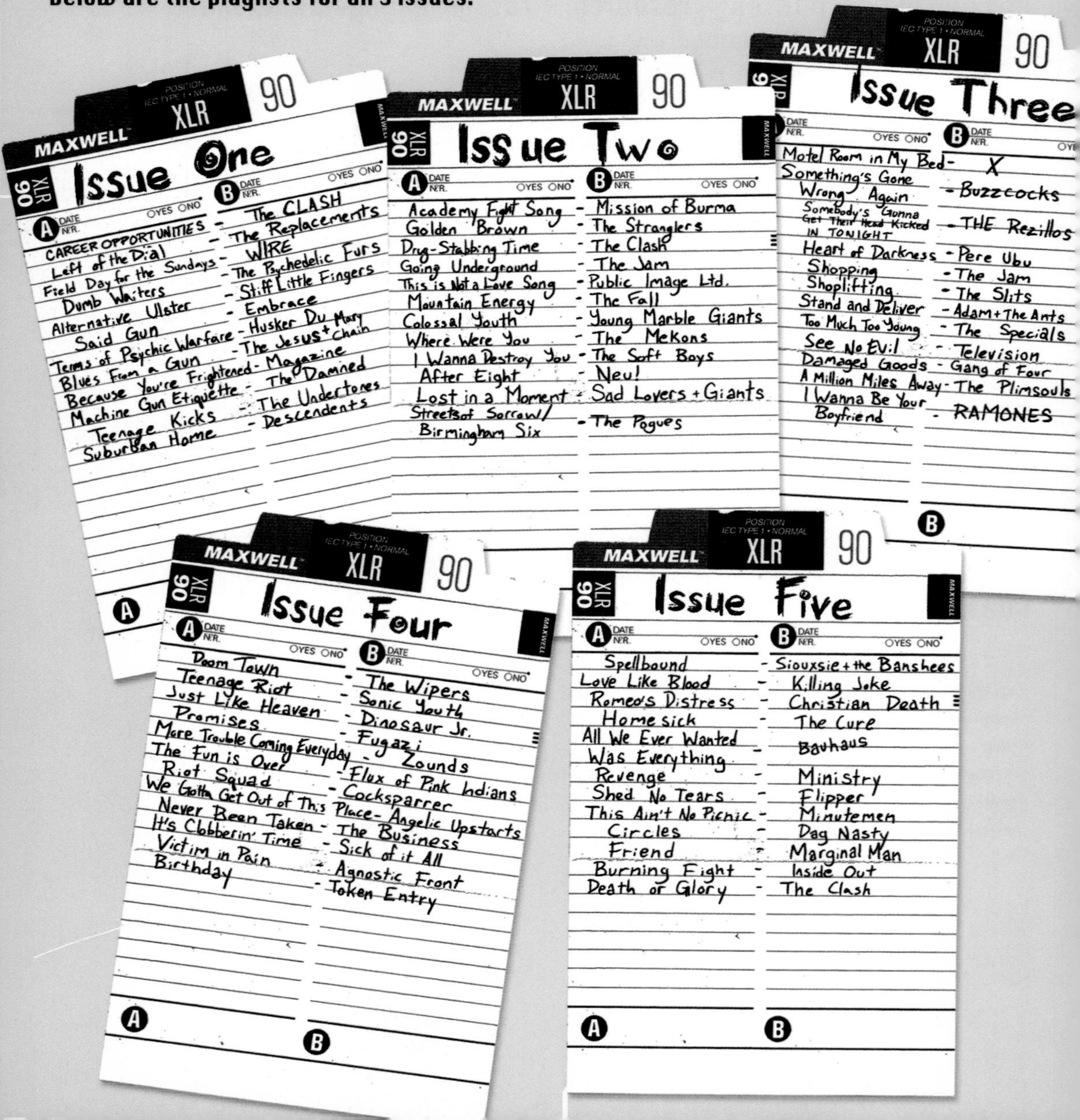
Issue One
CAREER OPPORTUNITIES - The CLASH
Left of the Dial - The Replacements
Field Day for the Sundays - WIRE
Dumb Waiters - The Psychedelic Furs
Alternative Ulster - Stiff Little Fingers
Said Gun - Embrace
Terms of Psychic Warfare - Husker Du
Blues From a Gun - The Jesus + Mary Chain
Because You're Frightened - Magazine
Machine Gun Etiquette - The Damned
Teenage Kicks - The Undertones
Suburban Home - Descendents
Issue Two
Academy Fight Song - Mission of Burma
Golden Brown - The Stranglers
Drug-Stabbing Time - The Clash
Going Underground - The Jam
This is Not a Love Song - Public Image Ltd.
Mountain Energy - The Fall
Colossal Youth - Young Marble Giants
Where Were You - The Mekons
I Wanna Destroy You - The Soft Boys
After Eight - Neu!
Lost in a Moment - Sad Lovers + Giants
Streets of Sorrow/ Birmingham Six - The Pogues
Issue Three
Motel Room in My Bed - X
Something's Gone Wrong Again - Buzzcocks
Somebody's Gonna Get Their Head Kicked IN TONIGHT - THE Rezillos
Heart of Darkness - Pere Ubu
Shopping - The Jam
Shoplifting - The Slits
Stand and Deliver - Adam + The Ants
Too Much Too Young - The Specials
See No Evil - Television
Damaged Goods - Gang of Four
A Million Miles Away - The Plimsouls
I Wanna Be Your Boyfriend - RAMONES
Issue Four
Doom Town - The Wipers
Teenage Riot - Sonic Youth
Just Like Heaven - Dinosaur Jr.
Promises - Fugazi
More Trouble Coming Everyday - Zounds
The Fun is Over - Flux of Pink Indians
Riot Squad - Cocksparrer
We Gotta Get Out of This Place - Angelic Upstarts
Never Been Taken - The Business
It's Clobberin' Time - Sick of it All
Victim in Pain - Agnostic Front
Birthday - Token Entry
Issue Five
Spellbound - Siouxsie + the Banshees
Love Like Blood - Killing Joke
Romeo's Distress - Christian Death
Homesick - The Cure
All We Ever Wanted Was Everything - Bauhaus
Revenge - Ministry
Shed No Tears - Flipper
This Ain't No Picnic - Minutemen
Circles - Dag Nasty
Friend - Marginal Man
Burning Fight - Inside Out
Death or Glory - The Clash

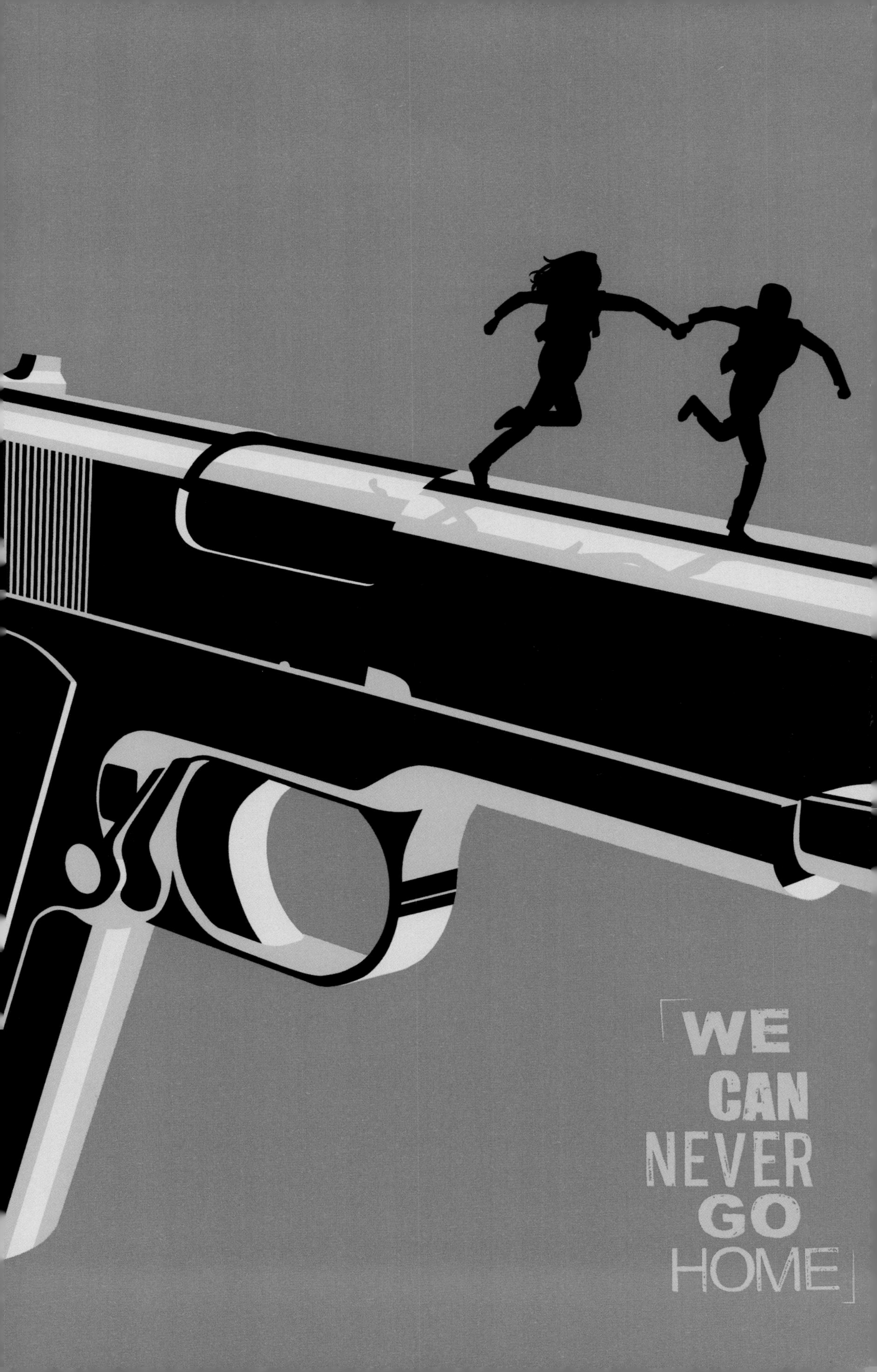
WE
CAN
NEVER
GO
HOME

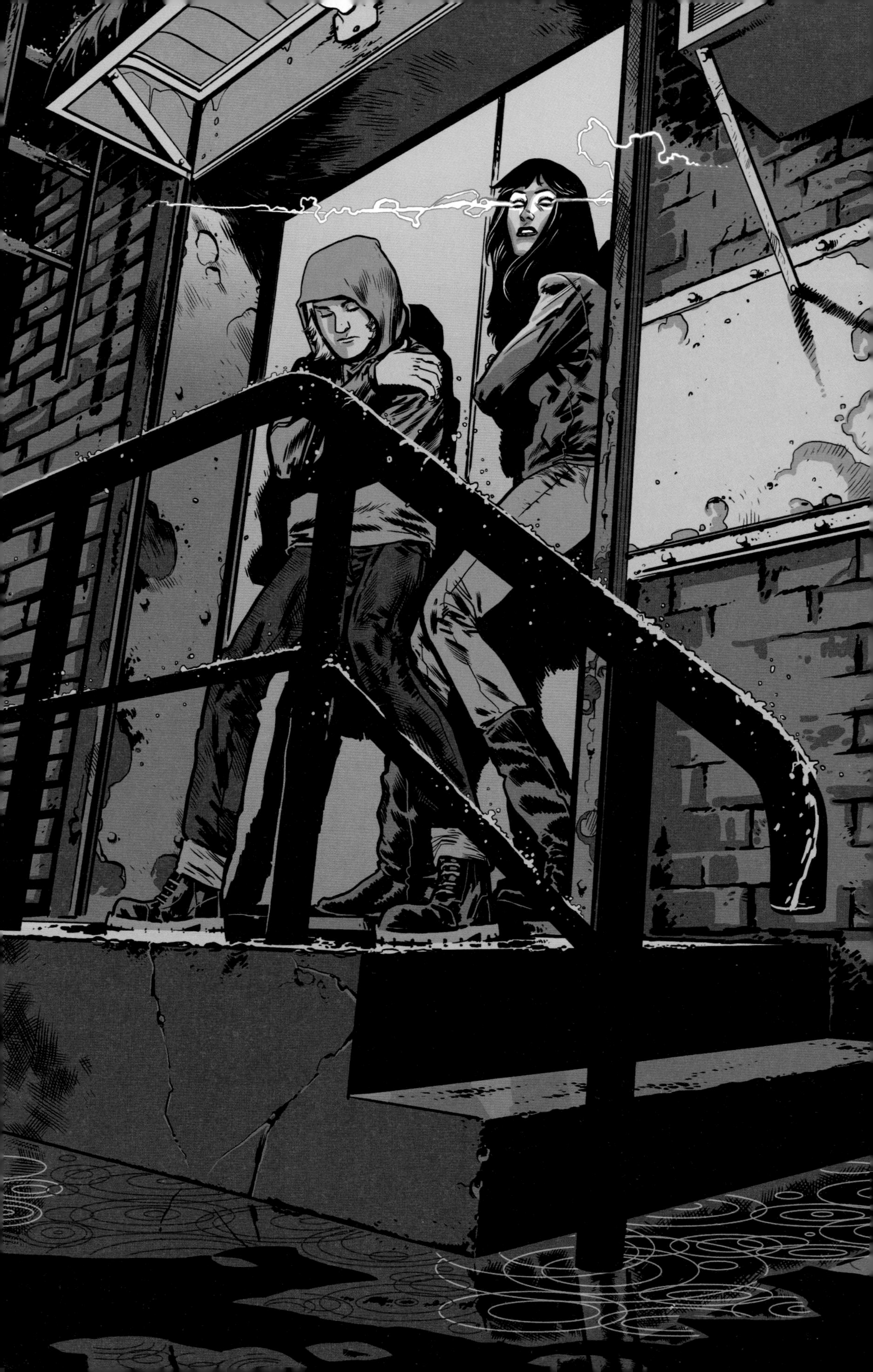

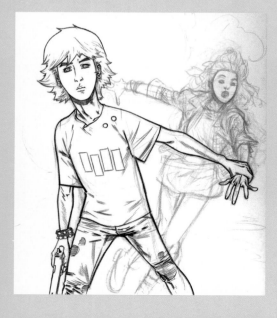

COVER GALLERY
This book had a lot of covers. Here they are.

age 140. Issue 1 cover by Michael Walsh.

age 141. Issue 2 cover by Michael Walsh.

age 142. Issue 3 cover by Michael Walsh.

age 143. Issue 4 cover by Michael Walsh.

age 144. Issue 5 cover by Michael Walsh.

age 145. Issue 1 cover by David Murdoch.

age 146. Issue 1 cover by Hana Nakamura & Josh Hood.

age 147. Issue 1 Baltimore Comic Con exclusive by Tyler Boss.

age 148. Issue 1 San Diego Comic Con exclusive by Alexis Ziritt.

age 149. Issue 1 cover for Larry's Comics by Rex Banner. Issue 1 super rare cover. Issue 1 over for the Phantom Comics network by Rex Banner. Issue 1 super rare cover.

age 150. Issue 1 cover for Third Eye Comics by Rex Banner. Issue 2 cover for Third Eye Comics y Rex Banner. Issue 1 cover for Beach Ball comics by Rex Banner. Issue 1 Emerald City Comic on exclusive cover by Rex Banner.

age 151. Issue 3 cover for Third Eye Comics by Taylor Cabaniss. Issue 1 cover for Ssalefish omics by Taylor Cabaniss. Issue 1 cover for Eh! Comics network by Rex Banner. Cover for For-idden Planet London by Tyler Boss.

age 152. Issues 1-3 covers for Books-A-Million / 2nd & Charles by Rex Banner. Issue 1 New ork Comic Con exclusive by Ramon Villalobos.

age 153. Issues 2-5 New York Comic Con exclusives by Ramon Villalobos.

age 154. Issues 1-3 connecting covers for Rick's Comic City by Amancay Nahuelpan.

age 155. Issues 1-3 connecting covers for Jetpack Comics / Forbidden Planet by Amancay ahuelpan.

age 156. Issue 1 2nd print cover by Josh Hood. Issue 1 cover for Forbidden Planet London & etpack Comics. Issue 1 Hot Topic cover by Dylan Todd. Issue 1 LCSD Exclusive Black Mask Box et cover by Amancay Nahuelpan.

ages 157. Issue 1 3rd print wraparound cover by Tyler Boss. Issue 2 2nd print wraparound over by Tyler Boss.

age 158. Issue 3 2nd print wraparound cover by Tyler Boss. Mixtape by Dylan Todd featuring rt from Michael Walsh & Tyler Boss.

ind all of these awesome folks here-
lichael Walsh- www.misterwalsh.tumblr.com
avid Murdoch- www.davidmurdoch-art.blogspot.com
ana Nakamura- www.mycoa.com
yler Boss- www.tylerboss.com
lexis Ziritt- www.aziritt.com
mancay Nahuelpan- www.annbonline.com
amon Villalobos- www.ramonvillalobos.tumblr.com
ylan Todd- www.bigredrobot.net
aylor Cabaniss- www.cargocollective.com/taylorcabaniss

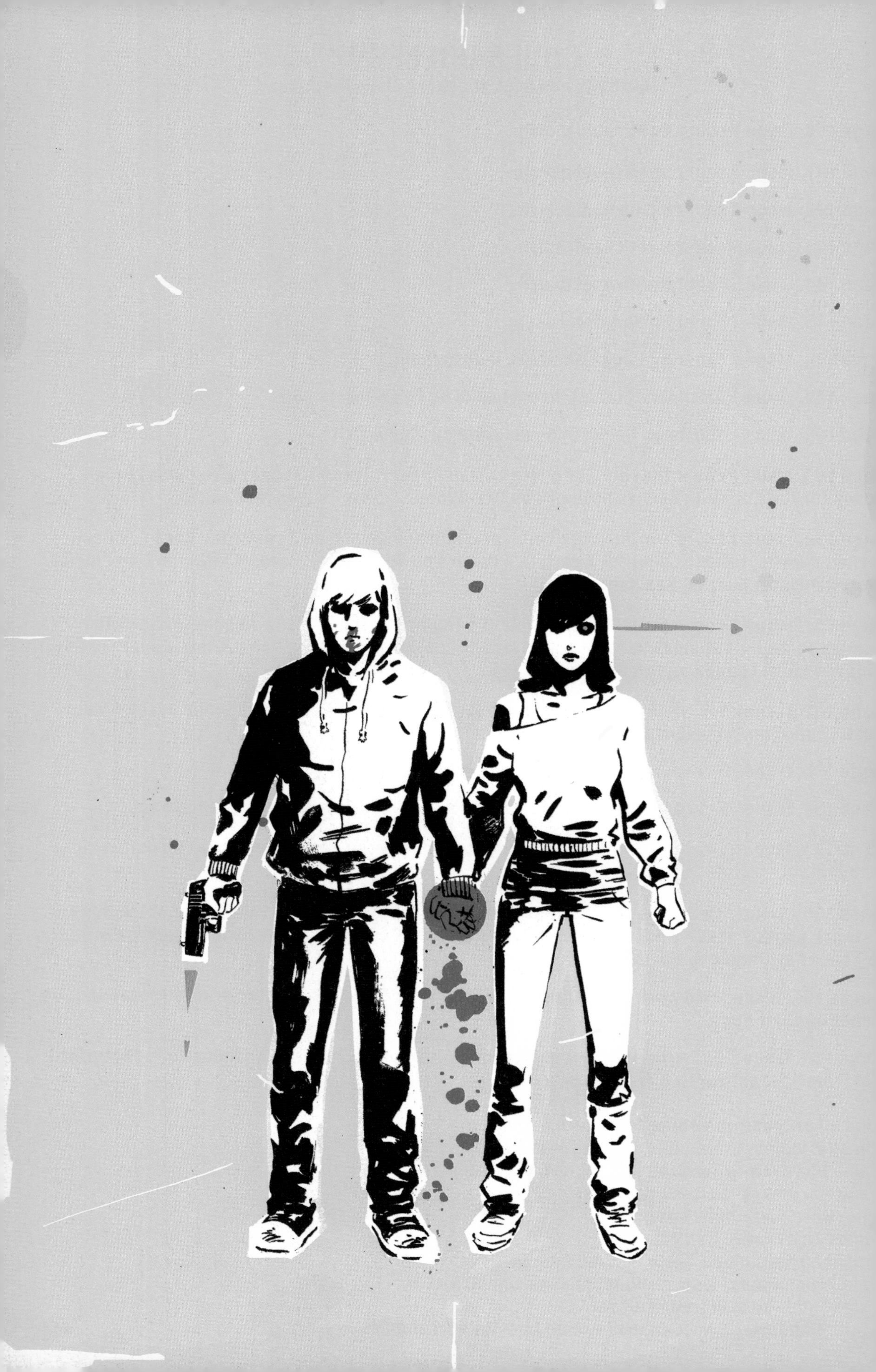

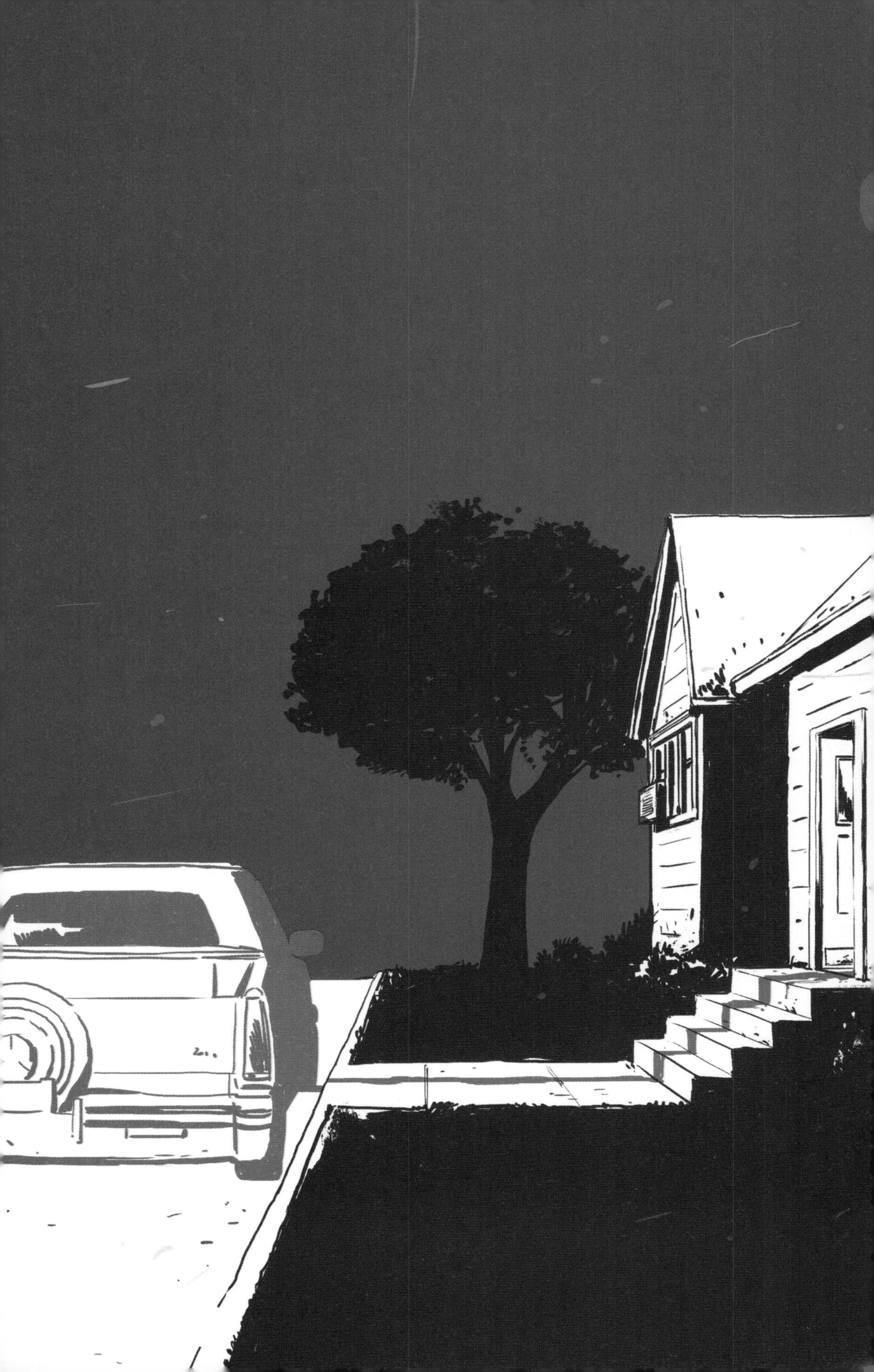

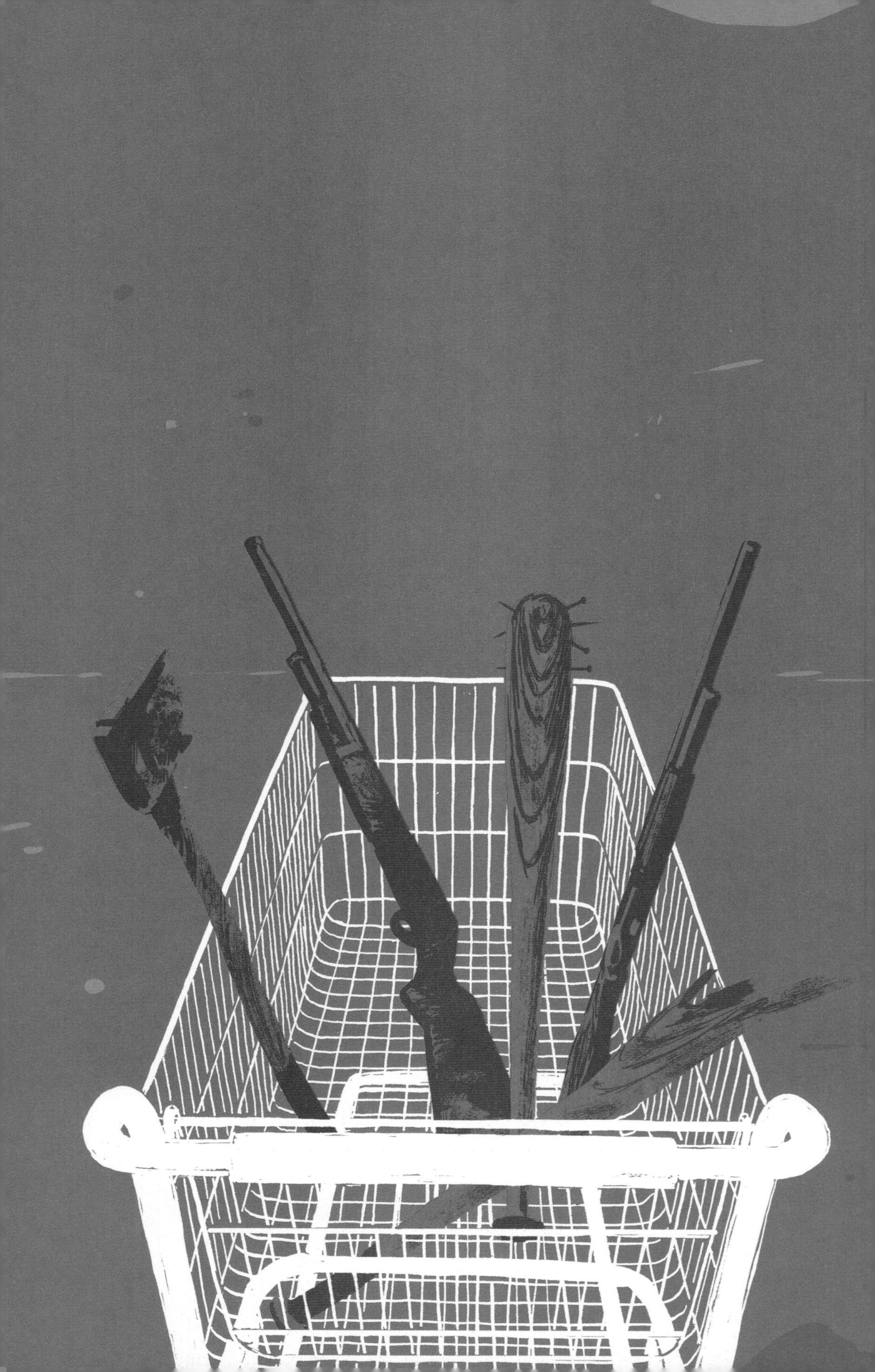

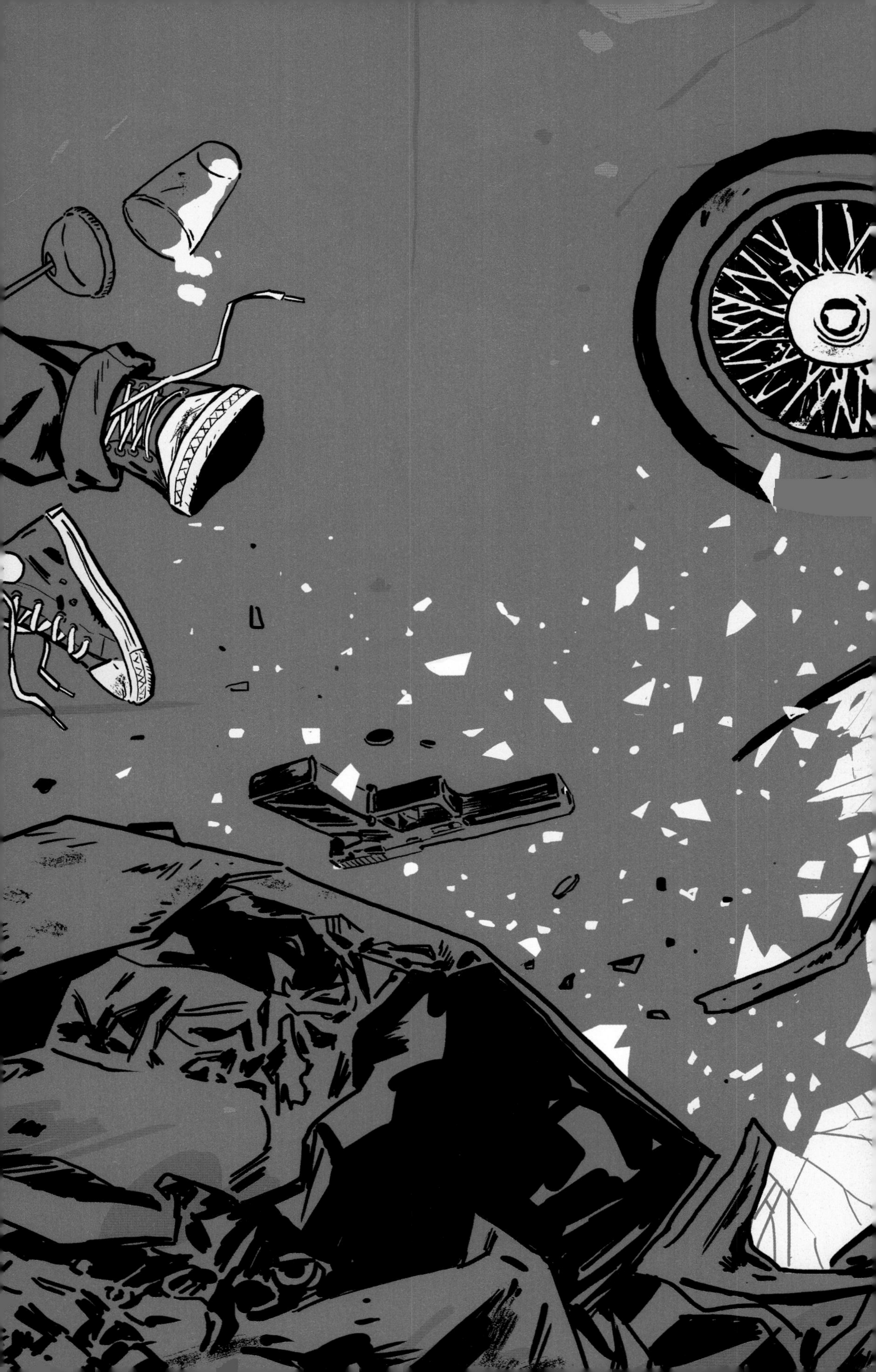

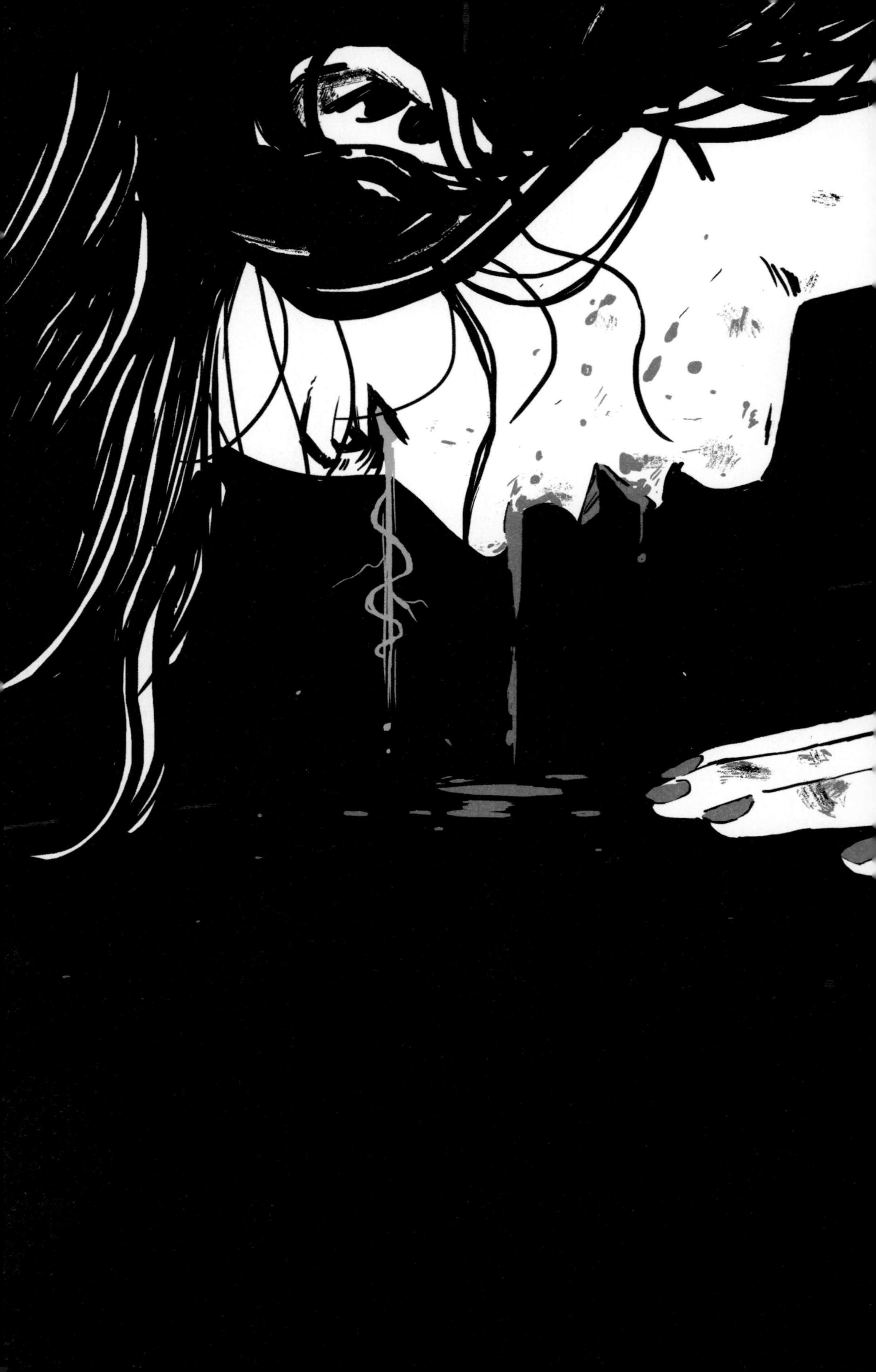

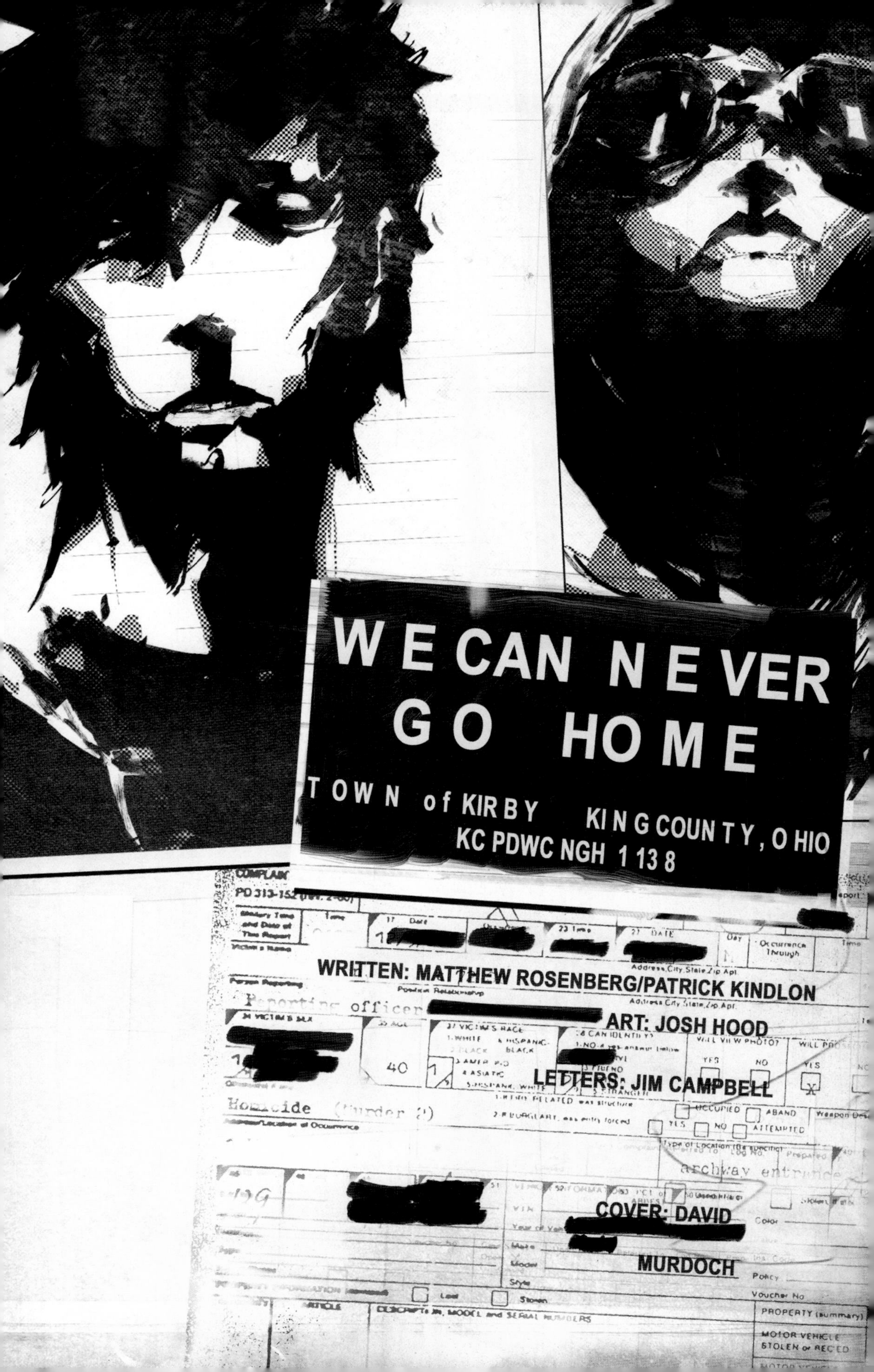
WE CAN NEVER GO HOME
TOWN of KIRBY KING COUNTY, OHIO
KC PDWC NGH 1138
WRITTEN: MATTHEW ROSENBERG/PATRICK KINDLON
ART: JOSH HOOD
LETTERS: JIM CAMPBELL
COVER: DAVID MURDOCH
Reporting officer
Homicide (Murder 2)
archway entrance
PROPERTY (summary)
MOTOR VEHICLE STOLEN or REC'ED

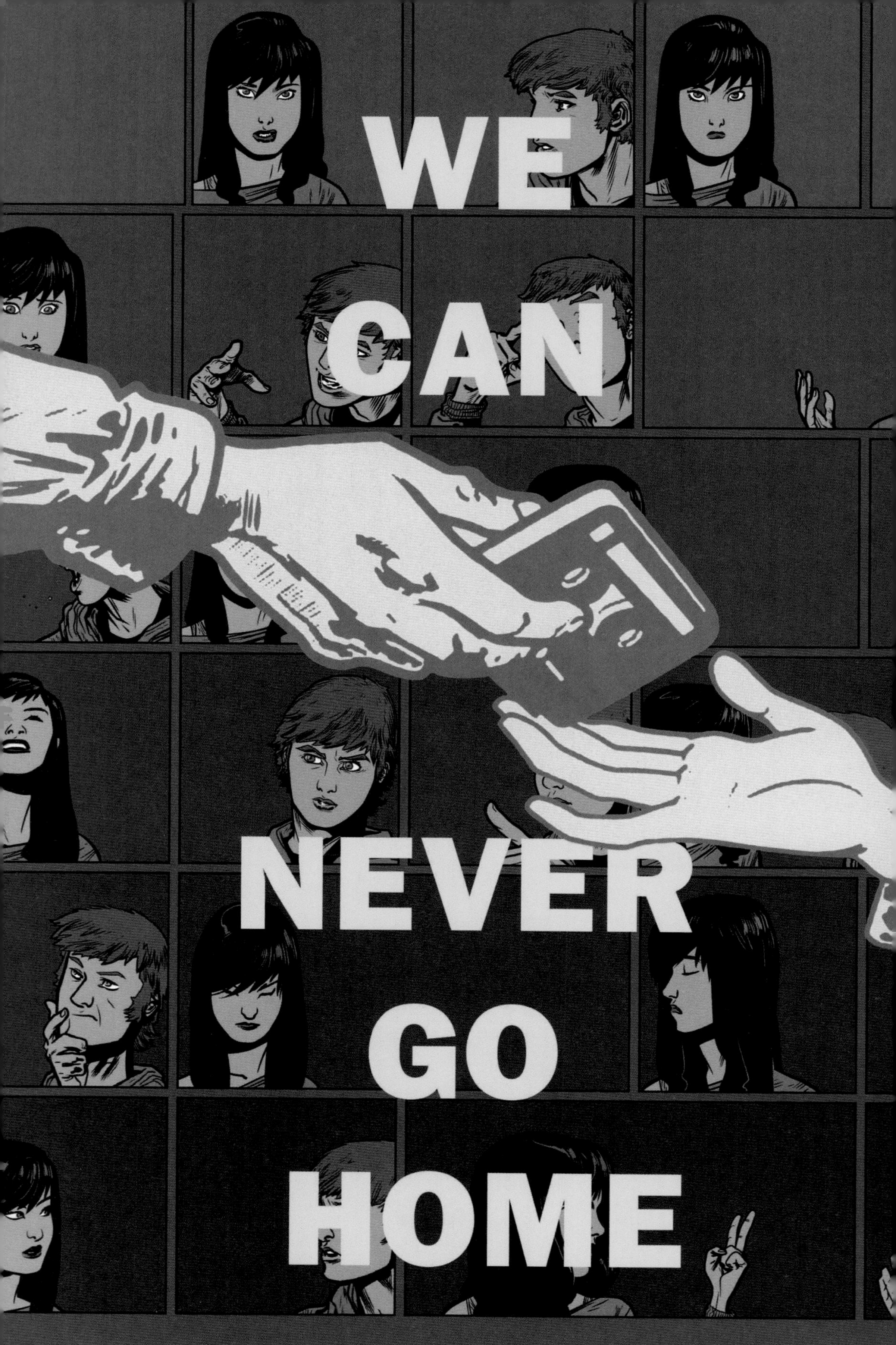

WE CAN NEVER GO HOME

Hood / Kindlon / Rosenberg / Scurti

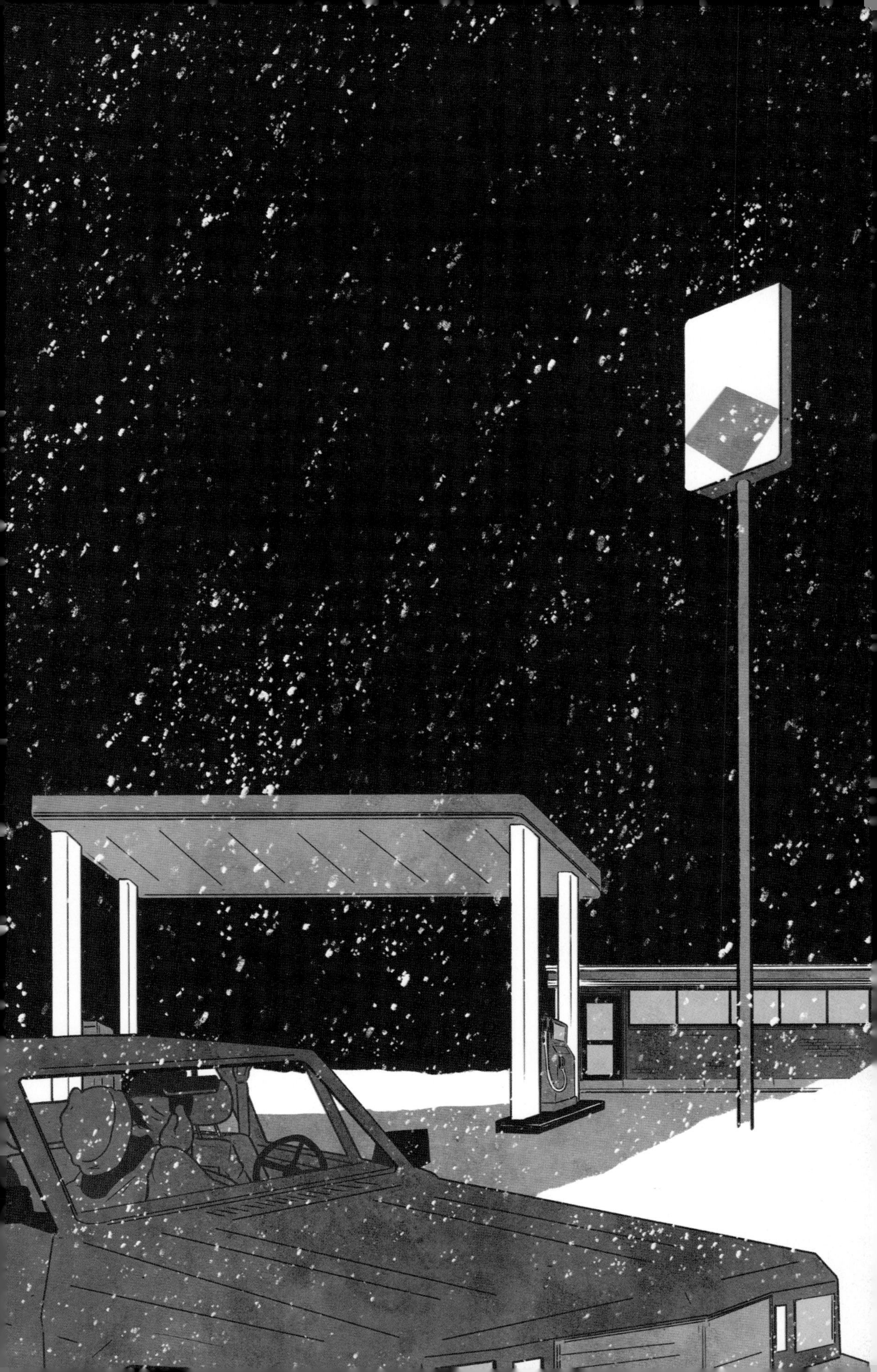

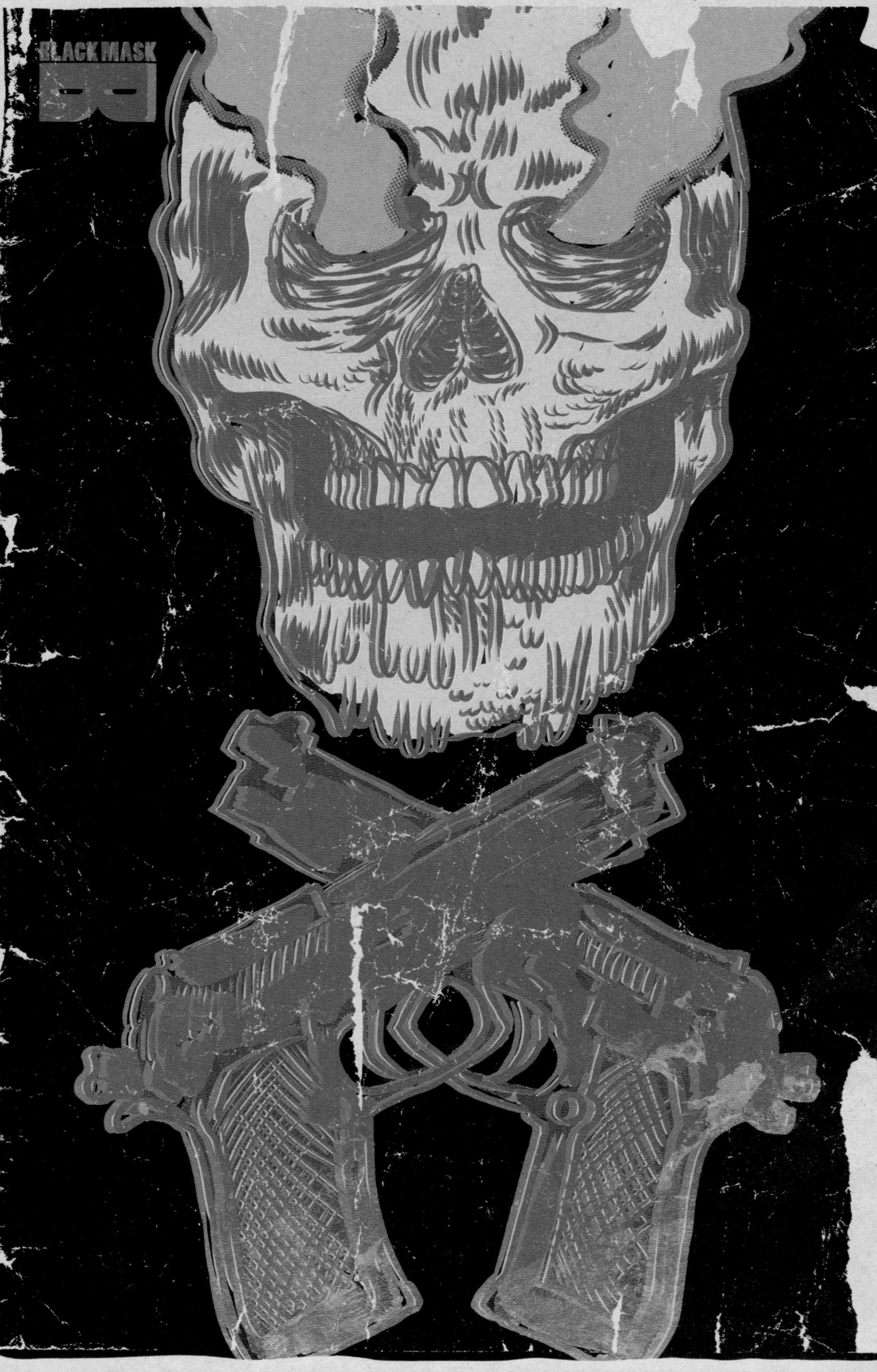
BLACK MASK

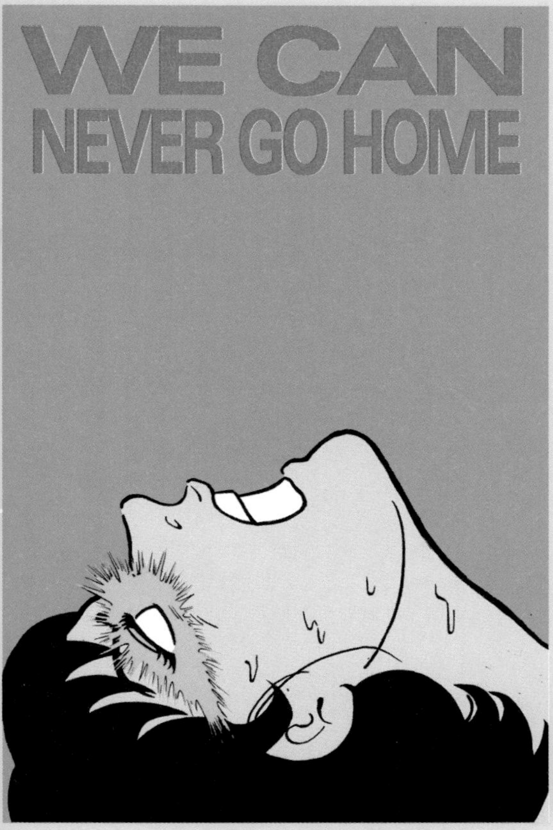
WE CAN
NEVER GO HOME
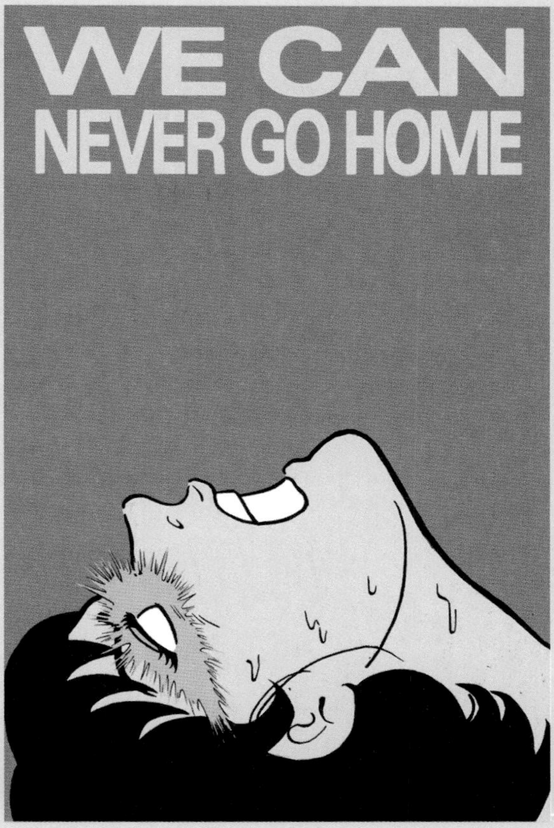
WE CAN
NEVER GO HOME
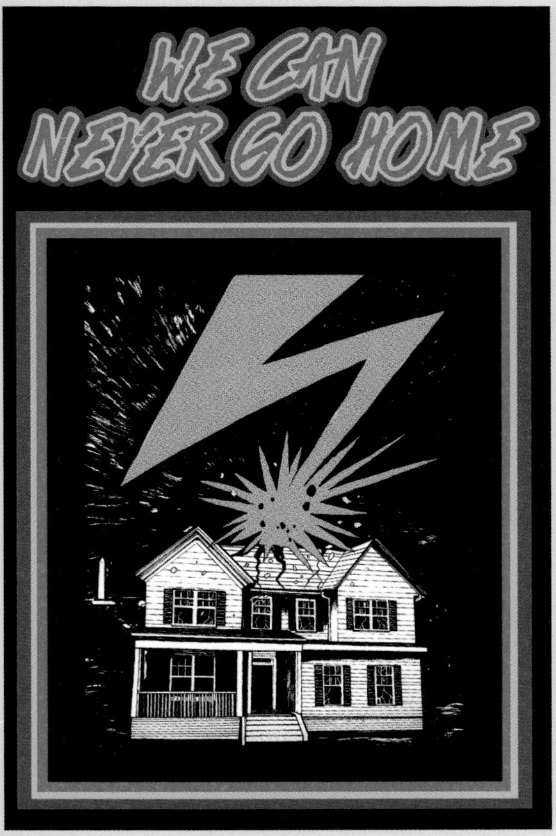
WE CAN
NEVER GO HOME
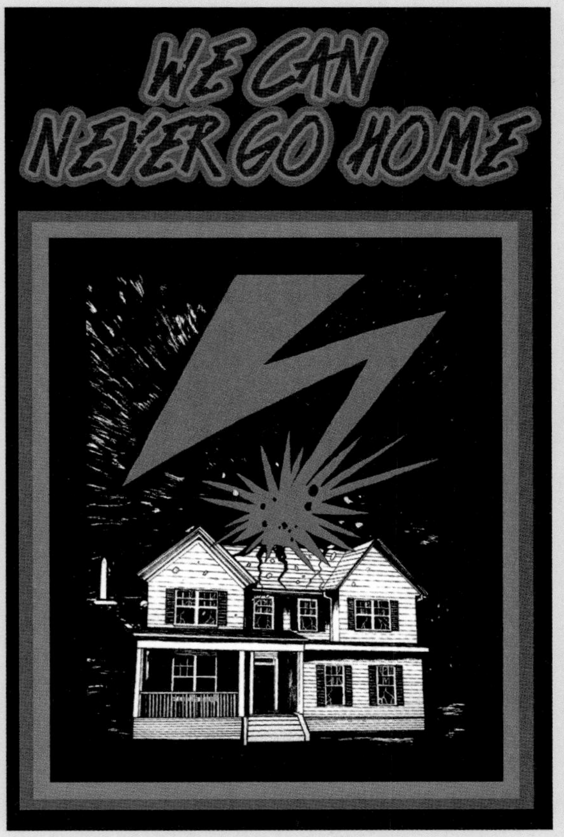
WE CAN
NEVER GO HOME

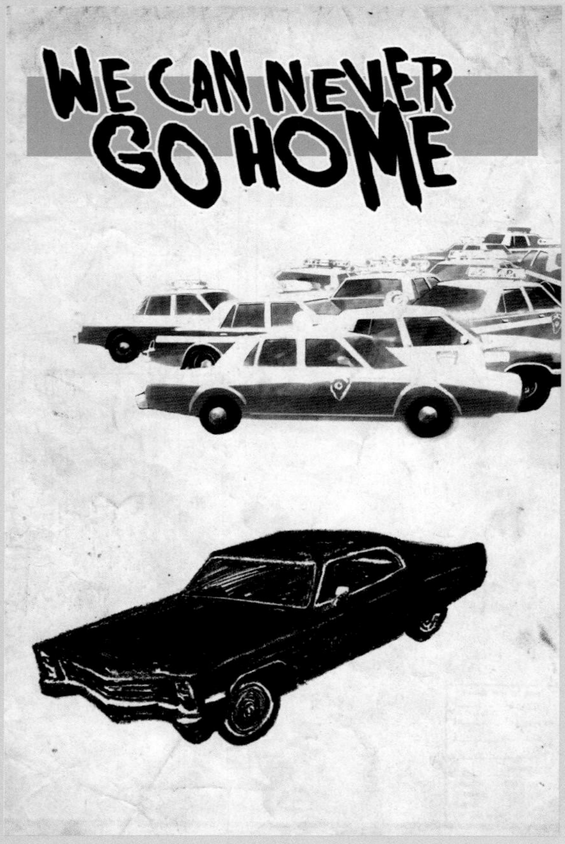
WE CAN NEVER GO HOME

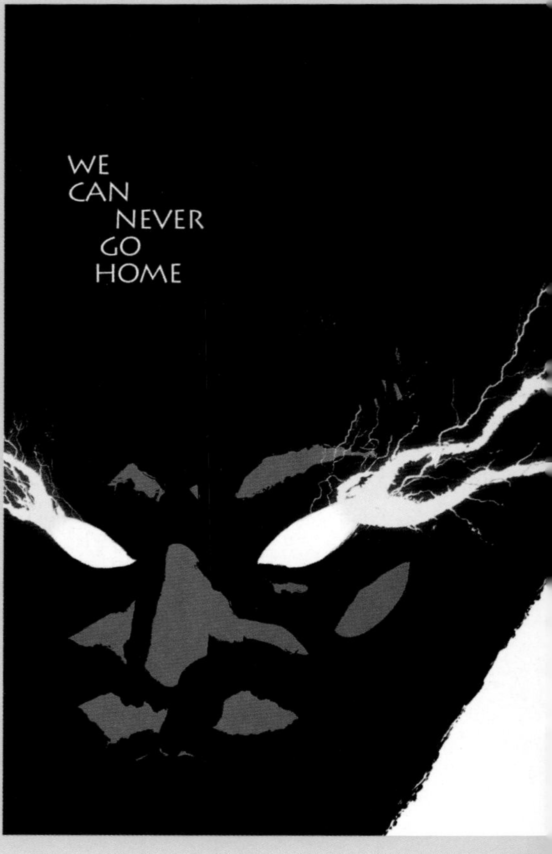
WE
CAN
NEVER
GO
HOME

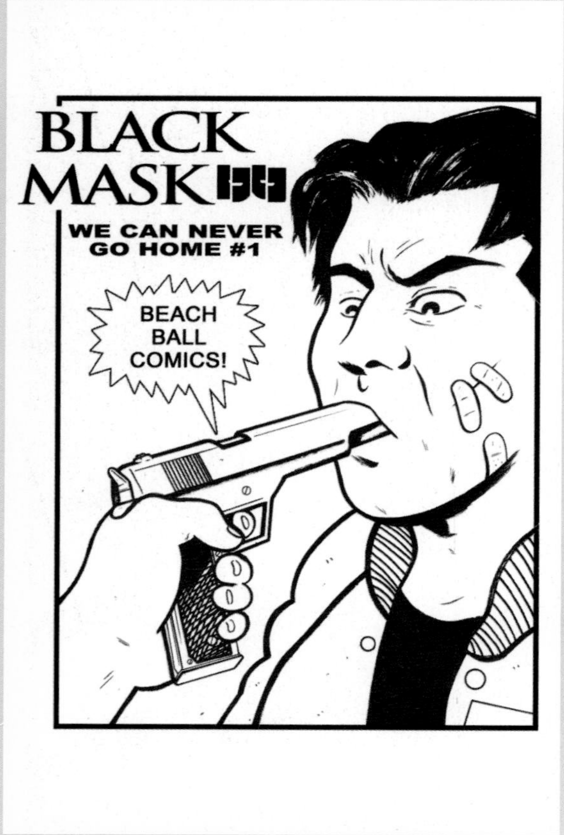
BLACK MASK
WE CAN NEVER GO HOME #1
BEACH BALL COMICS!

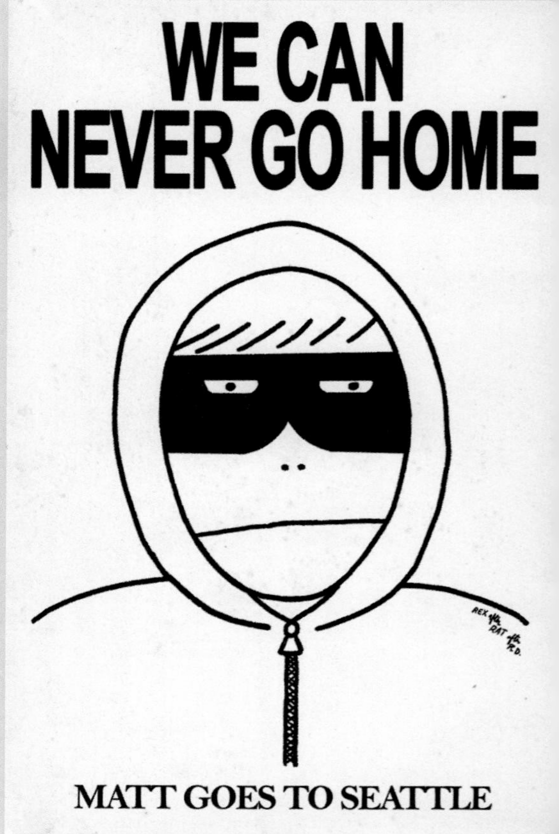
WE CAN NEVER GO HOME
MATT GOES TO SEATTLE

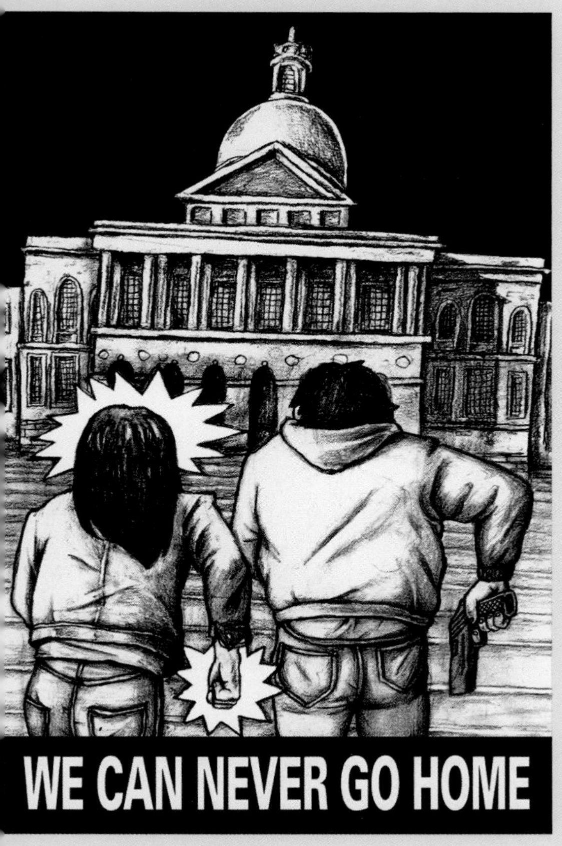
WE CAN NEVER GO HOME

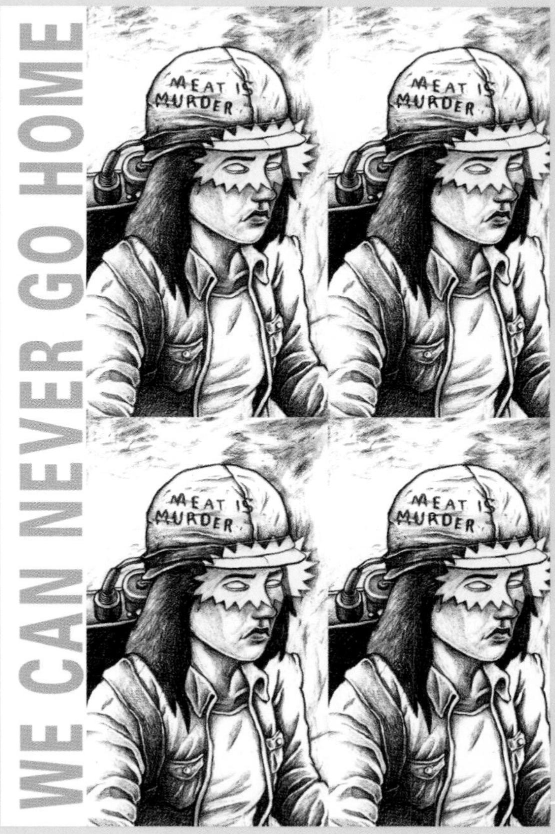
WE CAN NEVER GO HOME
MEAT IS MURDER
MEAT IS MURDER
MEAT IS MURDER
MEAT IS MURDER

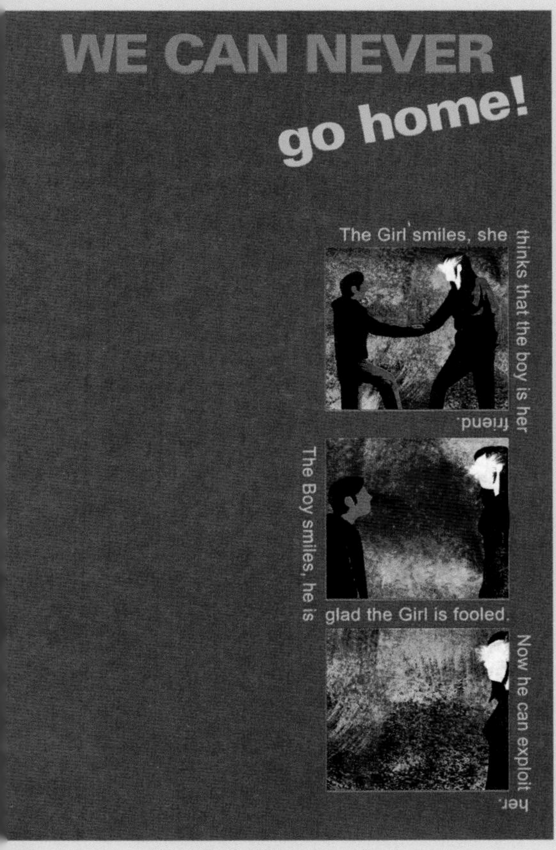
WE CAN NEVER
go home!
The Girl smiles, she thinks that the boy is her friend.
The Boy smiles, he is glad the Girl is fooled.
Now he can exploit her.

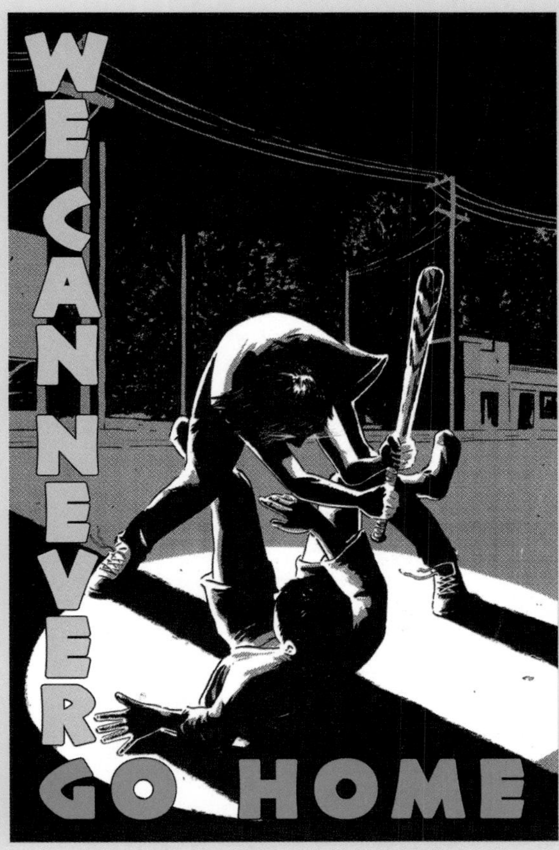
WE CAN NEVER GO HOME

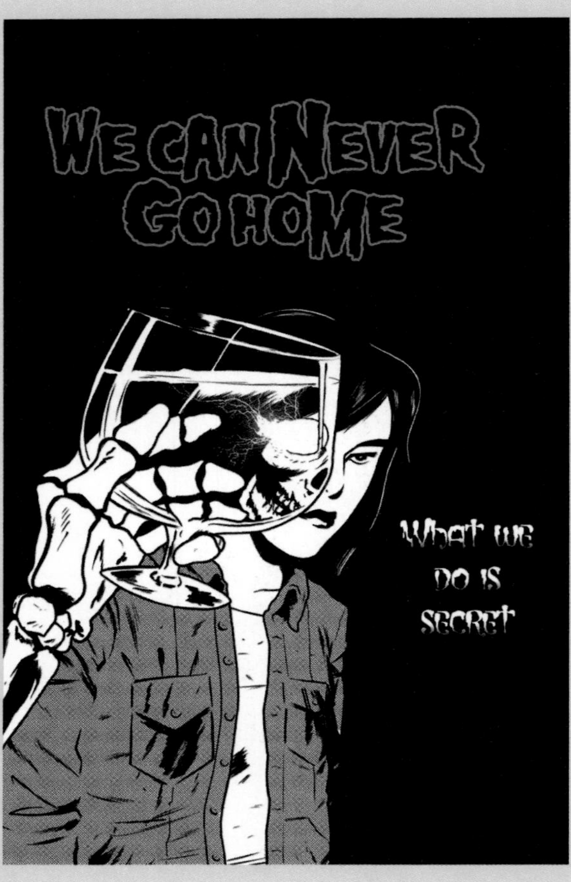
WE CAN NEVER GO HOME
What we do is secret

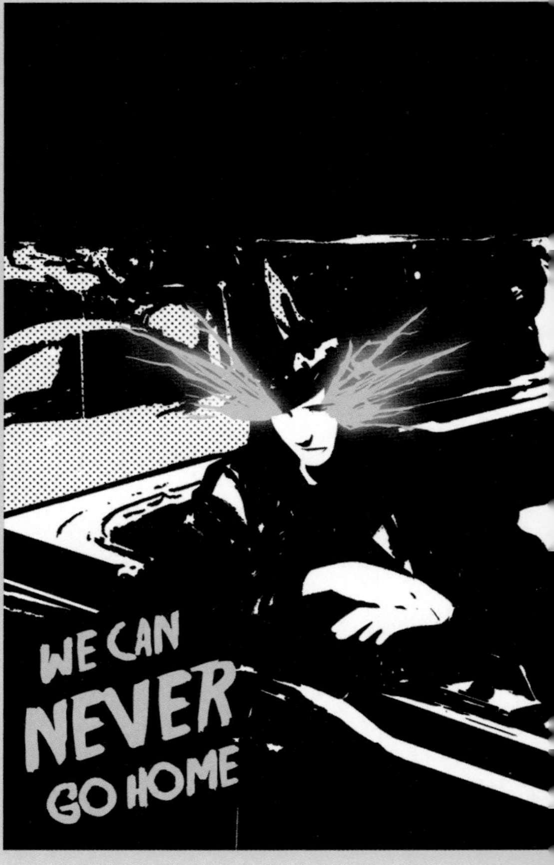
WE CAN NEVER GO HOME

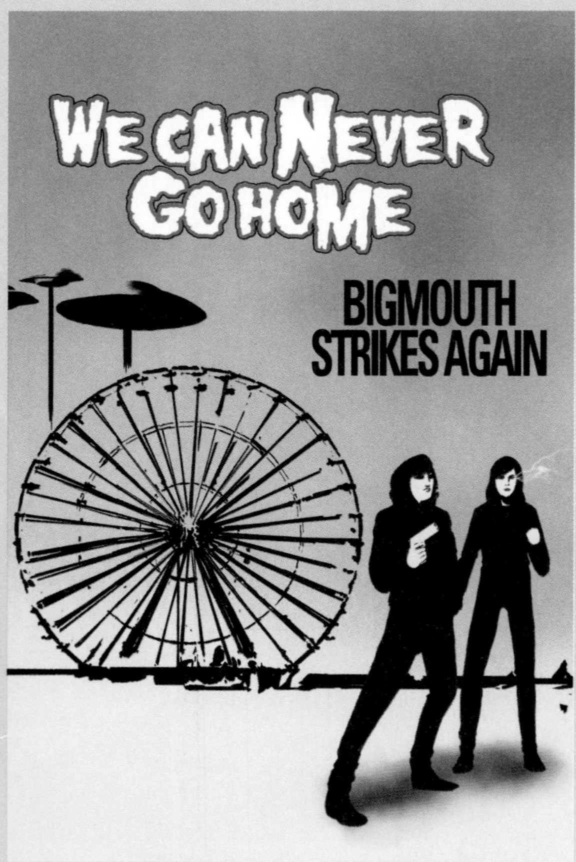
WE CAN NEVER GO HOME
BIGMOUTH STRIKES AGAIN

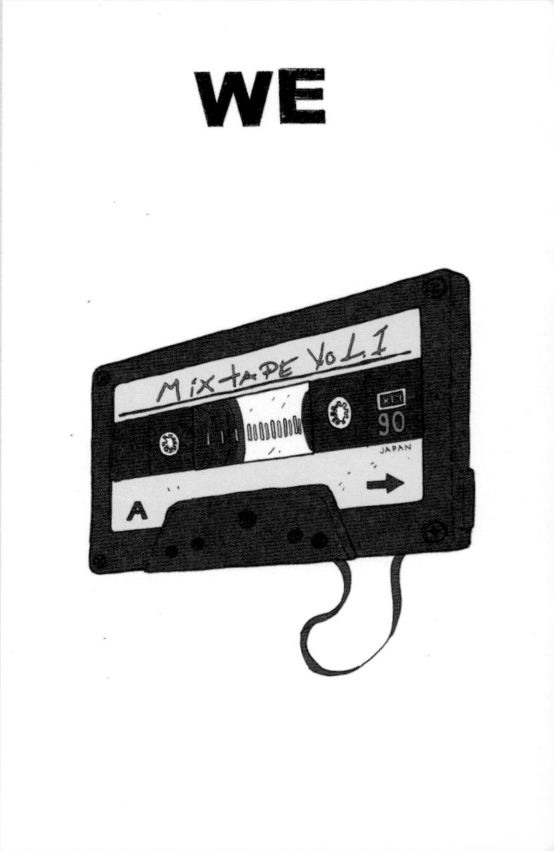
WE
MIX-TAPE VOL.1
90
JAPAN
A

CAN

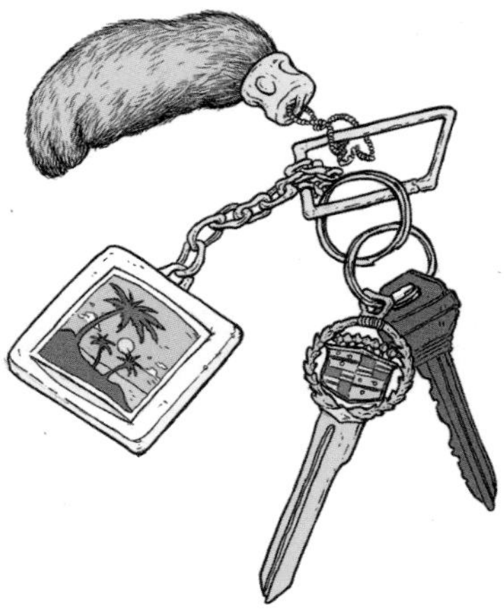

NEVER

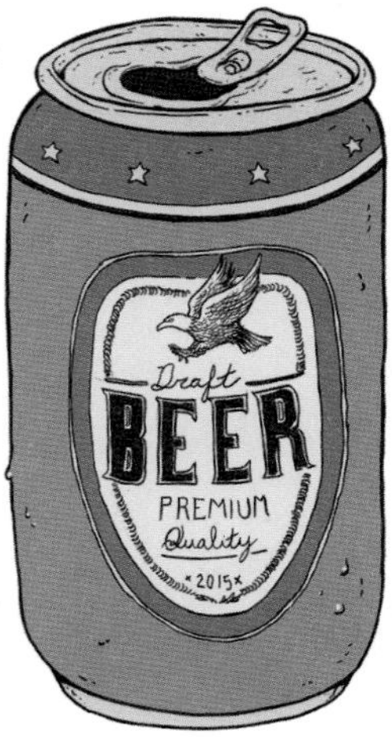
Draft
BEER
PREMIUM
Quality
2015

GO

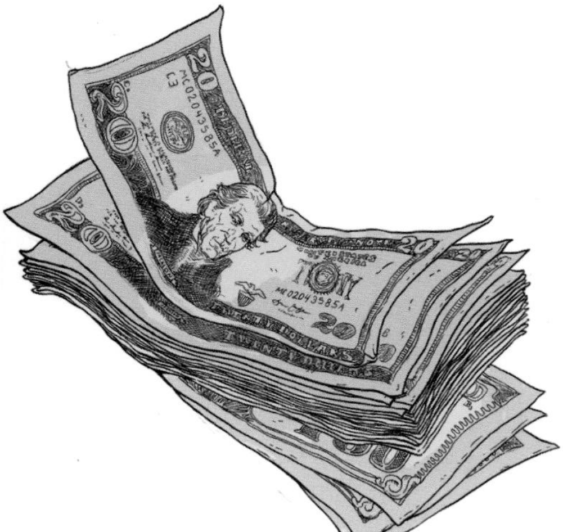

HOME

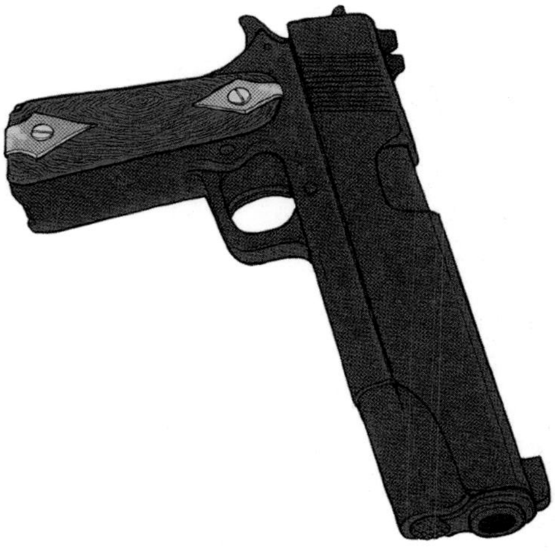

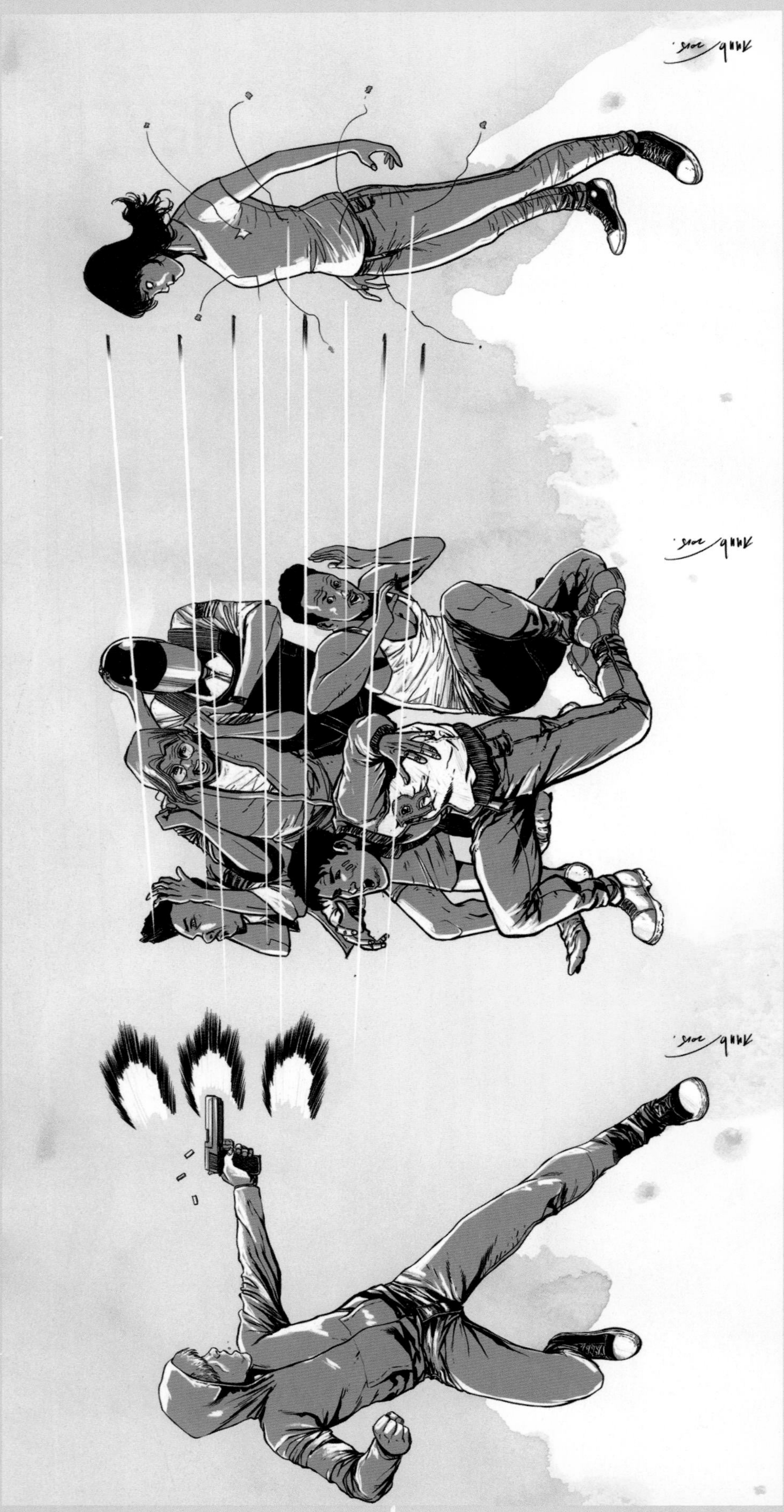

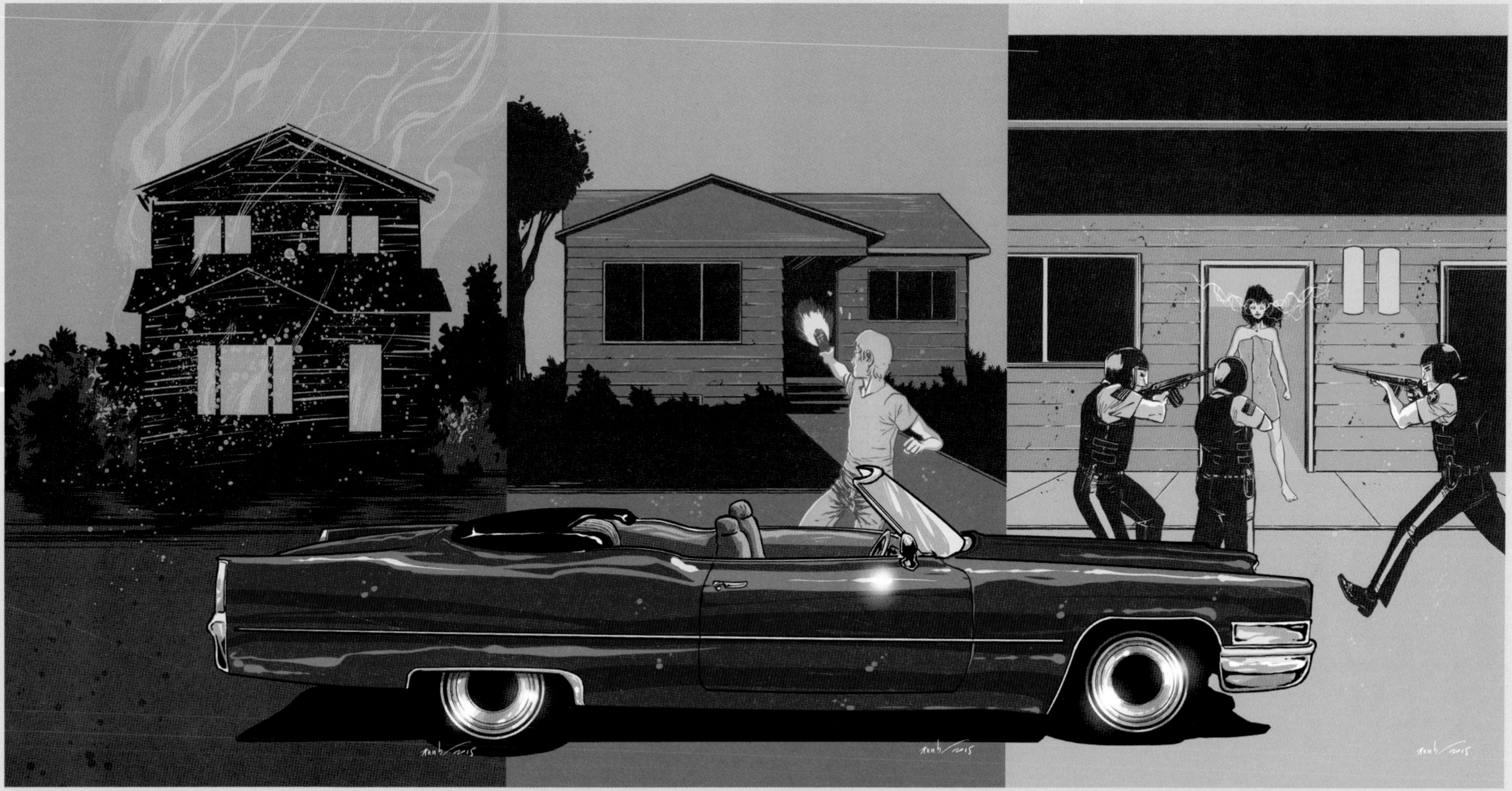

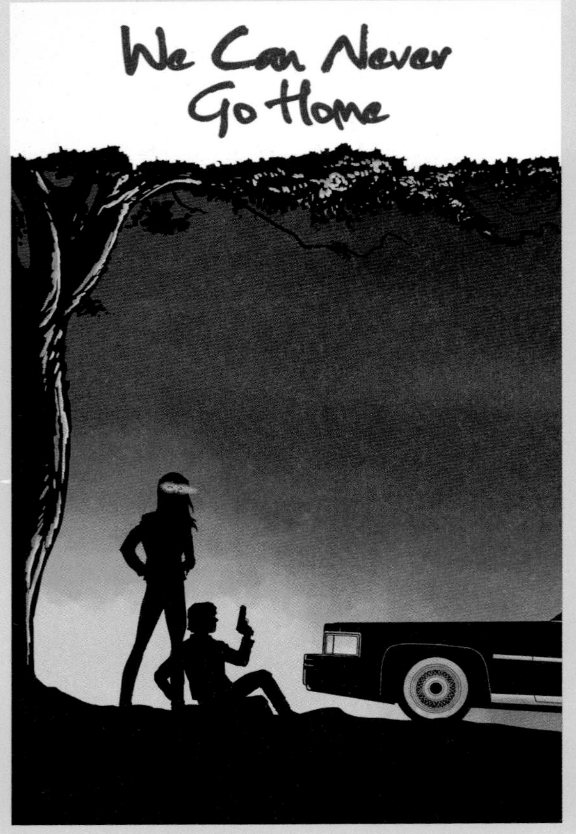
We Can Never
Go Home

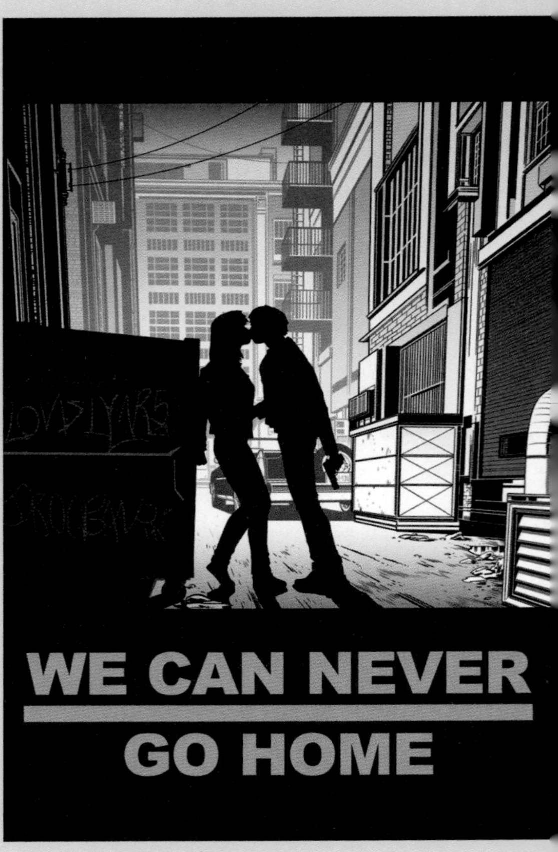
WE CAN NEVER
GO HOME

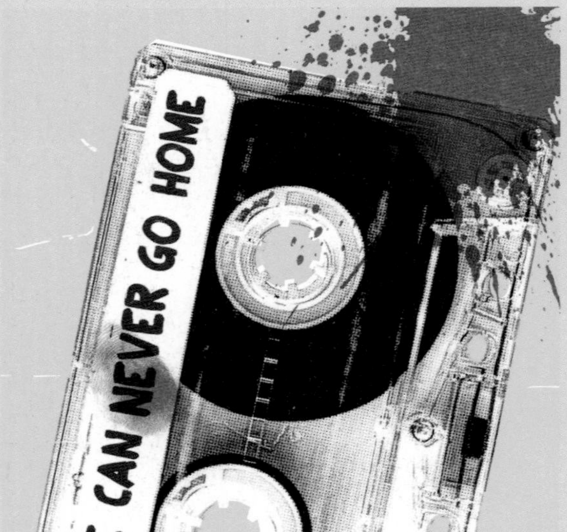
WE CAN NEVER GO HOME
B

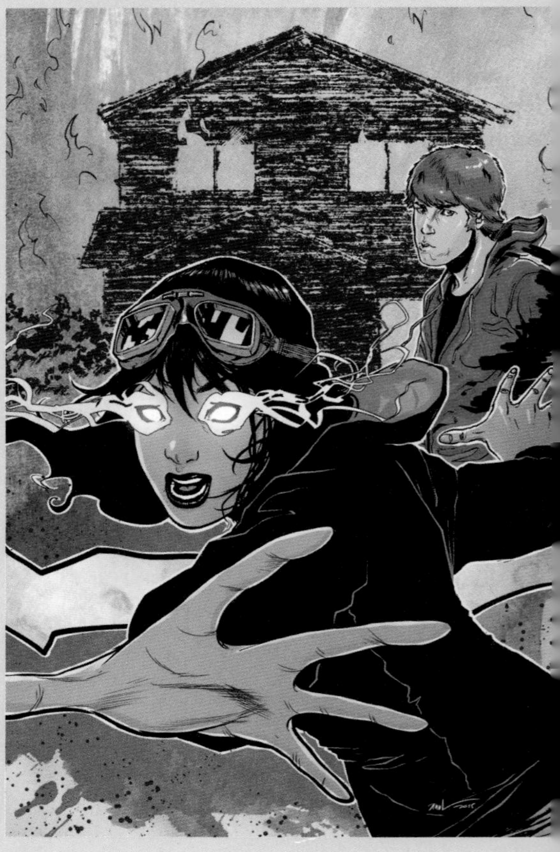

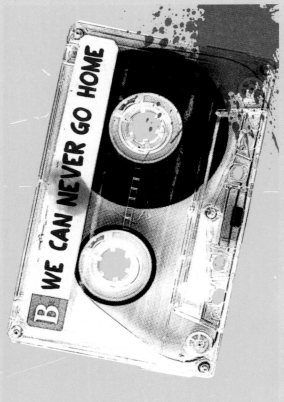

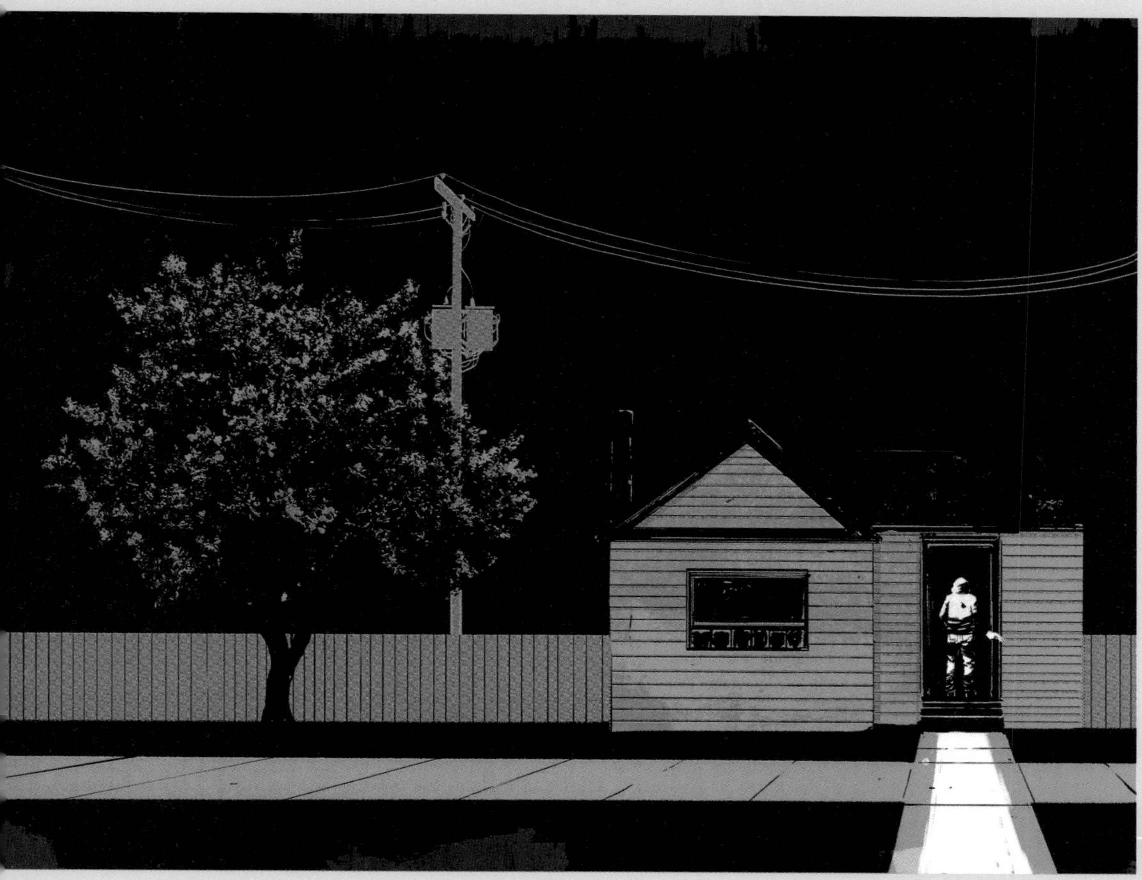

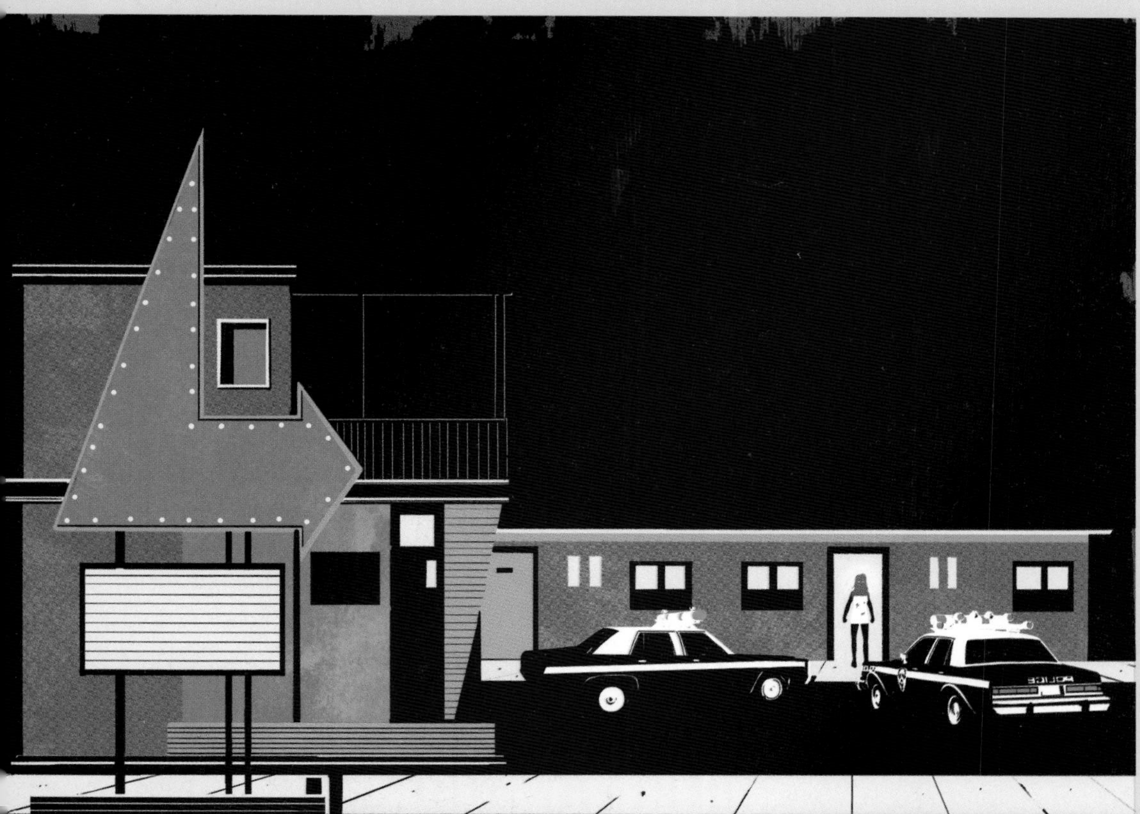

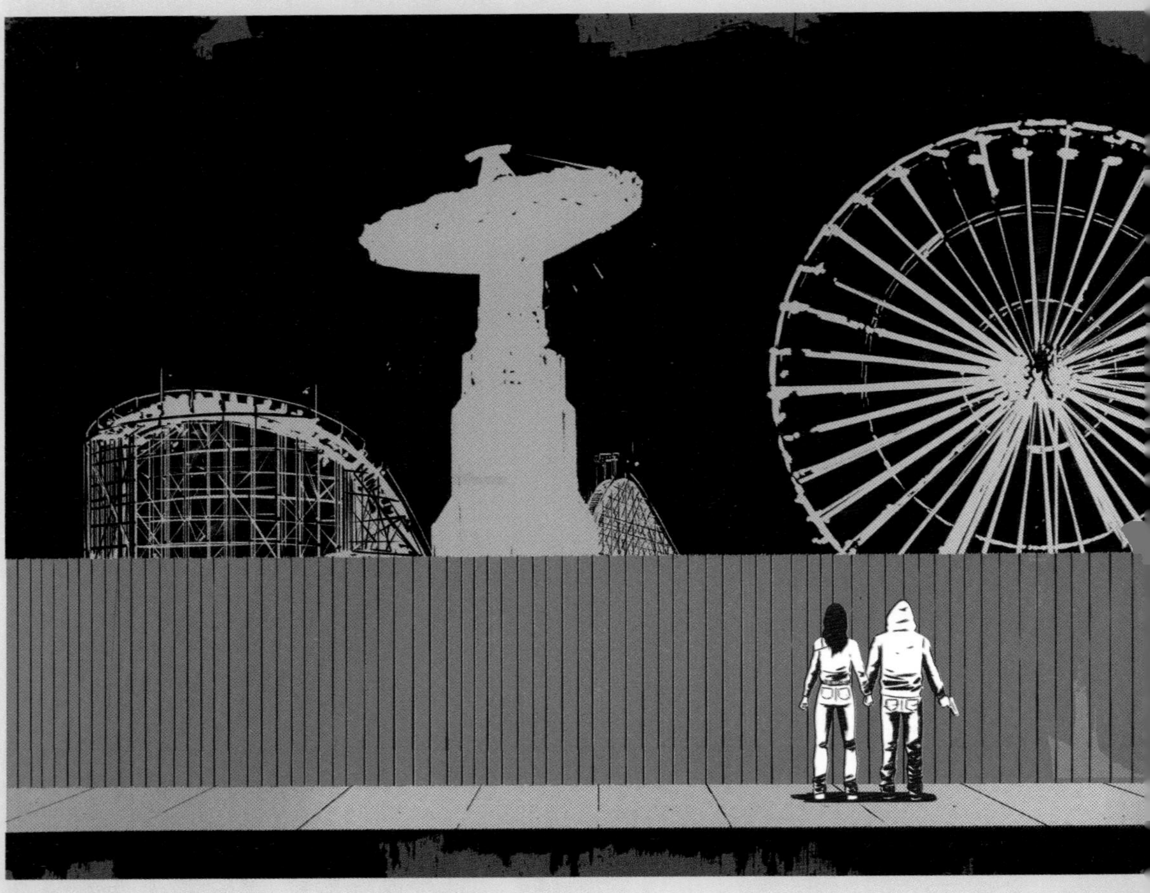

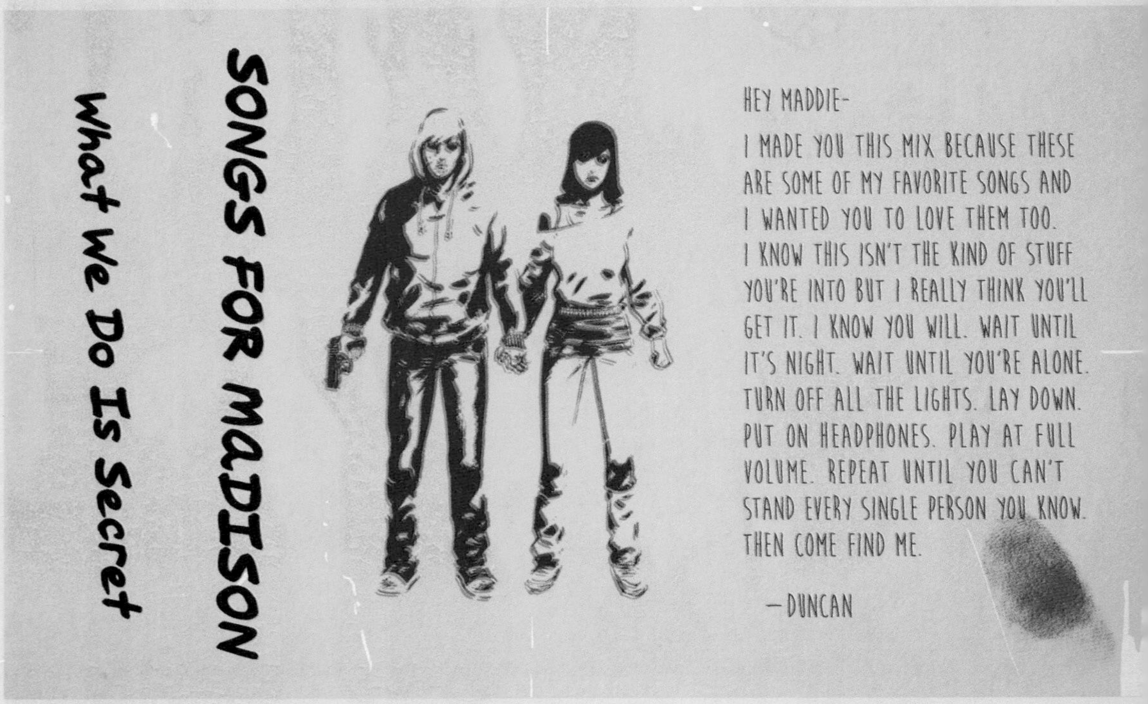
SONGS FOR MADISON
What We Do Is Secret
HEY MADDIE-
I MADE YOU THIS MIX BECAUSE THESE ARE SOME OF MY FAVORITE SONGS AND I WANTED YOU TO LOVE THEM TOO. I KNOW THIS ISN'T THE KIND OF STUFF YOU'RE INTO BUT I REALLY THINK YOU'LL GET IT. I KNOW YOU WILL. WAIT UNTIL IT'S NIGHT. WAIT UNTIL YOU'RE ALONE. TURN OFF ALL THE LIGHTS. LAY DOWN. PUT ON HEADPHONES. PLAY AT FULL VOLUME. REPEAT UNTIL YOU CAN'T STAND EVERY SINGLE PERSON YOU KNOW. THEN COME FIND ME.
—DUNCAN

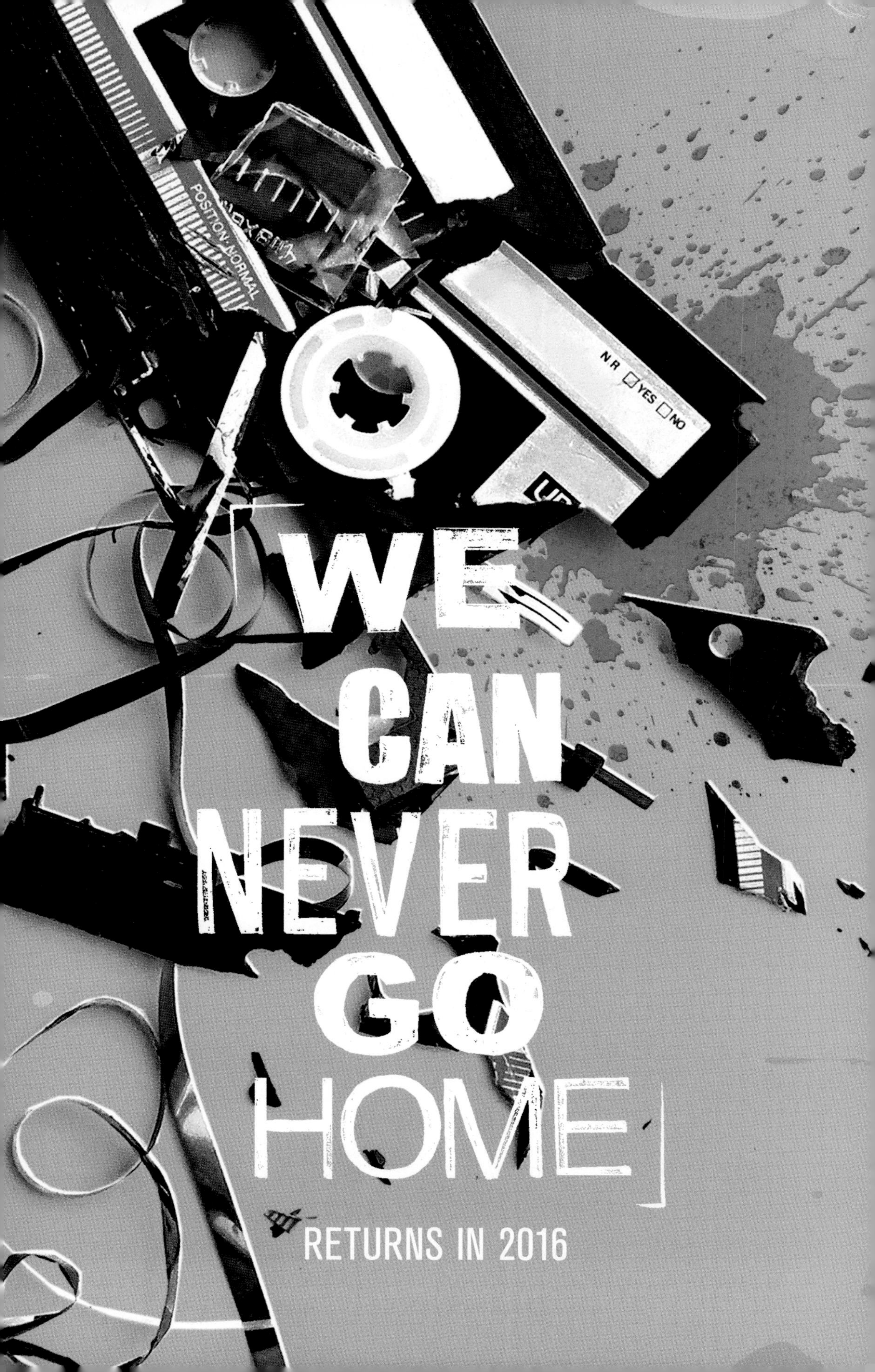
POSITION NORMAL
N R YES NO
WE
CAN
NEVER
GO
HOME
RETURNS IN 2016

WE CAN NEVER GO HOME

www.facebook.com/wecannevergohome

www.ashcanpress.com
www.joshhood.com
www.brianlevelart.wordpress.com
www.misterwalsh.tumblr.com
www.TylerBoss.com
www.AmandaScurti.com
www.clintflickerlettering.blogspot.com
www.hopkinsletters.com
www.BigRedRobot.net

BLACKMASK

www.blackmaskstudios.com
www.facebook.com/blackmaskstudios – www.twitter.com/blackmaskstudio
www.blackmaskstudios.tumblr.com